# A SEMANTIC AND STRUCTURAL ANALYSIS OF PHILIPPIANS

# A SEMANTIC AND STRUCTURAL ANALYSIS OF PHILIPPIANS

**JOHN BANKER**

**Summer Institute of Linguistics**

The Greek text used in this SSA is from the fourth edition of the United Bible Societies' *Greek New Testament*.

© 1996 by the Summer Institute of Linguistics, Inc.
ISBN: 1-55671-020-8
Library of Congress Catalog Card Number: 96-67037
Printed in the United States of America

Summer Institute of Linguistics, Inc.
7500 West Camp Wisdom Road
Dallas, TX 75236

# CONTENTS

Acknowledgments ................................................................................................................. 7
Abbreviations ........................................................................................................................ 8
General Introduction ............................................................................................................. 9
    Paragraph Pattern Chart ................................................................................................ 11
    Communication Relations Chart .................................................................................. 12
Introduction to the Semantic Structure of Philippians ....................................................... 13
    The Constituent Organization of Philippians ............................................................... 15
    Overview: Thematic Units and Their Theme Statements ............................................ 16
The Presentation and Discussion of the Semantic Units of Philippians ............................ 21
Philippians 1:1–4:23 (Epistle) ............................................................................................. 21
    Epistle Constituent 1:1–2 (Opening) ............................................................................ 22
    Epistle Constituent 1:3–4:20 (Part: Body) ................................................................... 25
        Part Constituent 1:3–11 (Expressive Section: Introduction to 1:12–4:20) ............. 29
            Section Constituent 1:3–8 (Nucleus$_1$) ................................................................ 30
            Section Constituent 1:9–11 (Nucleus$_2$) .............................................................. 40
        Part Constituent 1:12–26 (Expressive Section) ...................................................... 44
            Section Constituent 1:12–14 (Nucleus$_1$) ............................................................ 46
            Section Constituent 1:15–18e (Nucleus$_2$) .......................................................... 49
            Section Constituent 1:18f–20 (Nucleus$_3$) .......................................................... 54
            Section Constituent 1:21–26 (Nucleus$_4$) ............................................................ 59
        Part Constituent 1:27–4:9 (Hortatory Subpart) ....................................................... 67
            Subpart Constituent 1:27–30 (Introduction) ...................................................... 69
            Subpart Constituent 2:1–30 (Division: Appeal$_1$ of 1:27–4:9) ........................... 76
                Division Constituent 2:1–16 (Section: Appeal$_1$ of 2:1–30) ......................... 76
                    Section Constituent 2:1–4 (Appeal$_1$ of 2:1–16) ........................................ 78
                    Section Constituent 2:5–11 (Appeal$_2$ of 2:1–16) ...................................... 84
                    Section Constituent 2:12–13 (Appeal$_3$ of 2:1–16) .................................... 90
                    Section Constituent 2:14–16 (Appeal$_4$ of 2:1–16) .................................... 93
                Division Constituent 2:17–18 (Appeal$_2$ of 2:1–30) ..................................... 98
                Division Constituent 2:19–30 (Section: Appeal$_3$ of 2:1–30) ..................... 100
                    Section Constituent 2:19–24 (Commissive Paragraph) ............................ 101
                    Section Constituent 2:25–30 (Hortatory Paragraph) ................................ 105
            Subpart Constituent 3:1–4:1 (Hortatory Division: Appeal$_2$ of 1:27–4:9) ......... 112
                Division Constituent 3:1 (Introduction to 3:2–21) ....................................... 114
                Division Constituent 3:2–11 (Appeal$_1$ of 3:1–4:1) ...................................... 116
                    Section Constituent 3:2 (Appeal of 3:2–11) ............................................. 117
                    Section Constituent 3:3–4a (Basis$_1$ for 3:2) ............................................ 119
                    Section Constituent 3:4b–11 (Basis$_2$ for 3:2) .......................................... 122
                        Paragraph Cluster Constituent 3:4b–6 (Concession to 3:7–11) ............ 123
                        Paragraph Cluster Constituent 3:7–11 (Contraexpectation) .................. 127
                Division Constituent 3:12–21 (Hortatory Section: Appeal$_2$ of 3:1–4:1) .... 137
                    Section Constituent 3:12–16 (Appeal$_1$ of 3:12–21) .................................. 138
                    Section Constituent 3:17–21 (Appeal$_2$ of 3:12–21) .................................. 146
                Division Constituent 4:1 (Summary of 3:1–21) .......................................... 156
            Subpart Constituent 4:2–9 (Hortatory Section: Appeal$_3$ of 1:27–4:9) ............ 159
                Section Constituent 4:2–3 (Appeal$_1$ of 4:2–9) ............................................. 160

       Section Constituent 4:4–7 (Appeal$_2$ of 4:2–9) ............................................... 163
       Section Constituent 4:8–9 (Appeal$_3$ of 4:2–9) ............................................... 169
    Part Constituent 4:10–20 (Expressive Section: Nucleus$_3$ of 1:3–4:20) ............................ 174
       Section Constituent 4:10–14 (Reaction$_1$ of 4:10–20) .......................................... 175
       Section Constituent 4:15–17 (Reaction$_2$ of 4:10–20) .......................................... 182
       Section Constituent 4:18–20 (Reaction$_3$ of 4:10–20) .......................................... 187
  Epistle Constituent 4:21–23 (Expressive Section: Closing of the Epistle) ............................ 194
    Section Constituent 4:21–22 (Reaction$_1$ (greetings) of 4:21–23) ................................... 194
    Section Constituent 4:23 (Reaction$_2$ (benediction) of 4:21–23) ................................... 196
Bibliography ............................................................................................... 197

# ACKNOWLEDGMENTS

Many have contributed to *A Semantic and Structural Analysis of Philippians*. Of those who produced earlier drafts, Katharine Heyward is most noteworthy. She was ably assisted by John Callow as consultant. Though her work was never published, it has been used worldwide in prepublication form for a number of years.

I owe much to Heyward's work on the displays, though I thoroughly revised them. Also some of the notes in the "Introduction to the Semantic Structure of Philippians" are based on her work. The notes on the individual verses are almost completely my own.

Ellis Deibler reviewed my work on the SSA from a semantic perspective. James Mignard reviewed it from a Greek perspective and made many other valuable suggestions. Bruce Turnbull and Robert Smith also helped me in the analysis of the Greek. Copy editor Elizabeth Eastman has made this SSA much more understandable and accurate. Dick and Faith Blight have given valuable technical assistance in various areas and Alan Thomas has helped with keyboarding. I wish to thank each one for hours of effort on my behalf and the significant contribution each made to the SSA of Philippians. I am grateful, too, for those who have contributed to the semantic theory on which this SSA is based, most notably John Beekman, John and Kathleen Callow, and John Tuggy.

From a more general perspective, I thank my wife, Betty, who has so ably supported me, whether in working directly on the SSA or in innumerable other ways. Most of all I thank the Lord for his wisdom and strength, without which nothing of value could be accomplished.

# ABBREVIATIONS IN THE TEXT

| | |
|---|---|
| AGNT | *Analytical Greek New Testament* (Friberg and Friberg) |
| BAGD | W. Bauer, W. Arndt, F. W. Gingrich, and F. Danker, *Greek-English Lexicon of the New Testament and Other Early Christian Literature* |
| BDF | F. Blass, A. Debrunner, and R. W. Funk, *A Greek Grammar of the New Testament* |
| JETS | *Journal of the Evangelical Theological Society* |
| KJV | King James Version |
| LXX | Septuagint |
| MS/MSS | manuscript(s) |
| NAB | *The New American Bible* |
| NASB | *The New American Standard Bible* |
| NEB | *The New English Bible* |
| NJB | *The New Jerusalem Bible* |
| NIV | *The Holy Bible: New International Version* |
| NRSV | *The Holy Bible: New Revised Standard Version* |
| NT | New Testament |
| OT | Old Testament |
| REB | *The Revised English Bible* |
| RSV | *Revised Standard Version* |
| SSA | *Semantic and Structural Analysis* |
| SSWC | *Semantic Structure of Written Communication* or the theory which it presents (Beekman et al.) |
| TEV | *Holy Bible: Today's English Version* |
| TDNT | *Theological Dictionary of the New Testament* (Kittel and Friedrich) |
| TNT | *The Translator's New Testament* |
| UBS | United Bible Societies |
| UBSGNT | United Bible Societies' *Greek New Testament* (Aland et al.) |

# ABBREVIATIONS AND SYMBOLS IN THE DISPLAY

| | | | |
|---|---|---|---|
| * | a word being used in a sense other than its primary sense | idn | identification |
| | | inc | inclusive (includes addressees) |
| amp | amplification | [LIT] | litotes |
| CCL | CONCLUSION | [MET] | metaphor |
| CTX | CONTRAEXPECTATION | [MTY] | metonymy |
| dsc | description | ¶ PTRN | paragraph pattern |
| [DOU] | doublet | prc | procedural |
| emo | emotive | [PRS] | personification |
| [EUP] | euphemism | [RHQ] | rhetorical question |
| exc | exclusive (excludes addressees) | sg | singular |
| exp | expository | [SIM] | simile |
| hrt | hortatory | spf | specific |
| [HYP] | hyperbole | std | standard |
| [IDM] | idiom (special cases only) | [SYN] | synecdoche |

References to Greek words and their glosses in BAGD are made in the text by the following formula: page number, period, entry citation; e.g., BAGD, p. 405.I2bβ.

# GENERAL INTRODUCTION

**The theory on which a Semantic and Structural Analysis is based**

This analytical commentary on Paul's letter to the Philippian church is based on a theory of semantic structure set forth in *The Semantic Structure of Written Communication* (Beekman, Callow, and Kopesec 1981). More recently K. Callow's *Man and Message* (forthcoming) presents a broader basis for this theory. This Semantic and Structural Analysis (SSA) has been prepared with the needs of the Bible translator particularly in view, though it should be useful to all serious students of God's Word. Like other commentaries, it aims to arrive at the meaning the original writer intended to communicate to the original recipients. It differs from most other commentaries, however, in that it is consciously based on a theory of the structure of meaning. Consequently, a consistent and comprehensive approach to the analysis of the meaning is applied to the total document, whether that meaning is conveyed by the smallest segments of the written communication, such as words and their component parts, or whether it is conveyed by the largest segments, such as paragraphs and various combinations of paragraphs.

This SSA of Philippians does not include a detailed section on the theory and presentation of semantic and structural analyses as some of the earlier SSAs do (Colossians, 2 Thessalonians). The person who is building up his own collection of SSAs does not need this section in every SSA. So, for economy's sake, this section has been left out of the Philippians SSA, but the reader may refer to the Colossians or 2 Thessalonians SSA for this information. The Philippians SSA, however, does include a chart of communication relations and a chart of paragraph patterns for easy access to these important tools. At the date of this writing, a user's manual dealing with theory, presentation, and use of SSAs is in the process of being prepared.

Each semantic unit of Philippians will be presented in a display. The paragraph pattern and relational structure diagram appears at the left of the display, and the referential contents to the right. The reader should note the following:

1. Italics are used in the display text to designate implicit material that has been made explicit. Note, however, that in some cases it is difficult to decide what is implicit material and what is actually a component of meaning of the Greek word being translated.
2. Parentheses are used to enclose alternative renderings; for example, 'my God (*or*, God whom I worship)'. They are also used to enclose specifications for pronouns, for example, 'we(exc)' and 'we(inc)'.
3. Square brackets clarify references to antecedents, for example, 'him [Paul]', 'this [1:16a]'. They are also used to enclose abbreviations for the different types of figures of speech being used in the original text: '[MET]' for metaphor.
4. An asterisk following a word indicates that the word is not being used in its primary meaning in contemporary English.
5. In an orienter-CONTENT relationship where the CONTENT consists of more than one proposition, in most cases, the CONTENT label is not used, but a dotted line alerts the reader that an orienter-CONTENT relationship is intended. The CONTENT consists of everything on the vertical line to which the dotted line is attached, that is, each proposition of the multi-propositional unit immediately below the orienter.

In this SSA a distinction is made between communication relations on the lower propositional levels and paragraph pattern relationships on the highest level within the paragraph. The paragraph pattern type in any paragraph will be based on the author's intent for that paragraph. For example, when the author comes to a point in the discourse where he wants to directly bring to bear his efforts in affecting the audience's behavior, he will use a hortatory paragraph pattern. Because of this change of perspective from earlier SSAs, the reader will find that a supportive subparagraph unit in a hortatory paragraph which would have been labeled grounds in earlier SSAs is now labeled *basis*, and the corresponding supported unit will be called *APPEAL* rather than HEAD or EXHORTATION. Similar changes have been made in other types of paragraph patterns. For more information on paragraph patterns see Tuggy (1992) and the chart of Paragraph Pattern Subtypes in Various Discourse Genres on p. 11 of this book.

Other changes in this SSA include the following:

1. NUCLEUS is used instead of HEAD for nuclear units.
2. When a nuclear unit has a different relationship to two or more nonnuclear units on the same vertical line, each of the relationships held by the nuclear unit is labeled separately rather than only labeling HEAD or NUCLEUS as under the old system.

**The use of a Semantic and Structural Analysis**

For the translator, who must not only determine the exegesis of a passage but also resolve a myriad of translation problems, it is sometimes sheer drudgery to wade through the detailed reasoning backing up the exegetical decisions in the SSA or similar commentaries. On the other hand, the detailed reasoning is necessary to determine the best analysis. Any interpretation presented should be backed up with solid reasoning, and there is no way this can be done without adequate, detailed analysis, including reference to the Greek text. To determine whether or not the reasoning is solid, the translator must study the analysis which has been presented. Also the translator will want to consult the notes to see why any implicit item was supplied.

Does the translator who wants to use the SSA, then, have any other appropriate option than reading every part of the SSA? One is to use the display text of the SSA along with other commentaries, versions, and helps; and where there is obvious agreement, the translator may move ahead with confidence. Where there is a difference between the display and other texts, or there appears to be a number of alternatives, the translator may consult the notes in the SSA on the particular verse or portion of a verse being studied to see what factors led to the decision represented in the display. The translator should then be better able to make his own factually based judgment as to the best interpretation. In some cases the notes will provide an alternate propositionalization which may occasionally appear to the translator to be the better solution. Also, since the SSA is prepared with the needs of the translator in mind, the notes may supply needed information which is difficult to find elsewhere. If the translator is searching for such information as he works on a particular verse, it would be well for him to consult the SSA notes for that verse to see if the problem is dealt with.

To obtain the greatest benefit from an SSA, the notes should be consulted as consistently as possible. Just as a part of any book or discourse is best understood in its complete context, so discussion of a single point in the SSA in many cases will best be understood if the user has maintained access to the context of the SSA as a whole. Moreover, the display text and the notes work together to provide the information the translator needs for his work on any verse. Since the display text by its form is limited in the information it can provide, the notes contribute to the fuller understanding of what the display text is seeking to communicate. Where the display text is lacking, the notes seek to fill in.

**The SSA display text is not a translation in the common sense**

Finally, it should be understood that the SSA display text is not a translation in the common sense. It is a verbalization of the analysis of the meaning of the Greek text presented in propositional English surface-structure form and with various restrictions. For instance, abstract nouns are avoided as much as possible by changing them into propositional verbal form, and the finite form of the verb is normally used rather than participles. Words are used only in their primary senses. For live metaphors, the full meaning of the figure intended by the original author is given in the display text. As a result, the display text does not always sound natural, or "flowing," as a good translation should. The addition of implicit material may make it sound too overloaded with information and too interpretative for a translation. The display text's primary purpose, remember, is to be a source of information, not a model for word-for-word translation into any real language.

Nevertheless, in some of its patterns, the display text will more closely approximate patterns of non-Indo-European languages than of English or Greek. For example, if a language naturally uses abstract nouns in more or less the same way English or Greek does, it would be expected that translating using abstract nouns would in many cases be more natural and effective than following the propositional form of the display text. But if the receptor language does not normally use abstract nouns, the propositional form of the display text may be helpful since its patterns and obligatory elements are those of verbal constructions, rather than those associated with abstract nouns. But even in these languages a natural translation will avoid following the display text word for word; instead, it will follow its own patterns.

Likewise, a translator should not use all the implicit material presented in the display text, but only that material which would be considered valid or necessary in the particular language.

| | | SOLUTIONALITY | CAUSALITY | VOLITIONALITY |
|---|---|---|---|---|
| I D E A S | EXPOSITORY −sequence | +problem(exp)+SOLUTION ±evidence$_n$ ±(complication+SOLUTION) | +cause$_n$+EFFECT; +major+minor+INFERENCE; +evidence$_n$+INFERENCE; +application$_n$+PRINCIPLE | +justification$_n$ +CLAIM |
| | NARRATIVE +sequence | +problem+RESOLUTION ±resolving incident$_n$ ±(complication+RESOLUTION) | +occasion+OUTCOME | +step$_n$+GOAL |
| E M O T I O N | EXPRESSIVE −sequence | +problem(emo)+SOLUTION ±seeking/belief ±(complication+SOLUTION) | +situation$_n$+REACTION ±belief | +belief$_n$+CONTROL |
| | DESCRIPTIVE +sequence | +problem(dsc)+SOLUTION ±experience$_n$ ±(complication+SOLUTION) | +situation$_n$+REACTION | +description$_n$ +DECLARATION |
| B E H A V I O R | HORTATORY −sequence | +problem(hrt)+APPEAL ±basis$_n$ ±(complication+SOLUTION) | +basis$_n$+APPEAL; +APPEAL+application$_n$; +basis$_n$+COMMISSIVE | +motivation +ENABLEMENT$_n$; +motivation$_n$ +APPEAL |
| | PROCEDURAL +sequence | +problem(prc)+SOLUTION ±step$_n$ ±(complication+SOLUTION) | +APPEAL+outcome$_n$ | +STEP$_n$ +accomplishment |

**Paragraph Pattern Subtypes in Various Discourse Genres**

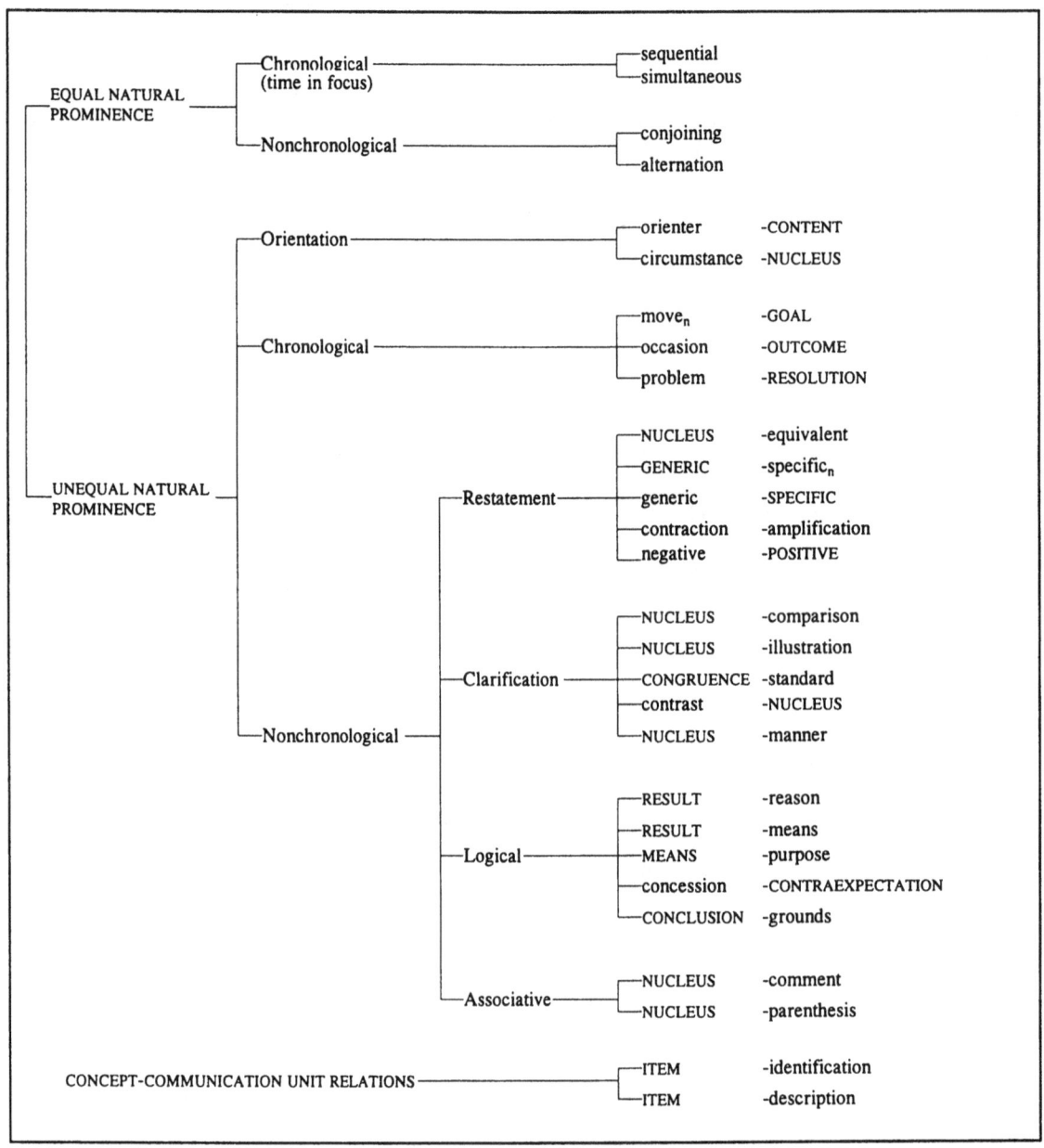

**Communication Relations**

Notes:
1. Since the Epistle to the Philippians is nonnarrative, not all the narrative relations are included in this chart.
2. The relations are given in the order in which they are most commonly found in the Greek of the New Testament; thus, a RESULT is usually followed by the reason for it, as signaled by ὅτι, γάρ, διά + accusative, etc.
3. The naturally prominent member of a paired relation is shown in caps. In one or two cases, one does not seem to be more naturally prominent than the other, e.g., contraction–amplification.
4. It should be noted that marked-prominence devices can be used to make the less prominent member of a pair as prominent as the one which is naturally prominent. And thematic prominence can reverse the natural prominence, so that, for example, a purpose will be of greater prominence than its means. This does not happen often, however.
5. Communication relation charts in the early SSAs also included macrostructure relations such as those of the epistle level (*opening-BODY-closing*) and those of the body level (*introduction-NUCLEUS-closure/summary*). In present theory these are classified separately.

# INTRODUCTION TO THE SEMANTIC STRUCTURE OF PHILIPPIANS

## Participants in the communication situation

The first three words of the discourse are Παῦλος καὶ Τιμόθεος 'Paul and Timothy'. They identify the participants involved in the sending of the epistle. As will be discussed in the notes for 1:1b, Paul alone is considered as the author of the discourse since all the verbs with first person endings in the body of the epistle are singular rather than plural.

As for genuineness of authorship, O'Brien (1991:9) says, "Apparently there was never any real question in the minds of the Church Fathers about the authorship or canonical authority of Philippians, for a number of them not only quote from the letter but assign it to Paul as well." The most significant opponent of its authenticity has been F. C. Baur of the Tübingen School in the 1840s. His view was based on his perception of Gnostic ideas in the hymn of 2:6–11; lack of motive, purpose, or leading idea in the epistle; and its being too repetitious. Also he argued that the polemic of 3:2–19 was a poor imitation of 2 Cor. 11:13–15 and that the statement about receiving repeated gifts (4:15–16) was against Paul's policy of not allowing his converts to support him (1 Cor. 9:15–18). These types of criticism are easy to raise but difficult to prove, and they have not been generally accepted by New Testament scholarship. In this analysis of the semantic structure, I will attempt to show that Philippians is a well-organized discourse with specific purposes in mind.

We first find mention of Timothy in Acts 16:2 in connection with Paul's second missionary journey. After the Macedonian call, Luke, Timothy, and Silvanus (Silas) accompanied Paul to Philippi, where the Philippian church was founded (Acts 16:13–40) around A.D. 52. When Paul and Silas left Philippi, it appears that Luke remained there and Timothy may have also, before joining Paul and Silas in Berea. Again, Paul and Silas went on before and Timothy later joined them in Athens and then was sent from there back to Macedonia (to Thessalonica; see 1 Thess. 3:1, 2, 6), although it is likely that he also went to Philippi. Timothy also was one of those who accompanied Paul on his journey from Corinth (via Philippi, Acts 20:6) to Jerusalem to take the collection there (Acts 20:4; 24:17). Seeing the connection Timothy had with the Philippian church gives us added insight into the passage about Timothy's being sent back to Philippi in 2:19–23.

We find Paul, at the writing of this letter, as a prisoner (Phil. 1:13, 14, 17). It has been generally conceded that he was imprisoned in Rome at the time, though some modern commentators have argued for Ephesus, Caesarea, or even Corinth. The major argument proposed against his being imprisoned at Rome at the time of the writing of Philippians is that there would have been insufficient time for all the trips alluded to in the epistle to have taken place if the imprisonment were in Rome. However, the amount of time would have been just as long for a trip from Caesarea to Philippi as from Rome to Philippi and there is no explicit reference in Scripture or elsewhere of Paul's being imprisoned in Ephesus. It seems best to understand Rome as the place where Paul was imprisoned when he wrote Philippians since it accords with tradition while the claims for other cities have serious problems. The fact that a trip between Rome and Philippi would take approximately forty days (O'Brien 1991:25) indicates that there would be sufficient time for several trips within the two-year period Paul was in Rome (Acts 28:30). See the commentaries for a much more detailed discussion of the different sides of the argument.

Philippi was located in the province of Macedonia, about ten miles inland from its harbor city, Neapolis, and not very far from Thessalonica. It was a Roman colony, and its citizens were primarily Roman. When Paul arrived in Philippi, he apparently did not find a synagogue there, but simply a place of prayer attended only by women. It is likely, then, that few Jews were in Philippi. In fact, the Emperor Claudius had ordered all Jews out of Rome at about this time, so we can assume that the Jews in Philippi were not highly favored either.

It was to this environment that Paul came on his second missionary journey. From the account in Acts 16, we find that Paul met with opposition in Philippi—being harassed by a servant girl with a divining spirit, then being thrown in jail and flogged at the request of her owners. Alford (prolegomena, p. 29) suggests as follows:

The cruel treatment of the Apostle at Philippi...seems to have combined with the charm of his personal fervour of affection to knit up a bond of more than ordinary love between him and the Philippian Church. They alone, of all churches [despite being quite poor (2 Cor. 8:2)], sent subsidies to relieve his temporal necessities, on two several occasions, immediately after his departure from them (Phil. iv. 15, 16; 1 Thess. ii. 2): and they revived the same good office to him shortly before the writing of this Epistle (Phil. iv. 10, 18; 2 Cor. xi. 9).

The epistle is not only addressed generically to all the saints in Philippi, but also specifically to the ἐπισκόποις καὶ διακόνοις 'overseers and deacons'.

Epaphroditus was also a participant in the communication situation since he was the bearer of the gift which occasioned the epistle (4:18) and most likely was the bearer of the epistle back to his fellow Philippian believers. He is mentioned in the New Testament only in Phil. 2:25-30 and 4:18. Since he is not mentioned elsewhere in the New Testament, our knowledge of his participation in the communication situation comes only from the content of the epistle itself. He is described by Paul in 2:25 as Paul's (Christian) brother, fellow worker, and fellow soldier, and as the Philippians' messenger and minister of Paul's needs. He is further described in 2:30 as having nearly died because of the work of Christ, risking his life in order to minister to Paul on the behalf of the Philippians. The analysis of the epistle will show that Paul presents the ministry of Epaphroditus as a selfless example of what God expects of all the Philippian believers.

## Occasion and purpose of the letter

While Epaphroditus was in Rome, or perhaps even on his way, he became very seriously ill. God, however, healed him. But the Philippians had been told of this serious sickness and Epaphroditus was distressed that they were worried about him. Also, he was apparently quite homesick: ἐπιποθῶν ἦν πάντας ὑμᾶς 'he has been longing for you all' (2:26). Thus Paul decided to send Epaphroditus back to Philippi and at the same time write a letter for him to take to the believers there, thanking them for their gift and expressing his concerns.

To determine Paul's purposes in the letter, it is helpful to examine those statements in the discourse which through grammatical form and resulting natural prominence are analyzed as forming the highest-level themes of the letter. These divide into two genre types, (1) expressive and (2) hortatory:

1. I rejoice because my adverse circumstances have advanced the gospel and because I know I will be victorious spiritually, magnifying Christ through life or death. I rejoice greatly because you have given me a very sufficient gift by way of Epaphroditus.
2. Love and humbly serve one another taking Christ as your example. Beware of false teachers and of those who live lustful lives. Instead, follow my example of dependence on and conformity to Christ. Rejoice always.

From this theme statement we may determine the following purposes:

1. To thank the Philippian church for its generous gift (4:10-20). There are also allusions to the gift in Paul's statements about partnership in 1:3-8.
2. To assure the Philippians of his joy in adversity and his confidence that he would triumph spiritually whether through life or death (1:12-26).
3. To encourage (i.e., exhort) the believers to be united, loving one another and humbly serving one another. While this is done generically for the most part (1:27-2:30), he applies it specifically to Euodia and Syntyche in 4:2.
4. To warn the believers against false teachers who are preaching circumcision and other legalistic practices (3:2-11) and to warn them not to follow people who live lustful lives (3:17-21).
5. Connected with 4, to present himself as a proper example to follow, both doctrinally (especially in regard to way of salvation) and ethically. Both of these are basic parts of constituent 3:1-4:1.
6. To encourage the believers to rejoice (scattered throughout the letter: 2:18; 3:1; 4:4a, b).

Though not prominent enough to be a part of the higher-level theme statement for the body of the letter, Paul had two other purposes as well: to ensure that Epaphroditus was received back properly (2:25-30) and to give news of his intention of sending Timothy to them as soon as he knew how his trial would turn out (2:19-23).

INTRODUCTION TO THE SEMANTIC STRUCTURE OF PHILIPPIANS 15

## THE CONSTITUENT ORGANIZATION OF PHILIPPIANS

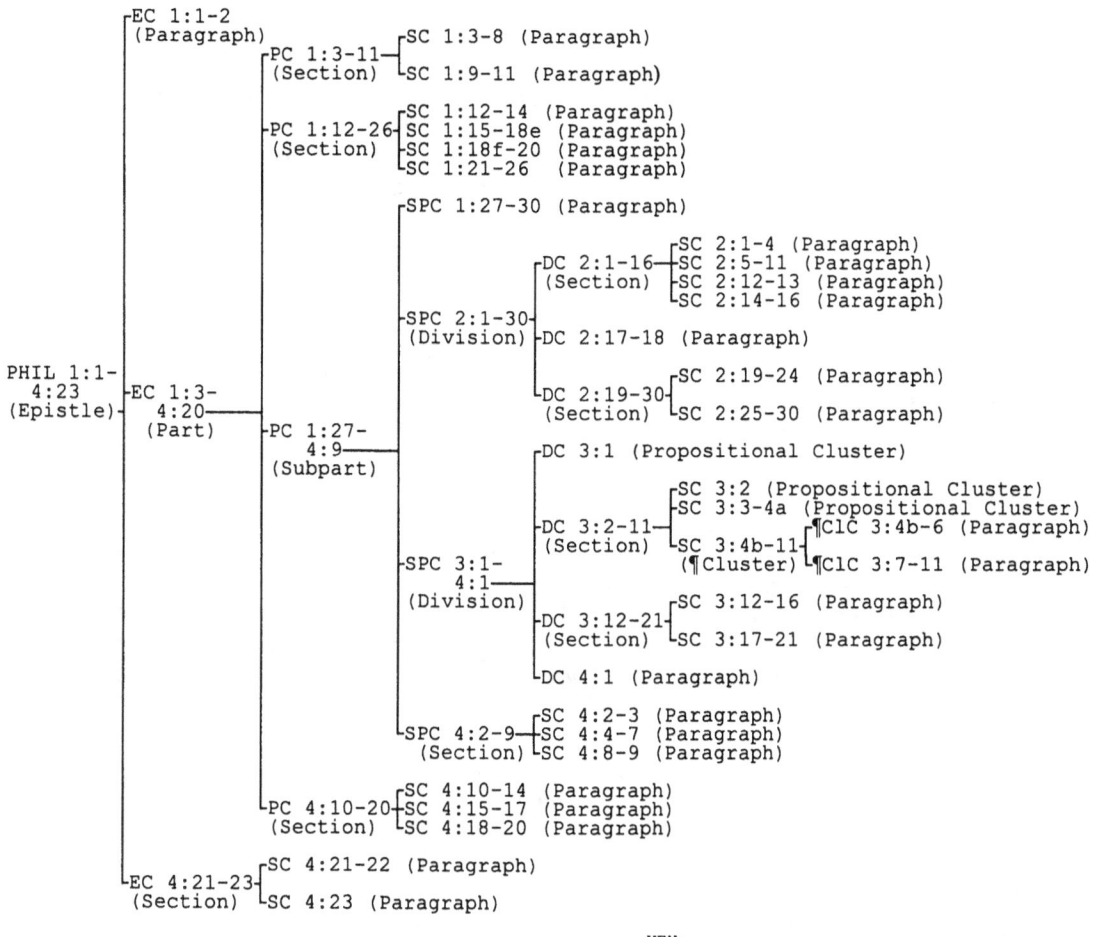

KEY:
EC       Epistle Constituent
PC       Part Constituent
SPC      Subpart Constituent
DC       Division Constituent
SC       Section Constituent
¶Cluster Paragraph Cluster
¶ClC     Paragraph Cluster Constituent

## OVERVIEW: THEMATIC UNITS AND THEIR THEME STATEMENTS

PHILIPPIANS 1:1–4:23 (Epistle)
*Theme: I, Paul, write to all of you who are God's people at Philippi. I rejoice because my adverse circumstances have advanced the good news and because I know I shall remain victorious spiritually. Love and humbly serve one another taking Christ as your example. Beware of false teachers and of those people who live lustful lives. Instead, follow my example of dependence on Christ alone and of striving to become more like him. Rejoice always. I rejoice greatly because you have given me a very generous gift by way of Epaphroditus. Greetings and the Lord's blessings to you all.*

    EPISTLE CONSTITUENT 1:1–2 (Paragraph: Opening of the Epistle)
    *Theme: I, Paul, write this letter to all of you who are God's people at Philippi. May God our Father and Jesus Christ our Lord bless you.*

    EPISTLE CONSTITUENT 1:3–4:20 (Part: Body of the Epistle)
    *Theme: I rejoice because my adverse circumstances have advanced the good news and because I know I shall remain victorious spiritually, magnifying Christ through life or death. Love and humbly serve one another taking Christ as your example. Beware of false teachers and of those people who live lustful lives. Instead, follow my example of dependence on Christ alone and of striving to become more like him. Rejoice always. I rejoice greatly because you have given me a very generous gift by way of Epaphroditus.*

        PART CONSTITUENT 1:3–11 (Expressive Section: Introduction to 1:12–4:20)
        *Theme: I joyfully thank God because you have been working together with me to make known the good news, and I pray that God will enable you to know how to love one another appropriately and to completely understand how you should believe and act.*

            SECTION CONSTITUENT 1:3–8 (Expressive Paragraph: Nucleus$_1$ of 1:3–11)
            *Theme: I thank God and rejoice because you have been working together with me to make known the good news from the first day until now.*

            SECTION CONSTITUENT 1:9–11 (Expressive Paragraph: Nucleus$_2$ of 1:3–11)
            *Theme: I pray that God will enable you to know how to love one another more and more appropriately and to completely understand how you should believe and act.*

        PART CONSTITUENT 1:12–26 (Expressive Section: Nucleus$_1$ of 1:3–4:20)
        *Theme: I rejoice because my adverse circumstances have actually advanced the good news and because I know I shall remain victorious spiritually and will magnify Christ through my life or my death. Though I desire to be with Christ, I know it is necessary for you that I remain alive in order to come and serve you and so you too will rejoice triumphantly.*

            SECTION CONSTITUENT 1:12–14 (Expressive Paragraph: Nucleus$_1$ of 1:12–26)
            *Theme: I want you to realize that as a result of my imprisonment many more people have heard the good news.*

            SECTION CONSTITUENT 1:15–18e (Expressive Paragraph: Nucleus$_2$ of 1:12–26)
            *Theme: Even though some believers proclaim the message about Christ because they are antagonistic toward me, at least they are proclaiming Christ, and so I rejoice.*

            SECTION CONSTITUENT 1:18f–20 (Expressive Paragraph: Nucleus$_3$ of 1:12–26)
            *Theme: I will continue to rejoice because I know that I will remain completely victorious spiritually since I earnestly expect to boldly honor Christ whether by life or by death.*

            SECTION CONSTITUENT 1:21–26 (Expressive Paragraph: Nucleus$_4$ of 1:12–26)
            *Theme: Though I desire to leave this world and be with Christ, it is more important that I remain alive to help you in your need. So I know that I shall remain alive and help you believe in Christ more firmly, and as a result you will rejoice triumphantly.*

        PART CONSTITUENT 1:27–4:9 (Hortatory Subpart: Nucleus$_2$ of 1:3–4:20)
        *Theme: Love and agree with one another, and humbly serve one another taking Christ as your example. Beware of false teachers and beware of those people who live lustful lives. Instead, follow my example of depending on Christ alone for salvation and of becoming more and more like him. Do not worry, but rejoice always.*

            SUBPART CONSTITUENT 1:27–30 (Hortatory Paragraph: Introduction to 2:1–4:9)
            *Theme: Conduct yourselves just as you learned in the good news about Christ, unitedly and fearlessly resisting those who oppose you and the good news, since God is helping you in all your struggles.*

SUBPART CONSTITUENT 2:1-30 (Hortatory Division: Appeal₁ of 1:27-4:9)
*Theme: Love and agree with one another, and humbly serve one another without arguing. Take Christ as your model in this. I dedicate my life to God together with you; therefore, let us all rejoice even though I may die. I expect to send Timothy to you soon and Epaphroditus right away. These are men who care for others' welfare, not their own. Welcome and honor such men as these.*

> DIVISION CONSTITUENT 2:1-16 (Hortatory Section: Appeal₁ of 2:1-30)
> *Theme: Love one another, agree with one another, and humbly serve one another since Christ has loved us and humbly given himself for us in death on a shameful cross. Obey God and your leaders always and never complain against them or argue with them, but witness in life and word to the ungodly people around you.*
>
>> SECTION CONSTITUENT 2:1-4 (Hortatory Paragraph: Appeal₁ of 2:1-16)
>> *Theme: Since Christ loves and encourages us and the Holy Spirit fellowships with us, make me completely happy by agreeing with one another, loving one another, and humbly serving one another.*
>>
>> SECTION CONSTITUENT 2:5-11 (Hortatory Paragraph: Appeal₂ of 2:1-16)
>> *Theme: You should think just as Christ Jesus thought, who willingly gave up his divine prerogatives and humbled himself, willingly obeying God though it meant dying on a shameful cross. As a result God exalted him to the highest position, to be acknowledged by all the universe as the supreme Lord.*
>>
>> SECTION CONSTITUENT 2:12-13 (Hortatory Paragraph: Appeal₃ of 2:1-16)
>> *Theme: Since you have always obeyed God, continue to strive to do those things which are appropriate for people whom God has saved, since he will enable you to do so.*
>>
>> SECTION CONSTITUENT 2:14-16 (Hortatory Paragraph: Appeal₄ of 2:1-16)
>> *Theme: Obey God and your leaders always and never complain against them or argue with them, in order that you may be perfect children of God, witnessing in life and word to the ungodly people among whom you live.*
>
> DIVISION CONSTITUENT 2:17-18 (Hortatory Paragraph: Appeal₂ of 2:1-30)
> *Theme: Because I and all of you dedicate ourselves together to do God's will, even if I am to be executed I rejoice and you should also rejoice.*
>
> DIVISION CONSTITUENT 2:19-30 (Section: Appeal₃ of 2:1-30)
> *Theme: I confidently expect to send Timothy to you soon. He genuinely cares for your welfare, not his own interests. I am sending Epaphroditus back to you. Welcome him joyfully. Honor him and all those like him since he nearly died while serving me on your behalf.*
>
>> SECTION CONSTITUENT 2:19-24 (Commissive Paragraph: Nucleus₁ of 2:19-30)
>> *Theme: I confidently expect that the Lord Jesus will enable me to send Timothy to you soon. He genuinely cares for your welfare, not his own interests. I am confident that the Lord will enable me also to come soon.*
>>
>> SECTION CONSTITUENT 2:25-30 (Hortatory Paragraph: Nucleus₂ of 2:19-30)
>> *Theme: Since Epaphroditus longs to see you and is distressed, I am sending him back to you. Therefore welcome him very joyfully. Honor him and all people like him since he nearly died while serving me on your behalf.*

SUBPART CONSTITUENT 3:1-4:1 (Hortatory Division: Appeal₂ of 1:27-4:9)
*Theme: Beware of those people who are trying to harm you by teaching that you must be circumcised. Also beware of those who are living lustful lives. Instead, follow my example of becoming more and more like Christ and depending on him alone for a right relationship with God. Our certain hope is that Christ will transform our earthly bodies to be like his heavenly body.*

> DIVISION CONSTITUENT 3:1 (Propositional Cluster: Introduction to 3:2-21)
> *Theme: As for the other matters, continue to rejoice and know that it is not tiresome for me and it is safe for you to mention them again.*
>
> DIVISION CONSTITUENT 3:2-11 (Hortatory Section: Appeal₁ of 3:1-4:1)
> *Theme: Beware of those unholy people who will harm you spiritually by insisting that you must be circumcised in order to become God's people. We are already God's*

*people not because we rely on ourselves at all but because we give up ourselves in order that we may know Christ and be united with him, relying on him alone to be made righteous and become his people, as my example shows.*

SECTION CONSTITUENT 3:2 (Hortatory Propositional Cluster: Appeal of 3:2-11)

*Theme: Beware of those unholy people who will harm you spiritually by insisting that you must be circumcised in order to become God's people.*

SECTION CONSTITUENT 3:3-4a (Expository Propositional Cluster: Basis$_1$ for 3:2)

*Theme: It is we who worship God through his Spirit and glorify Christ Jesus rather than depending on our own selves who are truly God's people.*

SECTION CONSTITUENT 3:4b-11 (Expository Paragraph Cluster: Basis$_2$ for 3:2)

*Theme: Although, if it were beneficial for salvation, I could rely upon my own attainments better than anyone else could, I consider all those attainments worthless because I want to know Christ and be united with him, made righteous through trusting in Christ alone.*

PARAGRAPH CLUSTER CONSTITUENT 3:4b-6 (Expository Paragraph: Concession to 3:7-11)

*Theme: If it were beneficial for salvation, I could rely upon what I have done and who I am better than anyone else could rely upon himself, since I was circumcised properly and have a purely Hebrew ancestry and I kept the law blamelessly.*

PARAGRAPH CLUSTER CONSTITUENT 3:7-11 (Expository Paragraph: Contraexpectation to 3:4b-6)

*Theme: I consider all these things which I used to think of as advantageous, and everything else as well, to be worthless because I want to know Christ and be united with him, made righteous through trusting in Christ alone.*

DIVISION CONSTITUENT 3:12-21 (Hortatory Section: Appeal$_2$ of 3:1-4:1)

*Theme: Follow my example of constantly striving to become more and more like Christ rather than following the bad example of those who are lustful and think only about earthly things. As for us, Christ will transform our earthly bodies to be like his heavenly body.*

SECTION CONSTITUENT 3:12-16 (Hortatory Paragraph: Appeal$_1$ of 3:12-21)

*Theme: Since you desire to be perfected and since you have my example of not considering that I am already perfect but of constantly striving to become more and more like Christ, follow my example.*

SECTION CONSTITUENT 3:17-21 (Hortatory Paragraph: Appeal$_2$ of 3:12-21)

*Theme: Imitate me and those who live as I do since there are many people who are bad examples as shown by their lustful behavior, thinking only about earthly things. As for us, Christ will transform our lowly earthly bodies to be like his glorious heavenly body.*

DIVISION CONSTITUENT 4:1 (Hortatory Paragraph: Summary of 3:1-21)

*Theme: My dear friends, on the basis of all that I have told you [3:1-21], continue to believe firmly in the Lord Jesus Christ according to what I have just taught you [3:1-21] and act accordingly.*

SUBPART CONSTITUENT 4:2-9 (Hortatory Section: Appeal$_3$ of 1:27-4:9)

*Theme: I urge Euodia and Syntyche to be reconciled with each other. Rejoice always and be gentle to everyone. Do not worry; pray instead. Think about all that is good and practice whatever you have learned from me and God will be with you and grant you peace.*

SECTION CONSTITUENT 4:2-3 (Hortatory Paragraph: Appeal$_1$ of 4:2-9)

*Theme: I urge Euodia and Syntyche to be reconciled with each other since they belong to the Lord, and I request that you, faithful comrade, help them in this since they have both proclaimed the good news faithfully together with me and my other fellow workers.*

SECTION CONSTITUENT 4:4-7 (Hortatory Paragraph: Appeal$_2$ of 4:2-9)
*Theme: The Lord is near. Always rejoice, be gentle to everyone. Do not worry about anything, but pray to God instead. As a result, God will grant you profound peace.*

SECTION CONSTITUENT 4:8-9 (Hortatory Paragraph: Appeal$_3$ of 4:2-9)
*Theme: Continually think about everything that is good and praiseworthy. Continually practice whatever you have learned from me. As a result, God will be with you and give you peace.*

PART CONSTITUENT 4:10-20 (Expressive Section: Nucleus$_3$ of 1:3-4:20)
*Theme: I rejoice greatly because, even though Christ enables me to be content in every situation, you have given me a very generous gift by way of Epaphroditus, just as you have helped me from the very beginning. God will abundantly supply your every need also. Let us praise him forever and ever.*

SECTION CONSTITUENT 4:10-14 (Expressive Paragraph: Reaction$_1$ of 4:10-20)
*Theme: I rejoice greatly because you have once again demonstrated your concern for me by giving to meet my needs, though it is true that Christ enables me to be content in every situation.*

SECTION CONSTITUENT 4:15-17 (Expressive Paragraph: Reaction$_2$ of 4:10-20)
*Theme: You Philippians yourselves know that in the early days of preaching the good news in your region you were the only congregation that sent me gifts; not that I desire your gifts but I desire that God would abundantly bless you for aiding me.*

SECTION CONSTITUENT 4:18-20 (Expressive Paragraph: Reaction$_3$ of 4:10-20)
*Theme: I have received your very generous gift; God is very pleased with this gift, and he will abundantly supply your every need also. Let us praise him forever and ever.*

EPISTLE CONSTITUENT 4:21-23 (Expressive Section: Closing of the Epistle)
*Theme: In closing, all of us here greet all of you. May the Lord Jesus Christ bless you spiritually.*

SECTION CONSTITUENT 4:21-22 (Expressive Paragraph: Reaction$_1$ (greetings) of 4:21-23)
*Theme: I and all of the rest of God's people here, including those who serve God with me and those who work at the emperor's palace, greet each one of God's people there.*

SECTION CONSTITUENT 4:23 (Expressive Paragraph: Reaction$_2$ (benediction) of 4:21-23)
*Theme: May the Lord Jesus Christ bless you spiritually.*

# THE PRESENTATION AND DISCUSSION OF THE SEMANTIC UNITS OF PHILIPPIANS

## PHILIPPIANS 1:1–4:23 (Epistle)

*THEME: I, Paul, write to all of you who are God's people at Philippi. I rejoice because my adverse circumstances have advanced the good news and because I know I shall remain victorious spiritually. Love and humbly serve one another taking Christ as your example. Beware of false teachers and of those people who live lustful lives. Instead, follow my example of dependence on Christ alone and of striving to become more like him. Rejoice always. I rejoice greatly because you have given me a very generous gift by way of Epaphroditus. Greetings and the Lord's blessings to you all.*

| MACROSTRUCTURE | CONTENTS |
| --- | --- |
| opening | 1:1–2 I, Paul, write this letter to all of you who are God's people at Philippi. May God our Father and Jesus Christ our Lord bless you. |
| BODY | 1:3–4:20 I rejoice because my adverse circumstances have advanced the good news and because I know I shall remain victorious spiritually, magnifying Christ through life or death. Love and humbly serve one another taking Christ as your example. Beware of false teachers and of those people who live lustful lives. Instead, follow my example of dependence on Christ alone and of striving to become more like him. Rejoice always. I rejoice greatly because you have given me a very generous gift by way of Epaphroditus. |
| closing | 4:21–23 In closing, all of us here greet all of you. May the Lord Jesus Christ bless you spiritually. |

## COHERENCE

The Epistle to the Philippians follows the established pattern of Greek letters of an opening, a body, and a closing, at this the highest level of the discourse. As J. Callow points out for Colossians (1983:23), "It is this formal structure of the total discourse that constitutes its organizational (or structural) coherence."

Some commentators take Τὸ λοιπόν, ἀδελφοί μου, χαίρετε ἐν κυρίῳ (3:1a) as meaning 'Finally, my brothers, farewell in the Lord' rather than 'As for the remaining matters, my brothers, rejoice in the Lord'. Based on this understanding of 3:1a, some see it as an intended closing to the epistle, after which Paul added more body-type information upon receiving new reports about the Philippians, while others see the epistle, as we now have it, as a compilation of more than one epistle. The position held in this SSA is that the epistle as we have it is one coherent discourse. This will be discussed more in the notes for 1:3–4:20.

## PROMINENCE AND THEME

While the body of a letter has more natural prominence since it carries the main message of the discourse, the opening is still highly thematic because of its function of identifying the writer and recipients. Also the well-wishing rapport elements of both the opening and closing are an integral part of the full discourse.

# EPISTLE CONSTITUENT 1:1–2 (Paragraph: Opening of the Epistle)

*THEME: I, Paul, write this letter to all of you who are God's people at Philippi. May God our Father and Jesus Christ our Lord bless you.*

| STRUCTURE | CONTENTS |
|---|---|
| ADDRESS — ITEM — description of 'Paul', 'Timothy' | 1:1a *I,* Paul, and Timothy *are* servants of Christ Jesus (*or,* men who serve Christ Jesus). |
| | 1:1b *I, together with Timothy, am writing this letter* to all *of you(pl),*** who are God's people *and who are united* with Christ Jesus *and who live in Philippi city, including you who are* overseers and deacons.* |
| BLESSING | 1:2 *We(dual exc) pray that* God, *who is* our(inc) Father, and Jesus Christ, *who is* our(inc) Lord, *will continue to* act graciously toward you *and will continue to* cause you to have peace/be peaceful.* |
| | **Unless otherwise marked, 'you' in the display text is always a plural reference in this SSA. |

## INTENT AND STRUCTURE

The ADDRESS and BLESSING are two quite different constituents. The ADDRESS has to do with referencing. Like any discourse, a letter must have some type of referencing at its beginning. While the BLESSING is not an obligatory feature of all letters, it is a component of expressive rapport found in many. (Expressive rapport occurs in an English letter with the use of *Dear* . . .)

Since these two components are different in import, they are in a conjoined (coordinate) relationship with one another. Difference in import of this kind would normally indicate that the relationship between v. 1 and v. 2 would be on the macrostructure level, but here there are important coherence features, such as the verbless form (except for the participle οὖσιν 'being') of the opening, that tend to mark all of the opening as one paragraph. Thus it is kept as one paragraph in the display. The two parts are given specific labels rather than representing them only as conjoined units, and the column's heading in the display is "structure."

## NOTES

The openings of letters in Paul's time were formalized, following a general pattern of the writer's identifying first himself and then those to whom he was writing, followed by giving a greeting. In Paul's letters this greeting takes the form of a prayer in which he prays that God will bless the recipients. In this stylized opening, we find certain characteristics: the writer gives his name in the nominative case, the recipients are mentioned in the dative case, and verbal forms are lacking, especially finite verbs.

**1:1a servants of Christ Jesus** 'Servants of Christ Jesus' is used in the display text rather than 'serve Christ Jesus' since 'servant of Christ Jesus' is a title and, in English and presumably in most languages where the concept of servant is known, the noun form more adequately expresses the total sense and collocational range of δοῦλος. For languages in which 'servant' does not occur as a noun or where its use would imply wrong connotations, 'men who serve Christ Jesus' would be a potential alternative.

**Christ Jesus** Both the order 'Christ Jesus' and 'Jesus Christ' are found in Philippians. It would be difficult to prove that there is a meaning difference between the two orders. Thus, in translating into a language in which it is inappropriate or unnatural to change the order each time it is changed in the Greek text, it is unnecessary to do so.

**1:1b *I, together with Timothy*** The conjunction καί in Παῦλος καὶ Τιμόθεος has been rendered as 'together with' rather than 'and'. The occurrence of Παῦλος καὶ Τιμόθεος at the beginning of this epistle does not indicate joint authorship. This is shown by the fact that all the verbs with first person endings in the body of the epistle are singular rather than plural. There is evidence in ancient Greek culture that the convention of coordinating two persons' names at the beginning of a letter was sometimes used to signal that one person was the author and the other person was in full agreement with what was being said and joined with the author in wanting to communicate the same message. The rendering 'Paul, together with Timothy', as opposed to 'Paul and Timothy', is meant to signal that Timothy's involvement in the letter is subordinate to Paul's and that he is not being regarded as an actual author.

***am writing this letter*** The first instance of a missing verb in the Greek text occurs here in 1:1, the verb which would relate the writers to the recipients. In some previous SSAs, 'send' has been proposed as the best choice of a verb to be supplied, while in others 'write' has been used. For propositionalization, 'write' may be better, since it is more basic to the actual communication of the message. This would be especially true for languages where 'send' does not potentially cover the total situation of writing and sending. If, however, the use of 'write' would imply that Paul actually penned the letter, then 'send' or some other appropriate word would presumably be a better choice, since Paul no doubt used an amanuensis.

**God's people** Concerning οἱ ἅγιοι, literally, 'the holy ones, the saints', J. Callow says in the Colossians SSA (p. 27), "The term 'saints'...is not used in the display because the biblical meaning is not its primary English sense any longer; it is replaced by 'God's people', i.e. 'saint' is understood to mean 'set apart for and belonging to God'." Although this basically is a good solution, one wonders if "holiness of heart and conduct" (Kennedy) would not also be signaled by ἅγιοι; that is, this component of meaning of ἅγιος would not necessarily be backgrounded in the use of οἱ ἅγιοι in this context. This would not necessarily imply that 'the holy ones' always displayed holy lives, but that hopefully they were striving toward such. Thus it would seem that 'God's holy people' would also be an acceptable translation, especially if such a translation in any language would not imply absolute perfection.

***who are united* with Christ Jesus** The phrase ἐν Χριστῷ 'in Christ' or ἐν Χριστῷ Ἰησοῦ in such a context as this is very widely held to mean 'incorporated into Christ' or 'united to Christ' (see p. 20 of the Colossians SSA).

**overseers** The Greek noun ἐπίσκοπος, often translated as 'bishop', does not correspond, of course, to our modern-day 'bishop'. The word is plural here, indicating more than one ἐπίσκοπος in the church at Philippi. It is often translated as 'overseer' as in the display. 'Leader' would also be acceptable. The ἐπίσκοποι probably had general oversight of the local body of believers including church-related financial matters (as 1 Tim. 3:3 and Titus 1:7 probably suggest). And since one purpose of Paul in writing is to thank the church at Philippi for their contribution to him, it may be that they and the deacons are specifically mentioned here because of their involvement in raising the funds for the gift.

The terms πρεσβύτερος 'elder' and ἐπίσκοπος 'overseer' are closely related (see Acts 20:17-28 and Titus 1:5-7). In Titus 1:5-7, these terms both refer to the same persons, according to most commentators, the first relating to their position and/or qualifications of experience and the second, to the work they are expected to perform.

**deacons\*** One question here is whether διάκονοι in this context refers to people with the same role as the deacons in Acts 6 (to care for the material needs of the Christian community) or some other, probably broader, role. At first the former might appear to be the correct answer. Note, however, Vincent's comment (p. 38): "Διακονία is applied to religious and churchly ministries of all kinds. In Eph. iv. 11, 12, Paul says that Christ gave apostles, prophets, evangelists, pastors, and teachers to the work of διακονία for the perfecting of the saints. Paul and Apollos, Timothy and the secular ruler, are alike διάκονοι (1 Cor. iii. 5; 1 Thess. iii. 2 [some texts]; Rom. xiii. 4)." An answer to this would be that these uses of the word do not denote a title as such. If this were applied to Phil. 1:1, then διάκονοι would refer to anyone in the church who had any type of role of service, from prophet to those ministering to the needy. And since ἐπίσκοπος would refer only to those having the function of overseeing, a specific term conjoined with a generic one would be somewhat of an unnatural collocation. It seems best, therefore, to take διάκονοι as referring to those who were ministering to the material needs of the congregation and, most specifically, were involved in the administration of this ministry. This is the view of Martin (1959): "The *diakonoi* took their name from those who, in the secular world, were responsible for certain welfare duties in the community (e.g. the distribution of gifts and food). The Christian deacon, whose origin is usually traced to the ministry of the Seven in Acts vi, though the actual title 'deacon' does not appear there, may be regarded as a person who had certain administrative tasks in the church..." While the role of deacon changed with time and became institutionalized, it may be best to understand it at this early date as referring basically to the administration of the ministry to the material needs of the believers.

The rendering of διάκονοι in the display is as a noun, with an asterisk to signify that our modern English meaning is not necessarily to be understood. For languages which must use verbal forms for this concept, the following are suggested: 'you who care for the material needs of the believers', 'you who care for believers who are needy', 'you who manage the ones distributing goods to needy believers'.

**1:2** *We (dual exc) pray that* This verse is regarded as a prayer, thus the implicit information 'We (dual exc) pray that' is included.

**act graciously toward you** This is Paul's familiar prayer that 'grace and peace' continue to be given by God and Christ to the recipients of the letter. J. Callow in the SSA of 2 Thessalonians says of 'grace' in a similar context:

> The question arises here, as it does also in the final verse of Paul's epistles, as to how "grace" (*charis*) should be understood. Does it have its full theological sense of God giving his blessings freely to those who can in no way merit them? Or does it have the more general sense of "bless," "do good to," "act kindly towards"? There is not as much difference as would appear at first sight, as, for Paul, "grace" is the word that characterizes all God's favorable attitudes and actions towards sinful men. Since it is a formal greeting, an expression should be chosen by translators which is appropriate to a greeting. (p. 24)

**cause you to have peace/be peaceful\*** As to εἰρήνη, Callow comments as follows (ibid.:24–25):

> To some extent, the same issue arises with the word "peace" (*eirēnē*). Again, it is very widely held that the choice of this word reflects the Hebrew greeting of *shalom* 'peace', which expresses much more than lack of strife, or even inner peacefulness. Rather it conveys the idea of "spiritual prosperity", "enjoying God's blessing", general "blessedness". In other words, it is the reciprocal of God's blessing, the recipients' state of blessedness. Hence, in translation some general word should be used that is appropriate for *spiritual* blessedness rather than material prosperity, which is not a New Testament emphasis.

## BOUNDARIES AND COHERENCE

The initial boundary of 1:1–2 coincides with the beginning of the epistle discourse.

These first two verses of the epistle follow the same basic pattern that Paul uses for the openings of his other letters. The ADDRESS (1:1) identifies the sender and his associate in the nominative case (Paul and Timothy) and the addressees in the dative case (all God's people at Philippi including the overseers and deacons). This is followed by the blessing (1:2), characteristically the last part of an *opening*. The formulaic structure of the *opening*, including the fact that it is verbless (except for the participle οὖσιν 'being'), strongly suggests that all of the *opening* should be understood as one grammatical paragraph. For that reason it seems best to also treat it as one semantic paragraph.

At 1:3 there is a change from a structure with no finite verbs (1:1–2) to one with a finite verb form, εὐχαριστῶ 'I thank', at the very beginning of v. 3. This verb also indicates that the subject matter changes from a blessing typical of an *opening* to thanksgiving.

## PROMINENCE AND THEME

The ADDRESS and BLESSING have distinctive roles in the *opening* of the epistle, and they are related by conjoining rather than by being in a supportive-type relationship. This means that the theme (see the theme statement at the top of the display) must be drawn from both of them. As far as the ADDRESS is concerned, only Paul's name is mentioned in the theme as the writer since, as argued in the introduction and in the notes on v. 1, Paul is the basic author of the epistle. The overseers and deacons are not mentioned specifically in the theme since they are included in 'all God's people' and reference to them is not forefronted in the text.

As for the theme of the BLESSING, 'bless' is used to represent granting of both grace and peace, and 'may' is substituted for '*we(dual exc) pray that*'.

# EPISTLE CONSTITUENT 1:3–4:20 (Part: Body of the Epistle)

*THEME: I rejoice because my adverse circumstances have advanced the good news and because I know I shall remain victorious spiritually, magnifying Christ through life or death. Love and humbly serve one another taking Christ as your example. Beware of false teachers and of those people who live lustful lives. Instead, follow my example of dependence on Christ alone and of striving to become more like him. Rejoice always. I rejoice greatly because you have given me a very generous gift by way of Epaphroditus.*

| MACROSTRUCTURE | CONTENTS |
| --- | --- |
| introduction (expressive) | 1:3–11 I joyfully thank God because you have been working together with me to make known the good news, and I pray that God will enable you to know how to love one another appropriately and to completely understand how you should believe and act. |
| NUCLEUS$_1$ (expressive) | 1:12–26 I rejoice because my adverse circumstances have actually advanced the good news and because I know I shall remain victorious spiritually and will magnify Christ through my life or my death. Though I desire to be with Christ, I know it is necessary for you that I remain alive in order to come and serve you and so you too will rejoice triumphantly. |
| NUCLEUS$_2$ (hortatory) | 1:27–4:9 Love and agree with one another, and humbly serve one another taking Christ as your example. Beware of false teachers and beware of those people who live lustful lives. Instead, follow my example of depending on Christ alone for salvation and of becoming more and more like him. Do not worry, but rejoice always. |
| NUCLEUS$_3$ (expressive) | 4:10–20 I rejoice greatly because, even though Christ enables me to be content in every situation, you have given me a very generous gift by way of Epaphroditus, just as you have helped me from the very beginning. God will abundantly supply your every need also. Let us praise him forever and ever. |

## INTENT AND MACROSTRUCTURE

If the BODY of the Epistle is analyzed as consisting of expressive and hortatory parts, the structure is seen to be quite simple. After the typical expressive introduction of thanksgiving and prayer (1:3–11), another rather long expressive unit (1:12–26) follows where Paul recounts his present situation, relating how he rejoices in spite of difficult circumstances because God is working them out for good. And he hopes that he will even be released from incarceration so that he may be with the Philippians again in order that they too may rejoice.

This section is followed by 1:27–4:9, the hortatory subpart of the epistle. Paragraph 1:27–30 is taken as the subpart's introduction since it has elements both of the theme of unity dealt with in 2:1–30 (especially in 2:1–11, with 12–30 highlighting unity's corollary of unselfish service to others) and of the theme of maintaining correct belief in the face of opposition dealt with in 3:1–4:1. The next hortatory unit is 4:2–9, which is a set of miscellaneous exhortations ending the hortatory part of the epistle. The 1:27–4:9 hortatory subpart is followed by an expressive section of gratitude for the gift that Epaphroditus had brought to Paul from the Philippians (4:10–20).

There is another possible analysis, however, which may be worthy of examination, though it is not the one this SSA presents. The unit 2:17–18 is different from the others here in that while it comes at the closing point of the main hortatory section on unity, it also ties in the basic elements of the theme of the expressive unit 1:12–26—rejoicing in the face of death. It thus acts very much like a summary or closure to these two units taken as a whole. As those two units are both expressive (1:12–26) and hortatory (1:27–2:16), so 2:17–18 is both expressive and hortatory. Heyward came to the conclusion in the earlier SSA work that 2:17–18 is closure for the unit 1:12–2:18 on the basis of semantic "sandwich structure" (inclusio); that is, Paul's rejoicing in adverse circumstances is discussed both in what would be the opening unit (1:12–26) of 1:12–2:18 and the closing unit (2:17–18). If the present analysis were to follow this viewpoint, the BODY of the epistle might be diagrammed as follows:

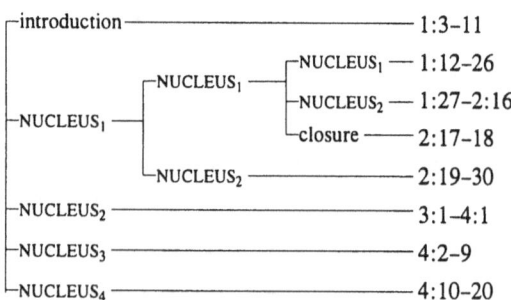

While this analysis has some good points, it is less simple because it mixes expressive material with hortatory material. And while some factors of unity and certainly of dedicated service to others occur in 1:12–26, one wonders if there is enough coherence between the two units to see them as more closely tied together than this hortatory section (1:27–2:30) is to the next one (3:1–4:1). As mentioned, 1:27–30 quite clearly functions as an introduction to the hortatory part of the epistle. Organizationally it would be peculiar for 2:17–18 to function as closure for 1:12–2:16 and 1:27–30 to function as introduction for 2:1–4:9, the hortatory part of the epistle. Because of this, it seems better not to take unit 2:17–18 as having a closure role.

This hortatory 'rejoice' unit (2:17–18) is similar to 3:1a, and even to 4:4a–b, in two respects. One is that even though the reference is expressive, the illocution is hortatory. The other is that their occurrence, especially in 2:17–18 and 3:1a and to some extent in 4:4a–b, seems somewhat difficult to tie in to the surrounding material. Two possible reasons for this are (1) that expressive material tends to be spontaneous and (2) that Paul is weaving into his whole discourse enough references to his motif of joy and rejoicing (whether his own reactions or his exhortations to them) that the Philippians will have cause to experience joy themselves. If this "weaving" characteristic of motif is not understood, there may seem to be a lack of coherence with the surrounding material in certain places.

It may seem somewhat strange to include the units in 2:19–30 on Paul's intentions of sending Timothy and Epaphroditus to the Philippians in the larger hortatory unit with its theme of unity. But as O'Brien (1991:315) states, with footnote references to Culpepper (pp. 350–51), Swift (p. 246), and Garland (1985:163): "There are striking verbal parallels between 2:19–30 and the christological confession of 2:5–11 with its related exhortations." Christ is the first and foremost example of lowly service, but also Paul has referred to the possibility of his own life being poured out as a libation for others (2:17). He now presents Timothy, who has slaved selflessly in the gospel (2:22; cf. 1:1, 7) and has a genuine concern for the interests of the Philippians (τὰ περὶ ὑμῶν, 2:20), and Epaphroditus, who almost died in the *service* of Christ (2:30), as godly examples of the way the Philippians should imitate Christ. (ibid., with footnote references to Culpepper [pp. 350, 353, etc.], Hawthorne [p. 108], Garland [1985:163])

This demonstrates that 2:19–30 functions not only as a travelogue but also points out examples of selfless service to others, examples that the Philippians are being encouraged to follow (cf. Watson, pp. 71–72). If we treat the epistle as a coherent unit, the fact that the travelogues are placed by Paul at this point, rather than at the end of the epistle where he normally would put them, strongly suggests that they are in some type of relationship to the hortatory section on unity and selfless service.

It is significant that my preferred analysis is amazingly similar to the results achieved by Watson in his rhetorical analysis of Philippians. Although I did build upon the suggestion of Watson (and others) that 2:19–30 is related in theme to 1:27–2:18, otherwise the results were reached independently. Following is a comparison of units in each analysis. Not all of the smaller units are included in the listing. The listing under rhetorical analysis is based, in most cases, on direct reference by Watson to these units and, in a couple of cases, on obvious implication from other comments on the structure.

| SSA | RHETORICAL ANALYSIS |
| --- | --- |
| 1:1–2 | 1:1–2 |
| 1:3–11 | 1:3–11 |
| 1:12–26 | 1:12–26 |
| 1:27–4:9 | 1:27–3:21 |
| 1:27–30 | 1:27–30 |
| 2:1–4:1 | 2:1–3:21 |
| 2:1–11 | 2:1–11 |
| 2:1–4 | 2:1–4 |
| 2:5–11 | 2:5–11 |
| 2:12–16 | 2:12–18 |
| 2:12–13 | 2:12–13 |
| 2:19–30 | 2:19–30 |
| 2:19–24 | 2:19–24 |
| 2:25–30 | 2:25–30 |
| 3:1–4:1 | 3:1–21 |
|  | 4:2–20 |

| | |
|---|---|
| 4:2-9 | 4:1-9 |
| 4:10-20 | 4:10-20 |
| 4:21-23 | 4:21-23 |

The major differences between the two analyses are (1) that the SSA takes 4:1 as a summary of 3:1-21 while the rhetorical analysis takes 4:1 as the beginning of the *repetitio* (4:1-9) and (2) the SSA groups 4:2-9 with the other preceding hortatory material and takes 4:10-20 as a separate expressive unit while the rhetorical analysis groups 4:1-9 with 4:10-20 as both parts of the *peroratio*. Watson (pp. 76-77) says of the *repetitio*, "Of the major methods of recapitulation that were recommended for the *repetitio*, the method used here is most akin to the standard method of briefly touching on each point by way of summation and proposing a line of action." Thus, while the SSA sees 4:1 as an independent summation of 3:1-21, the rhetorical analysis sees it as part of a summation unit of 4:1-9. And because Watson sees 4:1-9 as summation, he groups it with the emotive unit 4:10-20 following the rhetorical model of *repetitio* and *adfectus* as components of the *peroratio* (the concluding part of the discourse).

A final question is whether the expressive units of the *BODY*, in whole or in part, support the hortatory units. It is difficult to see an intended *basis-APPEAL* relationship between Paul's thanksgiving for the gift (4:10-20) and any of the hortatory units or the hortatory subpart as a whole (1:27-4:9). It is possible to see a *basis-APPEAL* relationship between the expressive units of 1:3-26 and the hortatory subpart, especially since Paul's experience and selfless desires recounted in the expressive units are an example of the attitude he asks the Philippians to take in the hortatory subpart. On this basis such an analysis has merit. On the other hand, μόνον 'only' at the beginning of the hortatory subpart does not clearly mark a *basis-APPEAL* relation and Paul appears to have encouragement of the believers in mind as the main purpose of the expressive section so the expressive and hortatory units of the *BODY* have been analyzed as being in conjoined rather than *basis-APPEAL* relationship.

## COHERENCE

Many recent writers have claimed that the Epistle to the Philippians as we now have it is really a compilation of more than one letter. Many contend that another discourse written at a different time is inserted at the beginning of chapter 3 (the exact place in vv. 1 and 2 is debated). Their reasons are: the travelogue normally occurs near the end of an epistle rather than in the middle as 2:19-30 does; 3:1 begins with τὸ λοιπόν, which may be translated as 'finally'; χαίρετε ἐν κυρίῳ in 3:1 could be translated as 'farewell in the Lord' (χαίρετε is appropriately translated as 'farewell' in 2 Cor. 13:11); 3:1-2 seems quite disjuncted in thought; and the tone of 3:2 and the following verses seems so much stronger than anything in the first two chapters. Views on where this insertion ends vary widely. Also, some feel that the thank you note in 4:10-20 must be the body of a separate letter in itself since it seems incongruous for Paul to wait to the very end of the epistle to thank the Philippians for their gift.

It is our position that the Epistle to the Philippians in the form that we have it, a form that can be shown to have existed as early as the beginning of the third or even late second century in the manuscript p46 (Silva, p. 14), is an integrated discourse. We have already mentioned a good reason for the travelogue's occurring in the middle of the epistle. As will be discussed in the notes for 3:1, τὸ λοιπόν does not necessarily mean 'finally', as shown by its use elsewhere in Paul's epistles (1 Thess. 4:1; 2 Thess. 3:1). And χαίρετε ἐν κυρίῳ is much more likely to have the meaning of 'rejoice in the Lord' rather than 'farewell in the Lord' because of the motif of 'rejoice' in the epistle and the similar occurrence of χαίρετε ἐν κυρίῳ πάντοτε 'rejoice in the Lord always' in 4:4. The presumed disjunction in 3:1-2 is discussed thoroughly under "Boundaries and Coherence" for 3:1-4:1.

As for the striking change of tone, Watson (pp. 86-87) argues in his rhetorical analysis of Philippians that "the tonal shift in 3:2 was not at all foreign to the rhetoric of Paul's day, but rather was conventional." Paul certainly knew how to handle changes in rhetoric as his Epistle to the Romans shows (note especially 2:1; 6:1; 7:1; 9:1).

There are elements of coherence in the Philippian epistle that demonstrate it to be a coherent whole: Lexical coherence is found in the motif of joy. The noun χαρά 'joy' and the verbs χαίρω 'rejoice' and συγχαίρω 'rejoice with' occur sixteen times: 1:4, 18e, 18f, 25; 2:2, 17 (twice), 18 (twice), 28, 29; 3:1; 4:1, 4a, 4b, 10. The argument that χαίρετε ἐν κυρίῳ means 'farewell in the Lord' in 3:1a and that chapter 3 is an insertion because it lacks any reference to 'joy' or 'rejoice' must deal with χαίρετε ἐν κυρίῳ πάντοτε in 4:4. Why take χαίρετε ἐν κυρίῳ to mean 'farewell in the Lord' in 3:1 when χαίρετε ἐν κυρίῳ πάντοτε in 4:4 obviously cannot mean 'farewell in the Lord always'?

Coherence is also shown by the exhortations to unity in 2:2 (τὸ αὐτὸ φρονῆτε and τὸ ἓν φρονοῦντες) and in 4:2 (τὸ αὐτὸ φρονεῖν). Paul has dealt with this topic generally in 2:1-30, and now at the place where individuals are usually referred to in an epistle he brings up the point again by specifically addressing two individuals who lack unity. Any theory that sees 3:1a as a statement of conclusion to the epistle must explain why Paul, after saying farewell, returns to what would seem an extremely relevant matter, related to what he had already said, and therefore a matter he intended to communicate from the beginning.

The structure of the epistle can be seen as symmetrical, something we would expect of a well-planned and orderly discourse, but not what we would expect of one that is a compilation of fragments or the result of a required change of tactics precipitated by something that happened while Paul was in the middle of writing the discourse. That it is a planned, symmetrical, discourse is supported by O'Brien (1991:16):

> The thematic unity of Philippians has long been recognized in relation to the introductory thanksgiving period of 1:3-11. Following and developing the seminal work of Paul Schubert, a number of scholars have concluded that the introductory thanksgiving paragraphs of Paul's letters have an epistolary function, namely to introduce and present the main themes of their letters.

O'Brien's footnote refers to Schubert, Funk (pp. 256-57), Jewett (pp. 40-53), Wiles (pp. 206-7), O'Brien (1977:19-46), Garland (1980:328-31), and Swift (pp. 234-54).

One of the most significant things Paul prays for in 1:9-11 is that the Philippians' love might increase in knowledge and all discernment. (Note that in propositionalization it is love which is the naturally prominent content; knowledge and discernment are the orienters.) Love is mentioned in 2:2, τὴν αὐτὴν ἀγάπην ἔχοντες 'having the same love', this statement being in effect equivalent to three other statements in the verse exhorting unity, τὸ αὐτὸ φρονῆτε, σύμψυχοι, and τὸ ἓν φρονοῦντες. (All three are idioms meaning 'be united'.) This piling up of exhortations to love and unity strongly suggests that this verse is the exhortation peak of the 2:1-30 unit on unity.

The second thing that Paul prays for is εἰς τὸ δοκιμάζειν ὑμᾶς τὰ διαφέροντα, literally, 'so that you may chose/approve that which is excellent'. Paul shows the Philippians what is excellent not only by his recounting of the example of Christ in 2:6-11 (including the principles implied in it) but also by his own acceptance of the only way of salvation, which, then, must be seen as superior to the way of the Judaizers. The excellent way, according to the apostle, is to strive continually to be conformed to Christ, rather than to do nothing, yet claim to be already perfect, as some of his opponents taught (3:12-16). And he chose to conduct his life with heaven in focus, rather than set his sights on earth as did the enemies of the cross of Christ (3:17-21). He wants them to follow his example and to think on whatever is excellent (4:8).

But we would also expect the opening words of the epistle's hortatory subpart (1:27-4:9) to be the best place where an introduction to the hortatory themes of the epistle might be found. The opening exhortation (1:27a), μόνον ἀξίως τοῦ εὐαγγελίου τοῦ Χριστοῦ πολιτεύεσθε 'only conduct yourselves worthily of the gospel of Christ', is generic, and it is thus difficult to prove that Paul intended to cover the more specific themes of the rest of the subpart. But the three coordinate components of the content construction oriented by ἀκούω 'I may hear' (namely, ὅτι στήκετε ἐν ἑνὶ πνεύματι, μιᾷ ψυχῇ συναθλοῦντες τῇ πίστει τοῦ εὐαγγελίου, καὶ μὴ πτυρόμενοι ἐν μηδενὶ ὑπὸ τῶν ἀντικειμένων 'that you are standing in one spirit, with one soul contending together for the faith of the gospel, and not being frightened in anything by the ones opposing', which function semantically also as exhortations) can be clearly seen as introducing the main themes of 2:1-30 and 3:1-4:1. The emphasis placed on the component of unity by the juxtaposition of the synonymous phrases ἐν ἑνὶ πνεύματι 'in one spirit' and μιᾷ ψυχῇ 'with one soul', together with the use of συναθλέω 'contend together, struggle side by side' with its συν- prefix indicating togetherness, shows that this is an introduction to the hortatory theme of unity and working together. This theme will be presented in 2:1-30 and may also be present in Paul's use of πολιτεύεσθε which could be translated as 'conduct yourselves as members of a community'.

The purpose of their struggling side by side is for the faith of the gospel (τῇ πίστει τοῦ εὐαγγελίου). They are to stand firm (στήκετε) in this struggle and not be afraid of their adversaries at all (μὴ πτυρόμενοι ἐν μηδενὶ ὑπὸ τῶν ἀντικειμένων). Certainly the theme of 3:1–4:1 deals with these ideas. Paul speaks of preserving the faith of the gospel in 3:2–11 as he warns against those who require circumcision for salvation and as he presents the true means of salvation. In 3:12–16 he urges them, as part of godly living, to strive constantly to be like Christ and not to relax in the assumption that they are perfect. In 3:17–21 he asks the Philippians to imitate him and those who conduct themselves like him, not those who conduct themselves as if they were enemies of the cross of Christ. Finally, in 4:1 he ends his theme on standing firm and contending for the faith of the gospel with the exhortation οὕτως στήκετε ἐν κυρίῳ 'thus stand firm in the Lord', which acts as a summary for 3:1–21.

The rest of the hortatory subpart is 4:2–9, a section comprising miscellaneous exhortations. It is not necessary to see them as introduced in 1:27–30 (4:2–3 is a specific instance of 2:1–30). They could, however, be seen as specifics of 'conduct yourselves worthily of the gospel' in 1:27.

In conclusion, it would be difficult to prove that Paul did not intend 1:27–30 to be an introduction to the themes of the 2:1–4:9 hortatory unit.

## PROMINENCE AND THEME

The theme for the *BODY* of this epistle is taken from each of the *NUCLEI* of the *BODY*, especially since the expressive units do not directly support the hortatory unit.

Since the theme of rejoicing is recurrent throughout the expressive 1:12–26 unit, it should be included in the *BODY*'s theme statement, and some indication of the reason for this rejoicing should also be given. As for the hortatory component of the *BODY*'s theme, the component of Paul's life as an example might be kept or not. But since it is the positive step to be taken following the negative prohibitions, it has as much prominence as they do, and so should be kept.

For the final expressive section, the central expression of thanks for the gift is the component included in the theme.

# PART CONSTITUENT 1:3–11 (Expressive Section: Introduction to 1:12–4:20)

| *THEME: I joyfully thank God because you have been working together with me to make known the good news, and I pray that God will enable you to know how to love one another appropriately and to completely understand how you should believe and act.* ||
|---|---|
| MACROSTRUCTURE | CONTENTS |
| *NUCLEUS*₁ (thanksgiving) | 1:3–8 I thank God and rejoice because you have been working together with me to make known the good news from the first day until now. |
| *NUCLEUS*₂ (prayer) | 1:9–11 I pray that God will enable you to know how to love one another more and more appropriately and to completely understand how you should believe and act. |

## INTENT AND MACROSTRUCTURE

The introduction to the body of a letter often seeks to establish or maintain rapport between the writer and addressees. Characteristic of many of Paul's epistles is an introduction containing both thanksgiving and prayer components. It is evident that the thanksgiving here (the first *NUCLEUS*) is a reaction to a situation in which the Philippians have shared and worked together with Paul. The prayer (the second *NUCLEUS*) can also be seen as an emotive reaction of good will to them.

## BOUNDARIES AND COHERENCE

This introduction of thanksgiving and prayer has structural coherence in the sense that it is formulaic. That is, it is characteristic of epistles.

## PROMINENCE AND THEME

Since the two paragraphs of this section are conjoined, significant parts of the theme of each are included in its theme.

# SECTION CONSTITUENT 1:3–8
## (Expressive Paragraph: Nucleus₁ of 1:3–11)

*THEME: I thank God and rejoice because you have been working together with me to make known the good news from the first day until now.*

| ¶ PTRN | RELATIONAL STRUCTURE | CONTENTS |
|---|---|---|
| REACTION₁ | NUCLEUS₁ — NUCLEUS | 1:3a I thank my God (*or*, God *whom* I *serve*) |
| | circumstance | 1:3b whenever *I* think about you. |
| | circumstance | 1:4a Every single time [DOU] I pray *for you*, |
| | NUCLEUS₂ — NUCLEUS | 1:4b I joyfully pray for all of you. |
| situation | | 1:5 *I thank God and rejoice* because you have been *working* together with me in order to *make known* the good news from the first day *you believed the good news* until now. |
| | orienter | 1:6a I am completely confident |
| REACTION₂ | CONTENT | 1:6b that God who has begun to work/perform in you what is good (*or*, that, *since* God has begun to work/perform in you what is good, he) will continue to perfect you until the day Christ Jesus *returns* [MTY]. |
| REACTION₁ | RESULT | 1:7a And indeed it is right that I feel about you all like this [1:3–5] |
| | reason | 1:7b because you are very dear to me |
| | circumstance | 1:7c *because* while I am a prisoner [MTY] and while I defend the good news *before people* and prove/confirm *to them* that it is true, |
| situation | NUCLEUS | 1:7d all of you share with me (*or*, help me) in this work *which God* graciously gave *to me to do*. |
| | prominence orienter | 1:8a God *can* verify |
| REACTION₂ | NUCLEUS | 1:8b that Christ Jesus causes me to *love and* long for all of you very much |
| | comparison | 1:8c *just as* Christ loves *you*. |

## INTENT AND PARAGRAPH PATTERN

Philippians 1:3–8 is the thanksgiving part of the introduction, a typical *REACTION-situation* paragraph pattern. Here, however, Paul's reactions to the Philippians' sharing with him in the gospel 'from the first day until now' (1:5), and especially in his present situation (1:7c–d), include not only thanksgiving and joy but also the reactions of stating a promise (1:6) and stating his fondness (1:7b), love, and longing for them (1:8).

## NOTES

**1:3a my God (*or*, God *whom* I *serve*)** The alternative 'God *whom* I *serve*' is presented in the display text since in many languages the word for 'God' cannot occur in a genitive relationship (especially if it is a name), and the role relationship, then, may have to be propositionalized. Another problem is that in some languages it would be identificational and exclusive, that is, 'my God rather than your God'. The basis for the propositionalization in the display text can be found in such passages as Acts 27:23, where Paul identifies his God as 'the God whose I am and whom I serve'. An alternative for 'serve' in the display would be 'worship'. (See Knox, Loh and Nida, O'Brien 1991.)

**1:3b I think about you** The noun μνεία most likely has the meaning of 'remembrance' here rather than 'mentioning (in prayer)'. The latter meaning is signaled in the New Testament only by the occurrence of μνεία with ποιεῖσθαι 'to make', as in Rom. 1:9; Eph. 1:16; 1 Thess. 1:2; Philem. 4 (see Vincent). In English, 'think about' is a better choice collocationally than 'remember' here, but in many languages an equivalent of 'remember' may be more appropriate.

The noun phrase τῇ μνείᾳ ὑμῶν 'remembrance of you, your remembrance' is more likely to refer to Paul's remembering the Philippians rather than the Philippians' remembering Paul. Vincent writes, "To make ὑμῶν the subjective genitive, 'your thought of me,' with an allusion to their gift, is against usage, and would require a definite mention of the object of remembrance." If I interpret him correctly, he is saying that since μνεία ὑμῶν is almost always used as an objective genitive, the author must give some explicit signal if he wants to show that a subjective genitive is in view.

**whenever** The preposition ἐπί can be taken temporally as expressing the relationship 'I thank my God *whenever* I remember/think about you' or it can be taken causally as 'I thank my God *because* of all that I remember about you'. Those taking ἐπί causally generally also regard the article in τῇ μνείᾳ 'the remembrance' as significant. The article, they claim, requires 'the remembrance' to be interpreted as definite ('in my whole recollection of you') and does not allow for an indefinite interpretation ('whenever I think of, or remember, you' [see Meyer]). But Robertson (p. 772) cites instances where an article may or may not be used with a substantive, and says that, in these cases there is little or no difference in meaning. For example, he says: "There is very little difference in idea between πάσῃ γνώσει ['all knowledge'] (1 Cor. 1:5) and πᾶσαν τὴν γνῶσιν ['all the knowledge'] (1 Cor. 13:2)." Instances such as these weaken Meyer's argument that an article requires a definite interpretation.

Both the causal and the temporal components of ἐπί appear to be present in 3b: If I thank God whenever I think of you (temporal), it is that which I remember about you that gives rise to my thanksgiving (an implied cause); and if I thank God because of all I remember about you (causal), one must assume the presence of a temporal element (i.e., this takes place at various times). The rendering in the display focuses on the temporal aspect following BAGD, pp. 287-88.II2 because of the closely connected and implied idea that it is Paul's entire recollection of the Philippians that gives rise to his thanksgiving whenever he thinks of them. "All of it comes to his mind whenever he thinks of them, and then his heart is grateful to God" (Lenski).

**1:4a-b Every single time [DOU] I pray *for you*, I joyfully pray for all of you** The phrase ὑπὲρ πάντων ὑμῶν 'for all of you' could be connected most closely with ἐν πάσῃ δεήσει μου 'in every prayer of mine', which immediately precedes it, or with μετὰ χαρᾶς τὴν δέησιν ποιούμενος 'with joy praying', which immediately follows it. If it is connected with what follows it, there is a possibility that Paul means, 'Every time I pray, no matter what else I am praying for, I always pray for all of you with joy' or 'In my daily time of prayer, I always pray for all of you with joy'. It would seem rather that the focus is more completely on prayer for the Philippians: 'Every single time that I pray for you, I pray for all of you with joy'.

**joyfully pray** The forefronting of μετὰ χαρᾶς 'with joy' shows that Paul is stressing the joyfulness of his prayer for all the Philippians. In Heyward's work on the Philippians SSA, she suggested as a propositionalization for v. 4 'Whenever I pray for all you, I always rejoice'. Although nothing is lost as far as content is concerned in this shorter version, it is not used in the display since the focus in the original seems to be on joyfully praying for all of the Philippians. However, in some languages it may be more difficult to follow the display rendering; the rejoicing may have to be expressed as a verb. However, it would be good to keep the stress on the fact that as he prays he feels a great sense of joy for all the Philippian believers.

**1:5 *I thank God and rejoice*** Is 1:5 the reason for Paul's thankfulness or for his praying joyfully or both? A glance at various versions will show that some connect 1:5 with Paul's thanksgiving to God while others connect it to Paul's praying with joy. We maintain that it applies to both for the following reasons:

1. The verb εὐχαριστῶ 'I thank' in 3a must have a content (i.e., reason for the thanksgiving). It would not be normal for it to be contentless since it is the main verb in the thanksgiving section of the letter.

2. There is no reason semantically (i.e., here logically) why 1:5 should not also be a reason for Paul's praying with joy.

3. The major objection to this solution is that there is only one finite verb here, εὐχαριστῶ 'I thank' ('praying with joy' is represented by a participial phrase, μετὰ χαρᾶς τὴν δέησιν ποιούμενος). Since they are not grammatically coordinate, can 1:5 be said to relate equally to both of them? The following considerations may override this objection: The thanksgiving and prayer unit in a number of Paul's epistles is almost formulaic with the thank orienter a finite verb (εὐχαριστῶ 'I thank' or εὐχαριστοῦμεν 'we thank') coming at the very beginning of the unit followed by the prayer orienter (or potential prayer orienter as here) in participial form. Note the occurrences in Col. 1:3, I Thess. 1:2, and Philem. 4:

In Col. 1:3 there is no expressed content of προσευχόμενοι 'praying':

Εὐχαριστοῦμεν τῷ θεῷ πατρὶ
We-thank      the God Father

τοῦ κυρίου ἡμῶν Ἰησοῦ Χριστοῦ
of-the Lord of-us Jesus Christ

πάντοτε περὶ ὑμῶν προσευχόμενοι
always for you praying

In 1 Thess. 1:2 there is no expressed content of the prayer:

Εὐχαριστοῦμεν τῷ θεῷ πάντοτε
We-thank     the God always

περὶ πάντων ὑμῶν, μνείαν ποιούμενοι
for all of-you, mention making

ἐπὶ τῶν προσευχῶν ἡμῶν
in the prayers of-us

For Philem. 4, which follows, Philem. 6 is the expressed content of the prayer (Philem. 5, the content of the thanksgiving, intervenes):

Εὐχαριστῶ τῷ θεῷ μου πάντοτε
I thank     the God of me always

μνείαν σου ποιούμενος
mention of-you making

ἐπὶ τῶν προσευχῶν μου
in the prayers of-me

A slight variation may be found in Eph. 1:16, where the content of the thanksgiving is in 1:15 preceding its orienter, and the content of the prayer is in 1:17–19 following its orienter. Both orienters are in 1:16: the pattern is similar to that of Col. 1:3, 1 Thess. 1:2, and Philem. 4.

Thus in each of these references, the verb 'thank' occurs first and is finite in form and 'pray' is participial in form. (In Eph. 1:16 εὐχαριστῶν 'giving thanks' is participial in form because it occurs with the finite παύομαι 'I cease', but this verbal construction as a whole equates with the finite form in the other constructions.) 'Thank' always has an explicit content while 'pray' may or may not. In the semantic structure, then, it would appear at the very least that in those cases where there is an explicit content of the prayer orienter, the thanksgiving and prayer are acting as conjoined units, though they are not formally conjoined. This suggests that some other factor is forcing the second proposition into participial form. It may be that everything is grammatically subordinate to εὐχαριστῶ 'I thank' (and its alternate forms) because it is the "anchor" of the thanksgiving and prayer section, or at least of the thanksgiving paragraph. Because of this the coordinate form one might expect between 'thank' and 'pray' is displaced by a finite verb and participle.

Vincent also sees a difference between the semantic relationships and grammatical form here. His note for μετὰ χαρᾶς 'with joy' is, "The petitions are accompanied with joy, the cause of which is indicated in vv. 5–7." His very next note, which is on ἐπὶ τῇ κοινωνίᾳ ὑμῶν 'for your fellowship', is, "Connect with εὐχαριστῶ ['I thank'], not with τὴν δέησιν ποιούμενος ['prayer making']...Neither should ἐπὶ τῇ κοινωνίᾳ ['for fellowship'] be connected with μετὰ χαρᾶς ['with joy'] which would require τῆς before ἐπὶ."

The rendering '*I thank God and rejoice*' for connecting 1:3–4 with 1:5 seems acceptable rather than '*I thank God and joyfully pray for you*' since μετὰ χαρᾶς 'with joy' is forefronted before the verbal phrase 'making petition' thus marking it prominent. The verbal phrase, of course, is part of the formula and so liable to be less prominent than its verbal form might otherwise indicate, especially since it does not act as an orienter with content, the actual prayer for the Philippians occurring in 1:9–11 with its own orienter.

**you have been *working* together with me in order to *make known* the good news** The basic meaning of κοινωνία has to do with sharing something with someone else or having a common basis. The preposition εἰς 'towards' following it indicates that the fellowship being discussed here is 'fellowship towards the gospel' (τῇ κοινωνίᾳ...εἰς τὸ εὐαγγέλιον) or 'fellowship which contributes to the gospel' (Muller). What the Philippians shared in common in regards to the gospel was working together with Paul in furthering it. In the other two instances where εἰς occurs with κοινωνία in the New Testament (Rom. 15:26; 2 Cor. 9:13), it has the similar idea of 'for, for the benefit of'. Hence 'to make known the good news' is an appropriate rendering.

There is no doubt an allusion here to the gifts that the Philippians have recently sent and for which Paul is thanking them in this letter (4:10–18, most specifically 4:18); ἄχρι τοῦ νῦν 'until now' at the end of 1:5 would indicate this. Likewise there is an allusion to their sending Epaphroditus to aid Paul; Paul calls him his fellow worker in 2:25. But Paul is referring to the times they have sent gifts to him and worked together with him in other ways as ἀπὸ τῆς πρώτης ἡμέρας 'from the first day' shows. In 4:15–16 Paul says, "And you Philippians yourselves know that in the beginning of the gospel, when I left Macedonia, no church entered into partnership with me in giving and receiving except you only; for even in Thessalonica you sent me help once and again" (RSV).

**from the first day** *you believed the good news* Some commentators feel that ἀπὸ τῆς πρώτης ἡμέρας 'from the first day' refers to the first day they received the gospel. Lenski has "the day he baptized Lydia, the day she insisted that he and his assistants lodge at her house." Others understand it to refer to their first sending of contributions to Paul. Since 'fellowship' or 'sharing' is taken here in the broadest sense, 'from the first day' is considered to mean 'from the very beginning of your believing the gospel'.

**1:6a I am completely confident** It is widely agreed that αὐτὸ τοῦτο 'this very thing' refers ahead to the ὅτι 'that' clause rather than referring backward. Stress is put on the τοῦτο 'this' by using αὐτό 'very' with it. Thus the content clause is marked as prominent: 'One thing I am sure of is that...', we might say in idiomatic English. What is actually being marked prominent in this context is the verity of the CONTENT clause. The rendering in the display makes the orienter stronger, 'I am completely confident that...'

**1:6b that God who has begun to work/perform in you what is good** The phrase ἔργον ἀγαθόν 'good work' has not been taken as referring only to the specific work of furthering the gospel mentioned in 1:5. As Hendriksen states, the Philippians' cooperation in advancing the gospel is included, but this 'good work' has broader implications in that it refers to the entire transforming work of God. There is no definite article with 'good work', the presence of which would have clearly indicated that there was a specific, previous referent in mind (such as 'partnership in the gospel' in v. 5). Compare also Rom. 14:20 where 'work' is taken in a broader sense, and Phil. 2:12–13.

Of the commentators who take 'good work' in the generic sense, most say that it is referring to some aspect of God's activity at the time of conversion coupled with his continued imparting of grace to the believers from that time on. But if one carries this thought further, the product of God's work of grace is that believers come to be better people and do more of what is good. This is the outworking of God's good work being done in them. The reason for understanding the inworking and outworking here is that the close lexical and structural parallels between v. 5 and v. 6 indicate an intended close semantic relationship. God has already done good things through them as 'your partnership in the good news' most obviously indicates. He will continue to work in them producing like good results until the day of Christ Jesus. It may not be necessary to explicitly indicate the outworking aspect in translation, but it is implicit in the Greek text.

The verb 'has begun' suggests a process rather than a one-time action. Related to the Christian life, this would indicate transformation, sanctification. In some languages 'work' has the more restricted sense of 'labor', so a suitable generic word may be difficult to find. In that case, a more specific word may be needed, for example, 'God who has begun to transform you will continue to transform you until the day Christ Jesus *returns*'. A suggestion that would maintain the outworking tie with v. 5 is 'God who has begun to transform you and help you do what is good will continue to do so until the day Christ Jesus *returns*'.

**(or, that,** *since* **God has begun to work/ perform in you what is good, he)** In Greek and many other languages a relative clause may be used to express semantic relationships other than description or identification. Here 'who has begun a good work in you' may function as grounds for the confidence that God would continue to perfect the Philippians. Since the grounds construction would equate better in some languages, it is given as an alternate in the display.

**will continue to perfect you** The verb ἐπιτελέω has a variety of senses in the New Testament: 'to end, bring to an end, finish, complete, accomplish, perform, bring about'. The form ἐπιτελέσει in this verse has been interpreted by commentators as having one or the other of the following senses:

1. Carry something out. KJV has "will perform it until the day of Jesus Christ."
2. Carry something out and perfect it in so doing but with the completion aspect focusing only on a perfecting during the whole time specified (i.e., 'until the day of Christ Jesus') and not on the end result.
3. Carry something out and perfect it in so doing, with the completion aspect focusing on

the perfect state those involved will experience on the day of Christ Jesus. Vincent says, "The sense is pregnant; will carry it on toward completion, and finally complete." He paraphrases, "God will perfect the good work which he has begun in you and will show it completed in the day when Christ shall appear" (p. 1).

The two verbal forms here are, at least in some contexts, members of a set: ἐναρξάμενος 'begin' and ἐπιτελέσει 'end'. Therefore we might expect the idea to be 'He that has begun a good work in you will end/complete it on the day of Christ Jesus'. However, instead of 'on the day of Christ Jesus', we find 'until the day of Christ Jesus'. Since 'he will end it until the day of Christ Jesus' does not make sense, the thought would seem to be "carry it on to completion until the day of Christ Jesus" (NIV). Another question remains: Since the use of 'until' (and 'has begun') forces us to understand a process over time, is the final end or product of the process also in focus or not? And by this I do not mean 'finish in time' but 'make the believer completely perfect'. In other words, does ἐπιτελέω have 'make perfect' as an obligatory component of meaning? We know that it does not have this meaning in every context (Heb. 9:6, for instance). It therefore seems best to propositionalize by using 'will continue to perfect' rather than 'will continue to perfect and make finally perfect'.

**the day Christ Jesus *returns*** In this metonymy 'day' stands both for the day and what will happen on it. The most common view is that it refers to the day Christ returns.

**1:7a And indeed** The word καθώς has a general meaning of 'as' and acts as a connector of units. It has the possibility of signaling at least the following roles (BAGD, p. 391): comparison, reason, circumstance, content. Its function in the majority of contexts has to do with comparison or some type of matching of units. In the context of 1:3-8, καθώς appears to signal a matching of meaning content, that is, a continuing of the same subject. Normally this would express the role of amplification or conjoining. Many versions do not translate καθώς here, though NEB uses "indeed" and Twentieth Century uses "and indeed." Either seems appropriate in this context: both express continuation of the same subject and mark an increase in emphasis on the new statements about the same general subject. The appropriateness of this increase in emphasis can be seen in the use of 'it is right' (ἐστιν δίκαιον), which also marks emphasis on what Paul is saying in 1:7.

**I feel about you all like this [1:3-5]** Normally when καθώς 'as' refers forward, it introduces a subordinate clause leading into a main clause. Here no main clause follows, so τοῦτο φρονεῖν 'to think/feel this', which καθώς 'as' introduces, must refer to something already said or implied; and whatever it refers to must have to do with Paul's expressive reactions toward them, based on the reasons or situations that follow.

Many commentators view τοῦτο φρονεῖν 'to think/feel this' as relating to 1:6. Note, however, the following considerations:

1. Though φρονεῖν is often thought of as having the primary meaning of 'to think', BAGD (p. 866.1) considers it to mean "*think* or *feel in a certain way about someone*" in this context. Michael says, "It signifies sympathetic interest and concern, expressing as it does the action of the heart as well as the intellect." All that Paul has mentioned in 1:3-5 (giving thanks for the Philippians, rejoicing as he prayed for them, being thankful for their fellowship in the gospel) has to do with Paul's feelings toward the Philippians, but 1:6 is largely about the character of God.

2. Paul goes on to say that it is right for him 'to feel this way' because he loves them ('has them in his heart' [1:7b]). It is more logical to say that Paul's love would be a justification for his general feeling of warm affection for them (1:3-5) than for his confidence that God would continue his good work in them. In fact, it is not logical at all to say that Paul can be confident that God will continue his good work in the Philippians because Paul loves them.

Based on these considerations, therefore, τοῦτο φρονεῖν 'to think/feel this' is taken as referring to 1:3-5, not so much to any particular thing in those verses but to the general feeling of affection communicated in them (cf. Moule). In other epistles, Paul thanks God for the church's faith and love (as in Col. 1:4; 2 Thess. 1:3; Philem. 5), sometimes adding hope. But here he talks about the church's relationship to himself (1:5). Where Paul talks about longing for the Romans it is not 'with the affections of Jesus Christ' mentioned here (1:8). It appears that Paul had a special bond with the Philippians that he did not have with the other churches. Summing up

Paul's frame of mind towards the Philippians in 1:3-5, we would say, then, that Paul had a special affection for them. When Paul says it is right for him to have this warm attitude, he is saying it is not an unsubstantiated feeling. He has warm feelings for them because they have a special place in his heart (1:7b) and this is because they are sharers (συγκοινωνούς) with him in his bonds and in the defense and confirmation of the good news.

**1:7b because you are very dear to me** Since both με 'I, me' and ὑμᾶς 'you(pl)' are in the accusative case in this infinitive construction, this construction, διὰ τὸ ἔχειν με ἐν τῇ καρδίᾳ ὑμᾶς 'because-of the to-have me in the heart you', could be rendered either as 'because I have you in *my* heart' or as 'because you have me in *your* heart'.

'Because I have you in my heart' is supported by the following:

1. To regard the first pronoun (με 'I, me') as the subject corresponds with the commonly held view that Greek is a VSO (verb-subject-object) language.
2. In a majority of the unambiguous instances where there are two accusative pronouns related to an infinitive, the first one is the subject.
3. In the next verse (1:8), Paul explicitly mentions that he longs for the Philippians, not vice versa, and γάρ 'for' at the beginning of that verse seems to more naturally go back to the general impact of the whole verse rather than just to 'It is right that I feel this way about you'.
4. The whole context is that of Paul's love for the Philippians. Also, it seems as though it would be more natural and less presumptuous to say, 'I have you in my heart', than to say, 'You have me in your heart'.

'Because you have me in your heart' is supported by the following:

1. BAGD gives three other instances of a construction consisting of ἔχω 'I have' plus a free subject plus an object plus an ἐν 'in' prepositional phrase: John 5:26; 2 Cor. 1:9; 1 John 5:10. A study of these shows that the object in these constructions always occurs immediately before or immediately after ἔχω. It should also be mentioned, however, that the subject always occurs before the other constituents.
2. Heb. 2:10 is an instance of a διὰ τὸ ... ἔχειν construction where the subject occurs after the object as the final constituent in the construction, as would be the case if ὑμᾶς 'you' were subject in Phil. 1:7.
3. Out of five instances of a διὰ τό construction plus the three references mentioned in point 1 above, only two of them had a VSO pattern, neither of which had ἔχειν as the verb. VSO, then, is not a major pattern in these constructions.
4. If we take φρονεῖν to mean 'feel' in 1:7a, then both the φρονεῖν construction and 'I have you in (my) heart' would be on the REACTION side of a REACTION-*situation* construction, whereas it is more probable that διά 'because' would signal *situation*. 'You have me in (your) heart' would represent *situation*.

The overwhelming majority of the commentaries consulted consider that 'I have you in (my) heart' is the correct interpretation. This interpretation is followed in the display, but rendered nonfiguratively. (The Greek is, of course, figurative.) See Loh and Nida.

**1:7c *because*** Most commentators would probably agree with the order 'I hold you in my heart, (for) both in my imprisonment and in the defense and confirmation of the gospel you are all partakers/sharers with me of grace'. However, some take ἐν τε τοῖς δεσμοῖς μου καὶ ἐν τῇ ἀπολογίᾳ καὶ βεβαιώσει τοῦ εὐαγγελίου 'in my bonds and in the defense and confirmation of the gospel' to relate most closely with what immediately precedes it, ἔχειν με ἐν τῇ καρδίᾳ ὑμᾶς 'I have you in my heart'. The reading would be, 'I have you in my heart both in my imprisonment and in the defense and confirmation of the gospel, for you are all partakers/sharers with me of grace'. There appear to be no indisputable signals in the syntax itself to indicate this connection rather than the one first mentioned above or vice versa. It is normal order for prepositional phrases to occur toward the end of a clause in Greek, but they are sometimes placed before the verb to emphasize them.

In propositionalizing, the order that seems somewhat more logical is: 'You are very dear to me, because while I have been a prisoner and while I have been defending the good news and proving that it is true all of you share with me in this work which God graciously gave me to do'. This is better than 'You are very dear to me while I am a prisoner and while I am defending the good news and proving that it is true, because all of you share with me in this work which God graciously gave to me to do'. In other words, it seems more logical or more effective if 'in my bonds and in the defense and confirmation of the good news' is seen as stressing the time of sharing rather than as stressing only Paul's time of holding them in his heart.

**while I am a prisoner** The phrase ἐν...τοῖς δεσμοῖς μου 'in my bonds' refers literally to Paul's state of being constantly bound in chains. From Acts 28:20 and 28:30 we know that Paul was in chains but was also in his own house during imprisonment in Rome. If that imprisonment is the same one in which Paul found himself when he wrote Philippians, such a situation would not normally be called 'prison' in English. It is possible his situation may have worsened later and he may actually have been in prison when he wrote the letter to the church at Philippi. Or it may even be that a wholly different time and situation are the background of this letter. It is probably best to use a term for 'in my bonds' that covers both situations. 'While I am a prisoner' is used for the display, but the rendering into other languages would depend on what would appropriately describe Paul's situation, which is difficult to describe accurately other than by either a specific reference to bonds or chains or a generic reference to confinement.

**while I defend the good news *before people* and prove/confirm *to them* that it is true** There are some very good reasons for understanding 'defense and confirmation' to allude to Paul's trial:

1. The words ἀπολογία 'defense' and βεβαίωσις 'confirmation' are terms used in legal proceedings: ἀπολογία is used in this sense by Paul in Acts 25:16; 2 Tim. 4:16; Acts 22:1; 1 Cor. 9:3; and 2 Cor. 7:11. Other than these references and those in Philippians (here and 1:16) ἀπολογία is found in the New Testament only in 1 Pet. 3:15.
2. Paul is undergoing a court trial at the time of the writing of the epistle as 1:19-27 shows.
3. 'Defense and confirmation' are collocated with 'in my bonds'. Paul's imprisonment is real, not figurative, and in real life it is closely associated with his trial.
4. In Phil. 1:16, where ἀπολογία 'defense' is also qualified by 'the gospel' (εἰς ἀπολογίαν τοῦ εὐαγγελίου κεῖμαι 'I am appointed/set for the defense of the gospel'), ἀπολογία appears to have a definite reference to Paul's trial and imprisonment experience.

Is Paul seeking here to emphasize the comprehensiveness of the help he mentions in 7d, or is he making a specific reference to help at a time of great need? If he had meant to be unambiguously comprehensive, he would not have used terms that in this context easily apply to specific situations. Certainly ἐν τοῖς δεσμοῖς μου 'in my bonds' is specific; it does not cover 'from the first day until now'. Of course, Paul could have had comprehensiveness in mind and shown it by using more than one specific, the total of which would equal comprehensiveness. But if he did have this in mind, he probably would not have used *contemporaneous* specifics.

There is no lexical or grammatical reason for taking 'in my bonds' and 'in the defense and confirmation of the gospel' as significantly distinct situations. The sequence τε καί is used to connect words that may have a single or very similar reference as in Heb. 5:1, δῶρά τε καί θυσίας 'gifts and sacrifices', and Heb. 5:7, δεήσεις τε καὶ ἱκετηρίας 'prayers and supplications'. Although in Phil. 1:7 τε and καί are not sequential, presumably τε...καί could signal the same. Or, if a distinction in reference is intended it could be between 'these bonds of mine' and 'the defense and confirmation of the gospel'. Being bound in chains and defending and confirming the gospel in court are recognizable as two different aspects of Paul's present situation. The first chapter of Philippians is full of references to Paul's conditions at the writing of the letter, so it is not out of line for 'defense and confirmation of the gospel' to be taken as referring to that situation.

If we take 'defense and confirmation of the gospel' to have at least some reference to Paul's court situation, we will not take τε...καί to refer to mutually exclusive situations as far as a general time period is concerned, since all of these things are happening during the same general period of time.

The propositionalization should perhaps specify to whom the gospel is being confirmed and before whom it is being defended. Without them we might propositionalize as 'while I am a prisoner and while I defend the good news and confirm that it is true'. To supply them, however, it must be determined before whom Paul was defending the gospel and confirming its truth. In Acts 25:12, Festus says to Paul, "You have appealed to Caesar; to Caesar you shall go" (RSV). But in 2 Tim. 4:17, in a court situation similar to that here, Paul says, "But the Lord stood by me and gave me strength to proclaim the message fully, that all the Gentiles might hear it" (RSV). This suggests that many heard Paul's defense in the imperial court. It may be appropriate, therefore, to be general in this regard: 'while I am a prisoner and while I defend the good news *before people* and confirm *to them* that it is true'.

**1:7d all of you share with me (*or*, help me)** A majority of commentators cited in Greenlee's work (1992) regard the enclitic μου 'of me' in the phrase συγκοινωνούς μου τῆς χάριτος 'participants of me of the grace' as relating to συγκοινωνούς 'participants' ('participants with me') rather than χάριτος 'grace' ('my grace'). The reasons given for not interpreting it as 'participants of my grace' are summarized by Vincent:

> Against this is the order of the pronouns, and the fact that when Paul speaks of the grace peculiar to himself he never says μοῦ ἡ χάρις or ἡ χάρις μου [both of which would be translated as 'my grace'], but ἡ χάρις ἡ δοθεῖσα μοι ['the grace given to me'] (Gal. ii. 9; 1 Cor. iii. 10; Rom. xii. 3; xv. 15); or ἡ χάρις αὐτοῦ ἡ εἰς ἐμὲ ['the grace of him to me'] (1 Cor. xv. 10).

**in this work *which God* graciously gave *to me to do*** There are many opinions as to what Paul intended by συγκοινωνούς μου τῆς χάριτος 'partakers/sharers with me of grace/the grace' here. (Note that although χάριτος 'grace' occurs with the article, the Greek article and English 'the' do not always equate.) It is basic to the understanding of Paul's intentions in this verse to determine the sense in which he used συγκοινωνός (usually translated here as 'partakers' or 'sharers'). In 1:3–5 (i.e., in this same thanksgiving section), he states that he is thankful for their participation (κοινωνία) in the gospel from the first day until the present. In 4:14 he says, 'It was kind of you to share [συγκοινωνήσαντες] in my troubles', where he clearly refers to the things he had received as a gift from them by way of Epaphroditus (4:18). In 4:15 he says, "...no church entered into partnership [ἐκοινώνησεν] with me in giving and receiving except you only" (RSV).

In the final part of the epistle where Paul usually deals with personal matters, he discusses their recent gift to him at length (eleven verses), thus showing the significance of the gift. It is highly likely, then, that he is at least alluding to this gift when he mentions συγκοινωνούς 'participants, sharers' in the opening rapport section of the letter, especially since χάρις is not limited to the sense of 'God's saving favor' nor συγκοινωνός to the sense of 'partaker'.

The purpose of 1:7c–d is to give the reason why Paul is so fond of the Philippian believers. It seems more probable, then, that it has to do with their participation/sharing in some specific sense of grace related to his present situation rather than referring only to their being fellow partakers (i.e., receivers) of the grace of God in salvation or some such general sense. The sense of 'partakers' is difficult to understand in this context since it would not seem to refer to the Philippians' initiative as much as 'participants' or 'sharers' would and one would think that Paul's warm feelings toward the Philippians in this context would more probably be because of something that they did under their own initiative rather than something that God did for them.

Also, the participation mentioned here has special reference to Paul's imprisonment and his defense and confirmation of the gospel. Their most recent gift and the service of Epaphroditus to Paul on their behalf occurred during Paul's imprisonment and the general time of his trial. It is very possible that the Philippians would read συγκοινωνούς 'participants' in the light of their participation in Paul's ministry through this service to him, or at least would see this service as the most concrete part of their participation.

But why does Paul here use χάρις, which has a primary meaning of 'grace', if he is referring to his ministry? In a few places (Eph. 3:8; Gal. 2:9; Rom. 5:1) χάρις has a specialized sense of 'God-given, God-enabled ministry/task'. It would appear, then, that he might be using it here too to stress the fact that it is God's ministry, not his own: they are not just helping him personally, they are participating in his God-given ministry. However, this specialized meaning of χάρις is more clearly signaled in the other three places. Also, he always mentions that this grace was given to him, or that he received this grace, while here he does not. Therefore, it is difficult to determine conclusively whether Paul intends τῆς χάριτος to specifically mean 'God-given ministry' here or not. In any case, this interpretation is followed in the display since it fits the context better and is much simpler in its reasoning than other interpretations.

It may be, however, that Paul does not mean to restrict the sense of 'grace' here to 'God-given ministry/task' in a narrow sense but to include other types of enablement for the Christian life (such as enablement to endure suffering, which is pertinent to the context). But it would seem that any 'participation' intended here would be not only partaking of the grace itself but also participating in the activity the grace enables one to do. This alternate sense might be propositionalized as, 'You are all participating with me in all those things which God is enabling us(inc)/me to do'.

**1:8a God *can* verify** The question here is whether Paul intends 'God is my witness' to function primarily as a prominence orienter or as an oath, which *The Random House Dictionary* defines as "a solemn appeal to God to witness one's determination to speak the truth or to keep a promise." The context suggests the former; an oath is not usually appropriate for an expression of one's feelings. Paul simply uses 'God is my witness' to show how strongly he feels about his readers. He has no reason to think they might doubt his fondness for them. 'God is my witness' in Rom. 1:9 is used similarly.

To simplify the semantic relationships represented in the literal 'God is my witness', 'God *can* verify' is used in the display.

**1:8b that ... very much** BAGD (p. 898-99) classifies the occurrence of ὡς here under IV4, "after verbs of knowing, saying (even introducing direct discourse: ...), hearing, etc.=ὅτι *that*." Thus ὡς, in effect, functions as an introducer of content in these contexts. Some commentators, however, contend that ὡς here should be translated as 'how'. From the use of ὡς in Rom. 10:15, 'Ὡς ὡραῖοι οἱ πόδες τῶν εὐαγγελιζομένων [τὰ] ἀγαθά 'How beautiful are the feet of those preaching [the] good news/things' (cf. 11:33), it is evident that ὡς can mean 'how...!', functioning as an intensifier of a quality or quantity in some contexts. Instances of ὡς listed by BAGD under IV4 are basically translatable as 'that', functioning as a marker of content, if the verb is not able to be intensified or if intensification would not have meaning in the context. But ὡς is potentially translatable as 'how' if there is an adjective or a verb that is able to be intensified in the clause introduced by ὡς.

In the New Testament, ὡς introduces the content construction of (at least) two other 'witness' orienters, Rom. 1:9 and 1 Thess. 2:10. In the latter ὡς translates as 'how': "You are witnesses, and so is God, of how holy, righteous and blameless we were among you who believed" (NIV). But in Rom. 1:9 ὡς is translated seemingly correctly (at least for English) by RSV as 'that': "For God is my witness...that without ceasing I mention you always in my prayers."

RSV translates ὡς as 'how' in Phil. 1:8 (NIV translates as 'how' in all three places). It makes sense in English to translate it as 'how' here since 'long for' or 'yearn' are verbs that may be intensified. However, 'how' in this sense (also translatable here as 'how much') is probably idiomatic in English. In the display this idiomatic usage is converted to 'very much': 'God *can* verify that Christ Jesus causes me to *love and* long for all of you very much'.

**1:8b-c Christ Jesus causes me to *love and* long for all of you all very much *just as* Christ loves *you*** To express how deeply he longs for the Philippians, Paul uses the prepositional phrase ἐν σπλάγχνοις Χριστοῦ Ἰησοῦ 'in/with the inward parts of Christ Jesus'. Vincent says that σπλάγχνα refers to "the heart, liver, and lungs...regarded collectively as the seat of the feelings, the affections and passions." In this sense, σπλάγχνα is comparable to the figurative sense of heart in English. Hendriksen says, "Paul's love is patterned after (cf. Phil. 2:5) and energized by Christ's indwelling love (Gal. 2:20)." It is difficult to argue against this two fold sense of 'in/with the heart of Christ Jesus'.

For the display, 'I long for all of you *just as* Christ Jesus loves/longs for you' might be a fair representation of the patterning after Christ (i.e., a comparison). The energizing sense might be added in this way: 'God *can* verify that Christ Jesus causes me to long for all of you just as he himself (Christ) longs for *you*'. The causing here is not being made to do something he does not want to do, but being enabled to have an even greater love than he could have in himself. But to use 'longs for' with Christ Jesus as the agent seems too specific and inappropriate in this context; and if the verb is changed to the more generic 'love', the comparison sounds unnatural, since usually the same verb is used in both sides of a comparison. To overcome this difficulty, the following propositionalization is offered: 'God *can* verify that Christ Jesus causes me to *love and* long for all of you very much *just as* Christ loves *you*'. (This is a language-specific solution for English and may or may not be helpful for other languages.)

Even many English translations (RSV, NIV, etc.) do not use a figure of speech to translate ἐν σπλάγχνοις Χριστοῦ Ἰησοῦ here, and in many other languages a figure will probably not communicate adequately. Moreover, the double sense of energizing and patterning may be difficult to translate even nonfiguratively. In such cases, it may be sufficient to translate the patterning (i.e., comparison) sense only: 'God *can* verify that I long for all of you *just as* Christ Jesus longs for/loves *you*'. Another option, to handle the problem of the two different verbs, is 'God *can* verify that I long for all of you *very much* because *I love you just as* Christ Jesus loves *you*'.

## BOUNDARIES AND COHERENCE

The initial boundary was discussed under 1:1–2. The final boundary is evidenced by the change of topic from Paul's thankfulness and affectionate attitude toward the Philippians to his specific prayer for them, initiated by the orienter καὶ τοῦτο προσεύχομαι 'and this I pray' at the beginning of v. 9. The explicit *situation-REACTION* relationship of 1:3–8 changes to the typical orienter-CONTENT relationship of prayer, where the prayer is a type of *REACTION* to the *situation* of Paul's relationship to them. This latter *situation* is implicit. Whereas both the thanksgiving and the prayer are expressive in import, there is a difference in the type of *REACTIONS* and in the explicit-implicit structure. It may be better, then, to see two distinct paragraph patterns here.

## PROMINENCE AND THEME

Constituent 1:3a is regarded as naturally prominent because it contains the only nonsubordinated finite verb in the unit, εὐχαριστῶ 'I thank'. (This is characteristic of the subgenre of a thanksgiving introductory unit.) As mentioned in the notes for 1:5 the idea of Paul's rejoicing in prayer for the Philippians is considered prominent, and it is thus included in the theme. In this *REACTION-situation* unit it is also necessary to include a representation of the *situation* in the theme. The first *situation* has a direct relationship with εὐχαριστῶ, which suggests that it should form at least part of the theme. It is significant that the second *situation* also has to do with the Philippians' working together with Paul: note κοινωνίᾳ 'fellowship' in v. 5 and συγκοινωνούς 'participants, sharers' in v. 7. Both of these verses also deal with the furthering of the gospel. And since v. 5 qualifies the time generically as 'from the first day until now' and v. 7 deals with a present situation (Paul's imprisonment and trial), 'until now' covers that present situation. Thus it would seem that though only v. 5 is included in the theme, the significant points of v. 7 are also covered. The more affectionate *REACTIONS* of 1:7b and 1:8 are not included in the theme. They are an extension of the concepts in 'I thank God and rejoice'.

# SECTION CONSTITUENT 1:9–11
## (Expressive Paragraph: Nucleus₂ of 1:3–11)

*THEME: I pray that God will enable you to know how to love one another more and more appropriately and to completely understand how you should believe and act.*

| RELATIONAL STRUCTURE | CONTENTS |
|---|---|
| ⎡orienter | 1:9a And this *is what* I pray: |
| ⎣MEANS₁ | 1:9b that *God will cause/enable* you to truly know and discern how to love *one another* more and more appropriately in every situation |
| MEANS₂ | 1:10a *and that he will enable* you to completely understand how you should believe and act. |
| ⎡purpose₁ | 1:10b *I pray this* [1:9b–10a] in order that you might be *spiritually* pure and faultless (*or*, completely faultless [DOU]) on the day that Christ *returns* [MTY] |
| ⎣purpose₂ —MEANS — RESULT | 1:11a *and in order that* you might act/live completely righteously |
|       ⎣means | 1:11b by means of Jesus Christ *enabling you to do so* |
|    ⎣purpose | 1:11c in order that *people will* honor God and praise him (*or, people will* praise God very much [DOU]). |

## INTENT AND PARAGRAPH PATTERN

As far as communication relations are concerned, this unit is purely a MEANS-purpose construction. Since it relates closely to the thanksgiving paragraph here, as it typically does elsewhere, it is likely also to be expressive in genre. One purpose in expressing one's reactions is to share them with others in the hope that they will be affected likewise. But prayer, good wishes, and blessings are slightly different. They call forth a blessing upon those who have caused the original situation. Therefore the situation calling forth the reaction of prayer is implicit as far as this paragraph is concerned. But it is explicit in the preceding thanksgiving paragraph and so there is carryover from the preceding paragraph.

## STRUCTURE OF 1:9–11

Both grammatically and semantically the content of the prayer could be analyzed as one long chain of purpose clauses built one upon another. At any point where there might seem to be a new start beginning a separate petition, a number of commentators will argue against it, pointing out a cause-effect relationship across the proposed break. The most obvious beginning of a new series of petitions would be at the second ἵνα (at the beginning of 1:10b), but, of course, ἵνα may introduce not only content but also purpose.

## NOTES

**1:9a And** This is the first καί 'and' in Philippians that connects constituents of a higher level than noun phrases. Its most obvious function is to connect as coordinate the thanksgiving paragraph with the prayer paragraph.

**this *is what* I pray** The role of τοῦτο 'this' here together with προσεύχομαι 'I pray' may very well be that of topic orienter. Paul has mentioned prayer for the Philippians earlier (v. 4), but he has not yet stated the content of that prayer; τοῦτο 'this' along with προσεύχομαι introduces the content of the prayer. The presence and forefronting of τοῦτο does indicate emphasis, emphasis in the context of topic orientation.

**1:9b *God will cause/enable*** If the prayer in these verses is seen as a true prayer to God, then it is best to propositionalize it with God as the one who is appealed to and who enables the action of the prayer to be carried out. In many languages this type of an appeal cannot be made without stating the grantor of the request of the appeal.

**truly know and discern how to love *one another* more and more appropriately in every situation** The expression ἡ ἀγάπη ὑμῶν ἔτι μᾶλλον καὶ μᾶλλον περισσεύῃ ἐν ἐπιγνώσει καὶ πάσῃ αἰσθήσει 'the love of you still more and more may abound in knowledge and all discernment' is interpreted several different ways by commentators. But most agree that the general idea is that love is to be directed in the right way by knowledge and discernment. When the ἐν prepositional phrase is propositionalized by changing it to adverbs (some types of ἐν phrases function like adverbs; see BDF § 219.4), this meaning association is clear: 'that you may love *others* more and more knowledgeably and perceptively/discerningly'. Such adverbs may not be universal across languages, so the ἐν prepositional phrase could be rendered as means: 'And this is what I pray, that you may love *others* more and more *correctly/appropriately* by means of your *coming to* truly know and discern *the best way to love them* in every situation'. For some languages it may help to change the order: 'that you may truly know and discern how to love *one another* more and more appropriately in every situation'.

Much prominence is signaled on 'love', 'knowledge', and 'discernment' in the Greek text by the piling up of words of similar meaning functioning semantically as modifiers, ἔτι μᾶλλον καὶ μᾶλλον περισσεύῃ 'in addition more and more may increase/abound', by the use of the intensive word ἐπιγνώσει 'full knowledge', and by the use of πάσῃ 'all' with αἰσθήσει 'discernment'. This prominence is conveyed in the display by using 'truly' before 'know and discern' and by using 'in every situation'.

Moore (p. 49) classifies 'knowledge and discernment' as a borderline case of a near-synonymous doublet.

**love *one another*** There are various interpretations as to the intended object of the Philippians' love. In the display it has been rendered 'love *one another*' since that is one of the main hortatory foci of the epistle (2:1–4 most specifically, but also implicit in 2:5–30; cf. 4:2–3).

**1:10a *and that he will enable*** There is a question as to whether 10a relates back to the ideas in 9b as a whole, i.e., discerning love, or basically only to knowledge and discernment. It is easy to see that God-given knowledge and discernment will enable a believer to determine what is excellent. In fact, when 1:9b and 1:10a are propositionalized, they appear to be quite parallel in meaning: Knowledge aids the believer to know how to believe and act, whether the action is described as the outworking of love or as making the best doctrinal and moral choices. Thus ἐπίγνωσις 'knowledge' and αἴσθησις 'discernment' are related to ἡ ἀγάπη 'love' (through περισσεύῃ ἐν 'may abound in') and also to δοκιμάζειν...τὰ διαφέροντα 'determining the things that are excellent' (through εἰς τό 'so that'). Now the question is, if 1:9b and 1:10a are parallel in meaning, are they conjoined (coordinate), even equivalent, rather than 10a being the purpose of 9b? To answer this, we need to ask if Paul sees 10a as a stage beyond 9b (whether or not we see it that way). Since the rest of the prayer seems to be a spiraling of purposes, would he not see 10a as the purpose of 9b? Not necessarily. But the question is not easy to answer. In the display 9b and 10a are conjoined. An alternate propositionalization of purpose would be: 'in order that you may be able to completely understand how you should believe and act'.

**completely understand how you should believe and act** Expositors are divided between possible renderings for δοκιμάζειν ὑμᾶς τὰ διαφέροντα. Two alternatives are given by Vincent:

1. 'To put to the proof the things that differ' [i.e., the good versus the bad], and so discriminate between them...
2. 'To approve the things that are excellent'...

But he adds, "The difference is not really essential, since, in any case, the result contemplated is the approval of what is good."

It is best to consider that Paul intends something quite generic in τὰ διαφέροντα 'the things that are excellent'. The reason is that his desire for them, as shown in the 1:27–30 introduction to the hortatory subpart, is that they will not only conduct themselves worthily of the gospel of Christ (1:27, and expanded in 2:1–30 and elsewhere) but will also contend for the faith of the gospel (1:27, as expanded in 3:1–4:1), holding to the gospel as the means of proclaiming salvation through Christ alone.

**1:10b *I pray this* [1:9b–10a] *in order that*** The conjunction ἵνα often introduces CONTENT constructions, as already done once at the beginning of the CONTENT of this prayer. This raises the question of whether ἵνα at the beginning of 10b introduces a second coordinate CONTENT of the prayer, or whether it is a purpose of the preceding construction. There is potentially a progression of purpose clauses in the prayer leading to a final goal in time (εἰς ἡμέραν Χριστοῦ 'until/for the day of Christ') and an ultimate goal (εἰς δόξαν καὶ ἔπαινον θεοῦ 'for the glory and praise of God'). Some commentators analyze this ἵνα construction as the purpose or result of the preceding phrase, while others state that it is the ultimate purpose of Paul's prayer. As far as semantic analysis is concerned, it seems best to understand it as a purpose construction (purpose rather than result since it is stated as a petition to be realized) relating to 1:9b and 1:10a, which would function as the MEANS. Being pure and faultless (εἰλικρινεῖς καὶ ἀπρόσκοποι) can easily be seen as the result of discerning love and knowledge-directed behavior. However, this and the following purpose construction are introduced here in the display with a repetition of the original prayer orienter since vv. 9–11 would be one very long sentence otherwise.

**faultless** Commentators are equally divided on whether ἀπρόσκοποι here means 'blameless' as in Acts 24:16 or 'not offending others' as in 1 Cor. 10:32. The context appears to favor 'blameless'. 'Blameless' like 'pure' is generic and deals primarily with the believer's relationship with God, while 'not offending others' is more specific and deals with one's relationship with others. Thus 'pure' and 'blameless' would be near synonyms in this context. Of course, no semantic rule states that they must be synonyms, but synonyms joined by 'and' are common in the Scriptures. And it is common to have synonyms in similar contexts to this where the idea of being pure, blameless, holy is in focus (although the word used here for blameless, ἀπρόσκοπος, is not found elsewhere in such contexts). See Eph. 5:27; Phil. 2:15; 2 Pet. 3:14. In Eph. 1:4 and Col. 1:22 the idea of being holy and blameless in the Lord's presence is mentioned as it is here in Phil. 1:11.

Also, εἰς ἡμέραν Χριστοῦ 'with reference to/for/until the day of Christ' suggests that the believer's relationship with Christ is in focus, rather than his relationship with other people. In the display the rendering is 'faultless' rather than 'blameless' since in English *blameless* is based on the transitive verb *blame* and may lead to unnecessary focus on the agent of the blame; *faultless* focuses on the believer himself.

Since 'pure' and 'faultless' are basically synonymous and Paul's use of this semantic repetition may have been for emphasis, an alternate propositionalization would be 'completely faultless'

**on the day that Christ *returns*** Most commentators cited by Greenlee (1992) take εἰς in εἰς ἡμέραν Χριστοῦ to mean 'with reference to, for': "that you may be pure and blameless in view of the coming day of Christ." Some versions, however, translate it as "until the day of Christ." Paul clearly intends that the Philippian Christians be pure and faultless now and always, right up until the day of Christ, but his focus here may very well be on their status on the day of Christ itself. The notion of being holy and blameless in the presence of the Lord is not an uncommon one, as Eph. 1:4 and Col. 1:22 show. Also, the fact that Paul uses εἰς here instead of ἄχρι (which clearly means 'until' and which he uses in 1:6, 'until the day of Christ Jesus') may indicate that he uses εἰς in the sense of 'with reference to'. However, εἰς does mean 'until' in some contexts (see Matt. 10:22, ὁ δὲ ὑπομείνας εἰς τέλος 'he who endures until the end').

Actually, there is not a lot of difference in meaning between 'with reference to' and 'until' in this context. The sense of 'until' is that from now right up until Christ returns they should be pure and faultless and it is left implicit that the believer needs to be ready for that day. The focus of 'with reference to the day of Christ', on the other hand, is on the readiness for the day of judgment while the sense of being pure and blameless now and always right up to that time is implied.

In view of all these considerations, the exegetical choice on which the rendering in the display is based is that the sense of εἰς 'for, with reference to' is in focus. But since 'with reference to the day of Christ' or even 'for the day of Christ' is quite abstract, 'on the day' is substituted.

In some languages 'to judge us(inc)' may need to be supplied after 'the day that Christ (returns)'. This would communicate the idea that being pure and faultless with reference to Christ's coming has to do with our standing before him. The temporal word 'on' in itself may not communicate this idea.

The translator should test for possible wrong implications: Would 'until' mean pure and blameless until the day Christ returns, but no longer than that? Would 'on the day Christ returns' imply that believers do not need to be especially concerned about being pure and faultless now?

**1:11a *and in order that*** There appears to be a semantic (and possibly grammatical) parallelism here between ἦτε εἰλικρινεῖς καὶ ἀπρόσκοποι εἰς ἡμέραν Χριστοῦ 'you might be pure and faultless unto/until the day of Christ' in 10b and πεπληρωμένοι καρπὸν δικαιοσύνης τὸν διὰ Ἰησοῦ Χριστοῦ εἰς δόξαν καὶ ἔπαινον θεοῦ 'having been filled with the fruit of righteousness which is through Jesus Christ unto the glory and praise of God' in v. 11. The εἰς 'unto' phrases indicate the goal in each of the parallel constructions. The question is whether the fact that the second construction is a participle depending grammatically upon the first construction would counterindicate such an analysis. It may be that the perfect participle is used here because 'having been filled with the fruit of righteousness' precedes (in people's lives) the day of Christ: the perfect participle would be the appropriate way to indicate that. This apparent parallelism in structure and the similarity between being pure/faultless and being righteous/doing good deeds suggest that these two constructions are conjoined (coordinate) purposes of 1:9b–10a.

**you might act/live completely righteously** To understand the meaning of 'fruit of righteousness', note first that 'fruit' here is a dead metaphor. Greenlee (1992) lists three interpretations of the semantic relationship in the genitive construction καρπὸν δικαιοσύνης 'fruit of righteousness'. The two major interpretations he cites are:

1. 'Righteousness' means righteous deeds or qualities, and these are the fruit...: fruit which consists of righteous deeds.
2. 'Fruit' is the result of righteousness.

Of those who take the second interpretation, some say 'righteousness' here refers to justification by faith in Christ while others say it refers to moral uprightness. Of course, if it refers to justification by faith in Christ, then 'fruit' would refer to the result of justification. In any case, the fruit must be the righteous deeds rather than only the state of being righteous. Justification does not seem especially in focus in this context, nor does the fact that 'through Jesus Christ' is connected with 'fruit' rather than with 'righteousness' favor this viewpoint.

As to whether 'fruit of righteousness' means 'fruit which consists of righteous deeds' or 'fruit which is the result of a righteous attitude of life', the propositionalization is based on the former since if 'righteousness' does not refer to justification here, there is practically no essential difference between being morally righteous and doing righteous acts.

The use of πεπληρωμένοι 'filled', a quantitative-intensive verb which also has qualitative-intensive connotations, marks 'fruit' as prominent. The connection of the phrase τὸν διὰ Ἰησοῦ Χριστοῦ 'which (is) through Jesus Christ' to 'fruit' rather than to 'righteousness' may be another marker of prominence on 'fruit'. In the display this intensification is communicated by 'completely'.

**1:11c in order that *people will* honor God and praise him** Many commentators say that grammatically this final construction of the prayer is related to πεπληρωμένοι 'filled' (1:11a), while others say it is related to everything back to the beginning of Paul's prayer. It may be that 'to the glory and praise of God' is intended to be the ultimate purpose of the prayer whether it is seen as more closely connected with πεπληρωμένοι or the prayer as a whole. However, because of the apparent parallelism of 1:10b and 1:11a–b the rendering in the display relates 1:11c to πεπληρωμένοι in 1:11a. Also, it is difficult to deny the potential connection between the Philippians' being filled with fruits of righteousness and God's being glorified and praised thereby.

A doxology at the end of a prayer was common in Jewish and Christian prayers (see O'Brien 1991:82) and also they "frequently appear as concluding formulas to...sections of letters" (ibid.:549). Thus, the body of the Epistle to the Philippians ends with a doxology. However, rather than forming thematically separate functions, both of these doxologies blend in with the themes immediately preceding them.

The noun δόξα 'glory' in the phrase εἰς δόξαν...θεοῦ 'to (the) glory...of God' may be propositionalized either as a verb such as 'honor', 'glorify', or 'praise' or as an expansion of this idea that will communicate the meaning of 'glory' in this context. Commentators variously define glory as the manifestation of God's character, majesty, power and grace, or redeeming nature (Greenlee 1992). God's intrinsic glory will not be enhanced by what man does; it is man's cognizance of God's glory that is in focus. An example of an expansion is '*People will* honor/glorify God *because he is able to make people holy and righteous*'. Such an expansion is probably not necessary in the propositionalization, though it may be needed in some translations.

**honor God and praise him** (*or, people will praise God very much* [DOU]) In this context δόξα 'glory' and ἔπαινος 'praise' are synonyms (Hendriksen, Loh and Nida, Louw and Nida). Moore (p. 49) classifies them as a near-synonymous doublet. The repetition of words with basically the same meaning is either for emphasis or rhetorical style. Neither of these functions could be denied in this context of glorifying God and prayer. The alternate given in the display consists of one verb plus intensification of that verb. In translating, this one verb without intensification may be appropriate in some languages, while in others some quite rhetorical form would be appropriate.

## PROMINENCE AND THEME

The two conjoined means constructions (9b and 10a) are the most naturally prominent units in the 1:9-11 paragraph and so form the central part of the theme. Here the orienter is also an integral part of the theme since it signals the genre (or subgenre) of the total construction.

# PART CONSTITUENT 1:12-26 (Expressive Section: Nucleus$_1$ of 1:3-4:20)

*THEME: I rejoice because my adverse circumstances have actually advanced the good news and because I know I shall remain victorious spiritually and will magnify Christ through my life or my death. Though I desire to be with Christ, I know it is necessary for you that I remain alive in order to come and serve you and so you too will rejoice triumphantly.*

| MACROSTRUCTURE | CONTENTS |
|---|---|
| NUCLEUS$_1$ | 1:12-14 I want you to realize that as a result of my imprisonment many more people have heard the good news. |
| NUCLEUS$_2$ (REACTION) | 1:15-18e Even though some believers proclaim the message about Christ because they are antagonistic toward me, at least they are proclaiming Christ, and so I rejoice. |
| NUCLEUS$_3$ (REACTION) | 1:18f-20 I will continue to rejoice because I know that I will remain completely victorious spiritually since I earnestly expect to boldly honor Christ whether by life or by death. |
| NUCLEUS$_4$ (REACTION) | 1:21-26 Though I desire to leave this world and be with Christ, it is more important that I remain alive to help you in your need. So I know that I shall remain alive and help you believe in Christ more firmly, and as a result you will rejoice triumphantly. |

## INTENT AND MACROSTRUCTURE

The four paragraphs in this section are in a conjoined (coordinate) relationship and they all express the theme of rejoicing. Although the first paragraph does not specifically mention rejoicing, it is evident that Paul's purpose in writing it is to provide grounds for the Philippians' rejoicing and encouragement. The two middle paragraphs deal with *Paul's* rejoicing, their REACTIONS juxtaposed in 1:18. In the final paragraph the accent is on the *Philippians'* rejoicing. Paul's statement in the first paragraph, 'I want you to know, brothers', suggests that the focus of this paragraph is on the grounds for this rejoicing. It could also be said that Paul's main intent in giving the reasons for, and the fact of, his rejoicing is to encourage the Philippians to rejoice.

## BOUNDARIES AND COHERENCE

The initial boundary was discussed under 1:3-11. The final boundary for this section is at the end of 1:26 as shown by:

1. A change from the indicative mood to the imperative mood at 1:27. This is a switch from the expressive to the hortatory genre.
2. A change from a preponderance of first person singular verb endings (Paul) in 1:12-26 to a majority of second person plural verb endings (the Philippians).
3. Constituent 1:27a is generic and functions to tell the reader Paul is now dealing with the new topic of Christian behavior and no longer with his attitude toward his circumstances in confinement and under trial.

There is a question as to whether 1:12–26 is made up of more than one section. But while 1:12–14 and 1:15–18e do both have reference to speaking the word (τὸν λόγον λαλεῖν in 1:14) or proclaiming Christ (1:15, 17, 18d) whereas this is not found in the other paragraphs, there is overlapping from each of these paragraphs into the next that unites them. The τοῦτο 'this' in 1:19a has reference back to either the preaching of Christ (Χριστὸς καταγγέλλεται in 1:18d) or Paul's present circumstances (τὰ κατ' ἐμέ in 1:12), and the alternatives of life and death of 1:20 are taken up in 1:21–26. Moreover, an expressive "feeling of joy" ties all of 1:12–26 together as a whole so that no subdivision is indicated. (In 1:12–14 joy is implicit; in the other paragraphs it is stated explicitly.)

## PROMINENCE AND THEME

Since the paragraphs of 1:12–26 are in a conjoined relationship, the section theme must be drawn from the theme of each paragraph. Basic to each is the concept of rejoicing, and that rejoicing, in the first three paragraphs especially, is in spite of adverse circumstances, because out of those circumstances God brings good results. The idea of giving up one's own desires in order to serve others is also retained since this is a main part of the theme of the immediately following unit, 1:27–2:30. (Since 1:27–30 is an introduction for both 2:1–30 and 3:1–4:1, it has, for that very reason, an integral relation with 2:1–30.)

Contrasting concepts or themes might appear to be within this general theme for the section—that is, the possibility of Paul's death contrasted with his statement that he knew he would remain alive and come to be with them. But we must remember that the most important thing of all to Paul was to honor Christ, no matter what it might cost him. He knew that he had to live by that principle and he wanted the Philippians to understand that. At the same time he felt that there was good reason to believe that he would be released since that would mean he would be able to continue to be of service to them.

# SECTION CONSTITUENT 1:12–14 (Expressive Paragraph: Nucleus₁ of 1:12–26)

| THEME: *I want you to realize that as a result of my imprisonment many more people have heard the good news.* |  |
|---|---|
| **RELATIONAL STRUCTURE** | **CONTENTS** |
| ┌ORIENTER | 1:12a Fellow believers, I want you to realize |
| │ ┌contrast | 1:12b that the *adverse* things *which have happened* to me *have not prevented me from proclaiming the good news to people.* |
| ┊NUCLEUS │ GENERIC | 1:12c Instead, *these adverse things* have caused/enabled even more people to hear the good news. |
| │ ├specific₁ | 1:13 *Specifically*, all the military guards who are stationed *in this city* and all the rest *of the people in the city* [HYP] *now* know that I am a prisoner [MTY] because *I proclaim the good news* about Christ. |
| │ └specific₂—RESULT | 1:14a And, *specifically,* most of the believers *here now* proclaim the message from God more courageously and fearlessly |
| │          └reason | 1:14b *because* they trust the Lord *more firmly to help/support them* because *they have seen how the Lord has helped me* while I have been a prisoner [MTY] *here*. |

## INTENT AND PARAGRAPH PATTERN

While it is obvious that 1:15–18e is expressive in intent based on Paul's statement 'I rejoice' in the most prominent construction of that unit, it is not quite so obvious that the 1:12–14 paragraph is expressive, though we might expect such a closely related unit to be of the same intent. As is often the case in expressive intent, Paul not only expresses his own emotions but also wants his addressees to share his feelings. Here he wants the Philippians to realize that his imprisonment has actually promoted the advance of the gospel; they should, therefore, have the same REACTION of joy as he has. (He does not, however, in 12–14 make explicit his desire for them to rejoice with him.)

Although the intent of the paragraph is expressive, the REACTION is not explicit; and therefore the explicit *situation* may consist of a different paragraph pattern or only of communication relations. Perhaps this *situation* unit (i.e., the grammatical paragraph) should be analyzed as having a CLAIM-*justification* structure (which is one of the typical expository types), or perhaps its structure is better analyzed as GENERIC-*specific*. The Greek signals do not clearly indicate that the paragraph is to be taken as CLAIM-*justification*. In fact, the Greek signal which introduces what would be the *justification* part of the paragraph, or alternatively the specific part of the GENERIC-specific construction, is one whose typical function is to introduce neither, but instead to introduce result: ὥστε. As will be discussed in the notes on v. 13, result does not seem to be signaled here since what is described in 13–14 is not something that is the result of the advance of the gospel but is specific instances of that advance. The question (a theoretical one) is, Should a unit that is not necessarily seen by the author as a CLAIM-*justification* unit be analyzed as such? One reason for not analyzing it this way is that the words introducing the *justification* (such as 'as evidence for this') in the display would appear to be overtranslation. Therefore the unit is diagrammed as GENERIC-specific.

## NOTES

**1:12a fellow believers** For many languages a literal translation of ἀδελφοί 'brothers' may be appropriate, but it is rendered here as 'fellow believers', which is the nonfigurative meaning.

**realize** The Greek word γινώσκειν, which is generally translated as 'know', is rendered in the display as 'realized'. Paul wants the Philippians to have not only a cognitive knowledge of these facts, but also joy that Christ's cause is being forwarded even in the midst of adverse circumstances. The word βούλομαι 'I want' may signal the fact that what Paul is saying is not only information, but something he wants them to act upon in their attitude toward his situation. In fact, it could almost be seen as a directive, though with an expressive purpose.

**1:12b the *adverse* things *which have happened* to me** The phrase τὰ κατ' ἐμέ 'the (things) concerning me' refers generally to Paul's imprisonment as shown by the fact that the specifics of τὰ κατ' ἐμέ are described as 'my bonds' in vv. 13 and 14.

**1:12b-c** *have not prevented me from proclaiming the good news to people.* **Instead,** *these adverse things* **have caused/enabled even more people to hear the good news** Commentators cited by Greenlee (1992) interpret μᾶλλον to have "the idea that what happened was contrary to what one would expect...: rather than being a hindrance, my circumstances have worked for the advance of the gospel." But some commentators say that μᾶλλον also has the idea that Paul's adverse "circumstances have worked for an even greater spread of the gospel" (ibid.:38). The fact that the specific restatement of 1:12b-c in 1:14a indicates that most of the brothers were now more courageously and fearlessly proclaiming the gospel suggests that Paul may have intended to state here that the advance of the gospel was even greater than before.

The contraexpectation signaled in μᾶλλον 'rather' has been propositionalized as *'have not prevented me from proclaiming the good news to people.* Instead...'. The increase in the spread of the good news is rendered by 'even more'.

Since 'adverse things have caused/enabled' is a personification of sorts, an alternate rendering for 12b-c would be 'that even though I am a prisoner, I am still able *to proclaim the good news to people.* In fact, even more people have heard the good news because I am a prisoner'.

**1:13** *Specifically* It is difficult to see how the spreading of the gospel message to all those in the praetorium and to all the rest and the encouragement other believers now have in proclaiming the message can be a result (the normal function of ὥστε, which occurs at the beginning of v. 13) of the advancing of the gospel rather than specific instances of that advance. Therefore vv. 13 and 14 have been displayed as specifics of 12c. (See 1 Cor. 5:1 for a similar instance of ὥστε being used to introduce a more specific explanation of what has immediately preceded rather than to introduce result.) Greenlee (1992) lists ten commentators as analyzing ὥστε as introducing "an explanation of the preceding reference to the advance of the gospel," and three who take it as indicating result.

**the military guards who are stationed** *in this city* Greenlee (1992) shows two basic interpretations of πραιτώριον 'praetorium/praetorian guard': (1) the military guard or (2) a building, either "the barracks of the military guard..., or the imperial palace if in Rome..., or the residence of the provincial governor if outside of Rome." Many commentators support the view ably researched and argued by Lightfoot that here πραιτώριον means the imperial guard. "This in fact is the common use of the term," says Lightfoot. This group was a more elite group than regular soldiers and their role was more that of guard duty rather than battlefield duty. Since in Paul's case they were guarding a prisoner awaiting trial, they cannot strictly be referred to in translation as 'men who guard the emperor'. Better would be: 'all the military guards stationed here/in Rome/in this city', 'all the military guards of the whole unit'. The number of praetorian guards in the unit stationed in Rome would have been in the thousands.

**all the military guards ... all the rest** *of the people in the city* Most likely ὅλῳ 'whole' and πᾶσιν 'all' are instances of hyperbole here. This is a difficult figure to adjust since its function is to intensify, and attempts to adjust it by restoring it to its exact measurement may decrease its intensity. Some languages may not accept hyperbole (one would need to translate as 'many' or 'most'); however, hyperbole of this type is more likely to be accepted.

**and all the rest** *of the people in the city* The Greek is καὶ τοῖς λοιποῖς πᾶσιν 'and all the rest'. It is difficult to know which specific group, if any, Paul has in mind. The rendering should probably be quite general. We know from Acts 28 that Paul had contact with a large number of people in the city. Furthermore Paul's intention in this paragraph is to show how much the gospel has been advanced. These factors suggest that no limiting specific should be put on Paul's reference, and so the generic 'in the city' is used in the display. A majority of the commentators cited in Greenlee (1992) take this view.

**because** *I proclaim the good news* **about Christ** It is generally agreed that ἐν in δεσμούς μου φανεροὺς ἐν Χριστῷ γενέσθαι 'my bonds have become known in Christ' signals the reason for Paul's imprisonment. However, by itself 'because of Christ' could be understood in various, even quite erroneous, ways. 'For the sake of Christ' would be better. In the display the prepositional phrase is rendered as a full proposition to more specifically represent the intended meaning.

**1:14a the message from God** There are some textual variants for what has been propositionalized as 'the message from God'. The UBSGNT has simply τὸν λόγον 'the word' (τολμᾶν ἀφόβως τὸν λόγον λαλεῖν 'dare fearlessly the word to speak'), whereas many other texts include the modifier τοῦ θεοῦ 'of God' or τοῦ κυρίου 'of the Lord'. Metzger (p. 544-45) in discussing the reason the UBS committee favored the shorter reading indicates that it was not due to τοῦ θεοῦ not being well substantiated but rather to the fact that the "position and wording of the genitive modifiers (τοῦ θεοῦ and κυρίου)" in the various manuscripts varied. Thus the UBS committee chose τὸν λόγον λαλεῖν 'the word to speak' "as that which best explains the origin of the other readings," admitting, however, that "it must be acknowledged that, on the basis of weight and variety of external evidence, the reading λόγον τοῦ θεοῦ λαλεῖν seems to be preferable" (ibid.). Whether or not 'from God' is explicit in the text, the notion is present semantically; based on that and on the external evidence for including τοῦ θεοῦ, it is included in the display as explicit information.

**1:14b they trust the Lord** The phrase ἐν κυρίῳ 'in the Lord' can be connected grammatically with either τῶν ἀδελφῶν 'the brothers' or πεποιθότας 'being confident/trusting'. But for the display the latter is chosen because Paul joins ἐν κυρίῳ unambiguously with πέποιθα 'I am confident' in 2:24, and because an ἐν phrase can precede πέποιθα as shown by 3:3, and because ἀδελφοί 'brothers' generally refers to Christians elsewhere without the addition of ἐν κυρίῳ.

Once this position is taken, one must decide the semantic relationship of πεποιθότας with both ἐν κυρίῳ 'in the Lord' and τοῖς δεσμοῖς μου 'in (i.e., dative) my bonds'. Both the ἐν construction and the dative with πέποιθα most often function as indicating the person or thing in which the trust or confidence is placed. And here this general relationship is possible with either construction, though the semantic relationships are different, especially since one of the "objects" represents a person while the other is a thing, Paul's bonds. But it is unlikely that both would act as the "object" of the confidence. Thus some commentators see 'the Lord' as the object of the brothers' confidence and Paul's bonds as the means or reason that encourage the confidence. Others see 'in the Lord' as the sphere or basis of the brothers' confidence while again 'in my bonds' in effect is the reason for that confidence.

The display rendering is based on the first interpretation but there is really not much difference in meaning between the two interpretations.

## BOUNDARIES AND COHERENCE

There is a question as to whether the final boundary of this unit is v. 14 or 18e. Verses 15-18e form a unified structure, as shown by (1) the chiastic structure of 15-17; (2) the two types of preachers that Paul talks about in 15-18e who are mentioned only generically in 14; (3) the contrast between good and bad motives found only in 15-18e, including the sandwich structure of Christ's being proclaimed from different motives in 15 and 18b-d; and (4) the threefold reference to the proclamation of Christ in 15, 17, and 18b-d. The tail-head transition from τὸν λόγον λαλεῖν 'speak the word' in 14 to τὸν Χριστὸν κηρύσσουσιν 'preach Christ' in 15 is a common feature at the boundary marking a new unit. It is valid as a boundary marker if there is sufficient evidence that the new unit is coherent in itself (as is true of the 15-18e unit).

It might be argued that vv. 15-18e are possibly a unit on the subparagraph level. The theme of 15-18d, 'Even though some believers proclaim the message about Christ because they are antagonistic toward me, at least they are proclaiming Christ', might be said to be a specific of a possible theme of 1:12-14, 'I want you to know that the adverse things that have happened to me have actually resulted in the advance of the good news'. However, 18e, 'and because of that I rejoice', is intricately connected to 15-18d, and is in fact more prominent than any part of 15-18d, so the final theme of 15-18e is *not* a specific of the theme of 12-14.

## PROMINENCE AND THEME

As the most prominent constituent of the unit, 1:12c provides the basic part of the theme. Since the orienter, 1:12a, has almost directive force it is also included in the theme. Instead of the generic 'these adverse things which have happened to me', the more specific phrase 'my imprisonment' is used, especially since Paul seems to be referring to that (cf. τοὺς δεσμούς μου 'my bonds' in v. 13 and τοῖς δεσμοῖς μου 'in my bonds' in v. 14) but including, of course, the trial.

# SECTION CONSTITUENT 1:15–18e (Expressive Paragraph: Nucleus₂ of 1:12–26)

*THEME: Even though some believers proclaim the message about Christ because they are antagonistic toward me, at least they are proclaiming Christ, and so I rejoice.*

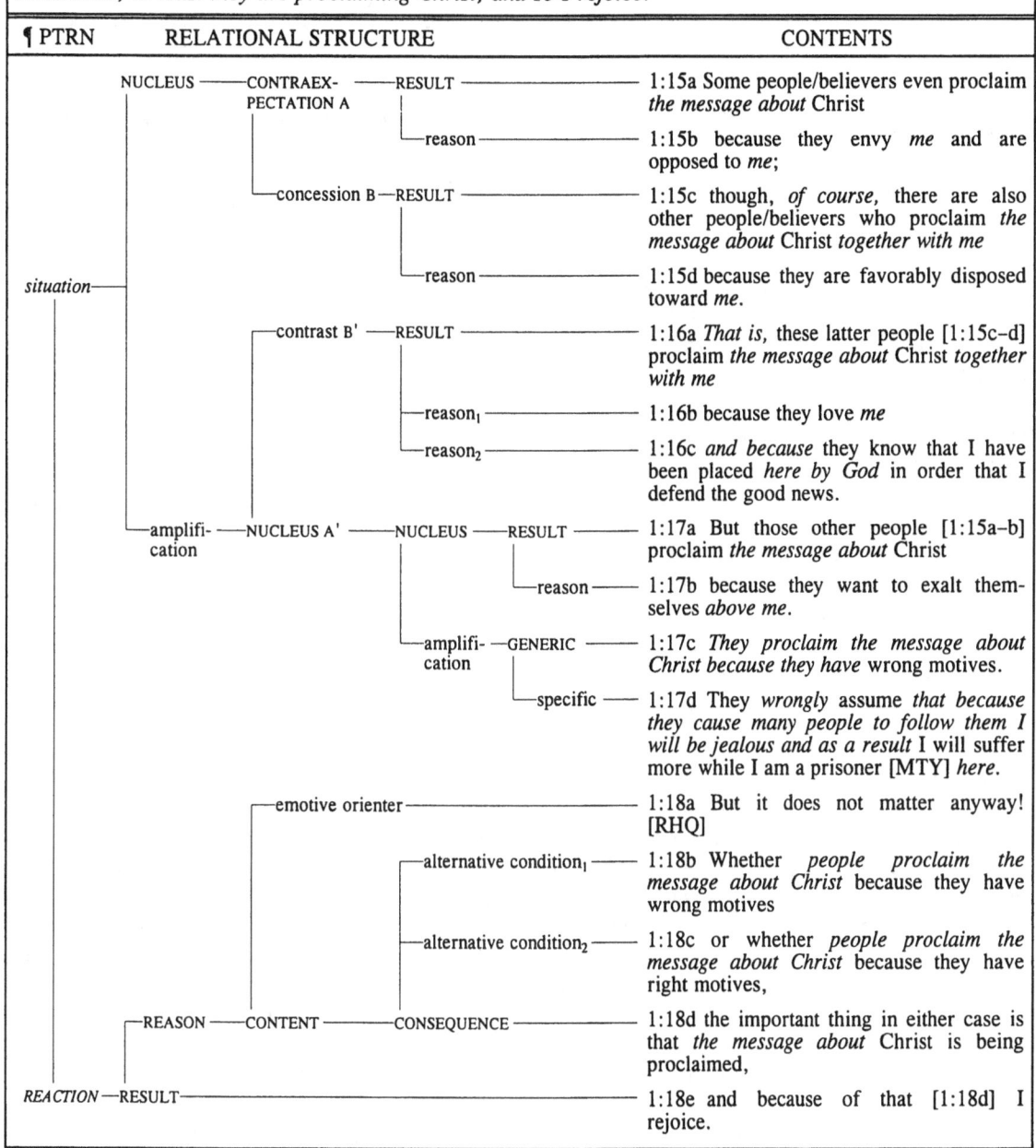

## INTENT AND PARAGRAPH PATTERN

Since the most naturally prominent constituent of this paragraph (καὶ ἐν τούτῳ χαίρω 'and in this I rejoice') is expressive in intent, the paragraph pattern is one of *REACTION-situation*.

The circumstance which underlies the *situation* is the activity of the two types of preachers, especially the preachers with wrong motives. Even though they are preaching Christ out of wrong motives, Christ is still being preached.

This is the *situation*. While 18e is obviously expressive with its use of 'I rejoice', the whole of 18a-e is *REACTION* to the *situation*. Paul's use of τί γάρ 'what then' is appropriate to an expressive *REACTION*. Vincent says of τί γάρ, "Interjectional, and called out by what immediately precedes." Within the *REACTION* a logical step is stated (18b-d) which shows the reason for Paul's being able to rejoice in otherwise bleak circumstances—Christ is being proclaimed.

## NOTES

**1:15-17** As the display indicates with the use of ABB'A', there is a chiastic structure here: 15a-b and 17a-d describe those who proclaim Christ out of bad motives, and 15c-d and 16a-c describe those who proclaim Christ out of good motives. A four-part chiasm like this usually marks prominence on the first and last elements, that is, on the people with bad motives in this case. This fits in with the contraexpectation orientation of this paragraph, 'Even though some believers proclaim Christ from bad motives, still Christ is proclaimed, and so I rejoice'. (See, however, the note on 1:16-17 regarding the fact that in the Textus Receptus and the Hodges and Farstad text the order is ABA'B'; that is, v. 15 remains the same but vv. 16 and 17 are in reverse order, as in the KJV. This would be an acceptable order for translation into other languages.)

Another possibility in translating into other languages would be to state all the facts about those with good motives first and then state all the facts about those with bad motives if such an order is required by the target language. One should seek, however, to maintain prominence at the most appropriate place in order to produce the same effect as the chiastic structure in the original Greek.

**1:15a Some people/believers** Through the centuries commentators have been divided as to whether τινές 'some' here refers to some of the ἀδελφοί 'brothers' mentioned in v. 14 who became bolder in preaching the gospel because of Paul's imprisonment or to people from some other group. But do the sets of participants in 12-14 need to coincide with the sets in 15-18e since the themes of the two units are different? In 12-14 Paul is talking about the majority of the believers who have been emboldened in preaching the gospel because of his imprisonment. Is there not a possibility that those people of whom he speaks in 15a-b are actually composed of some who were emboldened by Paul's imprisonment and others who have not been so affected by it? In point of fact, the composition of the group does not make much difference since Paul's theme is different in this new unit of 15-18e. It might be better, then, not to specifically identify the 'some' of 15a-b as a subgroup of the brothers of v. 14, but to be less specific: 'some believers/people proclaim the message about Christ'. That this is at least an option grammatically is supported by the following statement: "The two classes mentioned here are not subdivisions of the ἀδελφοί ἐν κυρίῳ ['brothers in the Lord'] above, who would more naturally be οἱ μέν and οἱ δέ..." (Alford).

Some commentators have maintained that the people preaching Christ from wrong motives were Judaizers. But it does not seem reconcilable that Paul would speak of the Judaizers with such condemning language in 3:2 while here he would virtually sanction their message, pointing out only that their motives were wrong. He even rejoices in their message (1:18)! These people are said to be proclaiming Christ. Eadie (p. 35) says, "Can it be supposed for a moment that the apostle could call any form of Judaistic teaching the preaching of Christ...?" Elsewhere (Gal. 2:21) Paul accuses the Judaizers of "subverting the gospel to such an extent, that upon their theory Christ had died in vain" (Eadie, p. 34).

**even** The μέν...δέ construction typically relates items in contrast to one another (Louw and Nida 89.136). Here the contrast is between those who proclaim Christ out of envy and rivalry and those who proclaim Christ out of good will. But there is also an element of contraexpectation here: it would not normally be expected that those who were proclaiming Christ would be doing so because they envied and opposed Paul. This instance of concession-CONTRAEXPECTATION most likely has two different realizations of concession. The καί in τινὲς μὲν καί represents the generic concession, 'Even though we would not think anyone (or anyone of these brothers) would proclaim Christ because they envy me'. The second realization of concession is 1:15c, τινὲς δὲ καὶ δι' εὐδοκίαν τὸν Χριστὸν κηρύσσουσιν 'some also proclaim Christ because of good will'. This is a specific realization of the concession and could be translated '*though* there are also other people/believers who proclaim Christ because they are favorably disposed toward me'.

In some languages the implicit generic concession may have to be fully represented: '*Although no one would think that fellow believers would proclaim Christ because they envy me and are opposed to me*'. In this case the CONTRAEXPECTATION would be, 'there are actually some believers/people who are doing this'.

**1:15b envy *me* . . . are opposed to *me*** That the envy and opposition mentioned here are directed toward Paul can be clearly seen from 17d: οἰόμενοι θλῖψιν ἐγείρειν τοῖς δεσμοῖς μου 'thinking to cause affliction in my bonds'. Likewise, evidence that the good will and love are directed toward Paul can be seen in 16a–c: 'they *preach the good news* out of *a motive of* love knowing that I have been appointed to defend the good news'.

Also we need to ask why these people are jealous of Paul. Presumably it is because of his position, influence, and/or success. Vincent says, "It may be, as Weiss suggests, that as the Roman church before Paul's arrival had no definite leadership, it was easy for ambitious and smaller men to obtain a certain prominence which they found menaced by the presence and influence of the apostle."

The reason the motives are forefronted before the occurrences of the verbal phrase 'preaching Christ' in 15–17 is to point up the contrastive motives.

**1:15c also** The καί in the δέ part of the μὲν...δέ construction makes sense translated as 'also': 'There are also others who proclaim *the message about* Christ because they are favorably disposed toward me'.

**1:15d favorably disposed toward** *me* Three motives are given for the second group for preaching Christ. These are εὐδοκία 'good will', ἀγάπη 'love', and εἰδότες ὅτι εἰς ἀπολογίαν τοῦ εὐαγγελίου κεῖμαι 'knowing that I have been set/appointed for the defense of the gospel'. Only in the third motive or reason is there an explicit reference to Paul, indicating that their motivation for preaching Christ is in some way connected with their feelings toward Paul. Certainly even Paul himself would not want to say that their only motivation for preaching Christ was their feelings toward him, whether their good will toward him, their love for him, or their sympathy expressed because of his appointment to defend the gospel (while imprisoned). While preaching Christ out of envy for someone else is an atrocious motive, preaching Christ with the primary motive of love for someone other than Christ could be seen as a questionable motive. So what is Paul saying? One answer is to understand Paul as saying that they work together with him in preaching the gospel because they are favorably disposed toward him and love him. This is in contrast to the others who are in opposition to him. The result of this line of thinking is in the propositions 15c–16c in the display.

There is much parallelism in the structure of 1:15–17, and in order to maintain the parallel structure semantic components and relationships are sometimes left implicit—even to the point that things appear skewed. Connected with this is the fact that Paul wants to retain 'proclaiming Christ' as most prominent, as v. 18 especially shows.

**1:16–17** Some manuscripts, including the Textus Receptus on which the KJV is based, have 1:16 and 17 in reverse order to that of the UBSGNT and most modern translations. The Hodges and Farstad text has the same order as the Textus Receptus. The Textus Receptus order continues the bad-good sequence found in 15. In other words, 15–17 are ordered ABA'B', rather than having the chiastic structure (ABB'A') for 15–17. It is easier to see why the chiastic structure would have been realigned to a parallel structure rather than vice versa.

**1:16c I have been placed** *here* The verb κεῖμαι 'be put, be appointed' is open to two interpretations. The first is that since these brothers know Paul has been appointed an apostle to defend the gospel, they should support him: they should stand with him rather than with those who out of selfish ambition want to be more prominent than Paul, not realizing, or possibly not acknowledging, God's appointment. The second is that Paul was placed in confinement to defend the gospel, and specifically before the Roman court. But would Paul have used κεῖμαι if he were making specific reference to the first option? It is not used elsewhere in the New Testament in the sense of being appointed to a position, though it is used in Hermas in the sense of "*be put in charge of someth.*" (BAGD, p. 426.2a). The forefronting of εἰς ἀπολογίαν τοῦ εὐαγγελίου 'for the defense of the gospel' before κεῖμαι would suggest that the defense of the gospel is more in focus than the act of being appointed, and the fact that God is not explicitly signaled as the agent of the appointment implies that God's agency in the appointment (rather than someone else's) is not especially in focus either. This is in contrast to the *opening* of some epistles where it is very much in focus (most notably Galatians). Also the second option would be supported by the fact that 'love' collocates well with that connotational sense of 'defense' that has to do with difficulty.

The sense of κεῖμαι here may be close to that of Luke 2:34, 'This child is destined/appointed for the falling and rising of many in Israel' and 1 Thess. 3:3, 'You know that we have been destined/appointed for [these trials]'. 'I have been placed/put *here by God*' would basically have this same sense. (Note that the agent of actions is uniformly included in propositionalization.)

These various considerations suggest that Paul has most specifically in mind here the sense of defending the gospel in his imprisonment and trial and all that is connected with that both on the physical and spiritual levels.

**1:17b they want to exalt themselves *above me*** Though BAGD (p. 309) acknowledges that the sense of 'strife, contentiousness' is possible as a gloss for the occurrences of ἐριθεία in the New Testament it goes on to say, "But *selfishness, selfish ambition*... in all cases gives a sense that is just as good, and perh[aps] better." In Phil. 1:17 no doubt selfish ambition is involved but that this selfish ambition includes or leads to rivalry with Paul cannot be denied as words such as φθόνος 'envy' and ἔρις 'rivalry' in 15 and 'supposing to cause me trouble in my bonds' in 17 show.

The ἐξ ἐριθείας 'out of selfish ambition' construction clearly expresses the motive for their preaching the message about Christ. In communication relation terms, this is a reason.

**1:17c *They proclaim the message about Christ because they have* wrong motives** The words οὐχ ἁγνῶς 'not sincerely' indicate that their preaching is from wrong motives. To express 'motive', an abstract noun, a good rendering may require a verbal form describing the wrong motives in this context more fully.

**1:17d They *wrongly* assume *that because they cause many people to follow them I will be jealous and as a result* I will suffer more while I am a prisoner *here*** The Greek here is οἰόμενοι θλῖψιν ἐγείρειν τοῖς δεσμοῖς μου, 'thinking affliction to raise up to my bonds'. "The meaning," according to Vincent, "is not that they deliberately set themselves to aggravate Paul's sufferings, but that their malice was gratified by the annoyance which their efforts to promote their own partisan ends caused him." It is not merely the proclaiming of Christ that they felt would make him jealous and so annoy him, but the winning of people to *their* Christian "party."

In the display 1:17d is shown as a particular specific of the more generic 1:17c.

***wrongly* assume** The word οἴομαι does not inherently mean 'to think mistakenly' as its use in John 21:25 shows ("I suppose [οἶμαι] that even the whole world would not have room for the books that would be written"). For a general definition, the gloss in Louw and Nida (31.29) for οἶμαι and similar words would seem appropriate: "to regard something as presumably true, but without particular certainty." As to Phil. 1:17, we can at least say that Paul does not intimate at all that they were accomplishing their purpose. Meyer suggests that Paul purposely chose οἰόμενοι to contrast with εἰδότες 'knowing' in 16 thus hinting "that what they imagine *fails to happen*." And the fact that Paul rejoices in these circumstances (18) would further suggest this to be true.

**suffer more** With τοῖς δεσμοῖς μου 'in my bonds' Paul is intimating that they hope to increase his troubles while he is imprisoned.

**1:18a But it does not matter anyway!** Most commentators and translators take the initial two Greek words in 1:18, τί γάρ, as a unit in itself, a rhetorical question. But they disagree on how it should be translated. Some translate τί γάρ as 'what then?', a rhetorical question introducing Paul's next point—his REACTION to the SITUATION he has just described. Others translate it as 'what does it matter?', which, though also introducing Paul's REACTION to the SITUATION, emphasizes his feelings about it, akin to our English idiom 'so what?', which is just as close a literal translation for τί γάρ as 'what then?'. However, we are not dealing here with literal translations but with idioms. In fact, γάρ itself in certain contexts signals a rhetorical question that indicates emphasis. Under entry 1f for γάρ in BAGD (p. 152) the example is given of "μὴ γὰρ οἰκίας οὐκ ἔχετε; *what! Have you no houses?*" (1 Cor. 11:22). BAGD classifies γάρ in Phil. 1:18 under entry 1f also and translates τί γάρ as "*what does it matter?*" The use of γάρ in this sense with only the question word τί would certainly seem to be an idiomatic way to signal strong emphasis. We would expect this type of emphasis in expressive import, especially at the beginning of a REACTION unit of the contraexpectation type.

In the display this rhetorical question is changed into the declarative statement 'But it does not matter anyway!' ('But...anyway' signals contraexpectation.)

As to the relationship between the proposition based on τί γάρ and the other propositions in 1:18, the options are that 18a is either an emotive orienter for 18b–d or a REACTION in itself. Since its position at the beginning of the REACTION unit is an appropriate position for an orienter, and since its idiomatic and interjectional nature suggest an emotive orienter rather than a full *REACTION*, it is considered to be an orienter here.

**1:18b because they have wrong motives** The noun πρόφασις 'false motive, pretext' is defined in the context (1:15–17) by the specific wrong motives for proclaiming Christ—envy, rivalry, selfish ambition, malice (shown by their assumption, which seems to be at least a hope, if not an intention, that Paul would suffer more while imprisoned through what they were doing).

**1:18d the important thing** BAGD (p. 669) categorizes πλήν as an "adv. used as conjunction...coming at the beginning of a sentence or clause" and gives 'only' as one of the glosses for πλήν (entries 1b, c). That seems to fit well in this context in a general sense, but to be more finetuned 'what is important, the important thing, the thing that matters' is better. In the propositionalization, 'the important thing' is delayed until 18d in order to relate it closely to what it describes, Christ's being proclaimed. And it preserves the prominence and is more understandable if the statement 'Christ is being proclaimed' comes right before 'and because of that I rejoice', even as it does in the Greek text.

**1:18e and because of that [1:18d] I rejoice** Paul rejoices because Christ is being proclaimed and made known to an ever-widening circle of people even though he does not appreciate the methods of the rival preachers.

## BOUNDARIES AND COHERENCE

The reasons for making a boundary in 1:18 between καὶ ἐν τούτῳ χαίρω 'and in this I rejoice' (1:18e) and ἀλλὰ καὶ χαρήσομαι 'but indeed I shall rejoice' (1:18f) include the following:

1. The present tense is used throughout 1:15–18e, then the future tense in 1:18f, with future tense again in the first part of 1:19 and twice in 1:20.
2. The participant references change in 1:18f and the following verses with no more reference to the different types of preachers.
3. In keeping with the participant reference change, the semantic domain of motives, good and bad, is no longer mentioned.
4. Both χαίρω 'I rejoice' and χαρήσομαι 'I shall rejoice' represent nuclear propositions with the support for each of them running in different directions linearly. That is, χαίρω is supported by propositions before it, while χαρήσομαι is supported by propositions occurring after it. Thus there must be some type of major boundary between them. In the display diagram it is shown that the support for the first one goes back to the beginning of the paragraph. The support system of the second verb runs to the end of 20.

## PROMINENCE AND THEME

In an expressive paragraph pattern, as in other paragraph patterns, both major components need to be represented in the theme. The most prominent part of the *REACTION* is 1:18e, but the theme is not communicated fully with the words 'I rejoice' alone. While all of 18 is the *REACTION* to 15–17, there is a logical step between the *situation* and Paul's expressive statement of 'I rejoice'. Without this step the theme does not make sense. Therefore the *REACTION* part of the theme should be based on 'I rejoice because the message about Christ is being proclaimed'.

As for the *situation* part of the theme, the outside parts of a four-part chiasmus are usually the more prominent parts; here that refers to the preaching from bad motives. This fits in well with Paul's overall theme of rejoicing in spite of adverse circumstances as found in 12–18e and even in 18f–20.

# SECTION CONSTITUENT 1:18f–20 (Expressive Paragraph: Nucleus₃ of 1:12–26)

*THEME: I will continue to rejoice because I know that I will remain completely victorious spiritually since I earnestly expect to boldly honor Christ whether by life or by death.*

| ¶ PATTERN | RELATIONAL STRUCTURE | CONTENTS |
|---|---|---|
| REACTION | | 1:18f Furthermore, I will continue to rejoice, |
| SITUATION—CLAIM | orienter | 1:19a because I know |
| | RESULT | 1:19b that these *adverse things which have happened to me* will *actually* result in my remaining completely victorious spiritually |
| | means | 1:19c by means of your praying *to God for me*, and by means of the *Holy* Spirit's helping *me, who was given to me by Jesus Christ*. |
| justification | orienter | 1:20a *I know that I will remain victorious* since I earnestly expect and confidently hope (*or*, I very confidently expect [DOU]) |
| | negative | 1:20b that in no way I will be ashamed *to honor Christ* |
| | POSITIVE RESULT | 1:20c but rather, just as I always *have done*, I will continue now also to very boldly/courageously honor Christ |
| | means — GENERIC | 1:20d by means of all that I do, [SYN, MTY] |
| | alternative specific₁ | 1:20e whether by means of *the manner in which I* live |
| | alternative specific₂ | 1:20f or by means of *the manner in which I* die. |

## INTENT AND PARAGRAPH PATTERN

Verses 1:19–20 are subordinate to 1:18f, and since 1:18f contains the expressive verb χαρήσομαι 'I will rejoice', this paragraph is expressive in genre, 1:18f being the REACTION to the 1:19–20 *situation*. The *situation* is signaled by γάρ 'because' at the beginning of 1:19a. This is future. Paul states that he will continue to rejoice because he knows that he will triumph spiritually whether his trial leads to life or death.

## NOTES

**1:18f Furthermore** The expression ἀλλὰ καί 'but also' can be used to connect noncontrastive conjoined units. BAGD (p. 38.3) describes it here as elliptical, that is, minus the οὐ μόνον 'not only' half of the construction but still meaning '(not only this) but also (that)' (cf. Luke 12:7; 16:21; 24:22). The basic function of ἀλλὰ καί is to signal emphasis. BDF (§ 448) describes it as introducing "an additional point in an emphatic way." Some type of emphasis would be appropriate in translation; however, ἀλλὰ καί at the beginning of a new paragraph (as here) would not necessarily mark the new paragraph as more prominent than the preceding one. 'Furthermore' is probably an adequate translation.

**1:19b these *adverse things which have happened to me*** The subject of the verb ἀποβήσεται 'will turn out to, will result in' is τοῦτο 'this'. But it is difficult to know for sure what the antecedent of τοῦτο is. When Ellicott says, "τοῦτο here can only mean the same as τούτῳ ver. 19 [v. 18 actually]—the more extended preaching of the gospel of Christ," he is speaking from a grammatical viewpoint only. Since τούτῳ 'in this' ('in this I rejoice') occurs in the preceding verse and nothing comes between these two occurrences of τοῦτο to serve as an antecedent for the second one, it would be natural to understand both occurrences as referring to the same thing unless it can be shown from the general context that this is incongruent. The first 'this' refers to Christ's being proclaimed. Many commentators feel that the context does in fact force τοῦτο 'this' to be understood as referring to τὰ κατ' ἐμέ 'the (adverse) things which have happened to me' in 1:12.

**will *actually* result in** BAGD (p. 88.2) glosses the figurative senses of ἀποβαίνω as "*turn out, lead* (to)." 'Lead to' might denote a cause-effect relationship and this is what we find in the only other figurative occurrence of ἀποβαίνω in the New Testament in Luke 21:13: ἀποβήσεται ὑμῖν εἰς μαρτύριον, which is translated by NIV as

"This will result in your being witnesses to them." The situational context there is quite similar to the context here. Another occurrence is in the Septuagint translation of Job 13:16, which contains a construction identical to the construction here in Phil. 1:19, τοῦτό μοι ἀποβήσεται εἰς σωτηρίαν 'this for me shall turn out/lead to salvation'. In the reference in Job, ἀποβαίνω signals a cause-effect relationship, as it does in Luke 21:13. (This is clearly seen in the NIV translation of that whole context.)

There are no doubt contexts where ἀποβαίνω in the figurative sense means 'turn to, change to' where no cause-effect relationship exists. The Septuagint rendition of Job 30:31 would be one: Ἀπέβη δὲ εἰς πένθος μου ἡ κιθάρα, ὁ δὲ ψαλμός μου εἰς κλαυθμὸν ἐμοί. Brenton translates this, "My harp also has been turned into mourning, and my song into my weeping."

**these *adverse things which have happened to me* will *actually* result in my remaining completely victorious spiritually** The most important factor in understanding the 1:18f–20 paragraph is the meaning of σωτηρία in this context. BAGD (p. 801) glosses σωτηρία with a general "*deliverance, preservation*" but then says that the predominant meaning in the New Testament is "*salvation,* which the true religion bestows" (entry 2). As Lightfoot says, "His personal safety cannot be intended here, as some have thought; for the σωτηρία, of which he speaks, will be gained equally whether he lives or dies (ver. 20)." The prior context (1:12–18e, and also 1:25) might appear to suggest that σωτηρία means acquittal here. But κατά 'according to' at the beginning of v. 20 is a clear, unambiguous signal of congruence between the statements of v. 19 and v. 20, so that 20, in effect, is a delimitation of σωτηρία. A σωτηρία that potentially includes death obviously does not refer to physical deliverance. Some commentators have tried to circumvent this and reach a solution in which σωτηρία does mean 'physical deliverance', but their solutions are not plausible.

At the same time, σωτηρία here cannot mean 'salvation' in the narrow sense of being declared righteous by God since that event happened in Paul's life long before this. Ascertaining the antecedent of τοῦτο 'this' and the meaning of σωτηρία are difficult problems, and commentators hold a variety of views. The two most probable solutions seem to be:

1. Take τοῦτο 'this' to refer to its most natural antecedent grammatically, which is τούτῳ 'this' in v. 18, referring to the proclaiming of Christ, and consider ἀποβήσεται to have a cause-effect relationship as in Luke 21:13 and Job 13:16. With the context of v. 20 clearly in mind, σωτηρία would refer generally to a spiritual victory for Paul in the context of his defense and trial. This victory would include his not denying or being ashamed of Christ in any way but rather honoring him whether by life or death. It would also include fulfilling Christ's purposes for him in every way; eternal salvation; the vindication of himself from a spiritual standpoint and the vindication of the cause of Christ; and his own personal spiritual development.

2. Take τοῦτο 'this' to refer to τὰ κατ' ἐμέ 'the (adverse) things which have happened to me' in v. 12 (in this case ἀποβήσεται would not signal a direct cause-effect relationship, but an indirect one) and take σωτηρία to refer to spiritual development and victory for Paul: 'I know that the outcome of these adverse things which have happened to me will be complete spiritual victory for me'.

In favor of the first solution is the fact that grammatically it is much easier to explain τοῦτο 'this' as referring to Χριστὸς καταγγέλλεται 'Christ is preached' in 1:18 than to τὰ κατ' ἐμέ 'my circumstances' back in 1:12, though it is true that the sense of 12–14 and 15–17 has to do with adverse circumstances. Semantically, however, taking τοῦτο 'this' to refer to Paul's circumstances seems more appropriate than taking it as referring to Christ's being preached since it is difficult to see how the preaching of Christ would be the means or cause of Paul's salvation or spiritual victory. Taking τοῦτο 'this' to refer to the adverse circumstances in Paul's life maintains the theme of bad things (τὰ κατ' ἐμέ) turning out for good as in 12–14 and in 15–18e; that is, (the right handling of) the adverse circumstances produces a development in the life spiritually. Most of the commentators cited in Greenlee (1992) take τοῦτο 'this' to refer to Paul's present circumstances.

The most common understanding of the good effect of bad circumstances in our Christian lives is the development of spiritual character. Lightfoot takes σωτηρία here in the specific sense of Paul's own spiritual development. Vincent takes it as "the whole saving and sanctifying work of Christ in the believer." In this context the focus of sanctification and spiritual development would be on learning how to come out on top spiritually in every situation. This might be propositionalized as 'I know that these *adverse things which are happening to me* will *actually* result in my remaining completely victorious spiritually', 'I know that these *adverse things which are happening to me* will *actually* aid me to remain completely victorious spiritually', or, 'I know that these *adverse things which have happened to me* will *actually* be profitable for me and as a result I will remain completely victorious spiritually'.

The word 'actually' has been supplied in 19b in the display to make it clear that the thought of adverse circumstances producing good results is a contraexpected one. It signals that the cause-effect relationship is not a direct, intended one.

**1:19c by means of . . . and by means of** Some commentators argue that since no article precedes ἐπιχορηγίας 'supply/help', this conjoined noun is modified by the article and the pronoun ὑμῶν 'your(pl)' that precede δεήσεως 'prayer'. Thus the Philippians would be involved not only in the praying but in the supply of the Holy Spirit: 'your prayer (for me) and (your) supply (to me, by that prayer and its answer) of the spirit of Jesus Christ' (Alford). Others take the position that the absence of the article does not mean that ὑμῶν 'your(pl)' modifies ἐπιχορηγίας 'supply/help'. Ellicott says of this verse, "Each substantive has its own defining genitive, and on this account the second may dispense with its article." Since the grammatical evidence is insufficient to prove that ὑμῶν 'your(pl)' must modify ἐπιχορηγίας in this case, and since such modification would produce a more complex train of thought (one that would not necessarily be in focus in this context), we have chosen the simpler solution, that is, that the prayer of the Philippians and the help of the Holy Spirit are two separate means.

**by means of the *Holy* Spirit's helping *me*** Following the majority view, we have taken ἐπιχορηγίας τοῦ πνεύματος 'help/supply of the Spirit' to mean 'the help which the Spirit supplies' rather than 'the supply which is the Spirit' (i.e., apposition). Note that even if the appositional interpretation is taken, an implied action would still be needed in this means clause relative to the Spirit's help in producing the salvation.

***who was given to me by* Jesus Christ** Regarding the relationship between τοῦ πνεύματος 'the Spirit' and Ἰησοῦ Χριστοῦ 'Jesus Christ', all commentaries consulted say that 'the Spirit' here refers to the Holy Spirit, not the 'spirit of Jesus Christ' in some other sense. But what is the intended implied event signaled by this genitive construction? Is it 'the Spirit given/sent by Jesus Christ', 'the Spirit belonging to Jesus Christ', 'the Spirit who indwelt Jesus Christ'? Meyer says, "Paul here designates the Holy Spirit thus, because Jesus Christ forms, in the inmost consciousness of the apostle, the main interest and aim of his entire discourse, ver. 18ff." One way of looking at this, then, is to understand 'Spirit of Jesus Christ' as a reference to the Holy Spirit with Jesus Christ in focus as giving the Spirit. In such passages as John 15:26 and Acts 2:33, the Holy Spirit is seen as coming from the Father and then given by the Son to believers. 'The Spirit who belongs to Jesus Christ' would be ambiguous. Since there is no strong evidence in the context that 'the Spirit who indwelt Jesus Christ' would be more in focus than 'the Spirit given/sent by Jesus Christ', it is better to understand 'the Spirit given/sent by Jesus Christ' here. But in translating into other languages, especially those in which a buildup of relative clauses can harm the focus and meaning of the sentence in general, but where a genitive-type reference to the Spirit of Jesus Christ is possible, a genitive-type reference may produce better overall meaning even if it is somewhat ambiguous.

**1:20a *I know that I will remain victorious*** It seems best to take v. 20 as relating most directly to Paul's confidence in his spiritual victory rather than to the effect the adverse circumstances produce. This is because v. 20 focuses more on Paul's own energies and commitment.

**since** Although κατά has several functions or meanings, here the causal sense (BAGD, p. 407.II5aδ) is applicable. The relationship between 1:19 and 1:20 is labeled CLAIM-*justification* rather than RESULT-*reason* since Paul is dealing with the future.

**I earnestly expect** Despite the various glosses of ἀποκαραδοκία in the commentaries and versions and the somewhat differing explanations of its etymology, a common component of intensity in regard to expectation is apparent in almost all of the comments, though that intensity may be verbalized in different ways. Two frequently used words are 'eager' and 'earnest'. Either of them would probably be appropriate as long as it is understood that the sense of 'eager' here is not that of impatient but passive waiting, but of earnest hope actively involved in bringing to pass what one hopes for.

**I earnestly expect and confidently hope** It would be very difficult to make a distinction in meaning between ἀποκαραδοκία and ἐλπίς in this context. In the propositionalization both verbs are kept to maintain the prominence that double verbs signal even in English. In some languages the use of synonyms or near-synonyms here may be impossible or impractical because of the paucity of synonyms for this concept or because the prominence would be signaled better with a verb plus some modifier signaling intensity: 'I very confidently expect'.

In the display 'confidently' is used to strengthen 'hope', since the English word 'hope' has a much weaker sense than ἐλπίς.

**1:20b in no way I will be ashamed *to honor Christ*** Some commentators and versions translate αἰσχυνθήσομαι as 'I will be ashamed'; others, as 'I will be put to shame'. The *Analytical Greek New Testament* (Friberg and Friberg) classifies the form of the verb in this verse as a passive deponent, that is, a verb which has no active counterpart, is unambiguously passive in form, but is active in meaning. In fact, AGNT maintains that this future form αἰσχυνθήσομαι was a deponent (i.e., active in meaning) in first-century Greek in general (pp. 814, 840).

The intended contrast of αἰσχυνθήσομαι with παρρησία 'boldness' in this verse is very evident. The contrast is signaled not only in the contrast between the meaning of the two words themselves but also syntactically with the use of ἀλλά 'but', and again lexically in the contrast of οὐδενί 'nothing' and πάσῃ 'all'. The word παρρησία 'boldness, courage', especially in its common sense of 'boldness in speech', expresses an active force by the subject rather than a passive one. The active sense of αἰσχυνθήσομαι, then, would be appropriate in this contrast: 'I will be ashamed in no way whatsoever but with complete boldness...'. When this is propositionalized with an active sense throughout, the contrast is even more evident: 'that in no way I will be ashamed *to honor Christ* but rather...I will very courageously honor him...'.

As for the communication relation of 20b with 20c, the contrast of antonyms is typical of a negative-POSITIVE relationship.

***to honor Christ*** 'Ashamed' describes the manner in which one performs an action and for this reason the proposition is not complete until the words describing that action are supplied. However, since the action is described in the following proposition, it may not need to be supplied in this clause in many languages.

**1:20c just as I always *have done*** Here ὡς signals comparison. Paul's hope is that he will continue to magnify Christ in his imprisonment and trial as he has always done. There is no verb in the comparison construction itself. The construction modifies μεγαλυνθήσεται 'he will be magnified/honored' in the more nuclear part of the predicate. Thus a generic form ('have done') is added in the comparison proposition. The generic form is used rather than 'I will honor' in order to maintain the prominence on 'honor Christ' in the more nuclear part of the sentence.

**now also** The ὡς...καί construction typically indicates comparison but not with an obligatory ascensive sense; that is, καί would normally be translated as 'also' rather than 'even' or 'especially' (cf. Matt. 6:10; Acts 7:51; Gal. 1:9). Paul, however, is focusing here on the present situation.

**very boldly/courageously** It is evident from its glosses in Louw and Nida and from its uses in Paul's writings (cf. Eph. 6:19) that one of the primary senses of παρρησία is 'boldness, courage', though it also has the sense of 'plainly, openly, publicly'. Kennedy's comment sums up the situation here succinctly: "We are inclined to believe that παρρησία has its literal meaning, boldness of speech, for he has before him the danger of denying Christ." That παρρησία means 'boldness, courage' here is the opinion of a majority of commentators.

**I will... honor Christ** The Greek text is μεγαλυνθήσεται Χριστός ἐν τῷ σώματί μου 'Christ will be magnified in my body'. Lightfoot remarks: "After ἐν πάσῃ παρρησίᾳ the first person might naturally be expected: but with sensitive reverence the Apostle shrinks from any mention of his own agency, lest he should seem to glorify himself." Though Paul is seeking to mark Christ and his greatness as prominent here, he does in fact mention his own agency when he says 'Christ will be magnified in my body'.

Also, ἐν πάσῃ παρρησίᾳ 'in all boldness' can only apply to Paul as agent, and the whole construction is better expressed within the SSA propositional rules in active form. This is because everything from the beginning of 1:20b until μεγαλυνθήσεται Χριστός 'Christ will be honored' is focusing on Paul's agency, specifically the manner of his action.

**1:20d by means of all that I do** The phrase 'in my body' is an example of synecdoche, 'body' standing for the whole person. It is the giving of the body in death or life that is the most significant gift a person can give, and so the whole person is included: I will honor Christ in my whole being, even my body. The following construction, 'whether by life or by death', clarifies the extent of that commitment.

Metonymy is also found here, 'the body' being substituted for what the body does, for with a means construction there must be at least an implied action. Adjusting these figures of speech in the propositionalization yields 'by means of all that I do'.

**1:20e-f whether by means of** *the manner in which I* **live or by means of** *the manner in which I* **die** That Paul is talking about the manner of his life and death is evident from the use of διά 'through'. In the context of imprisonment and trial, the manner of Paul's death has to do with the way he will courageously and triumphantly honor Christ even if condemned to die. And the manner of Paul's life has to do especially with the way he will conduct himself during the trial and imprisonment, though it may also refer to his further service for Christ.

## BOUNDARIES AND COHERENCE

As the displays make clear, 1:18f–20 and 1:21–26 are treated here as distinct paragraphs. Many commentators and versions do not make a break until the end of v. 26, but the theme of the last part of 18f–26 is different enough from the theme of the first part to warrant the interpretation that these are two distinct units.

The final boundary of 18f–20 is considered to be after v. 20 for the following reasons:

1. There is a change from future tense to present.
2. Verses 18f–20 are one Greek sentence.
3. Although it seems very logical for 1:21a to be a reason for 1:20, that is, 'It is my deepest expectation and hope that Christ will be boldly magnified in my body whether through life or death because for me to live is Christ', 1:21b would also need to be so connected. But 1:21b as a reason for 1:20 is not so obvious, 'It is my deepest expectation and hope that Christ will be boldly magnified in my body... even through my death because for me dying is gain'.
4. A choice between two or more options is implied by 1:22b ('and/so what I shall choose I know not'). If 22a were the beginning of a new unit, then there would have been only one option given so far in that unit, 'if I continue to live in my physical body, that will mean fruitful labor for me'.

It is true that a repetition of 21b could be supplied at the beginning of 22 thus forming a more coherent beginning to the new unit, '*For me to die is gain*, but if I do live on physically this will mean that I will serve *Christ* productively, so I do not know which to choose'. But the fact that this needs to be supplied as a repetition weakens the argument for such a solution.

Once we interpret v. 21 as the beginning of the new unit, it seems fitting to take 'whether by life or by death' as the tail in a tail-head link with the beginning of this next unit, which contrasts Paul's continued physical existence with his death. The theme switches at the beginning of v. 21, but with threads of the former theme carried over. And what really signals the switch of the theme is '(to me)... to die is gain'. This is different from the theme of death in the preceding verse where Paul says he is willing to give himself in death rather than shame Christ. Note that κέρδος 'gain' begins a series of statements of evaluation (all positive) relating to living and dying: καρπὸς ἔργου 'fruitful labor' (22a); πολλῷ μᾶλλον κρεῖσσον 'better by far' (23c); ἀναγκαιότερον δι' ὑμᾶς 'more necessary for you' (24).

## PROMINENCE AND THEME

The theme statement should contain elements of both the *situation* and REACTION. Since there is also an embedded expository paragraph pattern, the most prominent parts of the CLAIM and the most prominent parts of the *justification* also should be represented in the theme.

# SECTION CONSTITUENT 1:21–26 (Expressive Paragraph: Nucleus₄ of 1:12–26)

*THEME: Though I desire to leave this world and be with Christ, it is more important that I remain alive to help you in your need. So I know that I shall remain alive and help you believe in Christ more firmly, and as a result you will rejoice triumphantly.*

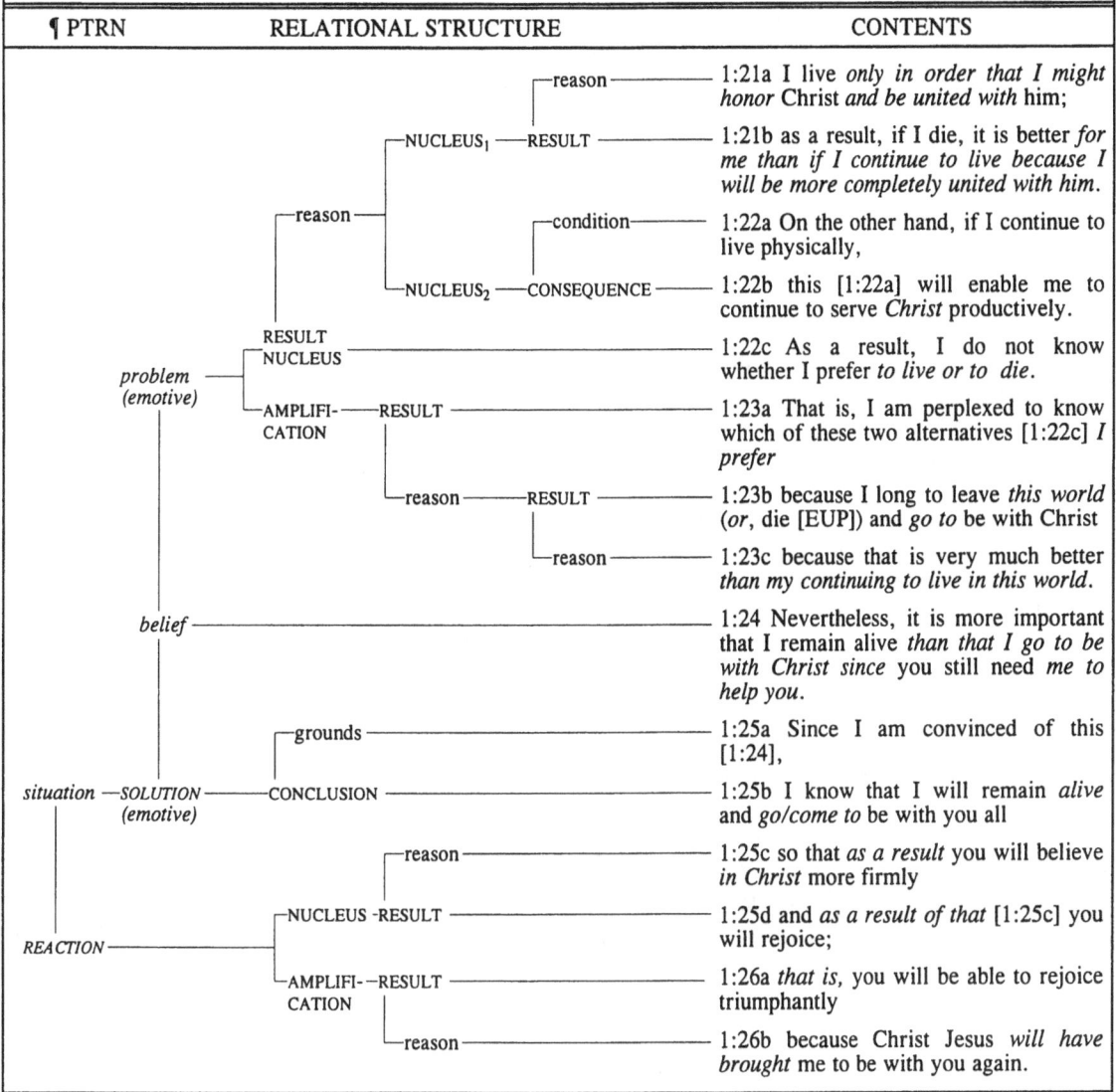

## INTENT AND PARAGRAPH PATTERN

In 1:21–23 Paul shows how he is caught between two desires. One is to die and be with Christ; the other is to live on and serve Christ productively on earth. But he comes to the conclusion in 1:24 that it is more necessary for the Philippians for him to continue to live. The whole section (1:12–26) is expressive and the conclusion reached in this 1:21–26 paragraph is not about something that has already happened but something expected to happen in the future. The conclusion also has to do with something personal with Paul. The problem in 1:21–25b of mixed emotions, which are then resolved, indicates a paragraph pattern of the expressive solutionality type (see the chart of paragraph pattern subtypes on p. 11).

To arrive at the resolution, Paul relies upon his belief that it is more necessary for the Philippians that he remain alive (τὸ δὲ ἐπιμένειν [ἐν] τῇ σαρκὶ ἀναγκαιότερον δι' ὑμᾶς, 1:24), a tenet in his belief system that it is more important to serve others than to seek one's own desires and interests. Based upon this belief his emotions are reconciled as stated in 1:25a-b: 'Since I am convinced of this [1:24], I know that I will remain *alive* and *go/come to* be with you all'.

The rest of the paragraph (1:25c–26b) might be diagrammed as the expected REACTION of the Philippians to Paul's hope that he will remain alive and come to be with them. Normally an expressive solutionality paragraph pattern ends with the emotional reconciliation of the person who had the mixed emotions, but here it ends with the emotions of other people, the addressees. Since the participants are different, there is probably embedding of expressive paragraph patterns (the final one being a *situation-REACTION* paragraph pattern) rather than one complex paragraph pattern.

## NOTES

**1:21a** The conjunction γάρ is not rendered in the display. Note that it is not a signal for a clearcut cause-effect relationship between v. 20 and v. 21 either on the verse level or on the paragraph level. Therefore it must signal a continuation of the same general theme or a related theme (see BAGD, p. 152.4). Another possibility is that it signals the reason for an implied statement, but an implied statement does not seem necessary here.

**I** Moule says, "'Ἐμοί ['to me'] is emphatic, with the force not of self-assertion but of intense personal experience."

**I live** *only in order that I might honor* **Christ** *and be united with* **him** Ellicott says, "τὸ ζῆν Χριστός] 'to live is Christ,' *i.e.* living consists only in union with, and devotion to, Christ; my whole being and activities are His." He goes on to say that the context shows "that Χριστός, beside the idea of union with Him, must also involve that of devotion to His service."

In v. 20, the previous verse, Paul states that it was of extreme importance to him to magnify Christ whether by life or by death. Since γάρ shows some type of connection of thought with v. 20, 'to me to live is Christ' would have something to do with magnifying Christ. On the other hand, the use of κέρδος 'gain' and what seems to be an amplification of 'to die is gain' in 1:23b, 'having the desire to depart and be with Christ which is better by far', suggest that 'to live is Christ' includes the idea of union with Christ, close fellowship with Christ, identity with Christ—something that would be gained by being in Christ's presence after death. This makes excellent sense on the basis of the close-knit parallel structure of 1:21. The opposite of 'to die' is 'to live'; thus physical life is the most obvious thing which death is better than, physical life being referred to in the first half of the verse. The union, identity, and fellowship with Christ that Paul experienced in his life here on earth would be better by far in the presence of Christ in heaven.

The construction ἐμοὶ τὸ ζῆν Χριστός 'to me to live (is) Christ' has no verb and, even with 'is' understood, is still very idiomatic. A verb or a verbal expression, therefore, should be used in the propositionalization, one which includes the sense of 'honor Christ' (which surely is intended to be carried over from the preceding verse) and also the sense of union, identity, or fellowship with Christ. The latter is demanded by the context of the new unit. Greenlee (1992) lists nine commentators who contend that dying would be 'gain' to Paul in that "he would be in more complete union with Christ." It is difficult, however, to find a verbal expression that would cover both of these aspects. The best we can do is to use two verbs, one to represent honoring Christ and one to represent being in union with him (alternates for the latter would be 'be associated with him', 'fellowship with him', 'be identified with him').

Note that it is not clearly evident that Paul intended to say that dying and being with Christ would promote the honoring of Christ more than living and honoring him, especially before unbelievers, which is the sense in v. 20. Therefore, to maintain the sense intended by 'gain', '*because I will be more completely united with him*' is used in 1:21b.

**1:21b as a result** When 'to me to live is Christ' is taken as referring to a close relationship with Christ and 'to die is gain' is taken as an advance in that relationship because death brings Paul into closer relationship with Christ in heaven, a reason-RESULT relationship takes place.

**if I die, it is better** *for me than if I continue to live because I will be more completely united with him* The majority of commentators understand 'to die is gain' as defined, or further amplified, by 1:23b, 'having the desire to depart and be with Christ which is better by far'. Greenlee (1992) categorizes this general view by answering the question "In what way would dying be 'gain' for Paul?" with such answers as he "would be in the presence of Christ" and "he would be in more complete union with Christ."

Martin (1959), however, representing a minority view, says:

The *gain*...is not only the apostle's own receiving of his heavenly reward in the presence of his Master (verse 23), but the promotion of the gospel in the witness which his fearless martyrdom for Christ will produce...In the context of this section we must emphasize equally the thought that death is *gain* because, as Barth puts it, it is a gain for the proclamation of the gospel; and Christ is magnified by the apostle's death as by his life (verse 20) because in both he is dedicated to the service of the Lord.

The view represented by Martin's comments would seem to be based on an expanded translation of 1:21 such as 'To me to live is to magnify Christ and to die is gain rather than loss since Christ will be magnified by my death'. The strongest evidence that I see against this view is that 1:23b for very apparent reasons functions as an amplification and explanation of 'to me...to die is gain'. The aorist articular infinitive phrase τὸ ἀποθανεῖν 'to die' of v. 21 equates with the aorist articular infinitive phrase εἰς τὸ ἀναλῦσαι 'to depart', meaning 'to die', of v. 23; κέρδος 'gain' equates with πολλῷ μᾶλλον κρεῖσσον 'better by far'. The significant amplificatory part is καὶ σὺν Χριστῷ εἶναι 'and be with Christ'. To Paul, to die is gain because it means that he can enjoy fellowship with Christ more completely.

The second reason that 'to die is gain' does not appear to me to focus on gain through magnifying Christ in death is that μεγαλύνω 'magnify' does not occur in 1:21a. If Paul did intend 'magnify' to be sharply in focus as the implied event here, this intent was confounded by not making 'magnify' explicit and instead creating a construction easily understood with a different meaning. Greenlee (1992) does not specifically list "magnify/honor Christ" as one of the answers to "What does Paul mean by 'to me to live is Christ'?" though he does mention this viewpoint under an earlier question. However, "magnify Christ" is probably part of the total meaning of 'to live is Christ'.

A related matter is whether 'to me to live is Christ and to die is gain' could mean 'to me to live is to magnify Christ and to die is gain over living since I will be with Christ'. One objection to this has already been given immediately above. Another is that this implies that Paul feels that magnifying Christ on earth is not as important, or profitable for him, as being with Christ in heaven.

Two elements are implied by 'gain': 'to die' and 'to live', the former being better than the latter. Although the latter element (living) is mentioned in 21a, it is mentioned again in the display rendering of 21b, for clarity's sake and because some languages may need to have both elements together.

**1:22a if I continue to live physically** Commentators disagree as to whether the protasis signaled by εἰ 'if, since' at the beginning of v. 22 ends at (1) σαρκί 'flesh' or (2) at ἔργου 'work'. The former would give 'If (I continue) to live in the flesh, this to me (means) fruitful work'. The latter would give 'If (by continuing) to live in the flesh I will produce fruitful work'. Many Greek commentators say that interpretation 1 is unlikely. Vincent, for example, says, "The awkward ellipsis required by the [first interpretation] appears quite inadmissible." On the other hand, an argument for interpretation 1 as against interpretation 2 is that interpretation 2 would have a καί beginning the apodosis, which as Vincent also says, "is of doubtful authority." He means that it is doubtful that καί has this function in the New Testament. It is difficult to find in the New Testament an exact correspondence to this sentence where καί begins an apodosis (James 4:15 may be the closest possibility), though it is found in other Greek literature.

When propositionalized fully, there is very little basic difference between the two interpretations. The full propositionalization of the two interpretations would be as follows:

1. If I continue to live physically, by means of my living physically I will serve *Christ* productively. As a result I do not know...
2. Since by means of my continuing to live physically, *if I do continue to live physically*, I will serve *Christ* productively, I do not know...

In the first interpretation, εἰ δὲ τὸ ζῆν ἐν σαρκί 'if I continue to live in the flesh' is presented as a true condition—Paul did not know whether he was going to continue to live or not. In the second, the conditionality is presented as implicit only (though there is no doubt that it is implicit). Again, in both interpretations, τοῦτό μοι καρπὸς ἔργου 'this to me (brings) fruitful labor' is translated basically the same. Thus, in both interpretations it is taken as a means-RESULT relationship. Some translations, such as TEV ("But if by continuing to live I can do more worthwhile work, then I am not sure what I would choose") clearly show the means relationship. This means relationship actually manifests itself in the Greek as a stative sentence (minus the stative verb): 'this to me (is) fruitful work', 'this' representing the first part of the sentence, literally 'if to live in the flesh'. In the phrase καρπὸς ἔργου 'fruit of work' (or more freely 'fruitful work') there is a dead metaphor, 'fruit', which is an abstract noun. There is also an abstract noun, 'work'. This phrase could be propositionalized as 'work productively' or, more specifically, 'serve *Christ* productively'. The clause τοῦτό μοι καρπὸς ἔργου can be quasi-propositionalized as 'this enables me to serve *Christ* productively'. In translations such as TEV (just cited), the means relationship is fully propositionalized, but τοῦτο 'this' is not translated, there being no necessity to repeat it. On the other hand, in translations where εἰ δὲ τὸ ζῆν ἐν σαρκί is taken as a true conditional (i.e., 'if I continue to live in the flesh'), the representation of the full means proposition would be cumbersome. For this reason the means is expressed as 'this will enable' or something similar, which is closer to the Greek text anyway.

The only real difference in the two interpretations is the focus. Interpretation 1 makes explicit the concept of two choices, which is central to the theme of the whole paragraph. Interpretation 1 is represented in the display, but interpretation 2 would be just as valid. In fact, there is no real difference in meaning. I have chosen to express interpretation 1 as, 'if I continue to live physically, this [1:22a] will enable me to continue to serve *Christ* productively', retaining as explicit the cause-effect relationship that is explicit in the Greek text. For some languages it may be necessary, or at least more appropriate, to translate as 'if I continue to live physically, I will continue to serve *Christ* productively', thus leaving the cause-effect relationship totally implicit.

**1:22b serve *Christ* productively** That the genitive construction καρπὸς ἔργου 'fruit of work' refers to Paul's continued productive labor, if he continues to live, makes excellent sense in this context. A result-reason relationship where the nominal not in the genitive, here καρπός 'fruit', is the result of the event signaled by the nominal in the genitive, ἔργου 'work, labor', is one of the categories described in Beekman and Callow's chapter on the genitive construction (p. 264). As already mentioned, the abstract noun 'fruit' is a dead metaphor; hence the phrase is propositionalized as 'work productively' or 'serve *Christ* productively'.

**1:22c As a result** Here Paul reveals how he feels about living and dying. Since for him living and dying both have advantages, the result is that he does not know which one to choose. Thus καί is signaling RESULT here (see BAGD, p. 392.I2f).

**I do not know** The Greek is γνωρίζω. While 'know' is the primary meaning of γνωρίζω in classical Greek, in all its other NT occurrences (over twenty times) it has the sense of 'make known, declare'. In the Septuagint, it is 'make known, declare' most commonly, but there are places where the sense of 'know, discern' is appropriate (e.g., Job 4:16; 34:25; Prov. 3:6). Here the sense 'know' fits the context very well, while 'make known (to you/others)' would not, on the surface anyway. The very fact that many commentators, including some expert exegetes, prefer the sense 'know' here in the face of all the occurrences of the sense 'make known' elsewhere in the New Testament, shows that the context strongly suggests 'know' as the appropriate meaning here.

**whether I prefer** The verb αἱρήσομαι is future indicative, 'I shall choose'. Some commentators hold that it has subjunctive force here. Viewed from a situational standpoint, Paul obviously does not see himself as the one to make the decision whether he shall live or die. On the human level the emperor would make the decision, but only as God willed. BAGD (p. 24.2) and Louw and Nida (30.86) gloss αἱρέομαι as 'prefer' in this verse, and this word is used in the propositionalization.

**1:23a That is** BAGD (p. 171.2) lists some occurrences of δέ under "very freq. as a transitional particle pure and simple, without any contrast intended...Esp. to insert an explanation *that is*." 'That is' fits the relational structure well here since 1:23a functions as a restatement of 1:22c.

**I am perplexed to know which of these two alternatives [1:22c] *I prefer*** Literally συνέχομαι means 'I am hard pressed'. It is a metaphor, though probably a dead one. Alford translates συνέχομαι here as 'I am perplexed', a very appropriate nonfigurative translation.

**1:23b because** Here Paul expands his reasons for being perplexed. The participle ἔχων signals reason, one of the potential functions of a participle. At first sight, it seems to make excellent sense that in 1:23b-c and 1:24 Paul is reiterating the two opposing reasons for his perplexity. But it is difficult to see how v. 24 can be both the basis for his perplexity whether to live or die and the basis for his confidence that he was going to live (cf. v. 25). If at the end of v. 24 Paul had said, I can now see that the most important thing is what is more necessary for you, then v. 24 as it now is would have been appropriate as the second reason for Paul's perplexity. The paragraph would have been uniform with the two opposing sides each presented once on both ends of the paragraph. But since he did not, a better way of understanding his logic is to take 1:24 as a CONTRAEXPECTATION of the 1:21-23 concession, or as what would be considered *belief* in the expressive paragraph pattern structure of this unit. *Belief* refers to an axiom held as true in an individual's belief system.

**I long** BAGD (p. 293) glosses ἐπιθυμία generally as "*desire, longing, craving*" and puts its occurrence in Phil. 1:23 under "*have a longing for someth.*" (entry 2). Though τὴν ἐπιθυμίαν is not modified by any intensive word or phrase and its occurrence before the participle ἔχων 'having' does not necessarily signal prominence, the context requires a meaning with intensive sense. The phrase συνέχομαι... ἐκ τῶν δύο 'I am hard pressed between the two' demands this. In fact, the integrity of the whole paragraph demands a strong word showing Paul's personal desire; otherwise it is hard to understand why Paul could one minute say he is perplexed about what to choose and the next have come to a decision on what should and would happen. In all likelihood, ἐπιθυμία is a stronger word than the English desire. Therefore, 'long' is used in the display.

**to leave** *this world* (*or,* **die** [EUP]) The verb ἀναλύω in its intransitive function means 'to depart, return'. It was also used by the Greeks as a euphemism for 'to die' (see BAGD, p. 57.2 for references to this euphemistic usage in other writings). Though possibly figurative in its original sense, as a recognized euphemism it would be a dead figure. Paul was hardly using an exotic live figure as some commentators indicate.

In the next two verses, Paul uses μένω 'remain' and two of its derivatives (ἐπιμένω and παραμένω). These also are dead figures; they refer to continuing to live physically.

Even in English the text sounds harsh when 'to die' is used instead of a euphemism, hence the euphemism for the display. In translating into other languages a euphemism may not be possible or appropriate here, so the alternate 'die' is given in the display.

**and** *go to* **be with Christ** A purpose construction may seem appropriate here, 'I desire to leave *this world* in order that I might be with Christ'; however, καί is what represents the semantic relationship between the two events and elsewhere καί is certainly not an easily recognizable signal for purpose constructions. (It comes nearest to that after imperatives.) Here it is more likely that it represents the connection between two events in a step-goal progression. In this context that idea is best translated as 'and'.

The words 'go to' are supplied as an implied link that would be required in some languages.

**1:23c because** Whether γάρ 'for, because, since' occurred in the original manuscript is disputed. (It is in brackets in the UBSGNT text.) But it is at least implied here semantically.

**that is very much better** Here, the simple comparative κρεῖσσον 'better' is heightened by another comparative, μᾶλλον 'more', and both are intensified by πολλῷ 'much'. This intensive sequence has been expressed in the display as 'very much better'.

***than my continuing to live in this world*** Describing an event as 'better' implies that it is better than some other event. Here, continuing to live on in this world is that other event. While it is true that being with Christ is very much better than living in this world for all Christians, this should be kept specific to Paul since this whole paragraph is intricately tied up with his own feelings and desires.

**1:24 Nevertheless** The conjunction δέ signals a contrast here as once again Paul weighs his options. But it is clear now, from 1:25a, 'Being persuaded of this (i.e., of v. 24)', that he has reached a conclusion in v. 24. He conveys this through 'this' (by itself instead of a full statement) and the participle πεποιθώς 'being persuaded'. Both together signal that the conclusion has already been stated. Thus v. 24 is taken to have the paragraph pattern role of *belief*.

**it is more important that I remain alive** ***than that I go to be with Christ since*** **you still need** *me* **to help you** It is not completely obvious that Paul is saying that it is necessary for him to depart and be with Christ and it is necessary for him to stay to help the believers, but it is more necessary for him to stay to help the believers. We do not know that Paul would say that it was necessary for him to depart and be with Christ. It is quite likely, at least from an English language perspective, that what Paul is saying is (1) that for him to remain alive is necessary or needful for the Philippians, as signaled in the basic meaning of the stem ἀναγκαι- 'necessary' plus δι' ὑμᾶς 'for you' and (2) that this is more important than the granting of his desire to go to be with the Lord, signaled by the comparative suffix -τερον. Based on this understanding, it sounds more like a conclusion to the argument, rather than just a presentation of the second side again. It may be that ἀναγκαιότερον covered this whole idea better in Greek than the English 'it is more necessary'. Note that TEV translates as "but for your sake it is much more important that I remain alive" and by so doing better signals this statement as Paul's conclusion than 'it is more necessary for you'.

**1:25a Since I am convinced of this [1:24]** The participial construction καὶ τοῦτο πεποιθώς 'and convinced of this' acts as a grounds for Paul's belief that he will remain alive and go to be with the Philippians. In other words, since he is convinced that it is more needful for them for him to remain alive, he knows that the Lord will work it out for him to remain alive and go to be with them.

**this [1:24]** As to τοῦτο 'this', the majority view is that it refers to the content of v. 24. A minority of commentators take τοῦτο to refer to the content of the following ὅτι construction, 'that I shall remain and abide with you all ...', but to do this the participle πεποιθώς 'being convinced' must be understood as an adverb ('I confidently know that'). In favor of the majority view Ellicott says, "καὶ τοῦτο πεποιθώς] 'And being persuaded, being sure, of this;' scil., that my ἐπιμένειν ἐν τῇ σαρκὶ ['remaining in the flesh'] is more necessary on your account. Πεποιθώς has thus its natural force and regimen (ver. 6), and is not to be explained away adverbially ..."

Another argument against the minority view is that it makes the passage abrupt and disconnected in thought. If this view were followed, Meyer says, "οἶδα would lack the *specification of a reason*, which is given in this very τοῦτο πεποιθ., as it was practically necessary."

**1:25b I know** Not only 1:19–23 but also 2:17 imply that Paul was still having to face death as a possibility. These verses strongly suggest that he uses οἶδα 'I know' to mean a knowledge based on the needs of the Philippians rather than prophetic revelation. Their need is what leads him to believe that he will be released and will be able to see them again in order to help them.

**I will remain *alive* and *go/come to* be with you all** Paul wants to communicate two ideas here: (1) that he is convinced that he will remain in this world ('body', 1:24) rather than depart to be with Christ and (2) that he will in some sense remain or stay with them. That the first is intended is clear from the context; that the second is intended is clear from the dative construction πᾶσιν ὑμῖν 'with you all'. Each of the verbs Paul uses here, μενῶ and παραμενῶ, is lexically capable of communicating either or both of these ideas, but in this context it would seem that μενῶ is intended to communicate the first idea and παραμενῶ the second. Based on all the lexical considerations, this would be more likely. It may be that he uses two words rather than one in order to emphasize each of these ideas.

But what exactly does Paul mean when he says, "I will remain with you all"? Is he being generic, meaning that he will stay on earth together with them where he can either encourage them by letter or come to see them, or is he being specific, meaning that he will stay with them in Philippi? Since the following context shows that he intends to go to be with them, τῆς ἐμῆς παρουσίας πάλιν 'my presence with you again, my coming to you again', this latter is at least partially in his mind when he says παραμενῶ πᾶσιν ὑμῖν 'remain with you all'. In fact, the part of v. 25 after παραμενῶ and all of v. 26 are so intricately connected semantically with the idea of Paul's physical presence with them again that it seems appropriate to propositionalize παραμενῶ πᾶσιν ὑμῖν as '*go to* be with you all', especially since some languages may require the missing chronological/directional step to be filled.

**1:25c** As to the relationship of the words within 1:25c, it is by far the majority opinion of commentators that ὑμῶν 'you(pl)' modifies both προκοπήν 'progress' and χαράν 'joy'. Most commentators also take τῆς πίστεως 'of the faith' to be connected with both προκοπήν 'progress' and χαράν 'joy'. The occurrence of only one article for προκοπήν and χαράν and only one explicit agent (ὑμῶν 'you(pl)') strongly suggests that ὑμῶν is the agent for both. Also, it is likely that προκοπήν 'progress' is modified by τῆς πίστεως 'faith, the faith', not only because there is only one article with προκοπήν καὶ χαράν 'progress and joy' but also because 'faith' would be the appropriate factor to be advanced as a result of Paul's coming.

**believe *in Christ* more firmly** Paul has said in v. 24 that his remaining alive is necessary for the Philippians. Therefore we would expect that τὴν ὑμῶν προκοπὴν ... τῆς πίστεως 'your progress ... of the faith' refers to what he will accomplish by teaching and encouragement. This is what he hopes to promote by being with them again (παραμενῶ πᾶσιν ὑμῖν 'remain with you all' in 25b and, as expanded, in 26b). It might be best, then, to take 'faith' to have the widest sense possible here, as presumably Paul could and would help them in each area. Hawthorne describes this as "... progress in the Christian faith, growing in their appreciation for and in their understanding and practice of those things taught by him as the truth of God ..." We might then propositionalize as 'understand, believe, and practice the true teachings about God more fully'.

However, there may be an added sense here. Martin (1959) says, "We may include the thought that their *faith* would be confirmed by the answering of prayer in his safe return. His 'coming to them again' (verse 26), if it were God's good pleasure, would certainly promote their joy." In other words, not only v. 26 but also v. 25 may be communicating this idea. For this reason it seems best not to be as specific as 'understand, believe, and practice the true teachings about God more fully'.

A few commentators state that τῆς πίστεως here means 'the faith' in the sense of 'what is believed, Christian doctrine' (Hawthorne, Lenski), but there is no lexical law that πίστις has such a meaning every time it occurs with the article. A check of even a few of the references in BAGD (pp. 662–64) in the various categories shows that there are many instances in the New Testament where πίστις with the article does not refer to 'what is believed'. Certainly in Phil. 1:25 'progress of/in the faith' must refer to the Philippians' commitment both mentally and practically to that person in whom they believe (Christ) and/or what they believe about him. The creed itself does not progress.

As to the relational structure, one must decide whether MEANS-purpose or reason-result is intended here and then follow up with that decision all the way through 1:25c–26b. Did Paul intend to present the effect of his coming as a purpose of that coming and a purpose of all actions explicit and implicit in which he is the agent in 1:25c–26b? Or did he intend to present the effect of his coming as a result of that coming? If the former, then we must propositionalize 1:26a as '*that is, I will cause you to* rejoice triumphantly by means of Christ Jesus bringing me back to be with you and help you again'. (See notes on 1:26b as to why it must be done this way.) In fact, if 1:25c–d is propositionalized as fully purpose it may need to be 'in order that *I may cause you* to believe *in Christ* more firmly in order that *I may cause* you to rejoice'. For the display reason-RESULT has been chosen rather than MEANS-purpose as the basic relationship in 1:25c–26b because it seems more appropriate to render τὸ καύχημα ὑμῶν περισσεύῃ as 'you will rejoice triumphantly' or 'you will be able to rejoice triumphantly' than as '*I will cause* you to rejoice triumphantly'. Also, the matter of rejoicing is given more natural prominence, which is in agreement with the previous two paragraphs in this expressive section (1:15–18e and 1:18f–20) where rejoicing is a nuclear part of the theme.

**1:25d and *as a result of that* [1:25c] you will rejoice** It seems appropriate to understand the genitive construction χαρὰν τῆς πίστεως 'joy of faith' as one in which the event signaled by the genitive (πίστεως 'faith') is the cause or means for the event signaled by the other noun (χαρὰν 'joy'). Ellicott calls this genitive "*gen. originis.*" Thus as the first event of 25c–d in which the Philippians act as agents, their faith grows: they believe more firmly or fully. In 25d they are to rejoice because of their believing. Thus there are potentially only two basic events, though there are three abstract nouns (προκοπήν 'advance' acts as an attribute here), and one of these events can be seen as the intended result of the other.

**1:26a *that is*** Here ἵνα is not taken in its primary sense of 'in order that', or even in its secondary sense of 'so that, as a result', because 1:26 appears to be a restatement of 1:25c–d. There are two conjoined statements both of which express the event 'rejoice' (each with its own reason, as can be seen in the display). The reasons have to do with the same general situation—Paul's presence (26b) and the resulting spiritual progress (25c).

**you will be able to rejoice triumphantly** The Greek noun καύχημα is often glossed as 'boast' or 'object of boasting', and in Greek it may have either a good or bad connotation depending upon the context. Since in English 'boast' tends to have a bad connotation, 'glory in, pride in' would be better than 'boast' in this context. In these words there is usually a component of elation and joy coupled with a component of triumph (sometimes wrongly expressed in a feeling of superiority over others). KJV and NIV focus on the state of elation, with 'rejoicing' (KJV) or 'joy' (NIV). Martin (1959) says, "*Kauchēma* is really 'glorying' (RV), or better, 'exultation'." The Funk and Wagnalls' dictionary defines exult as "To rejoice greatly, as in triumph; be jubilant: to exult in victory" and the verb glory as "To rejoice proudly or triumphantly; take pride" with a second entry of "To boast; brag." Hence, 'rejoice triumphantly' may be a good verbal phrase for the propositionalization, especially since the Philippians will rejoice in the triumph that Christ Jesus attains for Paul in releasing him from imprisonment and bringing him to be with them again.

But another component of meaning may be present in καύχημα here, especially in its relationship to (or combination with) ἐν Χριστῷ Ἰησοῦ 'in Christ Jesus', an additional sense of 'glorify'—glorifying Christ: 'You will be able to rejoice triumphantly and glorify Christ because *he will have brought* me to be with you again'. Perhaps the following will handle all these components: 'you will be able to rejoice triumphantly because of what Christ has done for me; *that is, he will have brought* me to be with you again'. Some translators have used 'glorify Christ Jesus' or 'praise Christ Jesus' but alone this does not seem to fit the meaning of καύχημα.

The basic meaning of καύχημα in the New Testament is clearly 'object or cause of glorying/boasting', and some commentators maintain that is the meaning here. It is true that the Philippians' cause for glorying in Christ will be increased by Paul's being brought to them again. This might be propositionalized as 'you will be able to rejoice triumphantly because Christ Jesus *will have brought* me to be with you again'. Since 'cause' is an abstract noun, 'cause for glorying' is rendered as 'be able to glory'.

The verb περισσεύῃ is glossed for this reference by BAGD under "*be present in abundance*" (p. 650.1aβ). The primary meaning of περισσεύω is not 'increase' and no lexical reason requires translating it as 'increase' here as some commentators and translations do. Here it functions basically as an intensifier of the event 'rejoice'. However, if we use 'triumphantly' in the propositionalization, it may not be necessary to add another intensive such as 'very'.

**1:26b because** Greenlee (1992) shows that commentators and versions are divided as to whether this διά with a genitive construction expresses reason or means. The normal propositionalized form of a means clause in this context in English would give us 'you will be able to rejoice triumphantly by means of Christ Jesus' *bringing* me to be with you again'. The means would help in the actual rejoicing process rather than being the direct cause of the rejoicing. But direct cause *is* in focus here, so this has been rendered as a reason proposition.

**Christ Jesus *will have brought* me to be with you again** The word καύχημα 'cause of glorying' presupposes someone or something to glory or take pride in. Where a person is the object of the pride, some event performed by that person is almost always what inspires the pride. The preposition ἐν 'in' often signals the person who is the object of the glory or pride. Here in Phil. 1:26 there are two persons mentioned in separate ἐν phrases, Christ Jesus and Paul. After these ἐν phrases a διά ('through, by means of, because of') phrase presents the event which in all likelihood the Philippians are to glory in, an event performed by at least one of the persons mentioned in the ἐν phrases—'through my presence with you again'. Since Paul would certainly honor Christ Jesus above himself and see him as the one who brings about glorious events in his life, we would expect Christ to be the causer or agent in bringing about the event and Paul as the (secondary) agent or beneficiary—'because Christ Jesus *will have brought* me to be with you again'. Both ἐν phrases are represented in this way in the propositionalization.

Some commentators make a point of the fact that ἐν Χριστῷ Ἰησοῦ 'in Christ Jesus' is to be connected with περισσεύῃ 'be abundant' rather than τὸ καύχημα 'cause of glorying'. However, that does not necessarily mean that they do not take the ἐν phrases as grounds for καύχημα. Vincent, for example, who says "ἐν Χριστῷ Ἰησοῦ: With περισσεύῃ, not with καύχημα," also says, "The ground of glorying is first, and comprehensively, in Christ; then in Paul as representing Christ; then in Paul's personal presence again with them."

## BOUNDARIES AND COHERENCE

The opening boundary has been discussed under 1:18f–20, and the final boundary under 1:12–26.

## PROMINENCE AND THEME

While the overall *situation-REACTION* paragraph pattern is naturally more prominent, most of the 1:21-26 paragraph is spent in describing the *situation*, which has an emotive *problem-SOLUTION* paragraph pattern embedded in it. Therefore the theme represents each of these components. The *belief* component (1:24), which is logically necessary to the theme, also is represented in the theme statement.

# PART CONSTITUENT 1:27-4:9 (Hortatory Subpart: Nucleus$_2$ of 1:3-4:20)

*THEME: Love and agree with one another, and humbly serve one another taking Christ as your example. Beware of false teachers and beware of those people who live lustful lives. Instead, follow my example of depending on Christ alone for salvation and of becoming more and more like him. Do not worry, but rejoice always.*

| MACROSTRUCTURE | CONTENTS |
|---|---|
| introduction | 1:27-30 Conduct yourselves just as you learned in the good news about Christ, unitedly and fearlessly resisting those who oppose you and the good news, since God is helping you in all your struggles. |
| APPEAL$_1$ | 2:1-30 Love and agree with one another, and humbly serve one another without arguing. Take Christ as your model in this. I dedicate my life to God together with you; therefore, let us all rejoice even though I may die. I expect to send Timothy to you soon and Epaphroditus right away. These are men who care for others' welfare, not their own. Welcome and honor such men as these. |
| APPEAL$_2$ | 3:1-4:1 Beware of those people who are trying to harm you by teaching that you must be circumcised. Also beware of those who are living lustful lives. Instead, follow my example of becoming more and more like Christ and depending on him alone for a right relationship with God. Our certain hope is that Christ will transform our earthly bodies to be like his heavenly body. |
| APPEAL$_3$ | 4:2-9 I urge Euodia and Syntyche to be reconciled with each other. Rejoice always and be gentle to everyone. Do not worry; pray instead. Think about all that is good and practice whatever you have learned from me and God will be with you and grant you peace. |

## INTENT AND MACROSTRUCTURE

The 1:27-4:9 unit is hortatory as seen from the initial imperative of the epistle, πολιτεύεσθε 'conduct yourselves' in 1:27a, to the final imperative of the epistle, πράσσετε 'do, practice' in 4:9a. Every paragraph except one is hortatory to some degree, and that paragraph, 2:19-24, is *COMMISSIVE*. K. Callow (forthcoming) categorizes *COMMISSIVE* as related to hortatory in the sense that it commits the speaker to future action while in hortatory the speaker is directing others toward future action. Section 3:2-11 is an expanded hortatory paragraph pattern with imperatives in its *APPEAL* paragraph. In all other paragraphs of 1:27-4:9, imperatives occur, except for 3:12-16, where φρονῶμεν 'let us think and τῷ αὐτῷ στοιχεῖν 'by the same thing behave' are the forms which the exhortations take.

## BOUNDARIES AND COHERENCE

The most important contributor to the coherence of the 1:27-4:9 unit is that it is hortatory in genre throughout.

## PROMINENCE AND THEME

An initial question is whether the first unit (1:27-30, most specifically 1:27-28a) is a generic representation of the specifics in the three *APPEAL* units of 2:1-4:9. In other words, is it comprehensive enough to cover their significant points? The answer is probably no, since 1:27-30 introduces ideas that Paul is going to take up in 2:1-4:9 but does not do so in a fully organized generic-specific manner. Thus the main basis for the theme statement should be the content of the three *APPEAL* units, and not that of the introduction. It is easy to see that Paul's exhortations on unity and humble service to others from the first *APPEAL* unit and resistance to wrong doctrine plus practicing right doctrine from the second *APPEAL* unit should be included in the theme statement. It is more difficult to know what other elements are prominent enough to be included in the theme statement of such a high-level unit. However, since the exhortation to rejoice is scattered five times throughout this unit (2:18 twice; 3:1; 4:4a, 4b), it should certainly be included.

Watson understands 1:27–30 as the *narratio* and the proposition of the discourse: it states that which the author wants the audience to make a decision on. The *probatio* (2:1–3:21) "provides proof for the proposition" (p. 67). Watson also says, "As is often the case, the proposition is reiterated at the beginning of each development: in 2:1–11 in vv. 1–4, and in 2:12–18 in vv. 12–13." These statements equate with the SSA in the sense that there is some type of restatement understood. This restatement relation, in the SSA, is taken as *introduction-APPEALS* (i.e., having elements of a generic-SPECIFIC$_n$ relation in this case) rather than as GENERIC-specific$_n$. Most likely Watson's analysis would be closer to GENERIC-specific$_n$.

# SUBPART CONSTITUENT 1:27–30
## (Hortatory Paragraph: Introduction to 2:1–4:9)

*THEME: Conduct yourselves just as you learned in the good news about Christ, unitedly and fearlessly resisting those who oppose you and the good news, since God is helping you in all your struggles.*

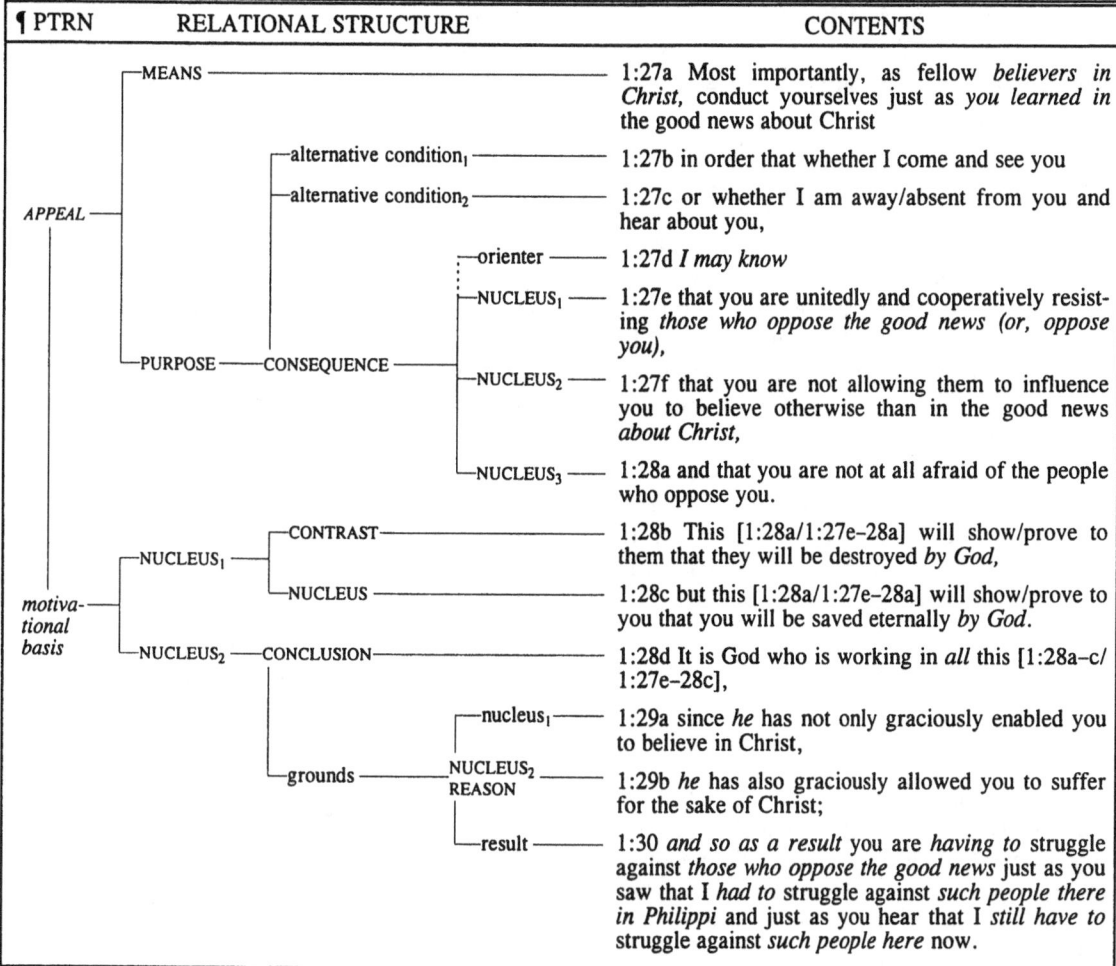

### INTENT AND PARAGRAPH PATTERN

This paragraph is obviously hortatory as shown by the imperative πολιτεύεσθε 'conduct yourselves' in 1:27a. While this is the only imperative form in the paragraph, the significant verbal constructions within the dependent ἵνα purpose construction (στήκετε ἐν ἑνὶ πνεύματι 'you are standing in one spirit', μιᾷ ψυχῇ συναθλοῦντες τῇ πίστει τοῦ εὐαγγελίου 'with one soul striving together for the faith of the gospel', and μὴ πτυρόμενοι ἐν μηδενὶ ὑπὸ τῶν ἀντικειμένων 'not being frightened in anything by the adversaries') are hortatory in the sense that they represent what Paul desires the Philippians to do.

We would normally expect a supporting *basis* for the 1:27–28 APPEAL. It appears that the supporting material after the complex APPEAL is thematically more closely related to the nearer "APPEALS in effect" than to the imperative itself. This suggests two things: First, it is not likely that each part of a multifaceted APPEAL will always be supported equally. Second, there may be a closer generic-specific or other overlapping relation between the APPEAL represented in the imperative and the following "APPEALS in effect" than is at first evident.

### NOTES

**1:27a Most importantly** Though BAGD does not mention the sense or function of μόνον 'only' in a grammatical context such as this, the meaning in this specific context is 'the one and only important matter above all other matters linked with it in the context'. This is not to say that those other matters are not important, but that this one is the *most* important. In other words, it marks prominence on 1:27a and whatever 1:27a may represent in the paragraph or larger unit. According to Watson (p. 65), "The adverb μόνον ('only'), which emphatically begins v. 27, marks the shift from *exordium* [the initial emotive part of the discourse] to *narratio* and indicates what is of central importance."

**as fellow *believers in Christ*, conduct yourselves** The verb here is πολιτεύεσθε, which originally had the meaning of 'be citizens, exercise your citizenship' but came to also have the meaning of 'live, conduct oneself, lead one's life'. Many commentators see the occurrence of this verb here in Phil. 1:27 as having at least some sense of its original meaning. Thus Vincent translates this verb and its immediate context in his paraphrase as "I exhort you to bear yourselves as becomes members of a Christian community." The paragraph is more coherent if some sense of the original meaning is present. That is, it is difficult to follow the train of thought from a broad, generic conducting of oneself worthily of the gospel of Christ to a realization of that conduct in basically only one specific—unitedly resisting those who oppose the gospel and believers. If πολιτεύεσθε to some extent focuses on the mutuality or corporateness of that conduct, then the relationship is much more obvious. Also, since the whole following section (2:1-16) and to some extent 2:17-30 as well deal with appropriate relationships between believers, and since a hortatory proposition at the beginning of a section or division often functions in a generic or introductory role for the unit as a whole, some element of proper relationship between believers would certainly be appropriate in this opening exhortation.

A further consideration is that elsewhere when Paul talks about conducting oneself worthily of someone or something he uses the verb περιπατέω 'walk' plus ἀξίως 'worthily' (Eph. 4:1; Col. 1:10; 1 Thess. 2:12). It is possible that he uses πολιτεύομαι here to indicate the need for a proper relationship between believers, though it is true that Eph. 4:1 also deals with this subject. In any case, it should be remembered that πολιτεύομαι does have as one of its meanings 'conduct yourselves as fellow citizens/fellow members of a (given) community'.

On this basis the rendering in the display is 'As fellow *believers in Christ*, conduct yourselves just as *you learned in* the good news about Christ'. Possible alternates are 'As fellow citizens *of Christ's kingdom*, conduct yourselves just as *you learned in* the good news about Christ' and 'Conduct yourselves according to the good news about Christ as you *live/work* together *as Christians*'.

**just as *you learned in* the good news about Christ** This might also be expressed as 'just as *we(exc) taught you in* the good news about Christ', 'just as you *were taught by us(exc) in* the good news about Christ'. As far as translation into other languages is concerned, if 'the gospel' or 'good news' collocates as an agent with 'teach' (i.e., if 'gospel' or 'good news' can be personified), then 'exactly like the good news about Christ *teaches us(inc)*' would be appropriate.

The genitive τοῦ Χριστοῦ 'of Christ' could mean '(the good news) about Christ' or '(the good news) from Christ', that is, '(the good news) Christ taught'. It would seem that 'the good news about Christ' is more appropriate than 'the good news from Christ' since it is more generic: What he taught and his life itself are examples for us to live by.

**1:27b-d in order that whether I come and see you or whether I am away/absent from you and hear about you, *I may know*** The Greek text is ἵνα εἴτε ἐλθὼν καὶ ἰδὼν ὑμᾶς εἴτε ἀπὼν ἀκούω τὰ περὶ ὑμῶν 'that whether having come and having seen you or being absent I may hear the things concerning you'. Vincent says of this, "The construction is rhetorically inexact... Ἀκούω ['I hear'], which in regular construction would be ἀκούων ['I hearing'] followed by γνῶ ['I may know'] or some similar verb, takes the finite form from the suggestion of the personal subject in ἀπὼν ['I being absent']. The construction is moulded by the thought of absence, which is last and most prominent in the writer's mind. The verb which would have been used on the supposition of his seeing them is dropped, and that which implies his absence is alone expressed." The unabbreviated form in a literal English translation would be 'whether having come and having seen you or whether being absent and hearing about you, I may know that you stand firm'. In a propositional rewrite of this type of abridgement it seems best to use the unabridged form, though in a translation into other languages an abridged form might be appropriate. It is not surprising that Paul would have used an abbreviated construction here since the εἴτε...εἴτε... construction itself is embedded and makes for a long sentence.

Note that 1:27b-28a is one long purpose construction signaled by ἵνα 'that, in order that' at the beginning of 27b. (The alternating conditions 27b and 27c are not as nuclear to the purpose construction as 27d-28a.) While it is true that 27e, f, and 28a are hortatory in intent, they function as purpose units within both the grammatical structure and communication role semantic structure.

**1:27b I come and see you** The participles ἐλθών 'having come' and ἰδών 'having seen' are in the aorist tense while the participle ἀπών 'being absent' is in the present tense. This may be because 'coming and seeing' are events that must take place first before Paul will know their present way of life, while 'being absent' is a state Paul is already in.

**1:27d *I may know*** See the note on 1:27b-d for the reason for the inclusion of 'I may know'.

**1:27e unitedly and cooperatively** The phrases ἐν ἑνὶ πνεύματι 'in one spirit' and μιᾷ ψυχῇ 'with one soul' are idiomatic, both having a common meaning which is translatable nonfiguratively as 'unitedly'. As far as translation into most languages is concerned, a literal translation would not be appropriate and so there is no need to discuss the contrastive meanings of πνεῦμα 'spirit' and ψυχή 'soul'. Translation will involve rendering these Greek phrases with whatever word or idiom may be used in the receptor language for the concept of 'unitedly'.

In the Greek text the two phrases that mean 'unitedly' each modify a different, though basically synonymous, verb. In the display, however, the two words for the sense 'unitedly' are presented as modifying only the first verb, simply because it is unnatural in English to use 'unitedly' or 'cooperatively' to modify the nonfigurative 'not allowing them to influence you to believe otherwise'. But this rendering still includes every obligatory component of meaning.

**resisting *those who oppose the good news (or, oppose you)*** The Greek verb στήκετε is usually translated literally as 'stand' or 'stand firm'. This is a dead metaphor, and to translate it nonmetaphorically the rendering would be 'persevere, be steadfast, resist (the opposition)'. The fact that both στήκετε 'stand' and συναθλοῦντες 'contending together' here presuppose real rather than totally figurative opposing forces is seen by the explicit reference to real opposing forces in the next verse, τῶν ἀντικειμένων 'opponents, adversaries'. In fact, the rest of the paragraph deals with real opposing forces.

The transitive 'resist' requires an object in the propositionalization. Since the next clause in the Greek text deals with 'contending for the faith of the gospel', 'those who oppose the good news' is one possible object. At the same time these adversaries are opposing the Philippians themselves, so that is shown as an alternative.

**1:27f that you are not allowing them to influence you to believe otherwise than in the good news *about Christ*** The verb συναθλέω means to 'contend' or 'struggle' as in an athletic contest or war, with the added thought that those referred to as agents are unitedly contending against a common foe. While it is true that some exegetes gloss συναθλοῦντες here as 'striving together' it should be noted that 'strive' in English has two senses: "1. To make earnest effort. 2. To engage in strife; contend; fight" (Funk and Wagnalls). It is the second sense that συναθλοῦντες carries here. Note that when the second sense is in focus, the first sense is also involved, while the opposite is not necessarily true.

The nonfigurative rendering of συναθλοῦντες 'contending, struggling' chosen for the display is based on the following considerations: The striving has to do with 'the faith of the gospel'; there is an important hortatory division of the book that deals with opposition to the doctrine of the gospel (3:1-4:1) which this verse is no doubt previewing; and one of the most prominent sets of exhortations in that division (3:2) is stated in negative defensive terms.

**believe... in the good news** There is much discussion in the commentaries on the relationship of τῇ πίστει 'the faith' to the genitive τοῦ εὐαγγελίου 'the gospel'. Here the propositionalization 'not allowing them to influence you' for συναθλοῦντες 'contending' causes us to render this genitive phrase as 'believe in the good news *about Christ*'. Even if Paul intended 'faith' to mean 'that which is believed', that sense is included in that it is basically synonymous with 'the good news about Christ' in this context, so nothing is lost in the propositionalization.

**1:28a and that you are not at all afraid of the people who oppose you** There is a question as to whether 1:28a should be rendered as an imperative, since this is in effect an exhortation for the Philippian believers to be unafraid of their adversaries. Nevertheless, it appears inappropriate to treat this third and final construction as an imperative because the two earlier constructions semantically coordinate with this one are expressed as the content of 'I may know'. The first of the coordinates, at least, must be translated as a content of 'I may know', and it does not seem fitting to switch to the imperative for the second and third, or third only.

**1:28b This [1:28a/1:27e–28a] will show/prove to them that they will be destroyed *by God*** This might also be propositionalized 'If/Since you are not afraid of them, they will know that they themselves will be destroyed *by God*'.

In Greek stative clauses, if the subject is a demonstrative or a relative that functions like a demonstrative its gender can be that of the complement. Thus ἥτις 'which' takes the gender of ἔνδειξις 'sign' here, and it is not necessary to take it as referring to the nearest feminine antecedent τῇ πίστει 'the faith' in 1:27. Since relatives tend to relate to the nearest semantically compatible antecedent, it is highly probable that ἥτις 'which' refers to the immediately preceding clause, 1:28a, rather than anything in 1:27 (unless that part of 1:27 can be generically included in the thought of 1:28a, which is possible since each of the coordinates have a similar meaning). This analysis agrees with that of a majority of commentators (Greenlee 1992). At least one version (NAB) takes ἥτις as referring to the opposition of the adversaries; the antecedent in Greek would then be τῶν ἀντικειμένων 'those opposing'. But τῶν ἀντικειμένων refers basically to a certain group of characteristic people rather than to their actions.

**show/prove** This, of course, is the verbal expression of the abstract noun 'sign'.

**destroyed *by God*** The most common sense of ἀπώλεια 'destruction' in the New Testament is 'eternal destruction' and that sense is appropriate here.

'God' is supplied in the display as the obvious agent of the destruction to fill out the case roles of a transitive-type event. It should be noted, however, that this event is of a type often handled with intransitive forms (i.e., patient plus event), even in some languages where there are no transitive passive forms.

**1:28c to you** There is a textual problem here. Some manuscripts have ὑμῖν δὲ σωτηρίας 'to you salvation', that is, 'a (sign of) salvation to you', while others have ὑμῶν δὲ σωτηρίας 'your salvation', that is, 'a (sign) of your salvation'. The Hodges and Farstad text has the former reading while the UBSGNT text has the latter and does not mention the former as a variant reading.

If the UBSGNT is followed, there is a problem in determining if the sign of the believers' salvation is a sign meant for the adversaries or the believers themselves. To reach a decision on this, it may be helpful to try to reconstruct what the Greek form of the construction might have been had Paul written it out completely:

ἥτις ἐστὶν αὐτοῖς ἔνδειξις
this is     to-them a-sign

(αὐτῶν) ἀπωλείας,
(of-their) destruction,

(ἥτις) δὲ (ἐστὶν αὐτοῖς/ὑμῖν
(this)   (is   to-them/to-you

ἔνδειξις) ὑμῶν σωτηρίας
a-sign)    of-your salvation'

For reasons of economy, Paul does not include the genitive form αὐτῶν 'their' in the first clause, though it is obviously implied. (Hawthorne thinks otherwise, however.) The dative form αὐτοῖς 'to them' in effect signals it. In the second clause, the dative form is missing, while the genitive form is present. Since the dative form is missing, we must expect it to be signaled either by αὐτοῖς 'to them' in the first clause, since Paul may be meaning the sign only for the adversaries and so signals to whom the sign is given only once. Or he may mean to indicate the believers as recipients of the sign of their own salvation. If so, his only chance to signal this in the construction he actually uses is through the word ὑμῶν 'your' (which modifies 'salvation'). From what one might call a universal grammatical viewpoint, αὐτοῖς 'to them' in the first clause signals the adversaries as the recipients of the sign for both clauses much more clearly than ὑμῶν 'your' signals the believers as the recipients of the sign for the believers' salvation.

On the other hand, there appear to be some strong reasons from the context of the rest of vv. 28 and 29 to understand the sign of the believers' salvation to be given to them to strengthen them in their persecution. If this is the case, one wonders if the ὑμῖν 'to you' reading is not the right one. While we might expect a scribe to make a correction in the manuscript to make the clauses more parallel (i.e., to change ὑμῶν to ὑμῖν) rather than the other way around, still a reading that is not congruent with the rest of the text seems to be at least open to question.

**will be saved eternally** The word σωτηρία is taken here in its most common meaning in the New Testament, spiritual or eternal salvation, rather than physical deliverance from the present persecution.

**1:28d God . . . is working** There seems to be an implicit reason for much of what Paul says in this paragraph. He wants to steer the Philippians clear of any false ideas regarding the reasons they are having to suffer and face such opposition. God is working in all this and certainly helping the Philippian believers since, if he allows his children to suffer (v. 29), he is certainly going to help them bear up under that suffering (28a) and use that suffering for his own purposes (28b). The fact that they are suffering and bearing up under it (28a) shows that they are God's children (28c).

*all* **this [1:28a–c/1:27e–28c]** It would not seem very likely that τοῦτο 'this', a neuter form, would refer only to the immediately preceding feminine form σωτηρίας 'salvation'. Moule says, "Τοῦτο of course does not refer properly to σωτηρία, which would require αὕτη..." The neuter τοῦτο 'this' is the form that is used for reference to quotations and syntactic constructions, a different function than that of the masculine, feminine, or neuter forms referring to antecedents or forward references of the same gender which are single words or nominal phrases. Some commentators take τοῦτο 'this' to refer to all the preceding part of the verse, while others take it to refer more specifically to ἔνδειξις 'sign'. Still others say it refers to ἀπωλείας 'destruction' and σωτηρίας 'salvation', or to σωτηρίας alone. (As noted above, this last interpretation is quite questionable.)

If ἔνδειξις 'sign' is the antecedent, the use of the neuter τοῦτο 'this' with this feminine antecedent might be explained by the fact that the feminine αὕτη 'this', had it been used, would refer to σωτηρίας 'salvation'. But even if the reference of τοῦτο is to ἔνδειξις 'sign', it is difficult to differentiate the sign from the activity the sign represents. How can the sign be from God but not the activity the sign represents? The lack of fear in itself is not significant unless the adversaries see it as a result of the believers' knowing that God is on their side. Thus it seems best to take τοῦτο as a more general reference to all that precedes it in v. 28. This, I believe, will also fit in better with the context of the ὅτι construction immediately following in v. 29.

Since 1:27e and f are very similar in meaning to 1:28a, their sense might also be included under τοῦτο.

An alternate propositionalization for 1:28d is 'It is God who is doing *all* this'.

**1:29a since** It is difficult not to see a connection in thought between καὶ τοῦτο ἀπὸ θεοῦ 'and this from God' and ὑμῖν ἐχαρίσθη 'to you has been granted', especially with ὅτι 'because, since' in between them in the text, with a possible translation of 'And this is from God since God has granted to you...'. Most commentators make this connection. A few, however, take ὅτι 'because' to signal 1:29 as motivational grounds for the implied exhortation(s) of 1:28a or 1:27e–28a.

**graciously enabled you to believe in Christ** As far as the primary action in the verb ἐχαρίσθη is concerned, it might normally be translated as 'it has been granted'. But when actions or events are being granted rather than material things, the idea is closer to 'caused', 'enabled', or 'allowed'. '*God* has caused you to believe in Christ' may suggest an action apart from the human will, so 'enabled' is used in the display.

For χαρίζομαι the gloss under entry 1 in BAGD (p. 876) is "*give freely or graciously as a favor.*" This brings out the verb's added component of meaning describing the manner of the action. This could be propositionalized as 'God has given you the privilege that you should believe in Christ'. However, 'privilege' is an abstract noun, and for the display it is rendered 'graciously'. But because many languages do not have an adverb that conveys this sense, it may have to be expressed in a separate phrase or clause, for instance, 'God is gracious/loves you and so...'.

**1:29b *he* has also graciously allowed you to suffer** For the relationship of ἐχαρίσθη with πάσχειν 'suffer', 'graciously caused you to suffer' seems too connotative of God's direct cause in the suffering. '*God* has graciously allowed you to suffer' may be nearer to the theological sense here.

There is definitely a component of contra-expectation here. Verse 29 might be expressed more fully as 'God has graciously enabled you to believe in Christ; although you might not expect that he would also graciously allow you to suffer, he actually does so, for the sake of Christ'. But since it seems unnecessary to include the concession in the display, the label concession-CONTRAEXPECTATION is not used. Rather, 1:29a and 1:29b are considered to be conjoined, with the second component more prominent.

**for the sake of Christ** Most commentators take τὸ ὑπὲρ Χριστοῦ 'for the sake of Christ' as connected with πάσχειν 'suffer', 'for the sake of Christ to suffer'. The phrase τὸ ὑπὲρ αὐτοῦ 'for his sake', which immediately precedes πάσχειν, is a repetition of τὸ ὑπὲρ Χριστοῦ, made necessary by the intervening οὐ μόνον τὸ εἰς αὐτὸν πιστεύειν 'not only to believe in him'. Lightfoot says, "τὸ ὑπὲρ Χριστοῦ] i.e. πάσχειν ['suffer']. The sentence is suspended by the insertion of the after-thought οὐ μόνον τὸ εἰς αὐτὸν πιστεύειν ['not only to believe in him'] and resumed in τὸ ὑπὲρ αὐτοῦ πάσχειν ['to suffer for his sake']." Some commentators take τὸ ὑπὲρ Χριστοῦ to be connected also with τὸ εἰς αὐτὸν πιστεύειν 'believe in him' (i.e., 'for the sake of Christ not only to believe in him but also to suffer for his sake'). However, there is a parallel structure in the οὐ μόνον...ἀλλὰ καί 'not only...but also' phrases:

οὐ μόνον τὸ εἰς αὐτὸν πιστεύειν
ἀλλὰ καὶ τὸ ὑπὲρ αὐτοῦ πάσχειν

'not only in him to believe
but also for him to suffer'

It would seem unnatural for τὸ ὑπὲρ Χριστοῦ 'for the sake of Christ' to modify both phrases when the parallel structure brings out a contrast between εἰς αὐτόν 'in him' and ὑπὲρ αὐτοῦ 'for him'. Since the function of the οὐ μόνον...ἀλλὰ καί 'not only...but also' construction is to place prominence on the ἀλλὰ καί 'but also' constituent, and since the parallel structure brings out the importance of ὑπὲρ αὐτοῦ 'for him' here, it would seem that the function of ὑπὲρ Χριστοῦ 'for the sake of Christ' would be to place more emphasis on the suffering for Christ.

**1:30** *and so as a result* Since πάσχειν 'to suffer' and ἀγῶνα 'struggle' are close in meaning, it is apparent that the thought of v. 30 follows directly on from v. 29 rather than being more closely connected with something earlier. It is true that the only verbal form in v. 30, the participle ἔχοντες 'having', has a nominative ending which would not be the normal grammatical form for relating to the ὑμῖν 'to you' dative of v. 29. But a majority of commentators do make this connection, citing the fact that such a change in case has many examples elsewhere. (Col. 3:16 is an example that is obviously similar to this one.)

Regarding the relationship indicated by the participial form ἔχοντες 'having', Greenlee (1992) presents only one option from the commentaries: "It further explains the meaning of the preceding word πάσχειν 'to suffer'." He interprets this relationship as, "to suffer for Christ by having the same struggle as I have." Vincent says, "ἔχοντες: 'you having,' or 'so that you have.'" Of the many relations a participle may signal, result is one of them. The obvious connection between the fact that suffering is a gracious gift from God and their present struggle is that the latter is a result of the former. It is also obvious that Paul wants to make the point that both he and they are involved in the same type of suffering and struggle. The purpose of Paul's reminder to them of the very real opposition from adversaries while he was with them in Philippi back at the beginning (Acts 16:16–40) and of the great opposition he is facing now is to prove to them that God does in fact graciously allow his children to suffer and also graciously helps them in that suffering.

**struggle against** *those who oppose the good news* The noun ἀγών assumes forces actively opposing a person, and it speaks of that person's reaction to the opposition, either active or passive. In 1 Thess. 2:2, ἀγών is used to describe Paul's experience in Thessalonica: ἐν πολλῷ ἀγῶνι 'in much opposition'. (NIV has "we dared to tell you his gospel in spite of strong opposition.") Although it is true that at both Philippi and the present situation in Rome Paul was actively involved in the struggle for the gospel, here, following ὑπὲρ αὐτοῦ πάσχειν 'suffer for his sake' in v. 29 and in the absence of any hortatory signal, the passive sense seems more appropriate than the active sense. (That the opposition is outside the person should be signaled, though.) Paul suffered, and still was suffering here, in the struggle brought on by the gospel's opponents.

## BOUNDARIES AND COHERENCE

The opening boundary of 1:27–30 has been discussed under 1:12–26. As for the closing boundary of this paragraph, 1:27–30 is one long grammatical sentence. At the beginning of 2:1 there is, in effect, asyndeton, since the conjunction εἰ 'if' marking the conditional clause relates forward to the imperative πληρώσατε 'fulfill' at the beginning of 2:2. This imperative marks a new *basis-APPEAL* paragraph pattern. Both 1:27–30 and 2:1–4 overlap lexically in terms of the semantic domain of unity (e.g., ἐν ἑνὶ πνεύματι, μιᾷ ψυχῇ 'in one spirit, with one soul' in 1:28; τὸ αὐτὸ φρονῆτε 'think the same thing', σύμψυχοι 'united in spirit' in 2:2). But 1:27–30 deals more with unity in opposing outside forces, while 2:1–4 (and the rest of the chapter also) focuses on unity within the body. The reason for this is that 1:27–30 introduces the subjects of unity and resisting outside forces and then in 2:1–30 Paul deals with the subject of unity before getting to the subject of resisting outside forces in 3:1–4:1.

## PROMINENCE AND THEME

Since the ἵνα purpose construction functions as hortatory in intent, its three coordinate NUCLEI are included in the *APPEAL* part of the theme along with the part of the *APPEAL* expressed by the imperative πολιτεύεσθε 'conduct yourselves'. The *basis* is also represented since it is an obligatory part of the paragraph pattern.

## SUBPART CONSTITUENT 2:1–30 (Hortatory Division: Appeal₁ of 1:27–4:9)

*THEME: Love and agree with one another, and humbly serve one another without arguing. Take Christ as your model in this. I dedicate my life to God together with you; therefore, let us all rejoice even though I may die. I expect to send Timothy to you soon and Epaphroditus right away. These are men who care for others' welfare, not their own. Welcome and honor such men as these.*

| MACROSTRUCTURE | CONTENTS |
|---|---|
| APPEAL₁ | 2:1-16 Love one another, agree with one another, and humbly serve one another since Christ has loved us and humbly given himself for us in death on a shameful cross. Obey God and your leaders always and never complain against them or argue with them, but witness in life and word to the ungodly people around you. |
| APPEAL₂ | 2:17-18 Because I and all of you dedicate ourselves together to do God's will, even if I am to be executed I rejoice and you should also rejoice. |
| APPEAL₃ | 2:19-30 I confidently expect to send Timothy to you soon. He genuinely cares for your welfare, not his own interests. I am sending Epaphroditus back to you. Welcome him joyfully. Honor him and all those like him since he nearly died while serving me on your behalf. |

### INTENT AND MACROSTRUCTURE

In the 2:1–30 division Paul begins his specific APPEALS. Note that even though the label APPEAL in the display is singular, each unit so labeled may consist of a number of APPEALS.

### BOUNDARIES AND COHERENCE

That 2:1–30 is a coherent whole can be seen from the many references to unity and selfless service to others. See the notes under 1:3–4:20.

### PROMINENCE AND THEME

Since the units in this division are in a conjoined relationship with one another, each of them should be represented in the division theme statement. To bring out Paul's stress on unity and selfless service to others, not only the travel components of 2:19–30 are included but also the examples of selfless service represented in Timothy and Epaphroditus.

## DIVISION CONSTITUENT 2:1–16 (Hortatory Section: Appeal₁ of 2:1–30)

*THEME: Love one another, agree with one another, and humbly serve one another since Christ has loved us and humbly given himself for us in death on a shameful cross. Obey God and your leaders always and never complain against them or argue with them, but witness in life and word to the ungodly people around you.*

| MACROSTRUCTURE | CONTENTS |
|---|---|
| APPEAL₁ (specifics) | 2:1-4 Since Christ loves and encourages us and the Holy Spirit fellowships with us, make me completely happy by agreeing with one another, loving one another, and humbly serving one another. |
| APPEAL₂ (model) | 2:5-11 You should think just as Christ Jesus thought, who willingly gave up his divine prerogatives and humbled himself, willingly obeying God though it meant dying on a shameful cross. As a result, God exalted him to the highest position, to be acknowledged by all the universe as the supreme Lord. |
| APPEAL₃ (urging) | 2:12-13 Since you have always obeyed God, continue to strive to do those things which are appropriate for people whom God has saved, since he will enable you to do so. |
| APPEAL₄ (specifics) | 2:14-16 Obey God and your leaders always and never complain against them or argue with them, in order that you may be perfect children of God, witnessing in life and word to the ungodly people among whom you live. |

## INTENT AND MACROSTRUCTURE

This first hortatory section of the division has four conjoined paragraphs each of which are labeled *APPEAL*. These *APPEALS* function somewhat differently, however. While 2:5-11 has its own exhortation, its dominant feature is the model of Christ's humility and service, and so it also functions as a motivational basis for the other hortatory paragraphs of the section. The 2:1-4 and 2:14-16 paragraphs consist of specific exhortations, while 2:12-13 appears to focus more on encouraging the readers to actually carry out the exhortations of the section.

## BOUNDARIES AND COHERENCE

The unity mentioned in 1:27-30 was associated with the threat from the outside since 1:27-30 is introducing both unity and opposition. In 2:1:16, and especially in 2:1-4, Paul deals with unity within the church and does not mention the opposition. Whereas it is easy to see 2:1-4 as an exhortation to unity and 2:5-11 as an exhortation to follow Christ's example of humility and service to others which promote unity, it is not quite so easy to see this in 2:12-13 (though 'do everything without complaining and arguing' in 2:14-16 can certainly be seen as promoting unity). 'Work out your own salvation' (2:12) on the surface does not seem to fit the theme of unity. On the other hand, ὥστε 'therefore' at the beginning of 2:12 most likely marks a relationship between 2:12-13 and the example of Christ, an example that is used as a basis to urge unity in 2:1-11 and 2:12-13. It is unusual for a support unit to provide support both backward and forward like this; it would be even more abnormal for it to support two completely different themes. On this basis it would appear that 2:12-13 should be taken as having some close relation with the theme of unity. It may be that its function is not so much one of supplying new information but of urging the addressees to carry out what has already been said. There are several things that suggest this. First, the exhortation in 2:12, τὴν ἑαυτῶν σωτηρίαν κατεργάζεσθε 'work out your own salvation', is generic. Second, it is the manner of carrying it out that is specific; in fact, it is quite strong, especially μετὰ φόβου καὶ τρόμου 'with fear and trembling', though μὴ ὡς ἐν τῇ παρουσίᾳ μου μόνον ἀλλὰ νῦν πολλῷ μᾶλλον ἐν τῇ ἀπουσίᾳ μου 'not as in my presence only but now by much more in my absence' may be much stronger than it would first appear. Also, the vocative ἀγαπητοί μου 'my beloved' at the beginning of v. 12 is appropriate to a strong exhortation.

The 2:17-18 unit contains two imperatives, χαίρετε καὶ συγχαίρετέ μοι 'rejoice and rejoice with me'; hence this unit has a hortatory paragraph pattern. But what is exhorted is expressive in nature and its *basis* is the embedded expressive unit with the *REACTION* being χαίρω καὶ συγχαίρω πᾶσιν ὑμῖν 'I rejoice and rejoice with you all'. Paul appears to be returning to elements of the expressive genre and content of 1:12-26. At the same time, as O'Brien (1991:315) and others have pointed out, when Paul refers to the possibility of pouring out his life as a libation for others, he may well be alluding to his own life and commitment as an example of selfless service, thus tying in with Christ's selfless example and the overall theme of unity and service to others. In Philippians Paul combines elements of expressive and hortatory nature. Note also 3:1 and 4:1.

Because of the uniqueness of 2:17-18, it seems better to see it as a paragraph separate from 2:14-16 and also as outside of the section 2:1-16. In it Paul focuses on himself, something which he has not done in 2:1-16, except in what may be seen as the tail of a tail-head link in 2:16b-c.

## PROMINENCE AND THEME

Since the four paragraphs that make up the 2:1-16 section are in a conjoined relationship, elements from each are included in the section's theme statement. Paragraph 2:1-4 is important to the theme statement since the intensive repetition of synonymous, specific terms all acting as exhortations indicates a peak in the hortatory intent of the section. Paragraph 2:5-11 is also significant in that it presents the model of Christ himself in very graphic form. Paragraph 2:12-13 appears to focus more on the component of urging than on specific content. In paragraph 2:14-16 'without complaining and arguing' fits into the theme of unity; the final *APPEALS* are also included.

# SECTION CONSTITUENT 2:1-4 (Hortatory Paragraph: Appeal₁ of 2:1-16)

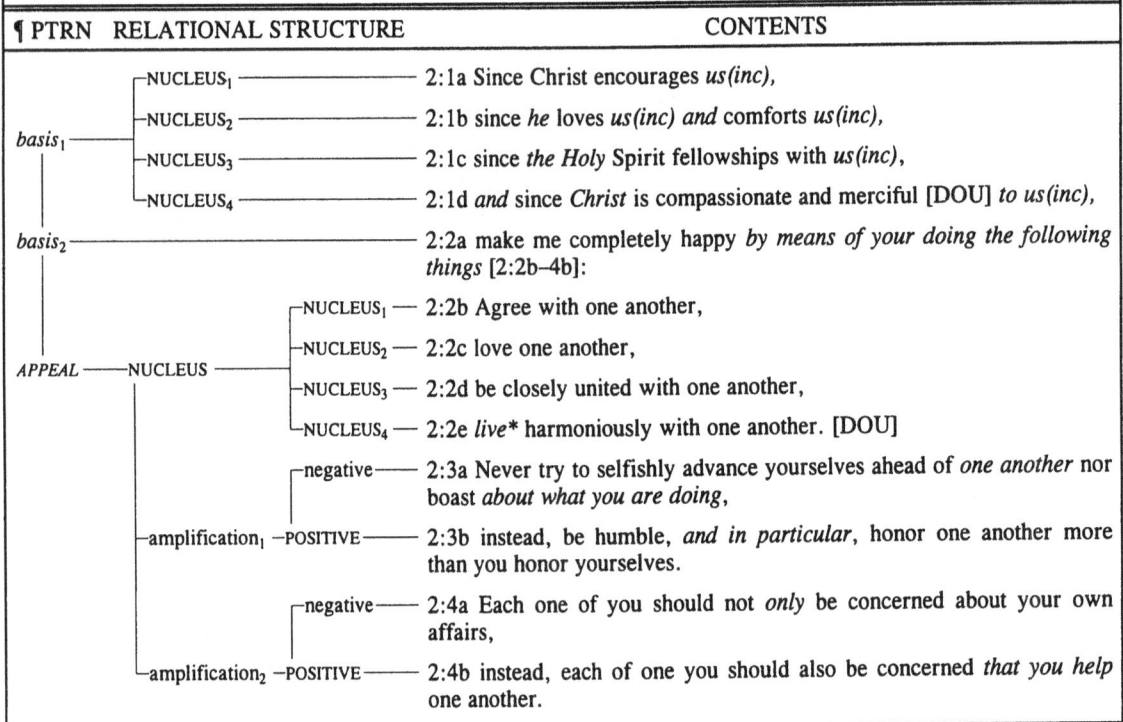

## INTENT AND PARAGRAPH PATTERN

Paul now takes up a full discussion of the need for unity among the Philippian believers, a subject he introduced briefly in 1:27. There is skewing between the grammatical and semantic structure of this hortatory paragraph. The imperative phrase of 2:2a, πληρώσατέ μου τὴν χαράν 'complete my joy', actually functions as a *motivational basis* for the *APPEAL*, while the ἵνα clause and subsequent participial phrases in 2:2-4 function as exhortations appealing for unity, love, and humility. Verse 2:1 also functions as a *motivational basis* for the *APPEAL*: Since Christ has treated us in such a loving manner, we need to treat our fellow believers in the same way.

## NOTES

**2:1** The relationship between 2:1-4 and 1:27-30 is marked in the Greek text by the conjunction οὖν. This conjunction may function in one of three ways (J. Callow 1983:153): it may mark an inference from the preceding material ('therefore'), or it may mark the resumption of the theme line, or it may mark the surface paragraphs in a hortatory section. The first of these functions does not fit because 1:27-30 and 2:1-4 are both hortatory and there is no evident relationship of direct inference, e.g., *basis-APPEAL*, between them. The resumption of theme idea does fit: The theme of 1:27-30 involves being united and standing firm in the face of opposition. These two elements are together in 1:27, but 1:28-30 goes on to deal with standing firm in the face of opposition. Clearly 2:1-4 then resumes the discussion of unity. Therefore the function of οὖν here is best understood as marking this resumption. The connection is not marked with 'therefore' in the display, but in translating οὖν it could be expressed as 'As for being united with one another'.

Verse 2:1 consists of four verbless clauses in which the actions, events, or states are encoded by abstract nouns. There is much conjecture as to what the relationship is between the participants: members of the Godhead, the Philippian addressees, Paul. Since 2:1 acts as a *basis* for the exhortations to loving action of 2:2-4, Paul is asking the Philippians to go above and beyond what they are now doing. Therefore if 'you' were the subject, for example in 2:1d, 'you are compassionate and merciful to one another', the *basis-*

APPEAL relationship would not seem appropriate. It seems probable that the *basis* is either (1) that members of the Godhead have shown these qualities to the Christians (so Christians should respond with the same qualities toward one another) or (2) that members of the Godhead enable Christians to have these qualities (so there is no reason why the Philippian Christians should *not* show these qualities to one another). Phillips would seem to support option 1: "Now if you have known anything of Christ's encouragement and his reassuring love...", and Bruce (1989) would seem to support option 2: "The resources that make...unity possible are available to the people of Christ in their fellowship with him."

It is difficult to decide whether option 1 or option 2 is intended. The English sense of 'if there is any encouragement in Christ' would tend to suggest that Christ is the agent of the encouragement: 'Since Christ encourages you because you are his followers'. The question is, Is this also the primary Greek sense? Or does it mean, 'Because you are followers of Christ, he gives you the grace of encouraging one another'? That is, Does 'in Christ' focus on the positional relationship of the believer as being 'in Christ', 'united to him', rather than on Christ as the agent of the action of encouraging?

The genitive construction in 1c, κοινωνία πνεύματος 'fellowship of (the) Spirit/spirit', would normally be understood to mean 'fellowship with the Spirit'. (A genitive following κοινωνία, unless it is a personal pronoun, normally refers to the one with whom there is fellowship.) This may seem to favor option 1: 'You enjoy the privilege of fellowship with the Holy Spirit, now make sure that you fellowship genuinely with your fellow Christians'. But 'fellowship brought about by the Holy Spirit' is also possible according to BAGD (p. 438-39.1), and this would be compatible with option 2.

A meshing of the two options is a possibility, though translating this into some languages would be complicated: 'Since Christ encourages us his followers and enables us to encourage one another', etc.

Option 1 is represented in the display. Option 2, which is also quite tenable, would be propositionalized as follows:

> (2:1a) Since Christ *enables us(inc)* to encourage *one another*, (1:b) since *he enables us(inc)* to love and comfort *one another*, (1c) since *the Holy Spirit enables us(inc)* to fellowship *genuinely with one another*, (1d) since *Christ enables us(inc)* to be kind and compassionate *to one another*

In the display, 'us(inc)' is used as the goal of the actions all through v. 1 rather than 'you(pl)', because the statements are true for all Christians, not the Philippian addressees only. The statements are inclusive rather than exclusive. Of course, in any language where the inclusive-exclusive distinction is not strong, 'you(pl)' could be used, and, in fact, would be more emphatic and appropriate to the clearly exclusive sense of 'you(pl)' in 2:2-4.

**2:1a Since** The Greek is εἴ τις 'if (there is) any', but the εἴ τις clauses here are not conditional in the sense that they express things in doubt. Quite often, in fact, εἰ is used to introduce the given in an argument. BAGD (p. 219) lists this use under III, "In causal clauses, when an actual case is taken as a supposition, where we also can use *if* instead of *since*." Since semantically these εἰ constructions represent reality and function as grounds, it is more appropriate to render them as grounds (*basis*) in the display. Whether or not they should be translated as conditional clauses in another language depends on whether grounds constructions in an argument such as this are appropriately translated as conditions.

**encourages us(inc)** The noun παράκλησις may mean 'exhortation' or 'encouragement'. With the context of loving action toward others in all of 2:1-4, 'encouragement' appears to be the better translation here.

There is also a possibility that παράκλησις relates most specifically to πληρώσατέ μου τὴν χαράν 'fulfill my joy': 'Since Christ has encouraged you/us so much, encourage me by doing the following'. Philem. 7 shows the close lexical relationship between παράκλησις 'encouragement' and χαρά 'joy': χαρὰν...πολλὴν ἔσχον καὶ παράκλησιν ἐπὶ τῇ ἀγάπῃ σου 'I have much joy and encouragement because of your love'. Although Paul may have intended this specific relationship between 2:1a and 2:2a, he also intends all of 2:1 as a whole to support 2:2-4 as a whole.

**2:1b since *he* loves *us(inc) and* comforts *us(inc)*** The word παραμύθιον 'comfort' is closely related in meaning to παράκλησις, and these two words in their cognate forms occur together elsewhere (see 1 Cor. 14:3; 1 Thess. 2:12). It also has the sense of 'exhortation, persuasion', but as with παράκλησις, the context, especially 2:1d and 2:2-4, shows that Paul's meaning here is 'comfort'.

Even though 'comfort' here may be seen as a state, it is most likely a state which is the result of the comforting action of someone else. In view of this and the more complicated structure of a result-reason construction, 'love' and 'comfort' are treated in the display as conjoined actions. A result-reason propositionalization would be: 'since *we(inc)* are comforted because *he* loves *us(inc)*' or 'since *we(inc)* are comforted because *we(inc) know that he* loves *us(inc)*'.

**2:1c *the Holy* Spirit fellowships with *us(inc)*** The Greek is κοινωνία πνεύματος 'fellowship of the Spirit'. Although this genitive would normally indicate the person with whom the fellowship is maintained, 'fellowship' has a completely reciprocal sense. We cannot experience fellowship with anyone without their doing likewise with us. Of course, it is the Holy Spirit who is the originator of the fellowship. In this context, then, the meaning might well be 'since we have the privilege of fellowshiping with the Holy Spirit' or 'since the Holy Spirit deigns to fellowship with us'.

**2:1d *Christ* is compassionate and merciful *to us(inc)*** Christ is considered to be in focus as the one showing compassion and mercy. (He had the same role in 2:1a–b.) In 1:8, Paul says, 'I long for you all with the affection (σπλάγχνοις, as here) of Christ Jesus'.

The word σπλάγχνα, which denotes the seat of the emotions, is equivalent to English 'heart'; οἰκτιρμός means 'compassion, mercy'. Therefore σπλάγχνα καὶ οἰκτιρμοί might be considered a hendiadys, and translated 'compassionate heart' (see BAGD, p. 561). However, 'heart' is figurative and σπλάγχνα, even in English translations, is often rendered as 'compassion, tender mercy, affection'.

**2:2a make me completely happy** The Greek is an imperative: πληρώσατέ μου τὴν χαράν, literally 'make my joy full' or 'complete my joy'. TEV has "make me completely happy," adjusting the abstract noun χαράν 'joy, happiness' to an adjective and maintaining the intensive idea in 'fill' or 'complete' with the adverb 'completely' and the causative idea in 'fill' or 'complete' with the verb 'make'. The display follows TEV, with 'make' rather than 'cause' since 'make' is more natural English. This is an appeal to the emotions, motivation for the APPEAL of 2:2b–4b. Paul is adding the personal touch by appealing to his beloved brothers and sisters, asking them to make him completely happy by their being totally united as one.

***by means of your doing the following things* [2:2b–4b]** Following the Greek imperatival clause is a construction introduced by ἵνα. Such a construction normally is a purpose or some type of content, but as far as SSWC relations are concerned, there is no doubt that the construction introduced by ἵνα here is a MEANS construction. In other words, ἵνα marks a RESULT-means relationship here, not a MEANS-purpose one. The structure is indeed complicated: not only is 'complete my joy' in imperative form in the Greek, but the ἵνα construction, which is *not* in imperative form, *is* hortatory (in the semantic structure). In an effort to preserve the hortatory form of both while also preserving the RESULT-means form to some extent, the display rendering is 'make me completely happy *by means of your doing the following things* [2:2b–4b]: Agree with one another, love one another ...'. An alternate propositionalization would be: 'In order that you might make me completely happy, agree with one another, love one another ...'.

**2:2b Agree with one another** The Greek is τὸ αὐτὸ φρονῆτε 'you should think the same (thing)'. We say 'think alike' in English but not as an imperative. We say that two or more people think alike but we would not tell a group of people to think alike. The better translation would be 'being of the same mind' (RSV) where 'same mind' is a figurative expression for 'agreement', but certainly not absolute conformity of thought. The nonfigurative rendering 'agree with one another' is used for the display.

**2:2c love one another** The Greek is τὴν αὐτὴν ἀγάπην ἔχοντες 'the same love having'. The intricately constructed 2:2b–e unit is composed of four parts, each of which has a lexical item of similar meaning, thus focusing on and accentuating the concept of unity: τὸ αὐτό 'the same', τὴν αὐτήν 'the same', συμ- 'together, one', τὸ ἕν 'the one (thing)' (see D. Black, p. 302). Like v. 1, v. 2 is a very compact unit. In fact, all of 2:1–4 is seen by some as having special literary character (ibid.:299 and O'Brien 1991:164–66). It is possible that these four lexical items are functioning not only within each individual phrase but also in relation to the unit as a whole such that the meaning of any one phrase cannot be fully understood without reference to the structure of the unit as a whole. The whole unit in this view is said to function as an idiom. If this is true, then τὴν αὐτήν 'the same' has the function of continuing to accentuate the idea of unity. Here in 2c it is unity in terms of mutual love. The translator does not need be concerned with what 'same love' might mean so much as what 'unity in love' means. Phillips translates this as 'live together in love'. There seems to be no English adverbial modifier for love which would be appropriate in this context but 'one another' does translate the sense of 'same' to some extent. Also, to maintain the lexical accent on unity throughout 2b-e 'one another' is used in each of the four phrases.

The 2:1-4 paragraph is one of the peaks of the hortatory subpart of the epistle. Its prominence is due to both the piling up of many nearly synonymous exhortations in v. 2 and the special literary style here.

**2:2d be closely united with one another** The Greek is only one word, σύμψυχοι 'united in spirit'. This is rendered in the display as 'be closely united with one another' since 'soul/spirit' here is figurative. 'Closely' renders the intensive sense found both in σύμψυχοι and in 2:2b-e as a whole.

**2:2e *live*\* harmoniously with one another** The first and last constituents of this four-part unit are very similar both in form and in meaning—τὸ αὐτὸ φρονῆτε... τὸ ἓν φρονοῦντες 'the same you should think...the one (thing) thinking'. The repetition suggests that the function of 2e is to emphasize unity rather than add some nuance of meaning not in τὸ αὐτὸ φρονῆτε. The rendering in the display is a synonym of 'agree together': '*live*\* harmoniously with one another'. The asterisk is on 'live' because it is not used in its primary sense of 'to be alive, exist' but "to pass life in a specified manner" (Funk and Wagnalls, entry 8), a sense not always translatable as 'live' across languages.

Moore (p. 50) takes the 2:2b, 2d, and 2e constituents as nearly synonymous.

**2:3-4** A generic-specific relationship might be suggested for the relationship between 2:2b-e and 2:3-4. But while this can be seen to some extent, there is not a clear overall pattern, and 2:3-4 is taken simply as amplification of 2:2b-e.

**2:3a Never try to selfishly advance yourselves ahead of *one another* nor boast *about what you are doing*** The Greek is μηδὲν κατ' ἐριθείαν μηδὲ κατὰ κενοδοξίαν 'nothing in accord with selfish ambition nor in accord with vainglory'. No verb occurs in the Greek text but since the accusative form μηδέν 'nothing' occurs as object, either the verb 'do' or the participle φρονοῦντες 'thinking', which immediately precedes μηδέν in v. 2, might be supplied. The two κατά constructions (κατ' ἐριθείαν 'according to selfish ambition' and κατὰ κενοδοξίαν 'according to vainglory') are either adverbial type modifiers of the supplied word indicating the manner in which the action is not to be done or they indicate the prohibited motivation for the action. The adverbial sense is in the display. The motivational sense might be rendered 'Never *do* anything because you want to get ahead of one another or because you want to boast about it' or 'Never *do* anything on the basis of your wanting to get ahead of one another or your wanting to boast about it'. The motivational sense seems more apt: The boasting is more easily seen as motivational than as the manner in which the action is carried out. But the propositionalization of the motivational sense forms a negative sentence ('Never *do* anything because...') not easily translated, so it is not given in the display. In languages where there is no problem rendering this negative motivational sentence, it would probably be the better choice as far as the thought patterns of the context are concerned.

The meaning of ἐριθεία is not especially self-evident from sources before New Testament times since it has been found in only one document, where it has the idea of 'selfish ambition'. Some believe it may be built on ἔρις 'discord, contention' and have the idea of 'contentiousness, strife', a meaning they feel is appropriate for New Testament occurrences (see BAGD, p. 309, and also the notes on 1:17). In this passage that treats relationship with others within the body of believers and also the right attitude toward one's own interests, it would appear that selfish ambition in its relationship to others within the body of believers is the appropriate meaning. Thus the display rendering is 'Never try to selfishly advance yourselves ahead of one another'. It also might be rendered 'Never seek to benefit yourselves at the expense of one another'.

The sense of κενός 'empty' in κενοδοξία 'vainglory' may be that the glorying is groundless or is a negative value. The focus here does not seem to be on a groundless glorying in the sense that one has not done the things he is boasting about. Rather it is on glorying for the wrong purpose—self-gratification. The negative connotation of 'boast' in English makes it an appropriate verb to use here. Because 'boast' is a speech orienter implying content of some sort, 'about what you are doing' is supplied. These words specify that the boasting is about their activities, which the context supports.

**2:3b be humble** The dative construction τῇ ταπεινοφροσύνῃ 'in humility' modifies either the verb ἡγούμενοι 'considering' or the verb phrase as a whole. It could be taken in an adverbial sense, 'humbly consider others as better than yourselves'. However, it seems simpler to propositionalize τῇ ταπεινοφροσύνῃ 'in humility' as 'be humble' and then take the following proposition built on the verb 'consider, honor' as either conjoined with it or a restatement of it. Since 'be humble' and 'honor one another more than you honor yourselves' overlap in meaning, the semantic relationship appears to be generic-specific: 'be humble; in particular, honor one another more than you honor yourselves'. Of course in translation, many languages would handle this with a simple coordinate or without any connective.

**honor one another more than you honor yourselves** Literally this is 'considering/regarding one another being superior to yourselves'. It does not seem probable that every Christian is asked to believe and consider every other Christian inherently superior to himself. This is hardly a valid assumption. Paul is talking about our actions toward one another, showing respect and deferring to one another. The construction might be translated 'treat one another as though the other person deserved to be honored more than yourselves' or simply 'honor one another more than you honor yourselves'.

**2:4a-b Each one of you should not *only* be concerned about your own affairs, instead, each one of you should also be concerned *that you help* one another** The verb σκοπέω, which is rendered 'be concerned' here, has to do with 'noticing, watching, looking out for'. The people (or things) to be looked out for may be ones to be avoided (Rom. 16:17), imitated (Phil. 3:17), or favored, as here. Thus it would seem that the verb has the sense of 'watching' or 'noticing' people or things in order to take some action based on what is seen, and 'be concerned' is an appropriate nonfigurative translation for σκοπέω.

There is no explicit noun in the Greek text as the object of 'look out for', only the plural accusative neuter article. Thus the implied noun would be 'things' or 'matters' if we want to retain the generic sense communicated by τά in itself. If we want to be more specific to the context, it would be 'affairs, interests'. But 'be concerned' in its primary meaning is neutral rather than an expression of only a caring attitude, so 'be concerned with the matters or interests of others' (second half of verse) could be interpreted as encouraging prying or undue attention in the affairs of others. (Loh and Nida also mention this possibility.) To avoid this, σκοποῦντες 'looking out for' has been propositionalized more specifically as 'be concerned *that you help*' in 4b.

**2:4b also** In the UBSGNT καί 'also' appears in square brackets indicating that its presence is not completely certain. Its absence in the original, if it was absent, might be due to hyperbole (in essence Paul would not be *prohibiting* the Philippians from being concerned about their own interests but this would be a hyperbole to emphasize his desire that they be less concerned about themselves and more concerned about one another). Therefore, if 2:4a expresses some personal matter that each believer must be concerned about, then 'only' might be supplied and 'also' would be seen as valid.

**one another** Though the primary meaning of ἕτερος is 'other', ἑτέρων is translated here as 'one another' since the focus is on the fellowship of believers in the whole context of 2:1-4 and since ἀλλήλους 'one another' occurs in the previous verse.

## BOUNDARIES AND COHERENCE

The initial boundary of 2:1-4 was discussed under 1:27-30. As to the closing boundary, there are some elements that signal a significant break at the end of 2:4, even though 2:1-4 and 2:5-11 are closely related. All the verbs in 2:2b-4 are grammatically subordinate to the verb πληρώσατε 'fulfill' in 2:2a. In 2:5, there is a nonsubordinate finite verb, φρονεῖτε 'think', which along with its full verbal phrase (ἐν ὑμῖν ὃ καὶ ἐν Χριστῷ Ἰησοῦ 'in you(pl) which also in Christ Jesus') is definitely connected with the following ὅς construction beginning in 2:6a. Also, Christ is the very evident principal character of 2:5-11. While 2:5-11 is closely related to 2:1-4 (especially to 2:3-4, in that it continues the discussion of humility with the example of humility in 2:5-11), 2:5-11 not only forms a very coherent whole in itself but is so outstanding in its subject matter and construction that it must be seen as a significant whole in itself.

The grammatical coherence of 2:1-4 is seen in the subordination of all of its clauses and phrases to 2:2a.

## PROMINENCE AND THEME

In view of the hortatory paragraph pattern of the 2:1-4 unit, the theme is drawn from the *APPEAL* and its two *bases*. The fact that there are many conjoined elements serving as the major components of the *APPEAL* and its *bases* makes it difficult to know which to choose to represent the equally prominent immediate constituents and at the same time maintain brevity. For the first *basis,* 'loves' has been chosen since it is one of the components of the *APPEAL* and is close in meaning to 'compassionate and merciful'. 'Encourages' has been chosen to represent itself and 'comfort'. To represent the *APPEAL*, 'agree' and 'love' are used ('agree' represents itself and 2:2d and 2:2e, which are close in meaning), and 'humbly serve' represents the POSITIVE constituents of the first and second amplification. (These constituents tie in with 2:5-11, a paragraph having a very close relationship to this one.)

# SECTION CONSTITUENT 2:5-11 (Hortatory Paragraph: Appeal₂ of 2:1-16)

*THEME: You should think just as Christ Jesus thought, who willingly gave up his divine prerogatives and humbled himself, willingly obeying God though it meant dying on a shameful cross. As a result God exalted him to the highest position, to be acknowledged by all the universe as the supreme Lord.*

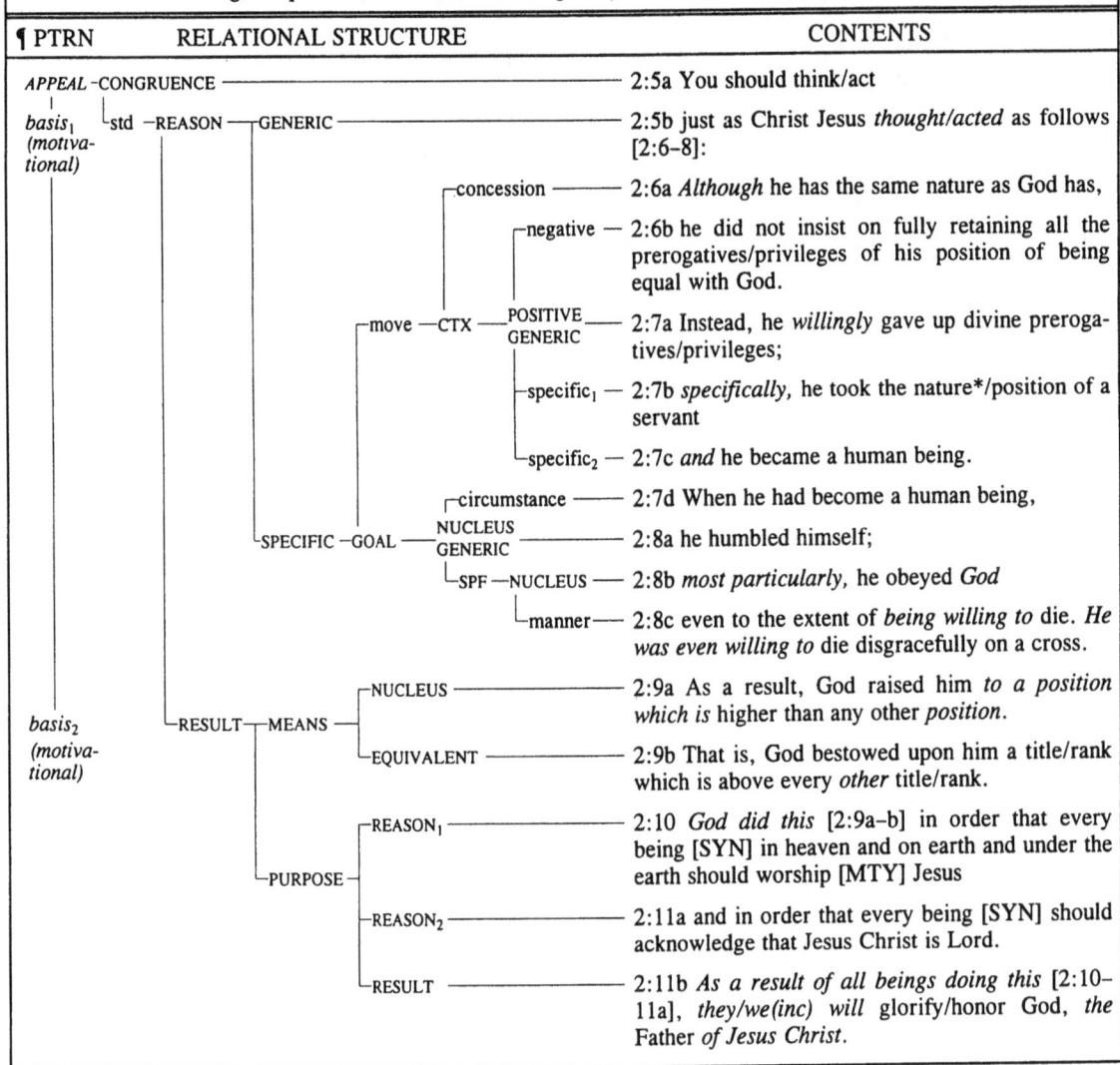

## INTENT AND PARAGRAPH PATTERN

The 2:5-11 unit is a hortatory paragraph as the imperative φρονεῖτε 'think' in v. 5 shows. Paul is asking the Philippians to imitate Christ's perspective on living for God in humility and obedience. Verses 6-8 describe that perspective, while vv. 9-11 describe the result of so living. The style of vv. 6-11 has led many commentators to believe that Paul is quoting a hymn about Christ's attitude of humility and obedience. This may be the explanation for the mismatch between the communication relation structure and the paragraph pattern structure. The communication relation structure is basically EXHORTATION-standard (CONGRUENCE-standard). At the same time the model of humility is motivational because it is the example of Christ himself and so it is considered as a motivational *basis* in the paragraph pattern structure. The result of Christ's model of humility is his exaltation (9-11). The RESULT has many prominence features, yet is not as obviously thematic as the model of humility. But it would seem that the RESULT can also be seen as a *motivational basis* for the APPEAL. The mismatch between the paragraph pattern and communication relation structure is best shown by double labeling in the display (e.g., *motivational basis*₂ = RESULT of standard).

## NOTES

**2:5a-b** In the Greek text for 2:5, τοῦτο φρονεῖτε ἐν ὑμῖν ὃ καὶ ἐν Χριστῷ Ἰησοῦ, literally 'this think in you which also in Christ Jesus', it is highly probable that the phrases ἐν ὑμῖν 'in you' and ἐν Χριστῷ Ἰησοῦ 'in Christ Jesus' express the same semantic relationships: one occurs on one side and one on the other side of a balanced, equationlike sentence. There is no explicit verb in the second half of the sentence. According to Alford and Lightfoot, the verb ἐφρονεῖτο 'was thought' is to be understood: 'this you should think in you which was also thought in Christ Jesus'. In a balanced, equationlike construction where there is no explicit verb in the second half but one is clearly implied, we would expect that verb to be the same as the one in the first half, unless there is some good reason not to do so. The demonstrative pronoun τοῦτο 'this' refers forward to the relative pronoun ὃ 'which', and ὃ in turn is explained specifically in vv. 6-8. At the same time there is at least an implicit reference backward to the APPEALS of 2:1-4: 'Have this attitude of love and humility toward one another, the same attitude which Christ Jesus had'.

**2:5a You should think/act** The most literal equivalent of φρονέω is 'think'. But in this context, it is more appropriately rendered in English by the abstract noun 'attitude' ('have the same attitude Christ Jesus had') since 'think' in English may not adequately cover this sense of φρονέω. In vv. 6-8 the example of Christ Jesus in regard to this attitude consists not only of an attitude of the mind but an outworking of that attitude in actions. Therefore, if 'think' in any language does not adequately cover the idea of an attitude leading to action, something like 'you must do just as Christ Jesus did' or 'you must act just as Christ Jesus acted' might be appropriate (cf. Loh and Nida). Of course, no human can think or act exactly as Christ thought or acted, but as Christians we are to seek the same general attitude and way of life that he exhibited as set forth in vv. 6-8.

**2:5b just as Christ Jesus *thought/acted* as follows [2:6-8]** This proposition is a generic introduction to Christ's model of correct attitude.

The interpretation taken here is that vv. 5-11 present Christ's life of humility as a model for believers. Some commentators, however, do not see it this way since the exaltation theme in vv. 9-11 does not seem relevant to a model of humility and vv. 6-11 seem to function well as a whole in describing some other theme or in describing humility only in the context of some other theme. There are good reasons, though, for taking vv. 9-11 as connected with Christ's humility. Jesus himself said more than once that 'everyone who exalts himself will be humbled and he who humbles himself will be exalted' (Luke 14:11; 18:14). Since there were people within the church seeking power and prestige (as ἐριθεία 'selfish ambition' and other characteristics named in 2:3-4 show), Paul is demonstrating that God's greatest good is reserved for those who will adopt an attitude of humbling themselves. If they seek for power and prestige according to the values of this world, they will find nothing of real value to themselves or anyone else. But, if they will humble themselves as Jesus did, God will shower upon them the only honor that matters, and it is incomprehensibly higher than any worldly power or prestige.

The model of 2:6-8 does not imply that the Christian is to precisely imitate the actions of Christ. Indeed it would be impossible to do so. Rather, it illustrates the principles to live by. In the same way, the exaltation of the Christian is not to be compared in degree with the exaltation of Christ, but the principle is nevertheless valid. Note that 2:9-11 is labeled as both RESULT of 2:6-8 and *motivational basis* for the APPEAL in 2:5a. This double function shows that 2:5-11 is an integral unit in itself. Paul uses both the model of humility and the exaltation as motivational *bases* for his APPEAL to act humbly as Christ acted.

Verses 6-8 are analyzed as specifics of 2:5b. They are specifics of the way Christ thought.

**2:6a *Although* he has the same nature as God has** This is a participial construction in the Greek text. Participial constructions of this type may function as concession or reason. Other roles are also possible. The whole sense of 2:6b-8 is that of CONTRAEXPECTATION, that even though Christ had the nature of God, he willingly went to the lowest human depths (for the sake of mankind). In the display 'although' signals the concession relation.

Regarding μορφή 'form', Vincent says that here it means "that expression of being which is identified with the essential nature and character of God, and which reveals it." In a rather lengthy study Lightfoot (pp. 127-33) comes to the conclusion that μορφή "must apply to the attributes of the Godhead" (p. 132), to "the true divine nature of our Lord" (p. 133). A comparison with μορφὴ δούλου 'form/nature of a servant' (v. 7) shows that the latter would be translated more appropriately in English as 'nature of a servant' rather than 'form of a servant' since the word 'servant' describes function and status more than outward form. If Paul had said μορφὴ ἀνθρώπου, then μορφή might be more appropriately translated as 'form'. In English we refer to elements of God's deity as 'nature' rather than 'form', since 'form' in English usually has to do with physical appearance. For these reasons 'nature' has been used in the display.

**2:6b he did not insist on fully retaining all the prerogatives/privileges of his position of being equal with God** The -μος ending in ἁρπαγμός would normally indicate 'the act of robbing', but there are many cases with other verbs where -μος endings do not indicate 'the act' but something more concrete. There are very few occurrences of ἁρπαγμός in any Greek literature, but BAGD (p. 108.2) gives two occurrences where it basically means 'prize' (cf. Lightfoot). The Greek fathers took ἁρπαγμός in Phil. 2:6 to mean "holding fast to a prize already obtained" though the sense "the appropriation to oneself of a prize which is sought after" (BAGD, entry 2a) is also possible. Concerning the latter sense Loh and Nida (p. 57) say, "It is difficult to conceive that Christ could have given up what he did not have (cf. v. 7)." The display follows the meaning 'holding fast to a prize already obtained'. This fits the referential and thematic context best.

In order to avoid the perception that Christ gave up his equality with God, the rendering in the display of vv. 6 and 7a describes what actually took place more specifically.

**2:7a Instead, he *willingly* gave up divine prerogatives/privileges** What did Christ actually empty (ἐκένωσεν) himself of? Primarily, he gave up those features that had to be divested to become a human being and function as a servant. Lightfoot says, "He divested Himself, not of His divine nature, for this was impossible, but 'of the glories, the prerogatives, of Deity. This He did by taking upon Him the form of a servant.'" The display tries to capture this idea by the use of 'divine prerogatives/privileges', but avoids saying '*the* divine prerogatives', since not every prerogative was given up.

It is true that the display text rendering loses some of the all-encompassing sense of surrender or renunciation signified by ἑαυτὸν ἐκένωσεν 'he emptied himself'. In translation into other languages, the translators should seek to maintain the emphasis on the inclusiveness of the self-surrender (humiliation), while at the same time not suggesting that Christ gave up things that it would have been impossible or inappropriate for him to give up.

*willingly* The word 'willingly' is supplied because this idea is implicit. "The emphatic position of ἑαυτὸν points to the humiliation of our Lord as *voluntary, self-imposed*" (Lightfoot).

**2:7b *specifically*, he took the nature\*/position of a servant** It is not easy to decide on the relationship between 7a and 7b–c. A number of commentators see 7b–c as the means of 7a (he emptied himself by becoming a human servant). At first this might seem correct, but note that the result is not an intended result—Christ did not became a human servant so that he could lose many of his divine prerogatives. It is closer to the truth that he gave up divine prerogatives in order to become a human servant. There is no overt, normal Greek marker of RESULT-means here.

Others see 'taking the nature of a servant, becoming like human beings' as implying the same action as 'he emptied himself'. If this is true, then 7b–c is some type of restatement of 7a. It is probably a type of generic-specific relationship where the specifics are stated in an opposite, though not contrastive, way to the generic.

While it is good to keep the lexical contrast between '*nature* of God' in 6a and '*nature* of a servant' in this verse, it may not always be possible in translation. Even in English it seems that the sense of 'nature' in 6a is different from that here in 7b. 'Nature of God' has to do with the inherent qualities of a certain type of being, while 'nature of a servant' has to do with the comparative status and function of members of the same type of being or between types of being.

**2:7c *and* he became a human being** This proposition is in a conjoined relationship with 2:7b, restating 2:7a in a second way. The Greek text translated literally is 'Having been born/ having become in likeness of men (i.e., human beings)'. In this context there is no real difference between 'having been born' and 'having become'.

The major question is, What is intended by ἐν ὁμοιώματι ἀνθρώπων 'in (the) likeness of men'? Many commentators make a point of the fact that 'likeness' reflects the idea that, although Christ was a real human being, he was not completely the same as a human being since he was divine as well. However, the focus of the passage is on the depth to which Christ lowered himself. He lowered himself to become a human being, not something higher than a human being. If one studies the other occurrences of ὁμοίωμα 'likeness' in the New Testament and other early Christian literature it will be evident that in at least some occurrences the idea is 'likeness' in the sense of 'sameness'. Note, for instance, the comment in BAGD (p. 567.1) regarding Rom. 5:14, ἁμαρτήσαντας ἐπὶ τῷ ὁμοιώματι τῆς παραβάσεως Ἀδάμ, "*sin in the likeness of Adam's transgression* (=just as Adam did, who transgressed one of God's express commands)."

Hence, the idea must not be communicated in translation that Christ was not a real human being, but only like one (see 1 John 4:2). It is not incorrect to translate as 'became a human being' as the preceding considerations have shown.

**2:7d When he had become a human being**
The Greek is καὶ σχήματι εὑρεθεὶς ὡς ἄνθρωπος 'and in appearance being found as a man'. It is difficult to know whether this is connected to ἐν ὁμοιώματι ἀνθρώπων γενόμενος 'having become in the likeness of men' or whether it begins a new sentence. The clearest presentation of the problem that I have found is that of Ellicott who takes καί 'and' as beginning what is in effect a new sentence rather than connecting the final clause of the previous sentence. He says that taking ἐταπείνωσεν 'he humbled' (2:8a) as the beginning of a new unit is too abrupt a separation "in a group of clauses which have a close logical and historical coherence" and that such an abrupt separation "is improbable, and apparently unprecedented." This abrupt separation is avoided by taking the καὶ...εὑρεθεὶς... 'and...being found...' participial construction as relating forward.

In the other view, the most apparent reason for connecting the three participial constructions (2:7b-d) closely together is their similarity in structure and meaning. However, one wonders if the third clause would not have had the participle at the end like the first two, if such close uninterrupted parallelism were intended. My conclusion is that the evidence and commentary support are slightly in favor of taking 'and in appearance being found as a man' with 'he humbled himself'. If this participial construction *is* taken with the following clause, the relation between the two is a temporal one, 'when he had become a human being'.

As to the relationship of 2:6-7c with 2:7d-8, many commentators see 'he humbled himself' as a further step after 'he emptied himself'. Greenlee (1992) gives the sense as "after emptying himself to become a man, he then humbled himself." This is a move-GOAL relation, a relation common to narrative genre but which sometimes manifests itself in other genres. This model of Jesus' life, though it is basically logical reasoning, of necessity has some elements of narrative in it. (For another instance of a move-GOAL (step-GOAL) relation in hortatory genre, see J. Callow, 1982:86.)

Commentators make much of the fact that σχῆμα refers to the outward appearance of an object. But what is in focus here is Christ's inherent nature as a human being, not merely how he appeared to others. Neither is there any component of meaning of εὑρίσκω 'found' that forces us to understand others as actively involved in the action; the meaning is not 'people saw him as a human being'. See the usages of εὑρίσκω in BAGD, p. 325.2, under the sense "*be found, appear, prove, be shown* (to be)."

**2:8a-b he humbled himself;** *most particularly,* **he obeyed God** Regarding the relation of 8a with 8b-c, in his life on earth Christ humbled himself in many ways. The humbling of himself in which he was obedient even to the extent of dying on a cross is one specific action (or one series of actions) within the many actions in his earthly life that may be described as a whole as 'he humbled himself'. This specific action is singled out as the most significant instance of Christ's humbling himself, hence the GENERIC-SPECIFIC labels in the display. Vincent says about 'becoming obedient', "The more general ἐταπείνωσεν ['he humbled'] is now specifically defined."

Another option would be to understand the statement about Christ's obedience here to refer not only to the extent of his obedience but also to the duration of his obedience (i.e., through his whole earthly life, till the point of death). If this is the case, then the relation would not be GENERIC-SPECIFIC but AMPLIFICATION of 2:8a. Most commentators understand μέχρι θανάτου to refer to the degree of the obedience and do not mention whether lifelong obedience would also be in focus (see the note on 2:8c).

Most commentators agree that the obedience involved here is obedience to God. It is God who responds to that obedience in v. 9. It is God to whom Christ said in the garden, "May your will be done" (Matt. 26:42, NIV).

**2:8c even to the extent of** *being willing to* **die** While μέχρι 'until' is commonly used to indicate a duration of time until a specified point, it also has a nontemporal sense of the extent of an action, 'even to the point of' (cf. 2 Tim. 2:9 and Heb. 12:4). Thus μέχρι θανάτου 'until death' here may be understood to mean 'even to the point of being willing to die'. This sense is preferred over the temporal sense because degree of obedience and humbling oneself are clearly in focus in the context and most specifically in the following statement, 'even death on a cross'.

***He was even willing to* die disgracefully on a cross** The words θανάτου δὲ σταυροῦ 'death of a cross' identify (or describe) Christ's death as that of death on a cross, the most humiliating death one could be subjected to in the Roman world. Thus the components of meaning of θάνατος σταυροῦ 'death of a cross' are not only death on a pole with a crossbar but also humiliating, painful death. For this reason, 'disgracefully' is explicit in the display.

**2:9a As a result** The literal gloss of διὸ καί is 'therefore also' but passages such as Acts 10:29 show that the sense of 'also' is so subtle and so intertwined with the reason-result meaning communicated by διό that the sense of 'also' does not normally need to be translated explicitly: the total phrase διὸ καί can be translated simply as 'therefore' or 'so', as many English translations do.

Since the communication relation here is REASON-RESULT, διὸ καί is rendered 'as a result' in the display rather than 'therefore', which is reserved for grounds-CONCLUSION relationships.

**God raised him** *to a position which is* **higher than any other** *position* BAGD (p. 842) glosses ὑπερυψόω as "*raise* τινά *someone to the loftiest height.*" The context clearly defines the meaning of ὑπερυψόω here, since the following construction says that God has given Christ 'a name/title/position which is above every name'.

**2:9b That is** The propositions 9a and 9b are equivalent. In such a relationship καί has the meaning 'that is' (see BAGD, p. 393.I3). Because of the occurrence of καί and because it is difficult to see any difference in prominence between 9a and 9b, 9b is labeled with a capitalized EQUIVALENT in the diagram.

**bestowed** As a basic meaning of χαρίζομαι BAGD (p. 876) has "*give freely* or *graciously as a favor.*" Several English versions use 'give' without 'freely'. 'Bestow' is used in the display since it is more specific than 'give', implying a gift of honor; however, the more generic 'give' is certainly a possible translation.

**title/rank** Rank is a basic component of the meaning of ὄνομα 'name' in τὸ ὄνομα τὸ ὑπὲρ πᾶν ὄνομα 'the name which is above every name'. As ὑπέρ 'above' clearly shows, this idea is in focus here (cf. Eph. 1:21, ὑπεράνω... παντὸς ὀνόματος ὀνομαζομένου 'far above... every name that is named'). Thus, ὄνομα signifies more than just 'name'—an appellation to distinguish one person or thing from another. For those languages in which 'name' connotes no sense of 'rank, position, title', some other word may have to be used.

**2:10** *God did this* **[2:9a–b]** *in order that* There is widespread agreement among commentators that ἵνα here means 'in order that'. It expresses a relationship of purpose: God exalted him to the highest position in order that every knee should bow and worship him (Jesus). But this is not the only purpose for which God highly exalted him. It would seem that the primary purpose was restoring him fully to the position he had from all eternity. However, the purpose stated in 2:10 is the one in focus in this context.

The comprehensiveness of the reference to those who will worship marks the purpose construction as prominent.

**every being in heaven and on earth and under the earth** 'Knee' is a synecdoche, the knee standing for the being as a whole. This phrase stresses the inclusion of all beings in the whole universe, both human beings and every type of spirit being. It is difficult to know whether 'beings under the earth' refers to human beings, demons, or both, or where, specifically, 'under the earth' is. For a language that requires a more specific word than 'beings', 'every human being and spirit being in heaven, on earth, and under the earth' might be one way of handling the translation. It seems best to use 'every being...under the earth' in the display rather than to specify a certain place such as hades or hell. If 'beings under/in the earth' is incomprehensible or has a wrong connotation, it is perhaps better to use an expression that describes the totality of the beings of the whole universe rather than trying to specify who the beings under the earth actually are.

**should worship Jesus** 'Bend/bow' is a metonymy, meaning worship.

Regarding ἐν τῷ ὀνόματι Ἰησοῦ 'in the name of Jesus', Greenlee (1992) lists ten commentators who take this phrase as "the basis for the worship and confession concerning Jesus which follows...: on the basis of the name of Jesus every knee will bow and every tongue should confess." Alford defines 'in the name of Jesus' here as "emphatic, as the ground and element of the act which follows." In some contexts, as here, what Alford means by "ground" and purpose are very similar in their relationship to the main clause: 'on the basis of the name of Jesus every knee should bow' and 'every knee should bow in order to honor Jesus' are not really different semantically. And 'at the name of Jesus every knee should bow' basically has the same meaning.

**2:11a acknowledge** Some exegetes hold that ἐξομολογέομαι means 'to confess or acknowledge publicly or openly' while others do not mention the component of openness. As far as translation is concerned, a representation of the latter idea ('publicly') is appropriate as long as the main point of the content of the confession, 'Jesus Christ is Lord', is kept in focus. Here, of course, the confession does not have to do with confessing one's sins but acknowledging Jesus Christ as Lord.

**Jesus Christ is Lord** Bruce (1989) says, "In the Greek OT that Gentile Christians read, Yahweh was denoted either by *theos* ('God') or (most often) by *kyrios* ('Lord'); they reserved *theos* regularly for God the Father and *kyrios* regularly for Jesus." In this present context where every being in the universe is to worship Jesus, κύριος is a divine title and therefore may be translated by using an appropriate divine title. Another option is to be more descriptive: 'acknowledge that Jesus Christ is the one who is the supreme Lord/Master over all beings'; 'acknowledge that Jesus Christ is the one who is supreme over all beings'.

**2:11b** *As a result of all beings doing this [2:10-11a], they/we(inc) will* **glorify/honor God,** *the* **Father** *of Jesus Christ* It is not surprising that the discourse of 2:6-11, called the "Christ-hymn" by many commentators, ends with a doxology (see the note on 1:11c). The form of this doxology is similar to that of the doxology of the prayer in 1:11c: 2:11b is εἰς δόξαν θεοῦ πατρός 'to the glory of God (the) Father'; 1:11c is εἰς δόξαν καὶ ἔπαινον θεοῦ 'to the glory and praise of God'. As to the role of 2:11b, result, rather than purpose, has been chosen in view of the context (vv. 9-12), the topic of which is the exaltation of Christ as a result of his humbling himself. If 11b is taken as the final or ultimate *purpose* of vv. 9-11, everything else in 9-11 is moving toward that purpose and so the exaltation of Christ is somewhat downplayed. As far as the theme is concerned in this context of the exaltation of Christ by both God and man, the glorification of God is not necessarily more primary than the exaltation of Christ. It is, however, the ultimate *result*.

Proposition 11b has been taken as more directly related to 10-11a than to 9 since it seems that the real honor comes when everyone acknowledges Jesus' lordship. It is possible that 11b (εἰς δόξαν θεοῦ πατρός 'to the glory of God the Father') relates only to 11a, but it has been diagrammed as relating to both v. 10 and 11a for the following reasons:

1. Both 10 and 11a are closely related semantically, being simultaneous, almost part of the same event, and broadly synonymous.
2. Grammatically, they are closely associated: both are governed by the same ἵνα 'that, in order that' and conjoined by καί 'and' (in the UBSGNT, which takes both verbs as subjunctive, though it is true that the reading of the second verb as subjunctive is given a C, i. e., uncertain, rating).
3. Both contain actions which would bring honor to the Father: in 2:10, every being worshiping Jesus; in 2:11a, every being acknowledging that Jesus is Lord.

Since v. 10 and 11a relate directly to the model of Christ's life, which is the theme of vv. 6-11, they are perhaps more prominent than 11b. Nevertheless, as indicated in the display, 11b is also considered prominent due to its reference to the ultimate result of the events in 10-11a, glorifying God the Father.

**God,** *the* **Father** *of Jesus Christ* The word 'father' implies that God is the father of someone. The most likely relationship here is the one between God as Father and Christ as Son, since the context indicates that the glorification has to do with the relationship between the Father and the Son.

## BOUNDARIES AND COHERENCE

The coherence of 2:5-11 is seen in the paragraph pattern of an *APPEAL* supported by two *motivational bases*. Verses 6-11 are a coherent whole in that they relate the experience of Christ's self-humbling and exaltation. In v. 12 a new exhortation is introduced. There is a vocative in v. 12 and more often than not a vocative marks the beginning of a new unit.

## PROMINENCE AND THEME

The theme of 2:5-11 is made up of the *APPEAL* and the *motivational bases*. In the first *motivational basis*, both parts of the move-GOAL construction are significant. In the second *motivational basis*, parts of the MEANS and the PURPOSE are included in the theme statement (the latter because of its marked prominence).

# SECTION CONSTITUENT 2:12-13 (Hortatory Paragraph: Appeal₃ of 2:1-16)

*THEME: Since you have always obeyed God, continue to strive to do those things which are appropriate for people whom God has saved, since he will enable you to do so.*

| ¶ PTRN | RELATIONAL STRUCTURE | CONTENTS |
|---|---|---|
| basis₁ | | 2:12a My dear friends, in view of this [2:5b-11], and since you have always obeyed *God*, |
| APPEAL | NUCLEUS | 2:12b each of you yourselves should reverentially/seriously [DOU] strive to do those things which are appropriate for people whom God has saved. |
| | —amplification— | 2:12c *You should strive to do these things* [2:12b] not only when I am with you, *you should strive even more to do them* [2:12b] now when I am not with you. |
| basis₂ | CONCLUSION | 2:13a *You are able to do these things* [2:12b], |
| | —grounds— | 2:13b since God *himself* causes you to desire to do what he wants you to do and also enables you to do what he wants you to do. |

## INTENT AND PARAGRAPH PATTERN

The 2:12-13 unit is a hortatory paragraph as signaled in the Greek text by the imperative κατεργάζεσθε 'work out'. The *bases* of the *APPEAL* are stated both before and after it. Paul is encouraging the Philippians to work out all the facets of their salvation in Christ, especially those in focus in this section: unity and selfless service to others. He is also showing them why they should do this and how they can do it through God's help.

## NOTES

**2:12a in view of this [2:5b-11]** Many commentators understand ὥστε 'so, therefore' as introducing the desired consequence of Christ's conduct just outlined in 2:6-11. On the other hand, Heyward, in the earlier work done on the SSA of Philippians, saw ὥστε "as resuming the hortatory line after the long departure of the example of Christ in 2:5-11, essentially meaning, then, 'back to commands'." As such, a representation of ὥστε was not made explicit in the display of the earlier work. It is true that the *APPEALS* of 2:5 and 2:12 are not in a *basis-APPEAL* relationship with one another, but 2:5b-11 could be seen as support for the *APPEAL* in 2:12, 'Since Christ was so completely obedient, so you also should continue to be obedient in completing/working out your own salvation'. There are two problems with this solution: (1) It would use one sub-unit of a paragraph as support for an *APPEAL* in a different paragraph. (2) Such a sense does not collocate well with the καθώς clause ('even as you have obeyed'): 'Since Christ was so completely obedient and even as you have always obeyed, work out your own salvation'. It seems to me that ὥστε is not signaling a direct *basis-APPEAL* relationship, but a more oblique one. At the same time, it seems that this relationship should be signaled explicitly and not left wholly implicit: 'in view of this [2:5b–11]'.

**since** The Greek text for the latter part of 12a is καθὼς πάντοτε ὑπηκούσατε 'as/just as you have always obeyed'. It does not seem quite correct to take 'as' or 'just as' as signaling the Philippians' past obedience as a model. The force of the imperative κατεργάζεσθε 'work out', complete' along with its prominent modifiers suggests that they are to go beyond what they have done in the past. Thus, 2:12a is motivational, and καθὼς might well be rendered 'since' and labeled as grounds or *basis*.

**obeyed God** The object of ὑπηκούσατε 'you obeyed' is not explicit in the Greek text. Some commentators have proposed that it means obeying Paul; others, to refer to God. The main argument given for regarding Paul as the object is that what follows (12c) deals with Paul; thus, he is the implicit object. An argument against this is that these clauses actually are connected with κατεργάζεσθε 'work out' rather than with ὑπηκούσατε 'you obeyed'. In favor of taking 'God' to be the object of 'you obeyed' is that this is also the most likely object of γενόμενος ὑπήκοος 'being obedient' in 2:8, which has a connection with ὑπηκούσατε 'you obeyed' here. While there is a sense in which one could say the Philippians had obeyed Paul, the ultimate sense here appears to be that of obeying God.

**2:12b** There is a difference of opinion as to whether μὴ ὡς ἐν τῇ παρουσίᾳ μου μόνον ἀλλὰ νῦν πολλῷ μᾶλλον ἐν τῇ ἀπουσίᾳ μου 'not as in my presence only but now much more in my absence' is subordinate to ὑπηκούσατε 'you obeyed' in 2:12a or to κατεργάζεσθε 'work out' at the end of the verse. Regarding the negatives οὐ and μή, BDF (§ 426) says: "Essentially everything can be subsumed under one rule for the Koine of the NT: οὐ negates the indicative, μή the remaining moods including the infinitive and participle." If this rule is valid, then one would have expected οὐ to occur here if the construction were to be connected with the preceding ὑπηκούσατε indicative clause. The occurrence of μή suggests that it connects with κατεργάζεσθε 'work out', an imperative, which, according to the above rule, would normally take a μή. Since a signal of some type is needed if the reader is to know where to connect this construction beginning with μή, it seems best to take the primary formal function of μή as such a signal.

Verse 12 in the Greek text is quite complex, especially with its forefronting of multiple phrases before the main verb. The phrases about Paul's presence and absence need to be reordered as amplification (12c) of the NUCLEUS.

**each of you yourselves** Some commentators state that τὴν ἑαυτῶν σωτηρίαν 'your own salvation' is used by Paul to point out that now that he is absent from the Philippians they are not to depend on him but to work out *their own* salvation.

**reverentially/seriously [DOU]** The Greek is μετὰ φόβου καὶ τρόμου 'with fear and trembling', an idiomatic expression. These words occur together often in the Septuagint and 'trembling' is obviously idiomatic in many of the places where they occur together (see 2 Cor. 7:15; Eph. 6:5, and compare 1 Cor. 2:3). Here the phrase is adverbial and it could be so translated ('work out your own salvation with reverential fear'); or it could be translated as a subordinate clause specifying the object of the fear ('strive to do those things which are appropriate for people whom God has saved lest you fail to do them').

**strive** The forefronting of the qualifying phrases before the verb marks emphasis on the effort the Philippians should give to carrying out the action. This is expressed by 'strive'.

**do those things which are appropriate for people whom God has saved** It is obvious that the meaning of σωτηρίαν 'salvation' here is not just being saved from hell, since we are saved in that sense only by God's gracious gift through faith. Greenlee (1992) interprets the majority view as "work for the full realization of your salvation in your life."

Some commentators take 'salvation' to refer to the spiritual well-being of the Philippian church as a whole. Martin (1980) says, "There cannot be an individualistic sense attached to salvation here since Paul has the entire Church in view. They are encouraged to work at their salvation, by which we should understand (following J. H. Michael, 'Work out Your own Salvation', *Expositor* 9th ser., 12, (1924), pp. 439–50) the health of the church which was sorely distressed by rivalries and petty squabbles." He also says, in regard to 'your own', that it "cannot mean that each church member is to concentrate on his own soul's salvation, since Paul has bidden them to do the opposite in 2:4." But Paul is not necessarily talking about salvation at all in 2:4. And in vv. 3

and 4 Paul's use of ἑαυτῶν 'yourselves' refers to their own individual interests, and it could mean their own individual salvation here in v. 12 (see Eadie and O'Brien 1991).

**2:13a** *You are able to do these things* **[2:12b]** Verse 13 may be seen as a type of *motivational basis* for the APPEAL in v. 12 since it shows the believers how they can fulfill that APPEAL: '*You are able to do these things* since God himself will enable you'. What is supplied in 2:13a is a missing logical step.

**2:13b** God *himself* There is no doubt that there is a contrast here between the ability of the Philippians in themselves to become what they ought to be and the ability of God to make them what they ought to be. Some see the occurrence of θεός 'God' first in the clause as also signaling this. The word 'himself' is supplied to indicate emphasis.

**causes you to desire to do what he wants you to do** BAGD (ἐνεργέω, p. 265.2) translates ὁ ἐνεργῶν ἐν ὑμῖν τὸ θέλειν as "*he produces the will in you.*" In propositionalizing, the abstract noun 'will' becomes 'to will, want, desire'; 'produces' becomes 'causes'; and 'you' becomes the agent of 'to will' instead of the object of 'in'. In translating this in some languages, a more specific, possibly figurative, phrase with a locative sense, such as 'he prepares/influences your heart', might be appropriate.

There is some question as to whether 'causes you to desire/want' is a universally acceptable collocation since 'desire' in some thought systems may always be considered as spontaneous, incapable of being influenced by an outside cause. Where this is the case, the meaning will have to be conveyed in some other way.

## BOUNDARIES AND COHERENCE

It seems best to see 2:12–13 as a separate paragraph from a unit beginning at 2:14 since 2:12–13 has its own hortatory paragraph pattern of an APPEAL with one *basis* before and one *basis* after. At the beginning of 2:14 is an imperative signaling another APPEAL and the following purpose construction in 2:15 acts as a *basis* for it. It is true that 2:14–15b might be seen as the manner of carrying out the APPEAL of 2:12, but this does not outweigh the fact that 2:12–13 has its own paragraph pattern.

## PROMINENCE AND THEME

The theme includes a representation of the APPEAL and both *bases*.

# SECTION CONSTITUENT 2:14–16 (Hortatory Paragraph: Appeal₄ of 2:1–16)

*THEME: Obey God and your leaders always and never complain against them or argue with them, in order that you may be perfect children of God, witnessing in life and word to the ungodly people among whom you live.*

| ¶ PTRN | RELATIONAL STRUCTURE | CONTENTS |
|---|---|---|
| APPEAL₁ (MEANS) | | 2:14 Obey *God and your leaders* in all things and never complain *about what God and your leaders want you to do* or argue *with God and your leaders*. |
| basis (purpose) | —NUCLEUS— | 2:15a *Act/Behave like this* [2:14] in order that you might be faultless and innocent and might be perfect children of God [DOU] |
| | —circumstance— | 2:15b *while you live* in the midst of people/a society who are wicked and perverted [DOU]. |
| APPEAL₂ (MEANS) | —NUCLEUS— —circumstance— | 2:15c *As you live* among them, |
| | —NUCLEUS— | 2:15d show them *clearly the way they ought to act/behave*, |
| | —comparison— | 2:15e just as the heavenly bodies show *an earthly road clearly to us(inc)*. [SIM] |
| | —AMPLIFICATION— | 2:16a Make known *to them* the message *that God can enable them to* live *spiritually/eternally*. |
| basis (purpose) | —RESULT— | 2:16b *I ask that you do this* [2:15c-16a] in order that I may be able to rejoice triumphantly on the day Christ *returns* [MTY], |
| | —reason— | 2:16c because *it will prove* I did not labor so hard *among you* in vain [DOU]. |

## INTENT AND PARAGRAPH PATTERN

The 2:14–16 paragraph begins with an imperative construction, πάντα ποιεῖτε 'do all things', acting as an APPEAL. This is normal for an imperative. However, instead of support for that APPEAL in a grounds construction beginning with a conjunction such as γάρ 'since' or ὅτι 'since', there is a ἵνα purpose construction. This purpose construction may therefore be a motivational purpose acting as the *basis* for the APPEAL. It describes the ideal to be strived for, 'perfect children of God'.

The verb form φαίνεσθε 'shine' in 2:15d, which may be indicative or imperative, is taken as an imperative in the display. The participle ἐπέχοντες 'holding forth' in 16a is also taken as an exhortation. At the beginning of 16b εἰς 'for' is taken as introducing a motivational purpose clause.

## NOTES

**2:14 Obey *God and your leaders* in all things and never complain *about what God and your leaders want you to do* or argue *with God and your leaders*** The imperative ποιεῖτε 'do' is the only verb in the verse, and the prepositional phrase χωρὶς γογγυσμῶν καὶ διαλογισμῶν 'without complaining and arguing' modifies it, stating the manner in which one should perform all things. In the propositionalization the abstract nouns are made into imperative verbs. The abstract noun γογγυσμῶν 'complaining, grumbling, murmuring' becomes 'complain'; the abstract noun διαλογισμῶν 'arguing' becomes 'argue'. Although the latter in some contexts has the positive senses of "*thought, opinion, reasoning, design*" (BAGD, p. 186.1), χωρίς 'without' shows that a negative meaning is meant here. For the negative meanings of this word, BAGD (p. 186.2) gives "*doubt, dispute, argument.*" In the context of 'complaint', the sense of 'dispute, argument' is clearly in focus rather than 'doubt'.

The grammatical structure and the semantic structure in πάντα ποιεῖτε 'do all things' are mismatched in that the Philippians are not being commanded to do all things. They are being commanded either not to complain/argue in whatever they do or, more specifically, to obey in all things without complaining or arguing. The first of these options might be propositionalized as 'In whatever you do, never complain or argue'. But in the context of vv. 12-13 (i.e., the context of doing God's will), the intended reference may be the more specific one. The word γογγυσμός 'complaining, murmuring' suggests a situation where the addressees are under the command of someone else and are unwilling to obey at least some of the commands. They may actually obey, but they are unwilling to do so. The use of γογγυσμός would call up the background of the Israelites in the wilderness who often murmured against Moses and God (see also 1 Cor. 10:10). That the Israelites are in mind can also be seen by the use in Phil. 2:15 of γενεᾶς σκολιᾶς καὶ διεστραμμένης 'a crooked and perverse generation', which is the same as the description of the Israelites in Deut. 32:5: γενεὰ σκολιὰ καὶ διεστραμμένη (LXX).

The ἵνα clause (15a) following the command of 2:14 reveals that the command's purpose is that the Philippians be blameless and innocent, children of God without fault. This reference to 'the children of God' might be taken as showing that the relationship of who is to obey whom involves the Philippians obeying God. However, διαλογισμός 'arguing, disputing' in v. 14 by its nature indicates that a relationship between people is in view: the people obeying their leaders. The wider context of 2:1–4 with its strong focus on unity of purpose among the brethren supports this, showing that what is being commanded in 2:14 could very well be intended to refer to preventing disunity. Another factor to be considered is that, as Exod. 16:7–8 shows, grumbling against God's appointed leaders is the same as grumbling against God. Therefore, in the proposition in the display, both 'God' and 'leaders' are supplied as ones to be obeyed.

**2:15a** *Act/Behave like this* **[2:14] in order that** In the grammatical structure vv. 14 and 15 are tied together: the ἵνα purpose clause at the beginning of 2:15 relates back only to the main clause of 2:14. They are also tied together in the semantic structure by the fact that obeying without complaining and arguing is related to being faultless, innocent, and perfect children of God. These concepts and wording are borrowed from the Old Testament (LXX), γογγυσμῶν 'complaining' (Exod. 15:24; 16:2; Num. 11:1; 14:2), γενεᾶς σκολιᾶς καὶ διεστραμμένης 'crooked and perverted generation' (Deut. 32:5), and even ἄμεμπτοι καὶ ἀκέραιοι, τέκνα θεοῦ ἄμωμα 'blameless and innocent, children of God without blemish'.

**you might be** The verb γένησθε can be translated either as 'you might become' or 'you might be'. In English, 'become' implies that the state enjoined has not yet been reached; 'be' is more neutral and possibly slightly more appropriate here.

**faultless and innocent and might be perfect children of God** The purpose for which Paul desires the Philippians' uncomplaining obedience is expressed with three basically synonymous Greek words: ἄμεμπτος 'blameless, faultless'; ἀκέραιος 'unmixed'; ἄμωμος 'without blemish'. Each of them in its literal sense is a negated negative and might be appropriately translated as a positive. Thus ἀκέραιος is often translated as either 'innocent' or 'pure', and ἄμεμπτος and ἄμωμος might either one be translated as 'perfect'. Note that ἄμεμπτος 'blameless' does not focus so much on the fact that no one would blame, or would have a reason to blame, but focuses, rather, on the desired inherent character of the Philippians. Thus it is not necessary to translate it as a verb with a supplied agent ('no one will be able to blame you for anything'), though that is a possible alternative.

In translating, if it is impossible or unnatural to use three different synonyms here, it would be valid to express the concept intended by Paul with just one or two terms. The use of three synonyms here indicates intensification, but it is difficult to know whether it is an intensification of the imperative aspect, 'in order that you *really* be perfect children of God', or of the lexical aspect, 'in order that you might be *completely* perfect children of God'.

**2:15b** *while you live* **in the midst of** The Greek is μέσον 'in the midst of', a preposition. For the display it could be rendered with a preposition only, but the implicit *'while you live'* has been supplied here.

**people/a society** BAGD (p. 154) classifies this occurrence of γενεά under entry 2, "basically, the sum total of those born at the same time, expanded to include all those living at a given time *generation, contemporaries.*" A crucial component of the word in 15b is pervasiveness, and thus 'generation' or 'a society' is an appropriate rendering in English. In languages where there is no appropriate word for this, the more generic 'people' may be sufficient if the pervasiveness of the surrounding society is communicated by 'in the middle of, in the midst of'.

**wicked** The first word used to describe the society that the believers live among is σκολιός, literally 'crooked'. This basically has a more generic sense than 'dishonest'. It describes the whole life of a person. In 1 Pet. 2:18 it is the opposite of ἀγαθός 'good' and ἐπιεικής 'considerate'. 'Morally corrupt', 'wicked', or 'evil' are possible translations.

**perverted** The second word used to describe the larger society is διεστραμμένης, the perfect passive participle of διαστρέφω. Its basic meaning in the sense used here is to turn away from what is right: 'to be perverted, perverse'. Because of the generic context, the perversion would appear to be focused on actual lifestyle, not just belief. It might be translated 'perverted', 'perverse', or 'depraved', or more generally as 'wicked' or 'evil'.

The words σκολιᾶς 'wicked' and διεστραμμένης 'perverted' may be interpreted as synonyms since they are used in a generic sense here.

**2:15c–d *As you live* among them, show them *clearly the way they ought to act/behave*** There are some good reasons for taking φαίνεσθε 'you shine' as an imperative, although its form here can be understood as either indicative or imperative. The genre of the 2:1–16 section is hortatory. The immediately preceding construction (2:14–15b) is a MEANS-purpose construction with the means encoded as an imperative and the purpose as a ἵνα clause, together expressing an EXHORTATION-motivational purpose relationship. It would not be uncommon for this to be followed by another EXHORTATION-motivational purpose, with the φαίνεσθε 'shine' clause and the ἐπέχοντες 'holding forth' participial phrase representing the MEANS and the construction beginning with εἰς representing the purpose (16b). It is easier to see the εἰς construction as motivational than as anything else, and motivation goes with exhortation.

The fact that the 2:15c–16 MEANS-purpose construction begins with a relative clause in the Greek text is no real problem. Relative pronouns and relative clauses certainly occur at the beginning of units even as large as paragraphs in Paul's writings. See, for instance, Eph. 1:11 where the NIV makes ἐν ᾧ 'in whom' the beginning of a new paragraph. See also Col. 1:13 in J. Callow's *Semantic Structure Analysis of Colossians* (1983) where good evidence is given that the ὅς construction begins a new paragraph.

The verb φαίνεσθε 'shine' or 'appear' is rendered nonfiguratively as 'show them' in the display.

**2:15e just as the heavenly bodies show *an earthly road clearly to us(inc)*** There is a division of opinion as to whether 'shine' or 'appear' applies here. (In one sense, heavenly bodies cannot appear without shining.) While the active form of the verb is usually used for the meaning 'shine', BAGD (p. 851.2a) and TDNT (vol. 9, p. 1) state that one of the meanings of the middle/passive deponent (the form here) is 'to shine' and give examples. TDNT (ibid.) states: "From Hom., e.g., Il., 8, 556 one finds the mid./pass. deponent φαίνομαι for 'to shine,' 'to gleam,' esp. 'to light up,' 'to arise and shine,' of heavenly bodies."

The immediately preceding context with its exhortation to holy living would suggest that the simile of shining as heavenly bodies among the ungodly refers to showing people by example how they ought to live at least as much as telling them by word of mouth.

The Greek text is ἐν οἷς φαίνεσθε ὡς φωστῆρες ἐν κόσμῳ 'among whom you shine as lights in the world'. The nonfigurative equivalent for 'shine' is not explicit in the Greek text. The point of similarity may be 'making something good appear to someone' or 'revealing something good to someone', hence 'show'. There is probably also an intended element of intensity since φωστήρ can be understood as a very bright light and the fact that a figure is used at all implies that it is to emphasize the action or attitude represented. Thus in the display 'clearly' is supplied in both the figurative and nonfigurative representations. One problem is trying to match the objects of 'show' in both. The solution for English that is in the display will not work in every language.

The noun φωστήρ 'light-giving body' is especially used of heavenly bodies. It is a generic term for the sun, moon, or stars (e.g., in the LXX text of Gen. 1:14 and 16). Many modern versions use 'stars' here (NAB, NIV, NRSV, REB, TEV). 'Stars' would be appropriate in representing the plurality of the believers, but not as appropriate in representing the amount of light given, which is important for the nonfigurative side.

**2:16a Make known** There is a difference of opinion as to whether ἐπέχοντες here means 'holding on to, holding fast' or 'holding forth, presenting'. Liddell and Scott (p. 619) give good evidence that ἐπέχω may have the sense of 'hold out to, present, offer', though 'hold on to, hold fast' is certainly another sense of the word. The reason the sense 'hold out to, present, offer' is used in the display (rendered 'make known') is that it parallels the sense communicated by φαίνεσθε 'shine' and the total clause in which it occurs.

If φαίνεσθε 'shine' in v. 15 is taken as an imperative, the participle ἐπέχοντες 'holding forth, holding fast', which immediately follows it here in v. 16, can also be understood as hortatory in function. The parallelism of the two constructions and the hortatory nature of the paragraph suggest that 16a is hortatory in function just as 15c-e is.

The relationship of 2:15c-e and 2:16a could be taken as either equivalent or amplificatory, but because 'word of life' is not explicitly expressed in 2:15c-e, 2:16a is here considered an amplification of the witness concepts of 2:15c-e. Because 2:16a is an exhortation, it is also prominent and its label in the diagram is in upper case letters.

**live** *spiritually/eternally* 'Life' here does not refer to physical life, which is the primary meaning of 'life' in English. The ungodly people with whom the word of life is to be shared already have physical life, so here it is 'spiritual life, eternal life' that is in view.

**2:16b** *I ask that you do this* **[2:15c–16a] in order that** The εἰς construction here does not express the primary intended purpose of Paul's injunctions. His primary purpose in encouraging them to be shining witnesses is not that he may boast or rejoice on the day of Christ, but that God's purpose of bringing unbelievers to himself might be accomplished. The εἰς construction thus expresses a secondary (though highly motivational) purpose.

Here, because ἐν οἷς 'among whom' is taken as beginning a new sub-unit, and because πάντα ποιεῖτε 'do all things' has its own ἵνα purpose clause, the εἰς purpose construction is then taken as a statement of purpose of the construction beginning with ἐν οἷς 'among whom'.

**I may be able to rejoice triumphantly** The notes on 1:26a give the reasons for rendering καύχημα as 'rejoice triumphantly'. While 'triumphantly' is an adverb that has reference to an event ('triumph') and therefore would not normally be used in the propositionalization, nevertheless it is used here because it states the intended type of rejoicing more appropriately than 'rejoice' alone would.

**on the day Christ** *returns* The phrase ἡμέρα Χριστοῦ 'day of Christ' refers to the day when Christ returns. An alternate would be, 'the time Christ returns'.

**2:16c because** The conjunction ὅτι generally introduces either a CONTENT construction (translated as 'that') or a reason construction (translated as 'because'). Here in 2:16, the decision in translation depends on whether καύχημα is rendered as a speech orienter such as 'boast' ('boast that') or as a verb of emotion ('rejoice triumphantly because').

*it will prove* **I did not labor so hard** *among you* **in vain** Very probably τρέχω 'run' is a metaphor not for activity or life in general, and not just a generic metaphor for 'work' or 'toil'. Here it means 'run in a race', not 'run' in general. The primary idea is to put all one's effort into running a race. It is referring to how any event might be carried out, that is, with great effort put into it. Thus it is less a live metaphor here and more a use of 'run' in its secondary meaning.

To support this, Paul's use of 'run in vain' in Gal. 2:2 is in a context where a live metaphor would not be especially appropriate or natural. TDNT states: "Gl. 2:2 and Phil. 2:16 are very similar with their εἰς κενὸν τρέχω ['in vain I ran'] (Phil. 2:16 irrealis). Since the circumstances are different one may assume that the combination of εἰς κενόν with the verb τρέχω was a common use of the apostle's" (vol. 8, p. 231). A 'common use' suggests a dead metaphor, that is, a secondary meaning. Note that TEV translates this nonmetaphorically: "all my effort and work have not been wasted" (Phil. 2:16).

In this sense 'run' is basically synonymous with 'labor'. The two are used together to signal intensity. Therefore they are rendered here as one verb, 'labor', plus the modifier 'so hard'.

An alternate propositionalization for 2:16c would be '*If you do not do these things*, I will have labored so hard *among you* in vain'.

The words 'it will prove' are supplied in the display to fill in a missing logical step.

The double negative, 'not...in vain', is probably an example of understatement, a device that might be expected when Paul is talking about his own accomplishments since he would want to prevent any suggestion of the wrong type of pride. At the same time the double negative signals emphasis on the importance of the fruit of Paul's labors.

The double negative might be expressed as a positive: 'I labored and toiled *among you* successfully/profitably'.

The words 'among you' have been supplied because the context indicates that Paul is speaking specifically about his labors among the Philippians.

## BOUNDARIES AND COHERENCE

The final boundary of the 2:14–16 unit has been discussed already under the 2:1–16 unit.

If we look at 2:14–16 strictly grammatically, it contains only one nonsubordinate finite verb, the imperative ποιεῖτε 'do' at the beginning of v. 14. However, φαίνεσθε 'shine' toward the end of v. 15 could be an imperative form. Immediately preceded by ἐν οἷς 'among whom', it could be either 'among whom shine' or 'among whom you shine'. The relative construction in Greek does not necessarily signal semantic subordination but in this context it at least is a grammatical signal of a rather close lexical or semantic tie, the matter of living holy lives in the midst of a depraved society being discussed both before and after φαίνεσθε 'shine, you shine'. It seems best then to take 2:14–16 as one paragraph, even though it is analyzed as having two sub-units each with a paragraph pattern.

## PROMINENCE AND THEME

Since this paragraph has two *APPEAL-basis* units, each is represented in the theme. The second *APPEAL* is expressed as a participle in the theme statement for the sake of brevity.

## DIVISION CONSTITUENT 2:17-18 (Hortatory Paragraph: Appeal₂ of 2:1-30)

*THEME: Because I and all of you dedicate ourselves together to do God's will, even if I am to be executed I rejoice and you should also rejoice.*

| ¶ PTRN | RELATIONAL STRUCTURE | | | CONTENTS |
|---|---|---|---|---|
| | | | specific₁ | 2:17a Perhaps I will be executed/killed *by the Roman authorities, and my blood will pour out just as* wine is poured out *by the priest* when he offers the wine to God. [MET] |
| | | | specific₂ | 2:17b *For your part,* you believe *in Christ firmly* and as a result you have given yourselves completely to God in order that you might do what he wills, *just as a priest* offers a sacrifice *completely to God.* [MET] |
| | situation | GENERIC | | 2:17c *Because I dedicate myself wholly to God* together with you *in this way* [2:17a-b], |
| | | | concession | 2:17d even if *the Roman authorities should execute me* |
| basis | REACTION | CONTRAEXPECTATION | | 2:17e I rejoice *because I am giving myself wholly to God* and I rejoice because you all *are giving yourselves wholly to God.* |
| APPEAL | | | | 2:18 In the same way, you too should rejoice *because you are giving yourselves wholly to God* and you should rejoice because I *am giving myself wholly to God.* |

### INTENT AND PARAGRAPH PATTERN

The successive imperatives in v. 18, χαίρετε καὶ συγχαίρετε 'rejoice and rejoice with/for', suggest that this paragraph has a hortatory intent. At the same time, the successive indicative words χαίρω καὶ συγχαίρω 'I rejoice and I rejoice with/for' suggest an expressive intent. Since hortatory constituents tend to be supported by other types of constituents rather than vice versa and the grammatical structure and semantic structure in this paragraph also suggest this is the case here, the *situation-REACTION* embedded constituent (2:17) is taken as supporting the *APPEAL* (2:18), and the paragraph as a whole is taken as hortatory. At the same time, the *APPEAL* itself is expressive in vocabulary.

### NOTES

**2:17a** At the beginning of v. 17 ἀλλά occurs, which usually signals contrast of some type. There is no contrast between paragraph themes but there is contrast across the paragraph borders on the lower level. There is potential contrast between the rejoicing of 2:16 and the threat of death referred to in σπένδομαι 'I am poured out as a libation' in 2:17a. In other words, ἀλλά introduces a situation here that contrasts with the one in 2:16. The problem is that even though Paul introduces this negative situation with 'but', he does not react to it negatively, but with rejoicing (17e). So the 'but' does not signal something in Paul's attitude but something on the lexical level. Therefore in the display the contrastive connective is dropped and it is left to the context to signal this minor contrast.

**Perhaps** A conditional element is signaled by εἰ 'if' in the Greek text.

**I will be executed/killed by the Roman authorities, and my blood will pour out just as wine is poured out by the priest when he offers the wine to God** The verb σπένδω means "*offer a libation or drink-offering*" (BAGD, p. 761) and is used here in its present passive form σπένδομαι. The image is being poured out as a drink offering; the topic is Paul's being executed; and the point of similarity is the pouring out of liquid (in Paul's case, blood) in offering to God. Although the Romans would act as the agents of the execution, Paul is the agent offering the libation to God.

**2:17b** *For your part,* **you believe** *in Christ firmly* **and as a result you have given yourselves completely to God in order that you might do what he wills,** *just as a priest* **offers a sacrifice** *completely to God* The word θυσία means 'sacrifice'; λειτουργία in connection with θυσία would refer to performing the religious rite of sacrifice (i.e., serving at the altar, offering the sacrifice). But what does τῇ θυσίᾳ καὶ λειτουργίᾳ τῆς πίστεως ὑμῶν 'the sacrifice and service *of your faith* mean? There are basically two interpretations of this genitive construction. One is that "their faith is the 'sacrifice' " and the other that "their faith is the motivation for their sacrifice" (Greenlee 1992). For the first interpretation, in which the Philippians' faith is understood as the sacrifice, 'their life of faith' would appear to be the more specific meaning (Bruce 1989). In fact, if we take the sacrifice to be their lives wholly committed to God, there is no real difference between 'life of faith' and 'life motivated by faith'. Some consider the sacrifice to refer to the gifts that the Philippians have sent Paul, but that would seem to be only a part of their total sacrifice to God.

The image, then, is a sacrifice being offered to God; the topic is complete dedication of oneself to God; the point of similarity is the whole of the entity's being dedicated to God.

**2:17c together with you** The preposition ἐπί 'upon' in εἰ καὶ σπένδομαι ἐπὶ τῇ θυσίᾳ καὶ λειτουργίᾳ τῆς πίστεως ὑμῶν 'even if I am poured out as an offering *upon* the sacrifice and offering of your faith' indicates that Paul's offering of himself is intimately mingled with the Philippians' offering of themselves to God.

**2:17d even if** The Greek is εἰ καί, for which 'even if' is a well-attested translation (see BAGD under εἰ, p. 220.VI4). The context shows that there is undoubtedly a concession-CONTRA-EXPECTATION relationship here. People do not usually see their own execution as a matter of rejoicing. At the same time, εἰ 'if' shows conditionality as well. However, the concession role, which is taken to be primary, is the one shown in the display.

**2:17e-18 I rejoice *because I am giving myself wholly to God* and I rejoice because you all *are giving yourselves wholly to God*. (18) In the same way, you too should rejoice *because you are giving yourselves wholly to God* and you should rejoice because I *am giving myself wholly to God*** The verb συγχαίρω is usually glossed as 'rejoice with (someone)'. In English the primary meaning of such a gloss is that both participants are rejoicing together. But here, after using συγχαίρω, Paul goes on to use the word again in v. 18 asking the Philippians to also perform this action. This implies that συγχαίρω in v. 17 does not indicate the sense of the Philippians already rejoicing together with him. Possibly the simplest explanation is that there are two different types of situations when people rejoice together, one when something good has happened to all of them, the other when something good has happened to one (or more) and all the others rejoice with that one. In the latter situation they could be said to 'rejoice for (someone)'. Thus Luke 1:58 says συνέχαιρον αὐτῇ 'they rejoiced with her' or 'they rejoiced for her' where the neighbors and relatives of Elizabeth rejoiced over the birth of a child to Elizabeth.

Taken with this meaning of 'rejoice for/because' rather than 'rejoice with', the use of συγχαίρω makes sense in this context. A second question follows: Is χαίρω 'I rejoice' basically a synonym for συγχαίρω in this context, laying stress on the concept of 'rejoicing', or is there a distinguishing sense between the two verbs here? The use of the two similar words whose distinguishing characteristics have something to do with the participants involved could certainly imply contrast. If συγχαίρω means 'I rejoice because of what is happening to you' (or 'because of what you are doing'), χαίρω may mean 'I rejoice because of what is happening to me'. Certainly the context forces us to take χαίρω as at least meaning 'I rejoice because of what will happen to me'. Therefore, if συγχαίρω means 'I rejoice for what is happening to you', the two verbs are representing different senses in this context. The only question remaining is, Does it make sense in this context for χαίρετε to mean 'you should rejoice because of your situation'. The answer is 'yes' in the sense that it fills out the parallel-structured argument that Paul has set up: 'If I am rejoicing for what is happening both in my own life and also in your lives, you too should be rejoicing for what is happening both in your own lives and also in mine'. Or possibly better, 'If I am rejoicing in my sacrificial service to God and in your sacrificial service to God, you too should be rejoicing in your sacrificial service to God and in my sacrificial service to God'. The parallel structure is understood better if θυσία 'sacrifice' is taken not only in its denotation of a complete dedication to God but also in the connotation of its costing something dear to the giver (cf. 1:29-30).

Otherwise, the χαιρ- forms could be taken as more general: 'I rejoice *because of all of this* [2:17a–d] and I *especially* rejoice because you all *are giving yourselves wholly to God*. In the same way you too should rejoice *because of all of this* [2:17a-d] and you should *especially* rejoice because I *am giving myself wholly to God*'.

The Greek phrase τὸ αὐτό at the beginning of v. 18 can be translated as 'in the same way' or 'for the same reason'. Either one would make sense in this context but since Paul is phrasing his statements on rejoicing in parallel structure, 'in the same way' may be the better translation here.

## BOUNDARIES AND COHERENCE

The initial boundary of the 2:17-18 unit was discussed under 2:1-16. The final boundary is marked by the change of topic in 2:19 where Paul begins to talk about sending Timothy to Philippi.

## PROMINENCE AND THEME

Elements of both the *basis* and APPEAL are represented in the theme statement. Since the *basis* is basically a paragraph pattern itself, that is, *situation-REACTION*, both of these latter components are represented. Paul's intimate bond with the Philippians can be seen in the idea of *his* being poured out upon the sacrifice and service of *their* faith and in the use of συγχαίρω 'rejoice with/for'. For the sake of brevity only the nonfigurative meaning is used in the theme statement.

# DIVISION CONSTITUENT 2:19-30 (Section: Appeal₃ of 2:1-30)

*THEME: I confidently expect to send Timothy to you soon. He genuinely cares for your welfare, not his own interests. I am sending Epaphroditus back to you. Welcome him joyfully. Honor him and all those like him since he nearly died while serving me on your behalf.*

| MACROSTRUCTURE | CONTENTS |
|---|---|
| NUCLEUS₁ (COMMISSIVE) | 2:19-24 I confidently expect that the Lord Jesus will enable me to send Timothy to you soon. He genuinely cares for your welfare, not his own interests. I am confident that the Lord will enable me also to come soon. |
| NUCLEUS₂ (APPEAL) | 2:25-30 Since Epaphroditus longs to see you and is distressed, I am sending him back to you. Therefore welcome him very joyfully. Honor him and all people like him since he nearly died while serving me on your behalf. |

## INTENT AND MACROSTRUCTURE

On the surface the 2:19-30 section deals with Paul's intentions of (1) sending Timothy to the Philippians as soon as Paul knows what will happen to himself and (2) sending Epaphroditus back to the Philippians, presumably carrying the epistle. However, in view of the allusions to Timothy and Epaphroditus as examples of selfless service, it is clear that Paul is continuing the thread of the theme of unity and unselfish service to others even in this "travelogue." (Normally a travelogue would come toward the end of an epistle; the best explanation for its being at the midpoint in this one is that Paul wants to use it to strengthen his theme.) For more on this subject, see "Prominence and Theme" for 2:19-24 and 2:25-30.

While the genre of 2:25-30 is clearly hortatory, that of 2:19-24 is probably best taken as commissive, a subcategory of a broad sense of hortatory (see the discussion on "Intent and Paragraph Pattern" under 2:19-24 on the next page).

## BOUNDARIES AND COHERENCE

The two topics concerning the sending of Timothy and Epaphroditus to the Philippians cohere in that they deal with very similar content

## PROMINENCE AND THEME

Since the two paragraphs that make up 2:19-30 are in conjoined relationship, elements from both are represented in the theme. The elements that continue the ideas of unity and selfless service are also included. The section is not simply a travelogue, but these ideas are purposively woven in to support the letter's overall intent.

# SECTION CONSTITUENT 2:19–24 (Commissive Paragraph: Nucleus₁ of 2:19–30)

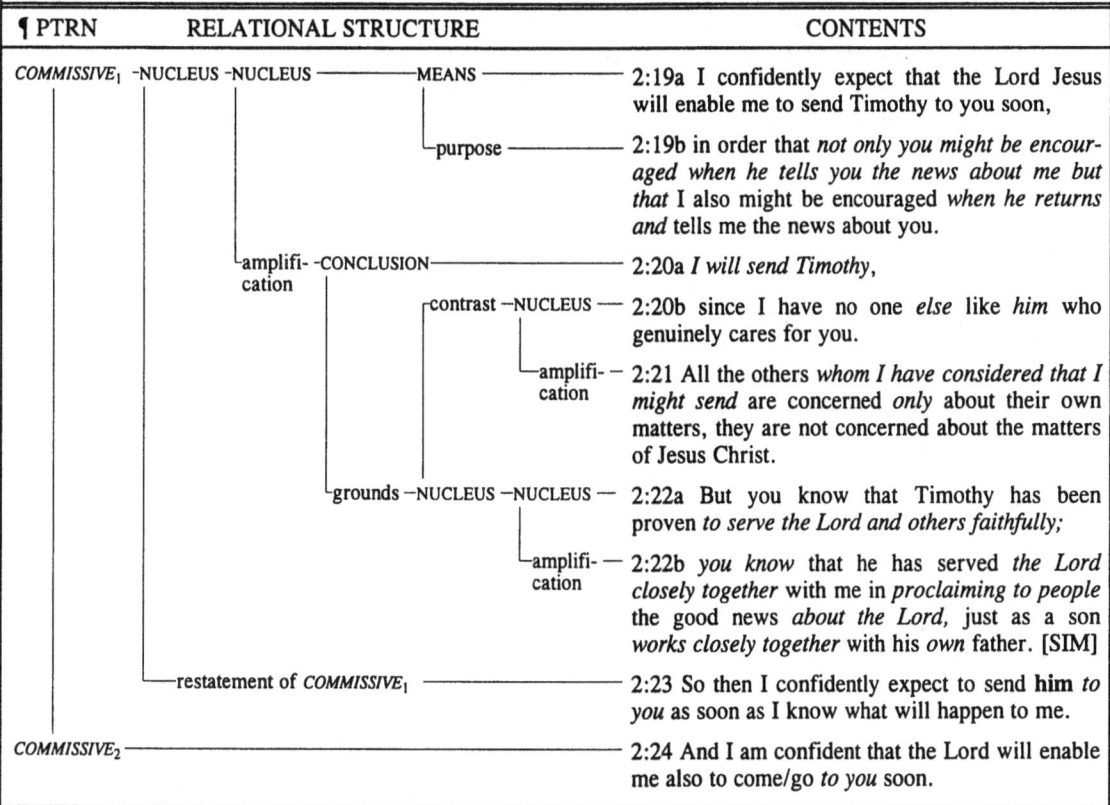

## INTENT AND PARAGRAPH PATTERN

In the 2:19–24 paragraph, Paul is committing himself to sending Timothy to the Philippians as soon as he sees how his trial comes out (2:23). This paragraph falls into a category that K. Callow (forthcoming) calls "commissive." It is akin to hortatory genre in that the speaker is committing himself to future action while in common hortatory genre he is directing others toward future action. In a second *COMMISSIVE* (2:24) Paul commits *himself* to coming to them.

## NOTES

**2:19a** The conjunction δέ at the beginning of this verse can be said to have a contrastive sense: the oblique reference to the possibility of Paul's death (σπένδομαι 'I be poured out as a libation') contrasts with his hope of sending Timothy to them and even of coming himself. However, it is more likely that δέ is marking a function on the paragraph level which could not be described as contrast and so it is not rendered as 'but'. It no doubt marks a switch to a new topic.

**I confidently expect that the Lord Jesus will enable me** Here Paul states that his basis of hope is in the Lord Jesus to fulfill his commitment; it is not in his own ability to do so. Some take ἐν κυρίῳ Ἰησοῦ 'in the Lord Jesus' as 'if the Lord Jesus wills'. But this would represent the provisio (i.e., condition) of the commitment rather than the strength of the intention. The word ἐλπίζω 'hope, confidently expect' indicates more confidence than English 'hope', and this word along with ἐν κυρίῳ Ἰησοῦ 'in the Lord Jesus' indicates a high level of commitment rather than a provisio.

**2:19b in order that *not only you might be encouraged when he tells you the news about me but that* I also might be encouraged** The word κἀγώ, a contraction of καὶ ἐγώ 'and I, I also', signals the implicit construction that is in italics here. Paul has already written much in the epistle to encourage the Philippians about his situation, including his immediately preceding words in 2:17–18. Now he emphasizes his desire to rejoice over *their* situation by not making explicit the part about their rejoicing over his situation other than signaling it with κἀγώ 'I also'. The implicit part has been supplied to indicate the full thought signaled by κἀγώ but it seems appropriate to mark the more focal part as prominent (i.e., that part which is explicit in the Greek text) by using 'not only…but also'.

**when he returns and tells me the news about you** The aorist participle γνούς 'knowing' in this context could be understood as indicating either circumstance, 'when I hear the news about you', or reason, 'because I will hear the news about you'. The word 'encouraged' implies that the news about them is good.

A chronological step is missing here, that of Timothy's return to Paul, which is how Paul will hear the news about them. This missing step is supplied in italics.

**2:20a–b** **I will send Timothy since** The conjunction γάρ 'for, because, since' does not introduce the grounds for the COMMISSIVE as a whole but gives the grounds for sending Timothy rather than someone else. To ensure the clarity of the argument, then, 'I will send Timothy', the sense of which is explicit in 2:19a, is repeated in italics in 2:20a.

**2:20b** **I have no one *else* like *him*** The rare word ἰσόψυχος 'of like mind, of like soul, of kindred spirit' necessitates the involvement of two different parties, but only Timothy is made explicit here. This leaves a question as to whether Paul means to say that (1) there is no one else with the same spirit as Timothy who really cares for the welfare of the Philippians; (2) there is no one other than Timothy who is of a kindred spirit *with Paul*, especially in his concern for the welfare of the Philippians; or (3) there is no one else who has a sympathetic spirit with the Philippians. Greenlee (1992) shows that commentators are basically split between the first two interpretations. Greenlee does not mention the third, though there are those who either support or mention it: Caird (p. 128) says there is much to be said for this position; Bruce (1989) and O'Brien (1991) mention it.

Some proponents of interpretation 1 point out that if interpretation 2 were meant, then Paul would have had to say, 'I have no one *else* who is like-minded'. But what he says is, 'I have no one like-minded', which if taken literally with interpretation 2 would mean, 'I have no one like-minded with me', excluding even Timothy. Therefore, the text would be easier understood to mean, 'I have no one like-minded to Timothy'. This is really a difficult statement to argue against, even though taking ἰσόψυχος this way (usually translated as 'I have no one like him') robs the word of its 'close fellowship' component.

If one of the other interpretations had been taken here, that would have required different components of meaning to be expressed explicitly in the display. But even though these interpretations were not followed, no meaning is lost because the components are explicit elsewhere (in the 2:20–22 grounds constituent).

Alternatives for 'I have no one like *him*' would be 'among my companions here there is no one like *him*', 'among those working with me there is no one like *him*'.

**2:21** The relationship of 2:21 with what comes before it is signaled by the conjunction γάρ, which may signal grounds, reason, or amplification of the same topic. The relative clause in 20b, 'who genuinely cares for your welfare', not only describes the attitude of Timothy toward the Philippians, it also describes the reverse attitude of 'the others'. They are not only *not* like Timothy but they also do *not* genuinely care for the welfare of the Philippians, the negative being found in οὐδένα 'no one'. Thus there are three parallel statements made concerning these 'others': They do not care about the Philippians, they care only about their own interests, they do not care about the interests of Jesus Christ. From this viewpoint, then, v. 21 appears to be a further description of these people, that is, an amplification.

It can also be seen that the reason Paul has no one else who cares for the Philippians' welfare is that all the others care only for their own interests, not for the interests of Jesus Christ. If Paul is focusing on the reason for their being the way they are, then γάρ should be taken as signifying reason. In that case, 2:21 would be a reason for 2:20b. Following is an alternate possibility expressing reason: 'because all the others are only concerned about their own interests'.

**All the others *whom I have considered that I might send*** The phrase οἱ πάντες 'they all' is defined by οὐδένα…ἔχω ἰσόψυχον 'I have no one like-minded', which is taken here to mean 'I have no one else like Timothy'. 'I have' indicates that the people in mind have some close relationship to Paul: they work with him and presumably are near enough to him geographically to be easily sent. In vv. 20-22 Paul contrasts Timothy with all the others that he has at his disposal to send.

**are concerned *only* about** The TEV translation "is concerned...with" is an appropriate nonidiomatic rendering for ζητοῦσιν 'they seek, look after, look out for'. (These glosses tend to be idiomatic in English.) A translation which includes the intensity of activity connoted by ζητέω would not be incorrect: BAGD (p. 339.2b) glosses this reference as "*strive for one's own advantage*" (emphasis added). The word 'only' in the display is used to fill in this component of meaning.

**their own matters ... the matters of Jesus Christ** The words τὰ ἑαυτῶν might be glossed as 'their own interests' or 'their own matters'. 'Interests' or 'matters' are abstract nouns, which in many languages would be translated *in this context* with a noun or noun phrase peculiar to the language (possibly idiomatic) rather than a verbal phrase. Some languages, however, would not use an abstract noun but a relative clause: 'they are only concerned about what they want to do, they are not concerned about what Jesus Christ wants them to do'.

**2:22a But** The contrast of Timothy's character with the character of all the others and the occurrence of the conjunction δέ show that the unit beginning with 2:20b and ending with 2:21 is in a contrastive relationship with 2:22.

**you know that Timothy has been proven *to serve the Lord and others faithfully*** For τὴν δοκιμήν, Beare, Hawthorne, and NASB all have 'proven worth', which sounds appropriate to the context. The Philippians knew (γινώσκετε 'you know') Timothy's worthiness to serve through having seen how he held up under trial while he was among them as Paul's co-worker (cf. Acts 16:1, 3, with 17:14). 'You know that Timothy has been proven *to be a good man*', or '...has been proven *to serve the Lord and others faithfully*' would be possible propositionalizations. In these propositions, however, there is a missing case role which would be obligatory in some languages. For these languages a more natural translation might be 'Timothy has proven/demonstrated to you *that he serves the Lord and others faithfully*'.

It is implicit that Timothy's proven worth or character is good. This does not need to be explicit in the Greek text, but it may have to be made explicit in some languages.

**2:22b *you know* that** The conjunction ὅτι could be taken as introducing a CONTENT ('that') after the orienter γινώσκετε 'you know', or it could be taken as indicating a reason ('because'). Since the result-reason relationship is not completely straightforward, the orienter-CONTENT relationship is perhaps the better solution. In this solution both 22a and 22b have orienter-CONTENT constructions and 22b is an amplification of 22a.

**he has served *the Lord closely together* with me ... just as a son *works closely together* with his *own* father** Many commentators say that ὡς πατρὶ τέκνον means 'as a child (serves) his father'. 'He has served with me' is the explicit, nonfigurative part of the comparison and so its meaning is of less conjecture than the figurative part, ὡς πατρὶ τέκνον 'as a child his father'. Thus it is appropriate to analyze the nonfigurative part first. In the phrase σὺν ἐμοὶ ἐδούλευσεν 'he has served with me', 'the Lord' is the implied object/goal of the service: 'he has served *the Lord* with me'. If πατρί 'father' were taken as the goal of ἐδούλευσεν on the figurative side, then πατρί would refer to the Lord, which is obviously not what Paul intended. Therefore, to avoid a defective comparison, it is best *not* to propositionalize the figurative part of the comparison as 'just as a child serves his father'. The following is better: 'he has served *the Lord closely* with me in proclaiming the good news, just as a son together with his father serve *their master*' or 'he has served *the Lord closely* with me in proclaiming the good news, just as a son *works closely together* with his *own* father'. If there are language constraints, 'serve' might be changed completely to 'work': 'he has worked closely together with me in proclaiming the good news, just as a son works closely together with his father' or 'he has worked as closely together with me in proclaiming the good news as a son works with his own father'.

***closely*** The implicit point of similarity between the two parts of the simile is that of working closely together.

**in *proclaiming to people* the good news *about the Lord*** For εἰς τὸ εὐαγγέλιον 'for the gospel', the renderings 'evangelize, proclaim the good news, make known the good news' would be fitting. These are a translation of the verb εὐαγγελίζω, which corresponds to the abstract noun εὐαγγέλιον.

Although others (Blight, Heyward, Miller and Rountree) have rendered εἰς τὸ εὐαγγέλιον 'for the gospel' as a purpose clause 'in order that *we(exc) might make* the gospel *known to people*' (Heyward), it may be more appropriate to see the relationship between 'serve/work' and 'proclaim the good news' as generic-specific. The reason for this is that 'serve' and 'proclaim the good news' refer to the same event, not two different ones. (A MEANS-purpose relation involves two different events.) In trying to translate this as a MEANS-purpose construction into another language, I have found the result to be incongruous.

Although my rendering in the display is not according to the normal rules for propositionalizing, it seems best to use this form since English has no other natural form for the generic-specific relationship in this context.

**2:23 So then** The conjunction οὖν signals the CONCLUSION of the reasoning in 2:20-22, but at the same time 2:23 is actually a restatement of the COMMISSIVE (2:19a). Unlike the structure of most of Paul's reasoning where the CONCLUSION is found either before or after the grounds, here the CONCLUSION is found both before and after the grounds. 'So then' is used in the display to signal the restatement of the COMMISSIVE after the statement of the grounds.

The COMMISSIVE of 2:19 and its restatement in 2:23 deal with more than just the fact that Timothy is the one to be sent. They deal with the purpose of the mission (19b) and the time of the mission (ταχέως 'soon' in 19a, ὡς ἂν ἀφίδω τὰ περὶ ἐμὲ ἐξαυτῆς 'as soon as I find out what will happen to me' in 23). Nevertheless, Timothy is especially in focus. Evidence of this is the forefronting of his name in v. 19a and the forefronting of the reference to him (τοῦτον) in v. 23, as well as, of course, the grounds for Paul's choice of Timothy, which is all of 20b-22.

**I confidently expect to send him** Since 2:23 is not only a statement of the CONCLUSION of the grounds for sending Timothy rather than someone else but also a restatement of the COMMISSIVE, the rendering in the display is better than 'So then he is the one I hope to send'. Note again that there is more to this statement than just the choice of Timothy. The time is also restated from 2:19a and expanded upon.

**I know** Although the literal meaning of ἀφοράω (ἀφίδω) is 'see', the idea of seeing how things turn out is somewhat figurative and so 'know' is used instead.

**what will happen to me** The phrase τὰ περὶ ἐμέ 'the things concerning me' means 'my affairs, my situation'. In this context where the result of Paul's trial is obviously in view, a good rendering would be 'what will happen to me' or even more specifically, 'whether or not I will be released' (Loh and Nida).

**2:24 the Lord will enable me** The reasons for translating ἐν κυρίῳ 'in the Lord' as 'the Lord will enable' are given in the note on 2:19a.

## BOUNDARIES AND COHERENCE

Verses 19-23 clearly form a unit of some kind since they deal with one topic, the sending of Timothy to the Philippians, a subject not mentioned before or after these verses. Although v. 24 deals with Paul's own visit to the Philippians, it is tied closely to v. 23 by the use of μὲν...δέ, a device that indicates close connection.

## PROMINENCE AND THEME

Both of the COMMISSIVES in the 2:19-24 paragraph should be included in the theme. As some writers have suggested, Paul's lengthy description of Timothy is for the purpose of using him as a further example of a correct Christian attitude. Thus the statement of Paul's intentions of sending Timothy has a dual purpose: it also lends support for his theme of unity and selfless service in 2:1-30. The word ἰσόψυχον 'like-minded' in 2:20 may even be an allusion to σύμψυχοι 'united in spirit' in 2:2 and μιᾷ ψυχῇ 'with one spirit' in 1:27. Also note the lexical similarity between οἱ πάντες...τὰ ἑαυτῶν ζητοῦσιν 'they all seek their own things' in 2:21 and μὴ τὰ ἑαυτῶν ἕκαστος σκοποῦντες 'not looking to your own things' in 2:4. Thus it would seem that some part of Paul's description of Timothy's character should be included in the theme. Normally that would be the NUCLEUS (2:22), which is more naturally prominent than the contrastive part (2:20b-21). But it is the latter that brings out the qualifications most specifically; so instead of using the vague wording of the NUCLEUS, the theme includes the wording of the contrastive part, but stated in positive terms to apply to Timothy.

# SECTION CONSTITUENT 2:25-30 (Hortatory Paragraph: Nucleus₂ of 2:19-30)

*THEME: Since Epaphroditus longs to see you and is distressed, I am sending him back to you. Therefore welcome him very joyfully. Honor him and all people like him since he nearly died while serving me on your behalf.*

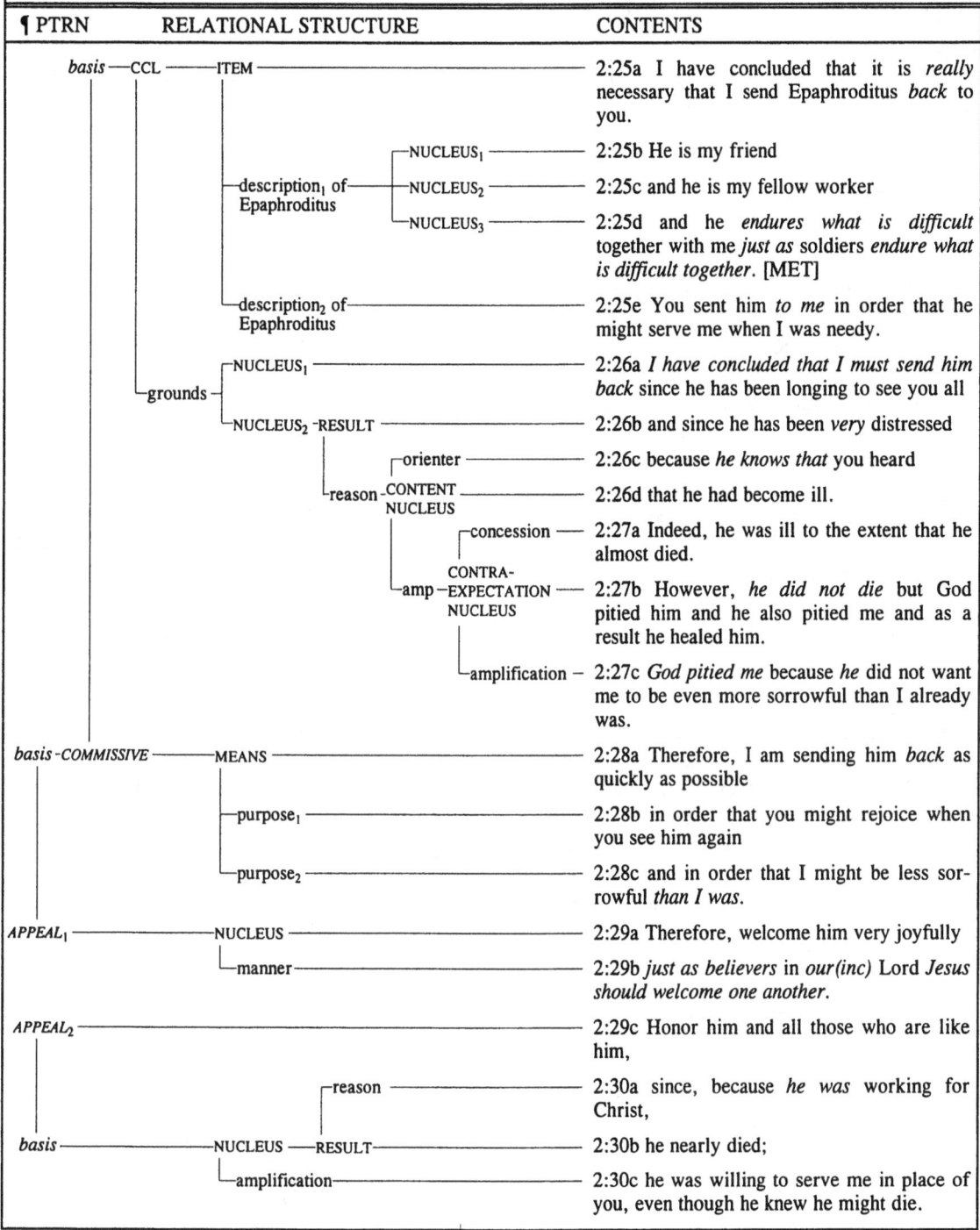

## INTENT AND PARAGRAPH PATTERN

The 2:25-30 paragraph has a hortatory pattern with a double-headed *APPEAL* requesting that Epaphroditus be welcomed home joyfully in the Lord and be held in honor along with all those who are like him. The *basis* for these two *APPEALS* is stated both before and after them. Both *basis* units could be taken to support both

APPEALS, but it seems better to take the first *basis* with the first APPEAL and the second *basis* with the second APPEAL.

In the first *basis* Paul comes to the conclusion that it is necessary to send Epaphroditus back to the Philippians, and based on this he commits himself to sending him back as soon as possible. (This COMMISSIVE is actually carried out by the time the Philippians read the epistle.) The APPEAL develops out of the COMMISSIVE.

This paragraph furthers Paul's theme of unity and selfless service to others.

## NOTES

**2:25a** The conjunction δέ at the beginning of this paragraph signals a switch of topic—the sending of Epaphroditus. There does not appear to be enough evidence that contrast is also intended.

**I have concluded** Whereas 'considered' is a more common gloss for ἡγέομαι, the fact that Paul has already come to a decision on sending Epaphroditus back to the Philippians shows that it may be translated as 'I have concluded, I have decided'.

**it is *really* necessary** The forefronting of ἀναγκαῖον shows that Paul is stressing the necessity of sending Epaphroditus back to the Philippians, hence 'really'.

**2:25b my friend** According to O'Brien (1991), "ἀδελφός...μου ('*my* brother') is not merely a synonym for 'Christian' (which Epaphroditus obviously was), but speaks of Paul's close personal relation with and affection for him as a believer." Michael and W. Michaelis (TDNT, vol. 7, p. 742, note 29) also hold this view. They take ἀδελφός in its larger figurative sense, not only in its specific figurative sense of 'fellow believer'. The phrase τὸν ἀδελφόν...μου is striking in that it is not really necessary. It may well be that it is included to emphasize that Epaphroditus is his *close* friend. Based on these considerations, 'he is also a believer as I am' would not be an appropriate translation. 'My friend' would be a possible translation, or even 'my close friend'.

As to the pronoun μου 'my', some have suggested translating it as first person plural inclusive: 'our(inc)'. But μου 'my' and ὑμῶν 'your' are juxtaposed indicating that they are contrastive and therefore the 'my' and 'your' relationships are to be thought of separately. Thus 'my' is better here. However, individual languages may have constraints that force the use of 'our(inc)'.

**2:25c my fellow worker** Other possibilities would be 'he/who works together with me', 'he works *for God* together with me'.

**2:25d he endures what is difficult together with me *just as* soldiers endure what is difficult together** The metaphor 'my fellow soldier' may be propositionalized in either of the following ways:

1. 'He *endures what is difficult* together with me *just as* soldiers *endure what is difficult together*'. This is based on the point of similarity's having more to do with the camaraderie of fellow soldiers to one another, rather than their soldier-like activity. In 2 Tim. 2:3 is an example of this metaphor with this meaning: "Endure hardship with us like a good soldier of Christ Jesus" (NIV).

2. 'He *defends the good news* together with me, *just as* soldiers *defend their country together*'. This is based on the point of similarity of defense by a joint effort. In Phil. 1:7 and 16 Paul talks about his defense of the gospel. In 1:27 he says the Philippians should contend as one man for the faith of the gospel.

There is a problem with the latter choice. It is activity oriented and therefore things tend to get out of focus if any attempt is made to render it less figuratively than 'defending the good news'. Therefore, all things considered, the first choice seems better.

**2:25e You sent him *to me* in order that he might serve me when I was needy** Paul is reminding the Philippians that Epaphroditus is one of them. They had sent him to minister to Paul's needs. As Paul has a close relationship and responsibility to Epaphroditus, so do they. As can be seen by the juxtaposition of μου 'my' and ὑμῶν 'your' and by the use of δέ, Paul is comparing and stressing his and their relationships with Epaphroditus.

The nouns ἀπόστολος 'apostle/messenger' and λειτουργός 'minister' refer not only to a person but also to certain events associated with that person: 'be sent' and 'minister, serve'. Hence they may be translated by verbs as in the display.

**serve** In the New Testament and other early Christian literature, λειτουργός 'servant' is always used with a religious connotation (BAGD, p. 471). It is used of pagan government officials (called λειτουργὸς θεοῦ 'servants of God' in Rom. 13:6), of heavenly beings, of priests, of Christ as the true high priest, of the prophets, of Paul as servant of Christ Jesus for the Gentiles, and of Epaphroditus. BAGD calls this last a figurative usage. This specialized sense of 'servant/minister' and its infrequent occurrence suggest that Paul is honoring Epaphroditus by its use, showing what an important position he has. This may be difficult to communicate in translation. In an attempt to communicate something of this sense, 'serve' has been used in the display rather than 'help', which some English translations use and which would be acceptable, especially in those languages where a literal translation of 'serve' would be impossible or inappropriate.

**2:26a** *I have concluded that I must send him back* **since** The conjunction ἐπειδή typically signals cause or reason (Louw and Nida 89.32). Because of the deep longing of Epaphroditus to see the Philippians and his distress over their thinking he is still ill (vv. 26–27), Paul concludes that he must send Epaphroditus back home. A summary of this CONCLUSION is repeated in the display at the beginning of 26a to show the logical steps that might be obscured by the long description of Epaphroditus that intervenes between the first statement of the conclusion and the grounds.

**he has been longing to see you all** There is a variant reading here of ἰδεῖν 'to see' after ἐπιποθῶν ἦν 'he was longing'. The word ἰδεῖν is not included in the UBSGNT text. The reading in the text is given a C rating indicating a considerable degree of doubt as to the absence of ἰδεῖν. In Rom. 1:11, the occurrence of ἐπιποθῶ ἰδεῖν ὑμᾶς 'I long to see you' shows that this is a natural Greek collocation (cf. 1 Thess. 3:6 and 2 Tim. 1:4).

In English, 'he longs to see you' is a more appropriate translation than 'he longs for you'. In other languages a more specific word than 'long for' may be appropriate in this context (e.g., 'miss, be lonesome for'), and 'see' may not be part of the phrasing at all.

O'Brien (1991) says of ἐπιποθέω 'long for': "The word group occurs thirteen times in the NT, eleven of which are in Paul, and each term has a positive connotation. The English rendering 'homesickness' does not quite catch Paul's meaning since it introduces a rather negative note. See the remarks of W. Schenk, 236 n. 55." Other commentators indicate that 'homesick' is a proper translation for ἐπιποθέω in this context (Hawthorne, Moule, Vincent). The sense of 'miss' (NJB, REB) or 'be lonesome for' may be a little closer to the meaning Paul intends since 'homesick' may connote an overly emotional state.

'He has been longing to see you all' is used in the display. A good alternate rendering would be 'he misses you *very much*', 'very much' being implied by the fact that ἐπιποθέω is a strong term (Hawthorne, Loh and Nida, Martin 1959, Silva).

**2:26b he has been *very* distressed** BAGD (p. 16) glosses ἀδημονέω as "*be in anxiety, be distressed, troubled.*" After using the same word in Matt. 26:37 to describe Jesus, Matthew reports that Jesus said, "My soul is overwhelmed with sorrow to the point of death" (NIV), which brings out the intensity of ἀδημονέω.

The imperfect tense of ἐπιποθῶν ἦν 'he was longing for' in 26a and of ἦν ... ἀδημονῶν 'he was distressed' here in 26b and the aorist tense of ἔπεμψα 'I sent him' in v. 28 are all examples of epistolary usage. The consideration of time is from the viewpoint of the addressees when they read the letter, not from Paul's viewpoint when he writes it. It is difficult to know how widespread this usage is among the world's languages and it is difficult to know which is the norm and which is the variant. But for the display the same tenses are used as in situations unaffected by epistolary usage. In translating, the tense will depend, of course, on the target language's own use for letters. Note that NIV, for instance, follows normal English usage and does not use the epistolary past tense.

In the display, ἔπεμψα (28a) is rendered as present tense, 'I am sending him'. However, the epistolary imperfect tense in v. 26 could be rendered either as present ('he is longing to see you all and he is *very* distressed') or as present perfect ('he has been longing to see you all and he has been *very* distressed'), since these verbs represent states rather than actions.

**2:26c because *he knows that* you heard** There is an implied step missing in the Greek text. His distress came from knowing that they had received news of his being ill.

**2:26d he had become ill** It may be appropriate to take the aorist tense of ἠσθένησεν as ingressive, 'he became ill, had become ill' (Muller). However, as far as the English translation is concerned, 'he was ill' is also appropriate.

**2:27a Indeed** The most common English translation for καὶ γάρ here is 'indeed'. An ascensive sense is signaled. That is, some meaning component of the construction introduced by καί is more intense than the immediately preceding construction: Epaphroditus's illness was *even more* severe than the Philippians had originally heard'. In the English translation, the ascensive sense is not signaled by the words 'indeed' or 'in fact' themselves so much as by the content of the rest of the construction. Rather, in this context these words basically deal with the truth value of the preceding statement, verifying that it is true. They do not necessarily indicate an intensity greater than that of the first statement. Although καί is different from 'indeed' in that it does not explicitly mark the truth value of the preceding statement, this meaning is implicit', and 'indeed' is therefore used in the display since it (or its synonyms 'in fact', 'in truth') is more appropriate for the semantic situation as a whole than any other English word. But for translation into other languages the semantic roles being signaled here must be kept in mind.

**he was ill to the extent that he almost died** The phrase παραπλήσιον θανάτῳ 'near to death' modifies the verb ἠσθένησεν 'he was ill'. This verb represents a state. Thus 2:27a could be translated into English as 'he was deathly ill'. However, since the adverbial phrase refers to an event, dying (though it is not realized in this case), there should be another proposition to represent the event of dying. The semantic relationship between the two propositions is represented in English by 'he was ill to the extent that he almost died'. It would seem that the proposition 'he almost died' (or 'to the extent that he almost died') is actually filling an adverbial position within the clause or verb phrase, even as relative clauses which contain a proposition act as adjectival modifiers.

**2:27b-c God pitied him and he also pitied me and as a result he healed him. *God pitied me because *he* did not want me to be even more sorrowful than I already was*** It would appear that ὁ θεὸς ἠλέησεν αὐτόν 'God had mercy on him' refers to both an attitude in God's mind and the resulting action, the healing of Epaphroditus. Although in English this might be rendered by 'God acted mercifully to him' or 'God mercifully healed him', 'mercifully' (an English device for representing the thought or attitude in God's mind) is not an option in some languages and can be represented only by a full clause. Thus the semantic structure is best represented by a full proposition rather than 'mercifully' alone.

Notice that there are two sequences, one for Epaphroditus and one for Paul: (1) God pitied Epaphroditus; as a result he healed Epaphroditus. (2) God pitied Paul; as a result he healed Epaphroditus and Paul did not have as much sorrow as he might have had. Unit 27c might be rendered as in the display or as 'God healed Epaphroditus in order that I might not be more sorrowful than I was'. However, one must be careful in translation not to imply that the only reason God healed Epaphroditus was for Paul's benefit.

**more sorrowful than I already was** Commentators tend to understand λύπην ἐπὶ λύπην 'grief upon grief' as referring to Paul's grief that would have come from Epaphroditus's death added to grief that he already had, whether from his captivity and its attendant circumstances or because of Epaphroditus's sickness. This can be translated as 'in order that I might not be more sorrowful than I already was', or 'because *he* did not want me to be even more sorrowful than I already was'. An alternative for languages where comparative constructions must be handled in more complex constructions than Greek or English would be, 'because *he* did not want me to be extremely sorrowful'.

**2:28a Therefore** This verse is a COMMISSIVE built upon the CONCLUSION of v. 25. The relationship is signaled by the conjunction οὖν 'therefore'. Note that as far as the addressees are concerned, by the time they read the letter the COMMISSIVE has already been carried out. That is, by then Paul will have already sent Epaphroditus.

**I am sending** See the note on 2:26b.

**as quickly as possible** For σπουδαιοτέρως here, BAGD (σπουδαίως, p. 763.1) gives a gloss of "*with special urgency*" under "*with haste.*" Another option for the meaning is 'very eagerly'. An adverb with a rather generic, intensive meaning, the meaning of σπουδαίως is influenced by the verb it modifies. When that verb deals with movement, as here with ἔπεμψα, a natural sense to expect is the haste of inception of that movement and/or haste of the movement itself. When Paul uses the cognate verb σπούδασον to modify Timothy's coming (ἐλθεῖν) in 2 Tim. 4:9, he is not saying 'be eager to come to me soon (ταχέως)', but 'do your best to come to me soon'. Thus in Phil. 2:28, an appropriate rendering is, 'I have done my best to send him back as quickly/soon as possible' or, more simply, 'I am sending him back as quickly as possible'.

There is nothing in the context that demands that 'eagerly' be used rather than 'quickly'. And the translation 'all the more eagerly I send him back to you' appears inappropriate because this would imply that Paul never wanted Epaphroditus to stay with him in the first place. However, the context implies that Paul is sending Epaphroditus back without reservation and he probably wants the Philippians to be sure of this so that they will also receive him back without reservation. (Note the imperative of v. 29, 'welcome him joyfully'.) Thus 'very eagerly' would be an alternate translation to 'as quickly as possible'.

**2:28b when you see him again** There is a question as to whether πάλιν 'again' modifies ἰδόντες 'having seen' or χαρῆτε 'you may rejoice'. Out of the twenty-three occurrences in the Pauline Epistles where πάλιν definitely modifies a verb, it comes before the verb seventeen times and follows it only four times. But here in v. 28 and once in 2 Cor. 3:1 it is difficult to tell which verb is being modified. Based on its most common order in the Pauline Epistles, it is more likely that πάλιν 'again' modifies χαρῆτε 'rejoice', which it immediately precedes, than ἰδόντες 'having seen', which it follows with αὐτόν 'him' in between: ἰδόντες αὐτὸν πάλιν. This does not necessarily prove that it is the correct solution, however.

From the standpoint of the most common semantic collocation, it would seem that 'see him again' is a more common collocation than 'rejoice again'. This is also more easily understandable in this context.

No matter which verb πάλιν 'again' does in fact modify, the 'again' sense is implied by the context as modifying the event represented by the other verb. They will see him again; and since they had heard that he was sick and so were saddened, they will rejoice again on seeing him home well.

The solution in the display is based upon what is likely to be the more common semantic collocation. This is the one the original readers most likely understood. But the view that πάλιν 'again' modifies 'rejoice' is just as valid.

**2:28c be less sorrowful *than I was*** BAGD (ἄλυπος, p. 41) gives as a gloss for ἵνα κἀγὼ ἀλυπότερος ὦ here "*in order that I might be less anxious* (than now=*free from all anxiety*)." But it is difficult to see how ἀλυπότερος, literally '*less sorrowful, less* anxious', can be taken to mean that Paul would no longer have any sorrow or anxiety. Lightfoot in regard to ἀλυπότερος ὦ says, "'*my sorrow may be lessened.*' The expression is purposely substituted for πάλιν χαρῶ ['I may rejoice again'], for a prior sorrow will still remain unremoved; comp. ver. 27 λύπην ἐπὶ λύπην."

**2:29a Therefore** The conjunction οὖν signals the APPEAL that is based on the COMMISSIVE of 2:28.

**welcome him** The verb προσδέχεσθε might be translated here as either 'receive' or 'welcome'. The latter fits the context very appropriately; it tends to have a more positive sense than the neutral 'receive'.

In some languages it may be necessary to supply 'when he arrives' to assure proper orientation. Note, however, that when the Philippian addressees read this, Epaphroditus would have already arrived bearing the letter.

**2:29b *just as believers* in *our(inc)* Lord *Jesus should welcome one another*** Ellicott says about ἐν κυρίῳ 'in the Lord', "Christ was to be, as it were, the element in which the action was to be performed." In many contexts this phrase can be taken as a periphrasis for 'Christian', and so here, as Ellicott says, "almost, 'in a truly Christian mode of reception'." In taking this a bit further, it would appear that when ἐν κυρίῳ occurs with an imperative, the sense is, 'according to the Lord's standard'. This might be propositionalized as, 'Welcome him very joyfully *just as believers* in *our(inc)* Lord *Jesus should welcome one another*'. Another possibility would be, 'Welcome him very joyfully *as the Lord Jesus taught us to welcome fellow believers/other believers in him*'.

There is a question as to what relationship proposition 2:29b has with 2:29a. Is it manner, comparison, or standard? In the Greek ἐν κυρίῳ 'in the Lord' describes the manner of the reception as does μετὰ πάσης χαρᾶς 'with all joy'. However, when all the components of meaning of 2:29a–b are related together semantically and represented in propositions, it is possible that 2:29a and b are in a CONGRUENCE-standard relationship (a subtype of comparison). The standard is that reception which the Lord expects those who believe in him to give one another.

**2:29c Honor him and all those who are like him** The Greek is τοὺς τοιούτους ἐντίμους ἔχετε 'such ones hold in honor'. A common English translation for οἱ τοιοῦτοι 'such ones' in this context is 'people like him'. But note that this translation tends to focus on the class ('people') rather than on the representative of the class. Here Epaphroditus is definitely in focus as one to be honored, and the *basis* for the APPEAL to honor him describes specific things he has done. One can hardly say 'Honor *them* since *he* has done such and such'. At the same time, τοὺς τοιούτους 'such ones' is plural rather than the singular Paul could have used if he was not also intending to exhort the Philippians at this point to honor all members of the class. Thus it seems best to keep Epaphroditus in focus as the one to be honored but also include all other members of the class: 'Honor him and all those who are like him'.

The fact that Paul is stressing the importance of serving one another in 2:1-30 would explain why Paul asks the Philippians to honor not only Epaphroditus but all who serve as he has served.

**2:30** There appears to be a chiastic structure here:

  **a**  because of the work of Christ
    **b**  he came near to death;
    **b'**  he risked his life
  **a'**  in order to make up for your lack of service to me

The two outer constructions (a, a') deal with Epaphroditus's ministry, while the two inner ones deal with the extent of his sacrifice for that ministry. This structure has been noted by Schenk (p. 239, as cited in O'Brien 1991). It suggests a NUCLEUS-amplification relationship.

**2:30a since** The connector ὅτι signals the *basis* for the APPEAL to honor Epaphroditus. This is, at least, the most direct relationship. It is true that 2:25-28 could be seen as the *basis* for both of the APPEALS and that 2:30 could be seen as a second *basis* for both APPEALS. Nothing grammatically or semantically prevents this. But there is a definite relationship between the reciprocals ἔπεμψα 'send' (v. 28) and προσδέχεσθε (first APPEAL of v. 29) and also between χαρῆτε 'you might rejoice' (v. 28) and μετὰ πάσης χαρᾶς 'with all joy' (first APPEAL of v. 29). Also, proximity and simplicity or directness of thought favor taking vv. 25-28 to most directly support the first APPEAL and v. 30 to most directly support the second APPEAL. Moreover, the concept of selfless service brought out in this *basis* fits very well with Paul's overall theme in 2:1-30 and thus relates well to the injunction to honor not only Epaphroditus but others who serve like him.

**because *he was* working for Christ** The abstract noun phrase τὸ ἔργον Χριστοῦ 'the work of Christ' is propositionalized here as 'because *he was* working for Christ'.

**2:30c he was willing...even though he knew he might die** The Greek participial phrase παραβολευσάμενος τῇ ψυχῇ 'having risked life' refers primarily to a commitment rather than to an actual happening: it indicates the extent of Epaphroditus's dedication. That this is a matter of the will is shown by its being followed by a ἵνα purpose construction. The previous clause, μέχρι θανάτου ἤγγισεν 'he was near to death', shows the extent to which that commitment was actually realized. Epaphroditus is worthy of honor not because he happened to fall deathly sick but because of the dedication that led to his sickness.

Since 2:25-30 is a close-knit unit, μέχρι θανάτου ἤγγισεν 'he was near to death' in v. 30 and ἠσθένησεν παραπλήσιον θανάτῳ 'he was sick near to death' in v. 27 clearly refer to the same general event.

As for the propositionalization of 'risking his life' or 'endangering his life', 'life' is an abstract noun, though it sometimes can be translated as 'one's body' or 'self'. While the idea of 'risk' or 'endangering' may not be all that complicated, putting its meaning into one verb is, and so it may be more simply represented by some other construction such as 'he was willing to serve me in place of you, even though he knew he might die'.

**serve me in place of you** The word λειτουργία is usually translated 'service'. In the New Testament and other early Christian literature it is used to refer either to ritual and cultic service or other kinds of religious service (BAGD, p. 471). Its meaning is analogous to τὸ ἔργον Χριστοῦ 'the work of Christ' in the first part of v. 30. Therefore the sense of 'service' or 'serve' in English, which fits these ideas, is appropriate for this context. Some translations have used 'help' (NIV, TEV, TNT). This would be an acceptable substitute, especially in languages where a literal translation of 'serve' is impossible or inappropriate to the context. But in general the idea of 'serve' or 'service' is more appropriate.

The word ὑστέρημα in this context is often glossed as 'lack'. It has a generic sense and when it occurs with ἀναπληρόω 'fill' and a noun indicating the specific event involved, ὑστέρημα indicates nonperformance of that event, while ἀναπληρόω indicates performance of that event by someone else. In using ὑστέρημα Paul is not saying that the Philippians have failed him. The Philippians had themselves sent Epaphroditus with their gift and as their representative. Also criticism of the Philippians in such a way does not fit the epistle as a whole; one of its functions was as a thank-you letter to the Philippians for their service. On the other hand, it seems very probable that Paul wants to stress that it was Epaphroditus who actually served him on their behalf so that they would honor him properly.

Since 'service' (λειτουργία) is the specific event here, the propositionalization might be 'serve me in place of you'. But 'if in place of you' is considered an elliptical expression, it could be rendered as 'representing you' or 'instead of you serving me' or 'when you could not serve me'.

## BOUNDARIES AND COHERENCE

Epaphroditus is the topic of the 2:25-30 paragraph; explicit references to him begin in 2:25a and end in 2:30. While it is true that there are two paragraph patterns here (a *basis-COMMISSIVE* and a *basis-APPEAL*), the *basis-COMMISSIVE* construction itself forms the *basis* for at least the first *APPEAL*; and thus these two paragraph patterns are tied closely together. Also, the first and second *APPEALS* are very closely tied together. So it is best to keep all that is said about Epaphroditus as one paragraph.

## PROMINENCE AND THEME

The overall *basis-APPEAL* paragraph pattern of 2:25-30 is basic to the theme. As was discussed under 1:3-4:20, this paragraph on sending Epaphroditus back is used by Paul to stress his theme of unity and selfless service to one another. The second exhortation, τοὺς τοιούτους ἐντίμους ἔχετε 'hold such ones honored' (2:29c), is much more easily understood when seen in the light of Paul's theme on practicing attitudes that contribute to unity. Otherwise it is difficult to see why Paul would include as beneficiaries of their honor, not only Epaphroditus, who is definitely in focus in the paragraph, but all who are like him. Even the following support for this *APPEAL* deals only with Epaphroditus, on the surface at least.

For other indications of references to the theme of unity, note the similar ideas in 2:3, 25, and 29c ('considering others better than yourselves', 'my fellow worker and fellow soldier', and 'hold such ones in honor'). Based on all these considerations, the theme statement should retain 'all who are like him' rather than mentioning Epaphroditus only.

The *basis* for the *COMMISSIVE* is briefly represented in the theme because of its length.

# SUBPART CONSTITUENT 3:1–4:1 (Hortatory Division: Appeal₂ of 1:27–4:9)

*THEME: Beware of those people who are trying to harm you by teaching that you must be circumcised. Also beware of those who are living lustful lives. Instead, follow my example of becoming more and more like Christ and depending on him alone for a right relationship with God. Our certain hope is that Christ will transform our earthly bodies to be like his heavenly body.*

| MACROSTRUCTURE | CONTENTS |
|---|---|
| introduction | 3:1 As for the other matters, continue to rejoice and know that it is not tiresome for me and it is safe for you to mention them again. |
| APPEAL₁ | 3:2-11 Beware of those unholy people who will harm you spiritually by insisting that you must be circumcised in order to become God's people. We are already God's people not because we rely on ourselves at all but because we give up ourselves in order that we may know Christ and be united with him, relying on him alone to be made righteous and become his people, as my example shows. |
| APPEAL₂ | 3:12-21 Follow my example of constantly striving to become more and more like Christ rather than following the bad example of those who are lustful and think only about earthly things. As for us, Christ will transform our earthly bodies to be like his heavenly body. |
| summary | 4:1 My dear friends, on the basis of all that I have told you [3:1-21], continue to believe firmly in the Lord Jesus Christ according to what I have just taught you [3:1-21] and act accordingly. |

## INTENT AND MACROSTRUCTURE

The 3:1–4:1 division is hortatory in intent and contains an *introduction*, two main sections and a *summary*, all of which contain APPEALS. Paul is now dealing with the topic of resisting outside forces who will harm the Philippians doctrinally and morally. Instead of following them the Philippians should follow the example of Paul.

## BOUNDARIES AND COHERENCE

One of the principal elements in the coherence of this unit is Paul's use of his life as a model for the Philippian believers. The first person singular forms in 3:4–17 represent this. Another important element is the domain of resistance to spiritual opposition. The words ἀσφαλές 'safe' (3:2) and στήκετε 'stand firm' (4:1) represent this, as do the following negatives: βλέπετε 'beware' (3:2), κύνας 'dogs' (3:2), τοὺς κακοὺς ἐργάτας 'the evil workers' (3:2), τὴν κατατομήν 'the mutilation', i.e., 'the mutilators', (3:2), τοὺς ἐχθροὺς τοῦ σταυροῦ τοῦ Χριστοῦ 'the enemies of the cross of Christ' (3:18).

Further coherence is seen in the fact that while 2:19–30 deals with certain individuals as topics of discussion and 4:2–3 presents exhortations to certain individuals, 3:1–4:1 does not deal with named individuals at all (except for Paul himself) and the exhortations are all general.

Although it might seem that 'rejoice in the Lord' in 3:1 is a wholly different subject from the following exhortations to beware of the Judaizers, there are some reasons to consider 'rejoice in the Lord' as part of the same unit. When it functions on the higher level, as here, the connector τὸ λοιπόν usually acts as a topic introducer. It is more likely that it would introduce here a fully developed topic rather than only χαίρετε ἐν κυρίῳ 'rejoice in the Lord', which, although certainly an exhortation and prominent in itself, is structurally very possibly acting as a motif; for there is no doubt that rejoicing is a motif in Philippians. (As mentioned before, an author tends to weave a motif into the framework of the discourse as often as he can and when the function of the motif is misunderstood it may seem to violate the coherence of the unit in which it occurs.)

Also, 'rejoice in the Lord', though it is an exhortation, is expressive in content. This would not be the only place where Paul mixes expressive ideas with his main hortatory or expository points. Phil. 4:1 is such a place: in the same verse he uses several vocatives with expressive content along with the exhortation 'stand firm in the Lord' ("Therefore, my brothers, whom I love and long for, my joy and crown, that is how you should stand firm in the Lord, beloved!"). Paul may have felt that the subject matter to be discussed in 3:2–30 was of such a type that he needed to encourage them to rejoice at this point.

Note that there is a possible connection between rejoicing *in the Lord* and glorying *in Christ Jesus* (3:3c). They had every reason to rejoice in the Lord for they belonged to him; they were his people (ἡ περιτομή 'the circumcision', 3:3a).

Watson states, "According to Quintilian, in a multisectional work it was a common and useful practice to use short introductions functioning as *exordiums*" (p. 84) and "The rejoicing *topos* is ... strategically distributed throughout the rhetoric, and is picked up from the close of the *digresso* in 2:28–29 and skillfully used in 3:1 as a transition to the third and final developmental section of the proposition in 3:1–21" (p. 85).

Of course, one can always postulate that Paul used τὸ λοιπόν to mean 'finally' here and was actually closing his letter, as in 2 Cor. 13:11, with a final exhortation to rejoice, but then thought of other things he needed to say. But it is much more probable that he had in mind all the remaining topics he discusses when he wrote Τὸ λοιπόν, ἀδελφοί μου, χαίρετε ἐν κυρίῳ, especially since the subjects in 3:1–4:1 are obviously very important and he has already previewed them in 1:28. (See the discussion on τὸ λοιπόν in the notes for 3:1a.) The more Paul's epistles are studied from a semantic structural viewpoint, the more it will be shown that they are well structured rather than fragmentary.

As for the connection between the latter part of v. 1 and v. 2, there is a potential semantic connection between ἀσφαλές 'safe' and βλέπετε τοὺς κύνας 'watch out for the dogs'. The absence of a connector at the beginning of v. 2 can be explained by the generic-specific relationship between τὰ αὐτὰ γράφειν 'to write the same things' and those specific "same things" written in v. 2. Note that there is no connective at the start of v. 5, which begins the list of the specifics of the generic in v. 4.

The generic exhortation to stand firm in the Lord (4:1), coming after units that deal with resisting the influences of those who are opposing the gospel, certainly has the appearance of a summary for 3:2–21. Thus the structure of 3:1–4:1 may be seen as consisting of an *introduction*, two hortatory sections, and a *summary*.

## PROMINENCE AND THEME

While it is true that a summary is a generic representation of specifics and so 4:1 as the summary of 3:2–21 would potentially be a good representation of the theme, generic units such as 4:1 are often too generic to convey much content. So the theme statement summarizes the negative and positive APPEALS of 3:2–21 in more detail. Also it seems fitting to include the significant *basis* of 3:20–21, which has parallels in 3:11 and 3:14b.

# DIVISION CONSTITUENT 3:1 (Propositional Cluster: Introduction to 3:2–21)

*THEME: As for the other matters, continue to rejoice and know that it is not tiresome for me and it is safe for you to mention them again.*

| STRUCTURE | CONTENTS |
|---|---|
| ┌─NUCLEUS₁ ─────────────── | 3:1a *As for* the other matters, my fellow believers, continue to rejoice because *you belong to* the Lord. |
| │         ┌─concession──── | 3:1b *Though* I *now* write to you those same matters *which I mentioned/ communicated to you before,* |
| └─NUCLEUS₂ ─CONTRAEXPECTATION─ | 3:1c *this* [3:1b] *is* not tiresome for me and will protect you from those who would harm you. |

## INTENT AND STRUCTURE

The 3:1 propositional cluster contains an imperative, χαίρετε 'rejoice'. However, there is no explicit connector between the APPEAL in 1a and 1b-c, nor is there an obvious APPEAL-basis relationship between these two constituents of the verse. It seems best to understand them as having different purposes: continuity in the 'rejoice' motif and orientation of the new subject. This might be expected of brief introductory material (cf. the *opening* of the epistle, 1:1-2).

## NOTES

**3:1a *As for* the other matters** The Greek is τὸ λοιπόν. Other uses of λοιπός show that 'the rest, the others' is the primary sense of the word. There is no doubt that τὸ λοιπόν in general is a high-level marker, either for a paragraph or a larger unit. Such markers and connectors have a function beyond their normal lexical content, and this function often tends to extend or change the lexical meaning. This is most likely the case here with τὸ λοιπόν. Its lexical meaning might be said to be 'the remaining thing', and so on this basis it might be translated literally into English as 'the final thing' or, more naturally, as the high-level marker 'finally'. However, Paul uses τὸ λοιπόν as a marker in places where 'the remaining thing' or 'finally' makes sense only when we postulate that Paul made a mistake or something has happened to the text! Many commentators and versions translate τὸ λοιπόν here as 'finally'; but of the five places Paul uses (τὸ) λοιπόν as a high-level connector (2 Cor. 13:11; Phil. 3:1; 4:8; 1 Thess. 4:1; 2 Thess. 3:1), only the use in 2 Cor. 13:11 can, in the context, be appropriately translated as 'finally'. In 1 Thess. 4:1, for instance, it is at the beginning of the hortatory section of the book, where it might better be translated 'as for the remaining matters I want to talk about' or 'as for the other matters I want to talk about'. In 2 Thess. 3:1, J. Callow (1982:86) translates τὸ λοιπόν 'as for the other matters'.

BAGD (p. 480.3b) gives the following glosses of (τὸ) λοιπόν for all of its different contexts: "*as far as the rest is concerned, beyond that, in addition, finally.*" With all these possibilities, I see no lexical, contextual, or structural reason why τὸ λοιπόν should be translated in Phil. 3:1 as 'finally'. Something along the line of 'beyond that' or 'as far as the rest is concerned' would be much more appropriate, and it has been rendered in such a way in the display.

**continue to rejoice because *you belong to* the Lord** 'Rejoice' is usually a representation for an emotive REACTION; therefore 'in the Lord' is no doubt a representation of the *situation* which causes the REACTION. No explicit event is signaled by the words ἐν κυρίῳ 'in the Lord' (though 'the Lord' represents the agent involved in whatever event or state there might be) and the context does not directly signal a specific event for the *situation*, so in view of this the *situation* is considered generic. Since there are reasons to take 'rejoice in the Lord' as part of the same general unit as the warnings to watch out for the Judaizers (see "Boundaries and Coherence" for 3:1-4:1), χαίρετε ἐν κυρίῳ 'rejoice in the Lord' might be propositionalized as 'rejoice because the Lord cares for you'. However, it may be best to propositionalize it more generically here. This might be done either on the basis of the Philippians' relationship to the Lord (e.g., 'rejoice because you belong to the Lord', 'rejoice because you believe in the Lord') or on the basis of what the Lord has done ('rejoice because of all the Lord has done for you').

A gloss such as 'be happy because of your union with the Lord' (Loh and Nida) is appropriate, not because ἐν κυρίῳ always means 'in union with the Lord', but because it is a generic way of representing what joy in the Lord is all about.

Because χαίρετε 'rejoice' is an imperative but represents a state, an emotional reaction, it is potentially problematical. In some languages it would be unnatural to use an imperative with stative words such as this; adjustments would need to be made in order to say "Rejoice!" or "Be happy!"

**Lord** It is more probable that 'Lord' here refers to Jesus than that it refers to the Father. If possible, the translator should leave it ambiguous, but if a choice must be made, the better choice is 'the Lord Jesus'. Some commentators say that κύριος 'Lord' always refers to Jesus in Paul's writings. But it may be that in some places at least, κύριος, when unmodified, implies no special distinction between the Father and the Son in Paul's thinking, even as in many Christians' minds today.

**3:1b** *Though* The infinitive phrase τὰ αὐτὰ γράφειν ὑμῖν 'to write the same things to you', which functions grammatically as a substantive in the clause, needs to be adjusted in the propositionalization. This is done by changing the infinitive phrase into a proposition with the role of concession, an appropriate role in this context.

**I *now* write to you those same matters *which I mentioned/communicated to you before*** In the construction τὰ αὐτὰ γράφειν 'to write the same (things)', 'same' implies that these things were communicated before. However, it is not indicated whether the former communication was also by writing or was oral. There is much discussion in the commentaries as to what was communicated before that is now being communicated again. One interpretation is that this second communication is 'rejoice in the Lord', which immediately precedes 'to write the same things'. Since the Philippians are urged to rejoice in 2:18 and there are several other references to rejoicing, this interpretation is plausible as far as the repetition is concerned, but not so plausible from other standpoints, as the other interpretation brings out.

The other interpretation is that the second communication is the warning against the Judaizers given in 3:2. The earlier mention of this same subject, then, would be either earlier in this epistle (1:27–30, for instance), in an earlier letter or letters, or by word of mouth. It is difficult to know which of these would be the intended reference. While it is more likely that Paul would excuse his repetition of the same subject in the same epistle, little of what he wrote earlier in the epistle is similar to 3:2. As far as communicating this same matter orally at an earlier time is concerned, if we take this epistle to have been written from Rome, Paul had not seen the Philippians for well over two years (Acts 24:27). It would hardly be necessary for him to feel that he should excuse himself for repeating the same subject after such a long period of time.

As will be seen in the analysis of 3:2, there could be a high degree of relationship between ἀσφαλές 'safe' and the warning regarding the Judaizers, βλέπετε τοὺς κύνας 'beware of the dogs'. It is more natural to understand the repetition of a warning to watch out for the dangerous Judaizers as a safeguard than it is to understand the repetition of a command to rejoice in the Lord as a safeguard. For this reason, the former has been taken as the basis for the rendering in the display.

Since it is difficult to know when or how Paul gave his first warning, it may be better to use a more generic word than 'write' or 'speak' for the earlier implied event, one which could include either of them: 'I *now* write to you those same matters *which I mentioned/communicated to you before*'. However, if the translator chooses to be specific, 'write' would be better than 'speak' for the earlier implied event: 'I *now* write to you the same matters *which I wrote to you before*'.

**3:1c *this* [3:1b] *is* not tiresome for me** A variety of English translations would be appropriate here: 'it is not troublesome for me', 'it does not bother me', 'I don't mind' (TEV).

**and will protect you from those who would harm you** The adjective ἀσφαλές 'safe' in this context is more clearly stated in verbal form.

## BOUNDARIES AND COHERENCE

Although 3:1a has a different purpose from that of 3:1b–c (see "Intent"), it seems best to consider them as one unit since they form a brief introduction to 3:2–21.

## PROMINENCE AND THEME

Since 3:1 has a double-headed structure, elements from both units are included in the theme.

## DIVISION CONSTITUENT 3:2–11 (Hortatory Section: Appeal₁ of 3:1–4:1)

> THEME: *Beware of those unholy people who will harm you spiritually by insisting that you must be circumcised in order to become God's people. We are already God's people not because we rely on ourselves at all but because we give up ourselves in order that we may know Christ and be united with him, relying on him alone to be made righteous and become his people, as my example shows.*

| MACROSTRUCTURE | CONTENTS |
| --- | --- |
| APPEAL | 3:2 Beware of those unholy people who will harm you spiritually by insisting that you must be circumcised in order to become God's people. |
| basis₁ | 3:3–4a It is we who worship God through his Spirit and glorify Christ Jesus rather than depending on our own selves who are truly God's people. |
| basis₂ | 3:4b–11 Although, if it were beneficial for salvation, I could rely upon my own attainments better than anyone else could, I consider all those attainments worthless because I want to know Christ and be united with him, made righteous through trusting in Christ alone. |

### INTENT AND MACROSTRUCTURE

This section consists of a blown-up hortatory paragraph pattern. The *APPEAL* in 3:2 is supported by two *bases*, 3:3–4a and 3:4b–11. Paul's purpose in this section is to warn the Philippians of the legalistic doctrine of the false teachers. The *basis* units for this warning are expository. Paul shows the Philippians that salvation is through faith in Christ alone, not through circumcision, nationality, or legal requirements.

### BOUNDARIES AND COHERENCE

As for the thematic coherence of 3:2–11, the exhortations of 3:2 are supported by the expositional material in 3:3–11. To prevent the believers from following the false teachers, Paul shows the extreme value of the true gospel. Beginning in 3:4b, he uses his own life as an example to show the great value and validity of the gospel. The example of his life can be traced in the surface structure by the occurrence of first person singular forms and the absence of second person forms. This surface-structure phenomenon runs through v. 14, though many versions and commentators make a major break at the end of v. 11. In fact, vv. 12–14 form the *basis* for the *APPEAL* in v. 15, and the 17–21 unit is closely tied to 12–16, in that the *APPEALS* are similar in content: 'Have this same attitude that I have' (v. 15) and 'Imitate me' (v. 17).

Thus 3:2–11 may be seen as a blown-up *APPEAL-basis* paragraph pattern, which actually forms a section. This unit is too complex to be seen as a single paragraph. The unit consisting of 3:4b–6, for instance, has a *CLAIM-justification* paragraph pattern wholly contained within it.

### PROMINENCE AND THEME

An *APPEAL* always forms a central part of a theme statement and this is the case for the 3:2–11 unit. The support for the *APPEAL* here is long and complex, especially the second *basis*, but there are at least two important truths that stand out here. One is that becoming righteous before God and thus becoming his child is not through reliance on one's own activities but through Christ alone. (This, of course, is the reason why Christians should beware of those who teach reliance on the flesh.) This truth is therefore included in the theme statement. Paul's refusal to rely on the flesh even though he had reason to, had it been beneficial (3:4b–6, the concession) and his trusting in Christ alone for righteousness (3:9) demonstrate this truth. But interwoven with this is the part of the theme concerning the worthlessness of all fleshly attainments as a means of having a vital personal relationship with Christ, that is, of knowing Christ (3:8b, 10a), gaining him, and being incorporated in him (3:8f, 9a). The knowledge of Christ is further defined in 10b–d. The implication is that this life is better by far ('the surpassing knowledge of knowing Christ' in 3:8b) than the life the circumcision advocates offer.

Paul presents much of the support for the *APPEAL* from his own life's example. However, since the *APPEAL* is to be carried out by the Philippians, there must be a tie-in between his example and their lives. This is made clear in the theme statement.

# SECTION CONSTITUENT 3:2
## (Hortatory Propositional Cluster: Appeal of 3:2–11)

*THEME: Beware of those unholy people who will harm you spiritually by insisting that you must be circumcised in order to become God's people.*

| RELATIONAL STRUCTURE | CONTENTS |
|---|---|
| NUCLEUS₁ —ITEM | 3:2a Beware of those *people who are dangerous and impure like dirty* dogs [MET]. |
| —description of 'people' | 3:2b They are *dangerous* evildoers. |
| NUCLEUS₂ | 3:2c Beware of them *since they are like people who* cut *other people's* bodies; *they will harm you spiritually by means of insisting that you must be circumcised in order to become God's people/children* [MTY, MET]. |

## INTENT

The 3:2 propositional cluster forms the *APPEAL* for the blown-up paragraph pattern of section 3:2–11. It consists of three strong imperatives in the Greek text which are rendered as two *APPEALS* in the display. The *bases* for these *APPEALS* are found in units 3:3–4a and 3:4b–11.

## NOTES

**3:2** There is a question in v. 2 as to whether the three different warnings in 2a, b, and c apply to three different types of people or to the same people. Some of the older commentators held the view that three different types of people were meant. However, they overlook the fact that the threefold repetition is for rhetorical effect, an emphasis of the seriousness of the command. Besides, no contextual or situational reason leads us to suspect that three different groups of people are meant. The question for translation is whether the threefold repetition can be kept without implying that three different types of people are meant. In some languages adjustments will need to be made to prevent that misunderstanding. This is probably true even for English. However, the rhetorical effect of the repetition (i.e., the emphasis) should be conveyed in some way, if possible. In the display only the first and third 'beware of' are retained.

A majority of commentators understand the people Paul warns against as "Judaizing Christians, those who preached at the same time Judaism and Christianity, but who corrupted the latter by saying that a man had also to keep the law of Moses and, especially, to be circumcised in order to be saved" (Heyward). Some commentators, however, think they were Jews who never had been converted to Christianity. But the warning of v. 2 is so strong that it suggests a more insidious attack than would be expected from a community totally outside Christianity. The Jewish community in Macedonia had vehemently attacked Paul's work physically (Acts 17:5-15), not in the matter of doctrine.

**3:2a Beware of those *people who are dangerous and impure like dirty* dogs** Some commentators say that βλέπετε as in βλέπετε τοὺς κύνας here does not mean 'beware of'. That, they say, would be expressed as βλέπετε ἀπό. They say βλέπετε means 'observe, pay attention to' (cf. 1 Cor. 10:18). In any case, the context implies 'observe them to avoid them and their teaching', the same meaning as 'beware of'.

Many commentators (e.g., Alford, Ellicott, Hawthorne, Meyer, O'Brien 1991, Vincent) understand impurity to be the point of similarity between 'dogs' and the people here compared to them. The term 'dog' was often applied to "Gentiles or lapsed Jews who were ritually unclean and thus outside the covenant...In an amazing reversal Paul asserts that it is the Judaizers who are to be regarded as Gentiles; they are 'the dogs' who stand outside the covenant blessings" (O'Brien 1991; cf. Garland 1985, pp. 167-68, and Silva). Because of the long association of 'dog' with this meaning, it may have become a dead metaphor and thus other characteristics of dogs may not have been signaled when it was used to refer to Gentiles or lapsed Jews. However, it does not seem to be "dead enough" to omit the word 'dogs' in translation. On the basis of this reasoning, 3:2a might be propositionalized as, 'Beware of those *people who are impure like* dogs *are impure*' or 'Beware of those *people who are like* dogs *because they are impure*'.

But there is another component of meaning also in view here. Paul's use of ἀσφαλές 'safe' and βλέπετε 'beware of' indicate that Paul intended to capture the ferociousness of dogs *in this context*. Meyer says, "...the earnest, demonstrative βλέπετε, as well as ἀσφαλές (ver. 2), can only indicate a danger which was visibly and closely threatening the readers."

A comparison of this verse with Matt. 7:6 may be helpful: "Do not give dogs what is sacred; do not throw your pearls to pigs. If you do, they may trample them under their feet, and then turn and tear you to pieces" (NIV). Based on the analysis of this verse as a chiasmus, which it clearly is, the points of similarity between dogs and certain types of people are taken to be impurity (contrast with 'sacred') and dangerousness ('turn and tear you to pieces'). Thus the word 'dog' in reference to human beings potentially connoted more than just impurity. Of course, in the context of 'safe' and 'beware', 'dogs' will probably connote 'dangerous' in most languages anyway.

It is difficult to know how to best propositionalize this complicated figure. Alternatives to the display rendering are: 'Beware of those *people who are impure like dirty* dogs' and 'Beware of those *unholy people who are seeking to harm you just like dirty* dogs *would bite you and harm you*'.

**3:2b They are *dangerous* evildoers** The second reference to these people is τοὺς κακοὺς ἐργάτας 'the/those evildoers/evil workers'. This could be taken as similar to ἐργάται ἀδικίας 'evildoers' in Luke 13:27 or, since the reference is to people who are propagating false doctrine, ἐργάται could be taken in the sense of missionary workers. The latter is one of the recognized senses of ἐργάται in the New Testament according to BAGD (p. 307.1b; cf. 2 Cor. 11:13 and 2 Tim. 2:15). There is a third option: ἐργάται could be taken as a play on words with τὰ ἔργα 'works', which the Judaizers would have stated as necessary for salvation. Paul would be referring to them as "work-ers" meaning 'those who insist on performing works in order to be saved'. Such a teaching is only deception and leads to a bad end; hence their ἔργα 'works' are evil (or they themselves are evil).

The problem with the third interpretation is that ἐργάται is not found elsewhere in the New Testament with this meaning. On the other hand, the other two meanings are established. Even if the third meaning *were* established, the other two are the primary meanings. For translation, then, only the first or second meaning is appropriate, though if the translator is convinced that the third interpretation was intended by Paul, he might translate the first or second interpretation in such a way that a play on words is suggested.

As to whether the first or second meaning is the more appropriate identification of the Judaizers, the sense of danger conveyed by the other terms applied to the Judaizers suggests that here in 2b 'those who do evil' is more forceful than simply 'evil workers/teachers' (though 'evil workers/teachers' is appropriate to the type of activity these people were engaged in).

As mentioned in the first note for 3:2, 'beware of' is not used in 2b of the display. 'Dangerous' is used instead to maintain the force represented in 'beware of'.

**3:2c cut *other people's* bodies** A common gloss for κατατομή given by commentators and versions is 'mutilation'. BAGD (p. 419) glosses this only occurrence in the New Testament and other early Christian literature as "*mutilation, cutting in pieces*," but glosses the references from other sources as "always 'incision, notch', etc." This latter information leads to the conclusion that the *physical* event referred to in κατατομή in Phil. 3:2 might be more precisely defined as 'cutting the body with the intention of harming'. The use of the English word mutilation, which in its literal sense means a very severe cutting, as in severing limbs, is justified only in the figurative sense of the harm it might cause.

*they will harm you spiritually by means of insisting that you must be circumcised in order to become God's people/children* In the context of ἀσφαλές 'safe' and βλέπετε 'beware of', κατατομή 'cutting, mutilation' is intended to refer to both a figure that is harmful and a real-world reference (topic) that is harmful. The figurative reference might be propositionalized as 'people *who* cut/mutilate *other people's* bodies'. The topic and point of similarity might be propositionalized as '*they will harm you spiritually by means of insisting that you must be circumcised in order to become children of God/God's people*'.

The abstract noun κατατομή 'mutilation' is a metonymy: it refers to the people who mutilate.

## PROMINENCE AND THEME

Although in v. 2 the Greek text has three exhortations to beware, only one group of people is being warned against. With each repetition of 'beware' they are described in different ways, so 'beware' is needed only once in the theme statement. The various descriptions of these people are summarized by describing their character generically (unholy) and their action specifically (demanding that people must be circumcised in order to become God's people, an untruth that makes them harmful people that the believers must beware of).

Note that 3:2 does not consist of a full paragraph pattern, only an *APPEAL*.

## SECTION CONSTITUENT 3:3–4a (Propositional Cluster: Basis₁ for 3:2)

*THEME: It is we who worship God through his Spirit and glorify Christ Jesus rather than depending on our own selves who are truly God's people.*

| RELATIONAL STRUCTURE | CONTENTS |
|---|---|
| ITEM | 3:3a *Those people* [3:2] call themselves "the circumcised people" to mean that they are God's people because they have been circumcised. But we(inc), *not they*, are *actually* "the circumcised people" *in that sense, since we(inc) are truly God's people, even though we(inc) have not all been circumcised.* [MTY] |
| —identification₁ of 'God's people' | 3:3b We(inc) worship God by means of his *Holy* Spirit *enabling/helping us(inc)*; |
| —identification₂ of 'God's people' | 3:3c we(inc) glorify Christ Jesus *because he has enabled us(inc) to become the people of God.* |
| —idn₃ —CONTRAEXPECTATION | 3:3d We(inc) do not believe *that God will consider/make us(inc) his people as a result of what has been done to our(inc) bodies or as a result of what we ourselves do* [MTY, SYN]. |
| —concession | 3:4a *We(inc) do not rely on these things* [3:3d], although I could very well rely on them *if that were beneficial.* |

### INTENT

The role of the 3:3–4a propositional cluster is identificational with an expository intent. It differentiates God's true children from those who call themselves his children on an invalid basis. It thus supports the *APPEAL* of 3:2 to beware of those who teach this invalid message.

### NOTES

**3:3a** Verse 3:2 is definitely an *APPEAL* and 3:3–11 definitely the *bases* for that *APPEAL*. The connector γάρ at the beginning of 3:3 is perhaps the most common signal of a *basis* for an *APPEAL*. However, the surface structure of the Greek text contains a definite relationship between τὴν κατατομήν 'the cutting/mutilation' and ἡ περιτομή 'the circumcision'; it would seem to be a lower-level relationship (between 3:2c and 3:3). That relationship might be considered *APPEAL-basis*, 'Beware of the cutters since we are the true circumcision'. Of course, this supposed grounds relationship is indirect; and because it *is* indirect and on the lower level at a higher-level boundary, it seems best not to mark either a higher-level *basis* relationship or lower-level grounds relationship in the display. While in some languages such relationships might be marked by generic support connectors similar to γάρ in Greek and 'for' in English, connectors used in the display are more precise.

It is interesting that of the nine NT versions cited by Greenlee (1992), five do not have a conjunction here.

***Those people*** [3:2] ***call themselves "the circumcised people" to mean that they are God's people because they have been circumcised. But we(inc),*** *not they,* ***are*** *actually* ***"the circumcised people"*** *in that sense, since we(inc) are truly God's people, even though we(inc) have not all been circumcised* The term ἡ περιτομή 'the circumcision' is used figuratively here. The act of circumcision is a metonymy standing for the people on whom the act is performed. At the same time, it denotes a group of people many of whom have never been physically circumcised. Hence ἡ περιτομή 'the circumcision' does not refer here to the event of being physically circumcised in the regular sense. It would appear that the point of similarity between the figure of circumcision and the real-world reference is either (1) some spiritual experience of Christians that is somehow similar to physical circumcision (a circumcision of the heart is mentioned in Deut. 30:6; Rom. 2:29; Col. 2:11) or (2) some state or relationship that is the same as the result of being physically circumcised (becoming God's people or salvation). In this case, 'circumcision' would be a metonymy in which the cause stands for the effect. In regard to interpretation 1, since the context is dealing with the means of salvation, which is definitely not works for the Christian, no act with the Christian as agent is intended. But even circumcision done by Christ (Col. 2:11), which J. Callow (1983:132) sees as meaning 'your entire evil nature was completely removed by Christ', does not seem to be in focus here since Paul is contrasting the Christian's position with the position claimed by the Judaizers. Note that the description of 'the circumcised' which immediately follows does not deal with the aspect of sin. So it seems better to understand the point of similarity as having to do with the result of circumcision.

The early Judaizers of Paul's day are described as teaching that the result of circumcision was salvation: "Unless you are circumcised according to the custom taught by Moses, you cannot be saved" (Acts 15:1b, NIV). In looking at Gen. 17:1-14 where the rite of circumcision was originally commanded by God, it appears that the result of circumcision was recognition by God as belonging to his people and coming under his covenant. In Gal. 6:16 Paul calls the church 'the Israel of God', and the Gal. 6:16 context is much like the one here.

Salvation (or justification) and becoming one of God's people were not really understood as different results of circumcision but the same result viewed from a different focus. Here it is probably best to focus on the result of becoming people whom God recognizes as his own. (Some languages would translate this as 'children of God'.) This status is what is in focus in the Greek text. It is the true people of God who are described in the rest of v. 3. That the status or identity of God's people is in focus is corroborated by the fact that the Jews (according to Eph. 2:11) called themselves ἡ περιτομή 'the circumcision'. Paul is contrasting the identities of the two groups, saying, in effect, "Those who insist on circumcision call themselves ἡ περιτομή 'the circumcised people of God', but we believers in Christ are the true people of God."

A full propositionalization needs to be based on the cause-effect relationship of the metonymy. Since this is a very complicated figure, the propositionalization is complex: *'Those people [3:2] call themselves "the circumcised people" to mean that they are God's people because they have been circumcised. But we(inc), not they, are actually "the circumcised people" in that sense, since we(inc) are truly God's people'*. An alternate for the last part is *'...since we(inc) are truly God's people, even though we(inc) have not all been circumcised'*.

**3:3b-d** The words ἡμεῖς... ἐσμεν ἡ περιτομή 'we are the circumcision' in 3a are followed by three participial phrases. Grammatically they are related to ἡμεῖς 'we' and describe important aspects of the spiritual life of those who are ἡ περιτομή, the true people of God. O'Brien (1991) says, "It is not that the 'Christian right to the title of the circumcision is grounded in the realities of Christian spiritual experience, in worship and in faith', as F. W. Beare puts it, as though the participial clauses give the reasons or grounds for this claim to be ἡ περιτομή." Paul does not use an overt marker to show reason or grounds, nor are participial phrases beginning with the article οἱ (which acts as a relative pronoun) a common way to mark reason or grounds. And as for the semantic content of these participial phrases, it is not what Scripture ordinarily defines as the means or basis for salvation or justification. This type of syntactical construction usually presents description or identification. Thus, in the sense that these participial phrases distinguish the true people of God from those who falsely claim such a relationship, they are identificational.

**3:3b We(inc) worship *God by means of his Holy Spirit enabling/helping us(inc)*** The verb λατρεύω means 'worship'. In Acts 26:7 this verb is used to refer to the twelve tribes' earnestly serving/worshiping God day and night. Thus, it has a more comprehensive meaning than just formal corporate worship. O'Brien (1991) gives the meaning as "a service of a comprehensive kind that includes not simply prayer or worship in a formal sense but the whole of life." This is brought out in Rom. 12:1, "offer your bodies as living sacrifices, holy and pleasing to God—this is your spiritual act of *worship*" (NIV, italics mine).

**3:3c we(inc) glorify Christ Jesus** *because he has enabled us(inc) to become the people of God* As O'Brien (1991) points out, 3c and 3d in the Greek text are in chiastic arrangement, the objects of the boasting ('in Christ Jesus') and confidence ('in the flesh') being juxtaposed to bring them out as contrastive. This suggests that the events represented by the verbs are parallel in thought. The participle καυχώμενοι 'boasting' is probably used to contrast with the Judaizers' boast of being circumcised (cf. Gal. 6:13b, "yet they want you to be circumcised that they may boast about your flesh"). In Phil. 3:3, 'boast' has two pertinent components of meaning: (1) confidence in (Christ Jesus) and (2) the effects of that confidence—boasting about this confidence in Christ Jesus. If καυχάομαι has the same general meaning as boast in English, the component of meaning of confidence is implicit. It is the effect of the confidence (i.e., boasting) that is explicit in the Greek, and this is for the purpose of contrasting it with the Judaizers' boasting. Also significant in this context is the reason for the confidence.

In the display 'glorify Christ Jesus' is used instead of 'boast in Christ Jesus' because 'boast in Christ Jesus' is not a natural collocation in English.

**3:3d We(inc) do not believe** *that God will consider/make us(inc) his people as a result of what has been done to our(inc) bodies or as a result of what we ourselves do* In the context of the explicit references to circumcision in 3:2c and 3:3a, the words ἐν σαρκί 'in flesh' certainly have a reference to physical circumcision, a rite in which the Judaizers placed their confidence. But, as the next three verses show, Paul has additional reasons for confidence in the flesh in mind here: "If anyone else thinks he has reasons to put confidence in the flesh, I have more" (NIV). A list of his specific reasons for confidence in the flesh follow: circumcision, right ancestry, his proven ability to keep the law. A general reference is thus needed in propositionalizing 'in the flesh', but at the same time it must be made clear for readers that physical circumcision is included. The phrase 'in the flesh', which is a metonymy, refers to either what has been done to the flesh (circumcision) or what the flesh does. 'Flesh' also stands for the person as a whole and so synecdoche is involved. These factors form the basis for the rendering in the display.

**3:4a *We(inc) do not rely on these things*** **[3:3d]** This statement is supplied in the display to make an appropriate transition from 'we *believe*' in 3d to 'I could very well *rely* on' in the latter part of 4a and the similar statement in 4b.

**although I could very well rely on them** *if that were beneficial* Here πεποίθησιν 'confidence' means 'reasons for confidence', since Paul has just said that he along with all other true Christians do not put confidence in the flesh. Since 'reasons' is an abstract noun, its sense is rendered by 'could very well rely'. The words 'if that were beneficial' are supplied to clarify that Paul does not really rely on who he is or what he himself has done.

## BOUNDARIES AND COHERENCE

As for the final boundary of this unit, many commentators consider that a new unit begins at 4a. However, 4a, καίπερ ἐγὼ ἔχων πεποίθησιν καὶ ἐν σαρκί 'though I have confidence even in the flesh', is a clause which is subordinate grammatically to the preceding clause, καὶ οὐκ ἐν σαρκὶ πεποιθότες 'and not placing confidence in the flesh', and it functions in a concession role to that main clause. (Note the punctuation in the UBSGNT and also in the Hodges and Farstad text.) It is true that the subject matter of 4a may seem more closely related to what follows than to what precedes, but that is because 'though I have confidence even in the flesh' is acting as the tail in a tail-head link, a device which, though appearing at the end of a unit, is a transition introducing the next unit. This at least partially explains why the rest of 3:4 is so repetitious of 3:4a; such repetition is basic to the structure of the new unit.

## PROMINENCE AND THEME

The 3:3–4a unit consists of nuclear propositional configuration 3:3a plus three constituents which identify the topic ('we(inc)', i.e., God's people) presented in 3:3a. These three constituents must be included in the theme since otherwise the participants would be identified by 'we(inc)' only and the argument would be useless.

# SECTION CONSTITUENT 3:4b–11
## (Expository Paragraph Cluster: Basis₂ for 3:2)

*THEME: Although, if it were beneficial for salvation, I could rely upon my own attainments better than anyone else could, I consider all those attainments worthless because I want to know Christ and be united with him, made righteous through trusting in Christ alone.*

| MACROSTRUCTURE | CONTENTS |
| --- | --- |
| ┌─concession─────── | 3:4b–6 If it were beneficial for salvation, I could rely upon what I have done and who I am better than anyone else could rely upon himself, since I was circumcised properly and have a purely Hebrew ancestry and I kept the law blamelessly. |
| └─CONTRAEXPECTATION─ | 3:7–11 But I consider all these things which I used to think of as advantageous, and everything else as well, to be worthless because I want to know Christ and be united with him, made righteous through trusting in Christ alone. |

## INTENT AND MACROSTRUCTURE

In the 3:4b–11 paragraph cluster Paul shows that although he has all the qualifications for becoming right with God under the Judaistic system, they are of no value in God's sight and so Paul considers them worthless because he wants to know Christ. Thus there is a concession-CONTRAEXPECTATION relationship between the two paragraphs.

## BOUNDARIES AND COHERENCE

The initial boundary of the 3:4b–11 unit has been discussed under 3:3–4a; the final boundary under 3:2–11. This unit is considered a paragraph cluster since it acts as a single unit (i.e., *basis₂*) within the blown-up paragraph pattern of 3:2–11. (See Beekman, Callow, and Kopesec, pp. 128–29.)

## PROMINENCE AND THEME

A concession-CONTRAEXPECTATION relation is not complete without both parts, so both parts are represented in the theme.

# PARAGRAPH CLUSTER CONSTITUENT 3:4b–6
## (Expository Paragraph: Concession to 3:7–11)

> THEME: *If it were beneficial for salvation, I could rely upon what I have done and who I am better than anyone else could rely upon himself, since I was circumcised properly and have a purely Hebrew ancestry and I kept the law blamelessly.*

| ¶ PATTERN | CONTENTS |
|---|---|
| CLAIM | 3:4b *In fact*, I could rely upon what I have done and who I am [MTY, SYN] better than anyone else could rely upon himself. *This is demonstrated by the following facts:* |
| justification₁ | 3:5a I was circumcised *by people* when I was one week old. |
| justification₂ | 3:5b I am from the race of Israel. |
| justification₃ | 3:5c I am from the tribe of Benjamin. |
| justification₄ | 3:5d I am completely Hebrew in every way. |
| justification₅ | 3:5e *As* a member of the Pharisee *sect*, I *strictly obeyed* the law *which Moses commanded*. |
| justification₆ | 3:6a I was *so* zealous *to propagate the law that* I persecuted the people who believe in Christ *because I thought they were seeking to abolish the law.* |
| justification₇ | 3:6b *Indeed*, as far as my obeying the law *which Moses commanded* is concerned, no *human being could* have accused me saying that I had transgressed that law. |

## INTENT AND PARAGRAPH PATTERN

The relational structure of the 3:4b–6 paragraph depends somewhat on the meaning of πεποιθέναι ἐν σαρκί. The statement ἐγὼ μᾶλλον 'I more' is elliptical: ἐγὼ μᾶλλον δοκῶ πεποιθέναι ἐν σαρκί is understood (Ellicott, Meyer, O'Brien 1991, Vincent). If πεποιθέναι ἐν σαρκί is taken to mean 'secure in the flesh' (i.e., 'I consider that I am more secure in the flesh'), then the relationship between 3:4b and 3:5a–6b is quite clearly CLAIM-*justification*. If the meaning is taken to be 'I consider that I (can) depend on the flesh more' or as it is more commonly translated, 'I consider that I have more reasons for confidence in the flesh', then the question arises as to whether the relationship between 3:4b and 3:5a–6b is generic-specific. Note that although μᾶλλον 'more' is an adverb in the Greek, its semantic function is to quantify separate items; hence the English translation 'I have more reasons' is appropriate. It might even be rendered 'I have more reasons for confidence, which are the following'. As far as the Greek structure signals are concerned, there is no conjunction at the beginning of 3:5; this would be more appropriate to a generic-specific relationship than a CLAIM-*justification* relationship. At the same time, the seven statements in vv. 5–6 appear to be *justification* for the CLAIM. In fact, according to Greenlee (1992) many commentators take the position that the seven statements are *justifications* for the CLAIM in 3:4b. It would seem that when an author or speaker presents something in the form of a CLAIM that is quantifiable, the quantifiable specifics function at the same time as *justification* for the CLAIM.

In the display, the paragraph pattern is shown as CLAIM-*justification*, and as a signal for the *justification* the words 'This is demonstrated by the following facts' are supplied. (It is standard procedure for a display to signal a relation by labels in the left-hand column and in the proposition at the right as well.)

## NOTES

**3:4b** *In fact* English discourse structure requires 'In fact' to explain the repetition of 3:4a that occurs in 3:4b. Some such device may also be required in some target languages.

**I could rely upon what I have done and who I am better than anyone else could rely upon himself** Or if the abstract noun 'reason' is used, an alternate propositionalization would be: 'I would have more reason to rely upon who I am and what I have done than anyone else would have'.

The words εἴ τις 'if anyone' may be translated as 'whoever' (BAGD, εἰ, p. 220.VII). In the construction here in 4b, εἴ τις...ἄλλος, ἄλλος lexically means 'other', but εἴ τις...ἄλλος still may be translated as 'whoever'. The condition-CONSEQUENCE relationship here is not the normal one in which the reality of the CONSEQUENCE depends upon the reality of the condition. The conditionality is a way to express the universality of the persons involved. Instead of a literal translation as condition-CONSEQUENCE, it might be more natural to translate 4b as 'I have more reasons for confidence in the flesh than anyone else may consider he has'.

It is most natural to understand ἐγὼ μᾶλλον 'I more' to be elliptical: the full clause would be ἐγὼ μᾶλλον δοκῶ πεποιθέναι ἐν σαρκί 'I think/consider/suppose I have more reasons for confidence in the flesh' (Ellicott, Meyer, O'Brien 1991, Vincent). Because of this and because all the specific reasons for confidence in the flesh that Paul gives are concrete ones and are confidently stated by Paul to be such, the meaning of δοκῶ would be more like 'consider' (one of the meanings given by BAGD for δοκέω, p. 201.1) than 'think' or 'suppose', which are other glosses given by BAGD for δοκέω. (The latter would not express as much confidence.) If the condition-CONSEQUENCE structure is kept, we might then translate as, 'If anyone considers that he has reasons for confidence in the flesh, I consider that I have more reasons for confidence in the flesh' or, in more natural English, 'I consider that I have more reasons for confidence in the flesh than anyone else may consider that he has'.

Although some commentators take δοκεῖ 'he (anyone) thinks' to mean 'erroneously thinks', this does not fit the context. Vincent says, "Nor does δοκεῖ imply that the advantage was only apparent (Chrysostom, Theophylact), or that they had only arrogated it to themselves (Theodoret); for Paul uses δοκεῖν of himself."

When the abstract noun 'reason' (i.e., 'reason to be confident', the meaning of πεποίθησις here) is changed to verbal form, the auxiliary verb 'could' replaces the sense of 'consider': 'I could rely upon who I am ... better than any one else could rely upon who he is'. 'Could' is also necessary to prevent the misunderstanding that Paul actually does place confidence in the flesh. It implies that Paul has the qualifications but knows they are of no use; it does not imply that there was a question as to whether he had the qualifications or not.

***This is demonstrated by the following facts*** These words are added to signal the *justification* part of the paragraph. See the discussion under "Intent and Paragraph Pattern."

**3:5a I was circumcised *by people*** The agent performing Paul's circumcision is out of focus in this context. However, in some languages the agent for an event is required, especially where a goal is involved. In a normal English translation, the lack of reference to the agent keeps the correct focus, and so it is somewhat unnatural to supply an agent in the display rendering. In translating into languages that require an explicit agent, that agent should be kept as nonfocal as possible.

**when I was one week old** Although περιτομῇ ὀκταήμερος would translate well into English as 'circumcised on the eighth day', it seems better to use an expression that is completely unambiguous, such as TEV's "when I was one week old."

**3:5b from the race of Israel** The Greek is ἐκ γένους Ἰσραήλ 'from race of Israel'. Commentators point out that what is significant here is the concept 'race' and that terms such as 'people' or 'nation' that are not wholly based on descent are inappropriate. Though some people have suggested adjusting the genitive form of γένος Ἰσραήλ to 'race called Israel', this would be a formula for introduction of *new* identificational information and would not be appropriate for the addressees of the epistle, who knew very well what the race of Israel was. The suggestions 'race descended from Israel' or 'race descended from ancestor Israel' may be good for translation into some languages, but for the display 'race of Israel' is used because it keeps the race as an entity in focus. From a semantic perspective, the genitive construction 'race of Israel' represents a classificational relationship below the propositional level, which is represented in many languages by juxtaposition.

**3:5d I am completely Hebrew in every way** The phrase Ἑβραῖος ἐξ Ἑβραίων 'a Hebrew from Hebrews' has been variously taken by commentators to refer (1) to Paul's pure Hebrew ancestry, or (2) to his being brought up speaking Hebrew and following Hebrew customs, or (3) to both. BAGD (p. 213) shows how the term Ἑβραῖος 'Hebrew' was used for Jews in contrast to Gentiles and also for Aramaic-speaking Jews in contrast to Greek-speaking Jews. Since 'Hebrew' was thus a designation for both ancestry and language/customs, then ancestry would be its primary meaning, since ancestry is more basic than culture, and especially so in this context. This and the fact that Paul has already said he was of the race of Israel and of the tribe of Benjamin show that Ἑβραῖος ἐξ Ἑβραίων must have at least an implicit meaning of ancestry.

If this phrase is taken to refer to ancestry, it is idiomatic since it is obvious that if Paul's ancestors (i.e., from his parents back) were Hebrew he would be a Hebrew. The function of this idiom most likely is to stress the completeness of his "Hebrewness." That, of course, is the function of all of 3:5a-d. Its position as the last of the specifics dealing with ancestry would be appropriate for summarizing the purity of his descent. We know that Paul spoke Aramaic (Acts 21:40; 22:2) and would have had knowledge of Hebrew from his religious training. The references in Phil. 3:5e-6 to his strict observance of the Mosaic law show that he was Hebrew in culture. Based on these considerations, it appears that Ἑβραῖος ἐξ Ἑβραίων 'a Hebrew from Hebrews' refers to ancestry, language, and culture, well expressed idiomatically in English by the idiom 'born and bred' (REB). It might be translated as 'I am completely Hebrew in ancestry, language, and culture' and propositionalized as 'I am completely Hebrew in every way'.

**3:5e** *As* **a member of the Pharisee** *sect***, I** *strictly obeyed* **the law** *which Moses commanded* The Greek is κατὰ νόμον Φαρισαῖος 'as far as the law is concerned, (I was) a Pharisee'. An underlying categorical syllogism is intended:

Major premise: All Pharisees are strict observers of the law.
Minor premise: I was a Pharisee.
Conclusion: Therefore, I was a strict observer of the law.

Only the minor premise is explicitly stated in full though Paul's reference to the law (κατὰ νόμον) signals the major premise he is concerned about here. Even though the conclusion of the syllogism is left implicit, it is highly important. Paul is basing his confidence not on the name but what the name represents. In fact, we could say that 'Pharisee' had a component of meaning of 'one who strictly observes the law' which was in focus whenever Pharisee was mentioned in connection with law.

The propositionalization in the display states the minor premise and the conclusion, and 'as' suggests the major premise since it identifies Paul as coming under the assertion made in that premise.

It is important that 'the law' be understood specifically as religious law, not any other kind. 'The law *which Moses commanded*' is used in the display for two reasons: On the one hand 'the law which God commanded' does not seem especially appropriate in this context; on the other hand, while some commentators make a point of the fact that the law referred to here is a law which has been added to by the scribes, that does not seem especially in focus. However, an alternate for the display would be 'Jewish law'.

**3:6a I was** *so zealous to propagate the law that* **I persecuted the people who believe in Christ** *because I thought they were seeking to abolish the law* In the construction κατὰ ζῆλος διώκων τὴν ἐκκλησίαν 'as to zeal persecuting the church', 'zeal' presupposes something for which to be zealous, which in turn presupposes an action to enhance whatever one is zealous for. 'Zeal in persecuting the church' in and by itself is not appropriate as a reason for confidence in the flesh. Since 'law' is mentioned in both the preceding κατά clause and the following κατά clause, zeal for the law may be the idea Paul intended to communicate here in 3:6a (cf. Acts 21:20, πάντες ζηλωταὶ τοῦ νόμου ὑπάρχουσιν 'they are all zealous [literally 'zealots'] for the law'). O'Brien, (1991:374-78) has a good discussion of 3:6a, in which he argues that zeal should here be understood as "zeal *for the law* and the ancestral traditions" (p. 375).

Based on Gal. 1:13b, "I persecuted the church of God and tried to destroy it" (NIV), it seems that Paul's primary purpose in persecuting the church was to destroy it rather than force the believers in Christ to follow the law. In contrast with persecuting the church for the sake of the law, the opposite type of action is appropriate for describing Paul's zeal in maintaining the law: 'propagate, promote, cause people to obey, the law', hence the propositionalization of 3:6a that is in the display.

While Paul does not explicate the reason his zeal for the law is expressed in persecuting the church, this is potentially a very confusing point for the uninformed reader.

**3:6b** *Indeed***, as far as my obeying the law** *which Moses commanded* **is concerned, no** *human being could* **have accused me saying that I had transgressed that law** Literally, this is 'as to righteousness which (is) in (the) law, having become blameless' (cf. Luke 1:6). The righteousness referred to here is different from the righteousness referred to in Rom. 3:10 where Paul quotes the Old Testament to make the point that "there is none righteous, not even one." How is 'righteousness' here in Phil. 3:6b different? In some sense it is less demanding. A person can be blameless or perfect as far as righteousness under the law is concerned while one cannot be blameless regarding God's standard.

Usually when law and righteousness occur together in distinctive senses, law refers to the rules of conduct and righteousness is how well one follows those rules. If a person's righteousness is said to be blameless, it implies that he observes every rule of conduct. There is no good reason to expect that Paul is referring here to a rule of conduct other than the Mosaic law, though it may include laws added through the centuries. The difference between 'righteousness under the law' and God's perfect righteousness appears to be in the definition of 'blamelessly righteous'. Here in 6b righteousness is being defined by νόμος 'law', which refers not only to a rule of conduct but to a standard of judging people as to how they keep that rule of conduct. It is a different standard from God's perfect standard. Silva says: "The word 'faultless' does not at all reflect any illusion regarding sinlessness; rather, it must be viewed as a fairly standard way of expressing exemplary conformity to the way of life prescribed by the OT." As Silva points out, when Paul says that he is faultless as far as the righteousness which is in the law is concerned, he must be referring to a standard that can be measured objectively, since his purpose is to present verifiable statements backing his claim that he has more grounds for confidence in the flesh than anyone else. What he means is, "As for the standard commonly used to judge people's conformity to the law, I was faultless." This might be propositionalized 'As far as my obeying the law *which Moses commanded* is concerned, *no human being could* have accused me of being unrighteous at all' or, '*could* have accused me saying that I had transgressed that law'. But 'as far as...is concerned' is a formula introducing obedience to the law as a new topic, and this topic was already introduced in the propositionalization of 3:5e. Therefore 'indeed' is used at the beginning of 3:6b to show that this topic has already been introduced.

In translation one must be careful not to imply that Paul kept the law blamelessly before God. This would be contrary to some of the main points of the gospel message he taught (e.g., "no one will be declared righteous in his sight by observing the law" in Rom. 3:20, NIV).

While commentators tend to gloss the aorist participle γενόμενος as 'having become', a comparison with a similar usage of γίνομαι in the aorist in 1 Thess. 2:10, ὡς ὁσίως καὶ δικαίως καὶ ἀμέμπτως ὑμῖν τοῖς πιστεύουσιν ἐγενήθημεν 'how holy, righteous, and blameless we were (not 'we had become') among you who believed' shows that the sense 'become' rather than 'be' is not demanded in Phil. 3:6b either.

## BOUNDARIES AND COHERENCE

This paragraph coheres as a CLAIM-*justification* paragraph pattern.

## PROMINENCE AND THEME

For a CLAIM-*justification* paragraph pattern, elements of both the CLAIM and *justification* are integral to the theme. However, since the *justification* here is made up of seven constituents, the ideas are combined. In the theme statement the second, third and fourth constituents, dealing with Paul's ancestry, are grouped as one and the last three, dealing with his observance of the Mosaic law, are grouped as another. Circumcision is included in the theme statement quite specifically because of its importance in the context.

In order to make it clear that Paul does not actually believe that relying upon his attainments is efficacious in becoming a child of God, 'if it were beneficial for salvation' is included in the theme.

# PARAGRAPH CLUSTER CONSTITUENT 3:7–11
## (Expository Paragraph: Contraexpectation to 3:4b–6)

*THEME: I consider all these things which I used to think of as advantageous, and everything else as well, to be worthless because I want to know Christ and be united with him, made righteous through trusting in Christ alone.*

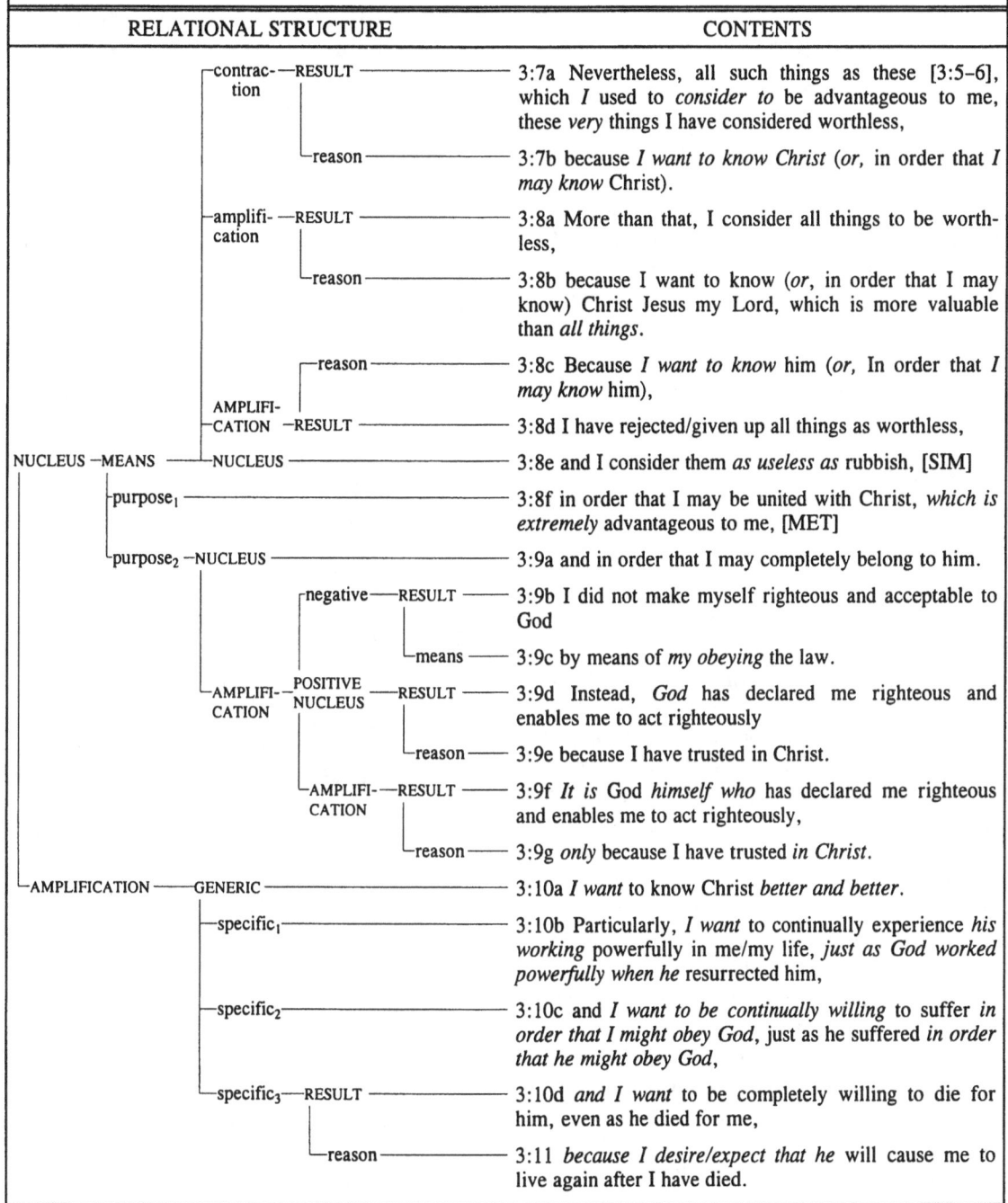

### INTENT

The sequence in the display chart of contraction, amplification, AMPLIFICATION, NUCLEUS shows that there is a four-fold repetition of the same general concept, 'I consider all things as worthless in order that I may know Christ, be united and incorporate in him'. The idea of being incorporate in Christ is amplified in 3:9b–g by statements that this relationship of being justified and righteous is through faith in Christ alone, not through Paul's own obedience to the law. 'Knowing Christ' is amplified in 3:10–11.

The manifold amplification indicates the significance Paul places on knowing Christ and on the fact that justification comes through him alone.

## NOTES

**3:7a Nevertheless** It is uncertain whether ἀλλά 'but' occurred at the beginning of 3:7 in the original text. (It is in brackets in the UBSGNT indicating that its presence is not completely certain; it occurs in the Hodges and Farstad text.) In any case, it is implied here, as shown by the strong contrast between what Paul once thought extremely important and the opposite belief he now holds as even more important. This contrast is of the contraexpectation type since Paul's new viewpoint is unexpected following upon his former viewpoint.

**all such things as these [3:5–6]** Regarding the meaning of ἅτινα, in general this relative pronoun means 'whatever' if it occurs without an antecedent. In such a usage it would normally be in the singular. If it occurs with an antecedent, it may have the idea of belonging to a certain class, 'of such a kind that', or it may just function as the simple relative pronoun ὅ (BAGD, ὅστις, p. 587.3), but it would normally be singular or plural depending on its antecedent. Phil. 3:5–6 lists seven gains for Paul, and these are clearly an antecedent to ἅτινα, which is plural. However, ἅτινα is connected with ταῦτα in a construction that would normally be translated as, 'whatever (things)...these (things)'. It appears, then, that there is a combination here of both functions of the word: 'whatever things of such a kind as this (3:5–6)'. REB translates this as 'all such assets' and TNT as 'all such advantages'.

**which *I* used to *consider* to be advantageous to me** In vv. 7–8, is Paul contrasting methods (supposed or real) of coming to God, or is he contrasting the value of knowing Christ over against the value of all the things he has mentioned in vv. 5–6 and anything else (πάντα)? There is, in vv. 3:4b–6, a reference to one supposed method of becoming children of God. Based on the concession of 3:4b–6, we might expect that the CONTRAEXPECTATION of 3:7–11 would be something like 'but all those things were worthless as far as enabling me to become a true child of God'. But that is not the case. Instead, the primary focus is on the contrastive value of the old advantages/gains (and anything whatsoever) and the surpassing value of *knowing* Christ.

Paul's ready willingness to consider all these things as worthless in order to gain Christ comes through in the many markers of intensification such as repetition, piling up of function words at the beginning of 3:8a, and the use of the lexically emphatic words τὸ ὑπερέχον 'the surpassing value' and σκύβαλα 'rubbish'.

A majority of commentators cited in Greenlee (1992) take ἦν μοι κέρδη 'were gains to me' as implying that the things mentioned in vv. 5–6 were actually gains to Paul previously. The question is, Is Paul stating that they were gains to him as far as the old carnal system was concerned, or is he saying that he used to consider them gains as far as attaining righteousness was concerned? It is true that they were advantageous to him for certain purposes and that they were real qualifications within the system that the Judaizers espoused. It is also true that Paul does not use the word 'consider' in 3:7a though he does use it three times in vv. 7–8. Therefore, a potential propositionalization would be, 'all such things as these [3:5–6] which used to be advantageous to me *in order that people would consider me righteous*'. Note that if the gain has to do with becoming righteous, becoming one of God's people, the idea of 'consider' needs to be included, either Paul himself considering them as advantages or other people considering them as advantages. If the gain does not have to do with being righteous, then it is questionable whether it would be in focus here.

**these *very* things** The inclusion of ταῦτα 'these things' following upon ἅτινα 'whatever things' and the position of ταῦτα before the verb emphasize that it is the very things that Paul once saw as gains he now considers to be losses. A similar construction occurs in Acts 7:35.

**worthless** BAGD (p. 338) states that ζημία in the New Testament and other early Christian literature is found only with the senses of "*damage, disadvantage, loss, forfeit.*" Here in Phil. 3:7–8 it is usually translated 'loss'. But, if these things were gains (or supposed gains) to him before, does ζημία mean that they have lost all their value and are now worthless to him, or does it mean that they are actually 'disadvantages'? While the general sense of the word would certainly allow for the meaning 'disadvantage' here and these things were actually hindrances to him as far as his coming to know Christ is concerned, there is at least one reason why ζημία may indicate that Paul is focusing on the fact that they have lost all their value to him rather than that they are hindrances. This reason is that in v. 8 he appears to equate ζημία with σκύβαλα, which BAGD (p. 758) glosses as "*refuse, rubbish, leavings, dirt, dung.*" These are the types of things which are usually thought of as worthless rather than as hindrances. In fact, the whole tenor of vv. 7–8 leads us to conclude that ζημία has the meaning 'loss' in the sense of 'worthless', not 'disadvantage'.

**3:7b because *I want to know* Christ (*or,* in order that *I may know* Christ)** In order to understand better the meaning of διὰ τὸν Χριστόν 'on account of/because of Christ', it is helpful to study the structure of vv. 7b–8:

ταῦτα ἥγημαι... ζημίαν
these I-considered loss

διὰ τὸν Χριστόν
because-of Christ

A ἡγοῦμαι πάντα ζημίαν εἶναι
I-consider all loss to-be

B διὰ τὸ ὑπερέχον τῆς γνώσεως
because-of the surpassing knowledge

Χριστοῦ Ἰησοῦ τοῦ κυρίου μου
of-Christ Jesus the Lord of-me

B' δι' ὃν
because-of whom

A' τὰ πάντα ἐζημιώθην
all(things) I-have-lost

A" καὶ ἡγοῦμαι σκύβαλα
and I-consider(them) rubbish

B" ἵνα Χριστὸν κερδήσω
that Christ I-may-gain

The parallelism brought out in this graphic representation of the chiasm suggests that the ἵνα clause and the διά constructions have a similar function. The semantic structure underlying the repetition in the chiasm is that of forfeiting one thing to gain another. The forfeiting as loss is brought out most clearly in the 'I consider them loss' constructions; gain is brought out most clearly in the MEANS-purpose construction: I consider (them) rubbish in order that I might gain Christ'. These considerations show that the διά constructions also indicate what is to be gained.

The διά constructions could be considered either reason or purpose in the propositionalization. Note that in MEANS-purpose constructions and in RESULT-reason constructions of this type, the purpose or reason construction does not indicate whether the action it represents has been accomplished already or not. This is signaled by the context. In this case, obviously Paul already knew Christ when he wrote the epistle though he continually wanted to know him better.

**3:8a More than that** At the beginning of 3:8 there is a piling up of function words, ἀλλὰ μενοῦνγε καί, three to five different function words depending upon how one breaks up the words (i.e., ἀλλὰ μὲν οὖν γε καί is a possibility). Like the more simple ἀλλὰ καί 'but also' construction, it is not a regular contrast or negative-POSITIVE sense that is being signaled, but an ascensive component; that is, something in the construction which ἀλλὰ μενοῦνγε καί introduces is greater or more intensive than that mentioned in the preceding construction. 'In fact' would be a good English translation but it is idiomatic so has not been used in the display text. 'More than that' is not idiomatic and is more to the point.

**all things** Some commentators maintain that πάντα refers only to ἅτινα... ταῦτα and means 'all these things'. But if that were true, then there would be no other contrast in intensification for ἀλλὰ μενοῦνγε καί to signal. Also, based on the absence of the article, it is more likely that πάντα means 'all things' rather than 'all these things'. Thus πάντα 'all things' represents the concept in v. 8 that is greater or more inclusive. It signals a more inclusive reference than ἅτινα... ταῦτα 'all such things... these things' does in 7a.

Some commentators maintain that a contrastive difference in the tense is being emphasized by ἀλλὰ μενοῦνγε καί; but since the perfect tense in v. 7 has reference to the *continuation* of Paul's state of mind (considering these things as worthless), no real change is signaled by the present tense here in 8a. It must be remembered that the piling up of function words signals a significant change in intensification between v. 7 and v. 8. As far as time and duration are concerned, the two tenses would signal not 'I did consider' and 'I now consider', but 'I have considered and continue to consider' and 'I continue to consider'. This is hardly a difference at all. Therefore it is evident that the intensification contrast between 3:7 and 3:8 has nothing to do with tense.

**3:8b know Christ Jesus** 'The knowledge of Christ Jesus my Lord' is referring to Paul's *experiential* knowledge of Christ. As v. 10 shows, it is a knowledge realized in close fellowship with

Christ. Thus 'the knowledge of Christ' is further defined there.

**which is more valuable than *all things*** The substantive phrase τὸ ὑπερέχον is constructed from the verb ὑπερέχω, which normally expresses the idea 'to surpass, to excel'. It could be translated as 'because I want to know Christ, which surpasses all things'. 'Surpass', however, may be figurative and not very specific, so 'is more valuable than' seems better.

As to the possibility of 'because I want to know Christ, who is more valuable than all things', the Greek text says that it is the *knowledge* of Christ that is of surpassing value. 'Know' indicates the relationship that Paul has with Christ. The relationship itself is important, though it is Christ who makes the relationship of supreme value. It would seem best to retain the connection between 'knowledge' and 'surpassing' in the propositionalization. In languages where this is difficult or unnatural, Christ might be directly indicated as of supreme value.

**3:8d I have rejected/given up all things as worthless** The obvious equating of the active form ἀπολέσας 'lose' with the passive form ζημιωθείς 'lose' in Luke 9:25 shows that there is a mismatch between the semantic sense 'lose' and the surface structure Greek forms by which it is represented. This may be because the concept of 'lose' is not necessarily one in which there is an implied agent who takes away the lost item. Therefore the use of the passive form ἐζημιώθην here in Phil. 3:8 was not necessarily based on Paul's wishing to indicate a sense of 'lose' in which he had no voluntary intention. The context—with its repetition of 'I consider(ed) these/all things loss'—strongly suggests that voluntary intention is involved. Notice also how close in graphic/phonological form ἡγοῦμαι πάντα ζμίαν εἶναι 'I have considered all things loss' is to τὰ πάντα ἐζημιώθην 'I have lost all things', strongly suggesting that one of the reasons Paul uses ἐζημιώθην is for repetitive parallelism. Thus ἐζημιώθην is rendered as 'I have rejected/given up as loss/worthless'. TEV translates it 'I have thrown everything away'. Greenlee (1992) cites four commentators who consider "the meaning is that Paul rejected these things." BAGD (p. 338.1) puts this occurrence of ζημιόω under "permit oneself to *sustain loss*" and translates the clause as "*for whose sake I forfeited everything.*"

'Loss', an abstract noun, is rendered 'worthless' in the display. That these things are a loss to Paul in the sense of being worthless is indicated by 3:8e, where he states that he considers them rubbish.

**all things** The Greek is a substantive phrase, τὰ πάντα, literally, 'the all (things)'. In English the article is never used with 'all things' and any explicit backward reference would be shown by a demonstrative, 'all *those* things'. However, the Greek article does not always act exactly like the English demonstrative in this type of construction. In Greek generally the first occurrence of an item that is being introduced as new information is represented without the article, while succeeding occurrences of the same item are with the article. If πᾶς 'all' usually functions in this same way also, then it may explain why the concept of 'all things (whatsoever)' first occurs without the article and then with the article. In the note under 'all things' in 3:8a it has been shown that the first occurrence of πάντα 'all things' means 'all things in general' or 'all things whatsoever', rather than as referring only to the type of things mentioned in vv. 5-6. Once this position is taken, it makes no sense to take the occurrence of τὰ πάντα 'all things' in 8d to refer to something less inclusive, especially since the structure of this paragraph is repetitive for the purpose of marking intensification.

**3:8e *as useless as* rubbish** BAGD (p. 758) glosses σκύβαλον as "*refuse, rubbish, leavings, dirt, dung.*" The figure here is basically a simile. The point of similarity between rubbish and all things which have only worldly value is the fact that they are both useless and worthless.

**3:8f in order that I may be united with Christ, *which is extremely* advantageous to me** The Greek is ἵνα Χριστὸν κερδήσω, literally, 'in order that I might gain Christ'. To arrive at a good rendering of this, the following facts are pertinent:

1. When we talk about possessing another person, we are actually referring to having some type of relationship with that person rather than possessing him or her as one might possess a car, for instance. Note BAGD's category (p. 332) under ἔχω 'have' I2b: "to denote the possession of persons to whom one has close relationships."

2. In some languages it may be difficult to state that one person can 'gain' another without expressing the kinship relationship one has with him.

3. Paul's use of 'to gain' here is influenced by his contrasting 'gain' and 'loss' in this carefully constructed repetitive structure. In fact, 'to gain' can be seen as somewhat metaphorical.

Thus, a good way to express the gaining of a relationship with Christ may be 'coming to know Christ' or 'becoming united to Christ'. The latter is closer to the idea of possession which 'gain' implies and also to the concepts communicated in the following verse. Paul seemingly intends to have such a close tie between the first part of the ἵνα clause (3:8f) and the second part (3:9). The rendering in the display retains the meaning of the metaphor by expressing it as an adjective (rather than as an abstract noun) and at the same time indicates the nature of the relationship Paul has with Christ.

**3:9a and in order that** In view of the conjunction καί 'and' at the beginning of v. 9 and the subjunctive form εὑρεθῶ 'I might be found' it is clear that εὑρεθῶ is part of the purpose construction that begins in 8f.

**I may completely belong to him** Regarding the use of εὑρεθῶ 'find' here Beare comments as follows:

> As in the French *se trouver*, the notion of 'finding' has virtually disappeared; the verb means little more than 'be in fact' (cf. Gal. ii. 17: 'But if while we are seeking to be justified in Christ, we ourselves also were found to be sinners...'; with Burton's note: 'It is clear from N.T. examples that *heurethēn* in particular had the sense "prove to be", "turn out to be", almost "to become", without special thought of the discovery of the fact' [*Galatians*, I.C.C., p. 125]).

It would appear that in a context like this, where 'found' acts like an orienter (equal to 'discover that') and the agent of the finding is not focused upon, the orienter is also not necessary semantically. It would hardly seem necessary to propositionalize it here as 'and in order that *God* would find that I belong to Christ'.

**completely belong to him** Some translate ἐν αὐτῷ here as 'united to him', 'in union with him'. A closer translation would probably be 'incorporate in him' (NEB), since καὶ εὑρεθῶ ἐν αὐτῷ 'and be found in him' appears to introduce the following discussion of righteousness or justification (i.e., a right relationship with God), a relationship whereby we become members of God's people. The more easily understood 'completely belong to' is used instead of 'incorporate' in the display.

**3:9b-c I did not make myself righteous and acceptable to God by means of** *my obeying* **the law** The participial construction here begins with μὴ ἔχων 'not having'. We would expect a present participle such as this, which expresses a stative sense, to signal either a descriptive or amplificatory relationship. The latter seems more appropriate in this context. It is true that 3:9b-g is descriptive of the relationship of being in Christ, but in an SSA, the descriptive relation modifies a non-abstract concept.

Eadie says, "The apostle characterizes it [δικαιοσύνη 'righteousness'] as his own—ἐμήν—as wrought out and secured by himself."

There are some good reasons to understand the meaning of δικαιοσύνη 'righteousness' in this verse to be more than simply 'be declared righteous, be justified':

First, it is more probable that a word will maintain the same basic sense in its occurrences in a close-knit context than that the meaning will be significantly different. If Paul had intended a different meaning for righteousness he would probably have at least used the noun δικαιοσύνην when switching from the topic of his righteousness to the righteousness that is through faith. However, he uses only the article τήν, functioning as a pronoun to imply the repeated 'righteousness'.

Second, it is difficult to see how δικαιοσύνη can mean 'be declared righteous (by God)' in ἐμὴν δικαιοσύνην 'my righteousness'. It is true that Paul in his previous way of life believed that God would justify him on the basis of his own ethical righteousness. But ἐμὴν δικαιοσύνην can hardly mean 'my justification' since the purpose of the ἐμήν is to indicate the effort of Paul, while 'my justification' would be objective, indicating that Paul was the one justified by God. So it would appear that either ethical righteousness or something more generic, including both ethical righteousness and God's justification, is intended.

Finally, when Paul describes his new life, if δικαιοσύνη refers only to justification, without any reference to the ethical righteousness God also imparts (i.e., enables the believer to achieve), then ethical righteousness is missing when Paul talks about righteousness through faith in Christ. Not that 'justification' is not of supreme value. But in a section where Paul is pointing up the falsity of the Judaizers' doctrine, it would seem that he would want to also stress the superiority of the ethical righteousness which comes through faith in Christ. In vv. 8–11 Paul is talking about the things which are of value far surpassing anything under the law. From that standpoint it is not inappropriate to take δικαιοσύνη with its full meaning. Liddon (p. 17) comments as follows:

> The δικαιοσύνη then which God gives includes these two elements; acquittal of the guilt of sin, or justification in the narrower sense of the word, and the communication of a new moral life, ἵνα τὸ δικαίωμα τοῦ νόμου πληρωθῇ ἐν ἡμῖν ['that the ordinance of the law might be fulfilled in us'] (Rom. viii. 4). These two sides of the gift of δικαιοσύνη can only be separated in thought; in fact they are inseparable...This true righteousness is one, not two or more.

The preposition ἐκ in 9c has the primary meaning of 'from, out of', and it signals some relationship between νόμου 'law' and ἐμὴν δικαιοσύνην 'my righteousness'. Whatever that relationship is, it must be somehow related to Paul's own experience. In Rom. 2:13 Paul describes the relationship between law and righteousness: "it is those who obey the law who will be declared righteous" (NIV). Though 'my righteousness' does not primarily refer to justification here in Phil. 3:9b, the principle that obedience to the law produces righteousness is the same. Since Paul is talking about his own righteousness, righteousness which he has "wrought out," a RESULT-means relationship is appropriate: 'I did not make myself righteous by means of my obeying the law'. Note that ἐκ often expresses some type of causative relationship (see category 3 under ἐκ in BAGD, p. 234).

**3:9d** *God* **has declared me righteous and enables me to act righteously** See the note on 3:9b–c regarding the meaning of δικαιοσύνη 'righteousness' in this verse.

**3:9e I have trusted in Christ** The grammatical relationship between πίστεως 'faith' and Χριστοῦ is genitive and so some commentators have taken this phrase to mean something other than 'faith in Christ', for example, "the faithfulness of Christ" (O'Brien 1991) and "faith which Christ kindles, of which He is the author, which, also, He nourishes and maintains" (Kennedy). However, most commentators take πίστεως Χριστοῦ to mean 'faith in Christ'. That such a sense is possible in a genitive relationship is shown by a comparison with such examples as ἔχετε πίστιν θεοῦ, literally, 'have faith of God' in Mark 11:22, which can hardly have any other meaning than 'have faith in God'. Since the genitive may convey such a relationship, and since "Paul never speaks unambiguously of Jesus as faithful...or believing" (Silva), and since the sense 'faith in Christ' is the primary sense in a context where God's granting righteousness is concerned, it is more likely that πίστεως Χριστοῦ means 'faith in Christ' rather than something else.

In this context, πίστις 'faith' has the sense of 'trusting, relying upon' more than 'belief'. Hawthorne comments as follows:

> Faith is...an admission that I cannot earn God's approval, but can only accept his free offer of forgiveness, grace and love...Faith...in its strictest sense is not intellectual assent to a series of propositions about Christ, but the act of personal trust in and self-surrender to Christ.

It is the contrast between confidence in oneself, which avails nothing, and the necessary confidence in Christ alone that brings out the 'trust, confidence, dependence' side of πίστις 'faith'.

**3:9f–g** *It is* **God** *himself who* **has declared me righteous and enables me to act righteously,** *only* **because I have trusted** *in Christ* Schenk (as cited in O'Brien 1991) has shown that the surface structure of 3:9b–g can be seen as chiastic. The chiasm brings out the sharp antithetical nature of the participial construction. The construction might also be presented in the following form:

μὴ ἔχων
not having

A ἐμὴν δικαιοσύνην
   my-own righteousness

B τὴν ἐκ νόμου
   the(one) from law

AA ἀλλὰ τὴν διὰ πίστεως Χριστοῦ
    but the(one) through faith of/in-Christ

BB τὴν ἐκ θεοῦ δικαιοσύνην
    the from God righteousness

AA' ἐπὶ τῇ πίστει
    on-the-basis-of the faith

While Paul's former righteousness was one of self-dependence (A), he now depends wholly on Christ (AA). This component of dependence on

Christ is so focal that he repeats it for emphasis in AA'. This is shown in the display rendering by 'only' ('*only* because I have trusted in Christ'); the emphasis is on faith alone as the prerequisite to being made righteous by God.

The display uses '*it is* God *himself*' to bring out the contrastive structure and the inherent superiority of God himself over the law or anything else. In the Greek text emphasis is expressed through surface-structure parallelism and abstract nouns; in the propositionalization it is expressed in other ways.

**3:10a *I want* to know Christ** The relationship of 3:10-11 to what comes before it is one for which many solutions have been put forward. Many variables are involved. One of the problems is that if τοῦ γνῶναι αὐτόν 'to know him' is taken as signaling 3:10-11 as a purpose construction it tends to make for a long, overextended subordinate construction. This is probably the reason why many modern English versions (e.g., Beck, NIV, NRSV, Phillips, REB, TEV, C. B. Williams) begin a new sentence here showing no explicit grammatical subordination to what has come before. There is, however, potential grammatical support for such a translation; it need not be seen as only based on English constraints. It is possible to understand the articular infinitive construction that begins with τοῦ γνῶναι αὐτόν 'to know him' as signaling amplification. BDF (§ 400) classifies this articular infinitive in Phil. 3:10 under "Often very little of the consecutive sense is left with τοῦ and the infinitive and its relationship to other elements in the sentence is very loose (epexegetical usage)." In Rom. 6:6 (ἵνα καταργηθῇ τὸ σῶμα τῆς ἁμαρτίας, τοῦ μηκέτι δουλεύειν ἡμᾶς τῇ ἁμαρτίᾳ 'so that the body of sin may be rendered powerless, that we no longer be slaves to sin') an articular infinitive follows a ἵνα clause and it may be understood either as purpose (Vincent) or epexegetical, that is, equivalence or amplification (BDF, ibid.). The semantic difference between real purpose and epexegesis can sometimes be so close that it would not be expected that an author would always use the "proper" grammatical form at these points. The same might be said of the semantic difference between parallel purposes, a series of purposes, and epexegesis following purpose. Another example is in Acts 26:17b-18; there the articular infinitive construction may be taken as equivalence or amplification.

It seems best, especially for the purpose of translation, to understand 3:10-11 as amplification of 3:7-9. The MEANS-purpose structure ('I consider all things loss in order that I may know Christ') is established earlier in the paragraph, so an amplification of the subject of knowing Christ is clearly appropriate. Although most commentators analyze 3:10-11 as a purpose construction because it is an articular infinitive, the construction of the paragraph as a whole is such that amplification appears to be a more suitable solution semantically.

**know Christ *better and better*** When Paul says he wants to know Christ (τοῦ γνῶναι αὐτόν 'to know him'), he is speaking more of an experiential knowledge than an intellectual knowledge. (For a similar use of γινώσκω 'know', see John 17:3; Gal. 4:9; 1 John 4:8.) In New Testament Greek, γινώσκω often implied a "personal relation between the knower and the known, involving the influence of the object of knowledge upon the knower" (Vincent). The constituents which follow 3:10b (3:10c-d) continue to talk about wanting to share in certain experiences of Christ's. A good alternative to 'know' is suggested by Loh and Nida, 'I want to be associated with Christ'. Since 3:10b-d are considered specifics of 'to know Christ', they will help the translator determine what should be the translation here for γνῶναι 'know' in any language.

Paul is not speaking of an initial knowledge of Christ. Hence 'better and better' is supplied in the display.

**3:10b Particularly** By far the majority of commentators in Greenlee (1992) do not take the καί immediately preceding τὴν δύναμιν τῆς ἀναστάσεως αὐτοῦ 'the power of his resurrection' as expressing simple coordination, but rather as an explanation of what Paul means in saying that he wants to know Christ. Each of the three following constituents focuses on Christ and relationship with him. There is a GENERIC-specific relationship between 3:10a and 3:10b-d. The specifics do not necessarily cover the total experience of knowing Christ, but they are the specifics that Paul wants to stress here. This is expressed by 'particularly' in the display.

***I want* to continually experience *his working powerfully* in me/my life, *just as God worked powerfully when he* resurrected him** If 10b, c, and d are specifics of 'know him', they will retain the focus on Christ that 'know him' has. The meaning of 'the power of his resurrection' will thus not focus on the power without noticeable reference to Christ himself. It is not just the benefits he might receive from Christ that Paul wants to experience; he wants to experience an intimate relationship with Christ himself.

The abstract noun 'power' that is here commonly refers to an attribute of an event ('he acted powerfully') or an attribute of a person or thing ('he is powerful'). In some languages this sense is not expressed as a noun or substantive, or, if it is, it occurs only in restricted environments. So we must ask what 'power' is an attribute of in the phrase here, 'the power of his resurrection'. The only explicit action in this phrase is that of 'resurrecting' (i.e., 'causing to live') or 'being resurrected'. If 'resurrect' is the intended action, it must have application to Paul's experience at the time of his writing of the letter, since his present experience is in focus. Paul is no doubt saying that he wants to continually experience Christ's powerfully giving him new life, as in Rom. 6:4, "We were therefore buried with him through baptism into death in order that, just as Christ was raised from the dead through the glory of the Father, we too might walk in newness of life."

A number of commentators see resurrection here as referring to new life given by Christ. Greenlee (1992) lists eight commentators under the classification, "It is the power to give new life and enable Christians to live the new life in Christ." This takes 'resurrection' figuratively. But of course it is literal as far as Christ's own resurrection is concerned, so in the display both the figurative and nonfigurative senses are represented.

**in me/my life** In some languages 'live' refers only to physical life. Therefore some generic representation for 'living spiritually' may be needed such as 'I want him to make me a new person in every respect just as he was made new when God powerfully resurrected him'.

**3:10c** *I want to be continually willing* **to suffer** *in order that I might obey God,* **just as he suffered** *in order that he might obey God* The word κοινωνία 'fellowship, participation, sharing' implies doing something with someone or, in this case, being willing to accept adverse treatment along with someone else or being treated in the same way someone else has been treated. Since Christ suffered at a different time than Paul did, 'be willing to suffer just as Christ suffered' is more appropriate than 'be willing to suffer together with Christ'.

The words 'be willing' are added to make clear that it is an active participation on Paul's part that is intended, not a passive acceptance of something that one can really do nothing about. Filling out the Greek surface structure here would yield a literal translation of 'I want to know the participation/fellowship of his suffering' or, better, 'I want to experience participation in his sufferings'. There does not seem to be a meaning difference between this and '*I want to be continually willing* to suffer just as he suffered'.

The words 'in order that I might obey God' are supplied to help delimit the suffering. This is suffering that involves Christian experience.

Since Paul was undergoing suffering as a prisoner at the time he wrote these words and the prospect of death by execution was real, it is difficult to see these words as having only a mystical sense, as some commentators maintain. In fact, the mystical and real-life senses converge. This can be seen in 1 Cor. 15:30, "Why do we endanger ourselves every hour?" where actual death is being talked about and 15:31, "I die every day," where mystical conformity to Christ's death in the sense of putting his own desires to death is meant.

**3:10d** *and I want* **to be completely willing to die for him, even as he died for me** It is difficult to understand how 'death' can be taken only in a figurative sense if 'sufferings' is taken in a physical sense, as some commentators do. O'Brien (1991) does set forth a substantial argument for taking figurative death as that which is in focus here, summing it up with the following statement:

> It is not in the fellowship of Christ's sufferings as such that Paul is conformed to Christ's death; rather, it is by participating in those sufferings (which he experiences in the course of his apostolic labours) *and* as strengthened to do so by the power of his resurrection that he is continually being conformed to Christ's death.

But in the context of Paul's experience of suffering and possible imminent death in the book as a whole and the immediately preceding context that refers to physical suffering, it seems quite obvious that the addressees will understand 'being conformed unto his death' as referring to Paul's willingness to be conformed to Christ even to the point of dying for his sake and not only to Paul's putting to death his sinful nature. While it is true that a person might be willing to die for Christ but unwilling to die to his own passions for Christ's sake, the whole thrust of Paul's life and teachings requires that the addressees understand Paul's commitment here to be to every area of his life.

Alternate renderings for 3:10d are 'even to the point of dying for him' or 'even to the point of my being willing to die for him just as he died for me'. The former retains by carryover implication from 3:10c the concept of conformity with Christ; the latter keeps it explicit.

**3:11** *because I desire/expect that* The Greek is εἴ πως. There has been much discussion as to the meaning of these words which literally mean 'if somehow'. The question is whether it implies any doubt in this context, and if so, what is the content of the doubt. From examples in the LXX (3 Kingdoms 21:31; 4 Kingdoms 19:4; Jer. 28:8) and New Testament (Acts 27:12; Rom. 1:10; 11:14), it is obvious that εἴ πως does express some degree of doubt, at least in some contexts. In Jer. 28:8 (LXX) the degree of doubt is very high, probably to the point of sarcasm, θρηνεῖτε αὐτήν, λάβετε ῥητίνην τῇ διαφθορᾷ αὐτῆς, εἴπως ἰαθήσεται, translated by Brenton as "lament for her; take balm for her deadly wound, if by any means she may be healed." However, in Phil. 3:11, the opposite is true. According to the context of the epistle, especially 1:23 and 3:20-21, and from Paul's writings in general (see especially Rom. 6:5), he does not doubt that he will attain the resurrection of the dead. In fact, the stating of such doubt at this point would weaken his argument for the validity of the gospel he preached.

The two interpretations that appear to provide the best solution for the meaning of εἴ πως in this context are:

1. In 3:12-14 the focus is on continually striving to accomplish Christ's purposes. One of Paul's aims in that unit is to show the believers that there is no time in the Christian life on earth where the Christian has reached perfection and may rest from all his labors. This idea is introduced in v. 10 when Paul mentions 'the fellowship of his suffering' and 'being conformed to his death', and εἴ πως then carries the idea on. In the New Testament especially, εἴ πως seems to focus on striving in expectancy to accomplish some difficult task more than on doubt that it will be accomplished. Greenlee (1992) describes this sense of εἴ πως as "emphasizing the need of constant vigilance."

2. The meaning of εἴ πως here is 'by whatever means'. O'Brien (1991) says: "On this view the element of uncertainty lies with πως (= 'somehow, in some way'): he might reach the resurrection through martyrdom (or by some other kind of death), or he might be alive at the coming of Christ (cf. Phil. 1:20-26)."

While the second interpretation is certainly a possible one, it is a secondary sense of εἴ πως, and something in the context would signal that a secondary rather than a primary sense is in focus here. What that signal might be is not evident. It seems best, therefore, to understand interpretation 1 as closer to the meaning Paul intended, though it also requires taking εἴ πως with a secondary meaning. But in this case the context does suggest a good reason for the secondary meaning.

Another question is what communication relation is intended by εἴ πως here. Bruce (1989) says that in general εἴ πως introduces "a clause of purpose where the attainment of the purpose is not altogether within the subject's power." In two references (Acts 27:12; Rom. 11:14) of the other three where εἴ πως occurs in the New Testament the relation involved is purpose. Because the attainment of the purpose is not altogether within the subject's power in this case in Phil. 3:11 and because a purpose clause might imply that being willing to die for Christ is a prerequisite for salvation (signified here by 'resurrection'), purpose does not seem the most appropriate relation here. Instead, in the display a reason proposition is used that includes the normal marker ('because') plus 'I desire/expect'. This type of proposition is closely related to purpose, yet does not directly imply that the reason is the effectual means of accomplishing the result.

Verses 3:10b-11 appear to have a chiastic structure—power of his *resurrection*, fellowship of his *suffering*, being conformed to his *death*, if somehow I may attain unto the *resurrection* from the dead. Loh and Nida say, "The chiastic structure of verses 10 and 11 shows that this clause [v. 11] is to be taken with the clause immediately preceding." Meyer also takes v. 11 as connected to 10d.

Since, according to the view that we have taken, εἴ πως communicates a sense of striving, which is very difficult to communicate in propositionalizing v. 11, it is possible in this case to transfer that sense to 10d: '*I want* to be completely willing to die for him, even as he died for me, *because I desire/expect that he* will cause me to live again after I have died'.

**he will cause me to live again after I have died** In the phrase καταντήσω εἰς τὴν ἐξανάστασιν τὴν ἐκ νεκρῶν 'I might attain the resurrection from the dead (people)' the focus is not on *people*, so this element is not required to appear in a propositionalization or translation (e.g., 'he may cause me to live again after I have died and have been like/with other dead people'). In fact, the expression 'resurrection of/from the dead' borders on the idiomatic. Note that in Rom. 1:4 Christ's own resurrection is called ἀναστάσεως νεκρῶν 'the resurrection of/from the dead'. The word νεκρῶν 'dead (people)' here may carry the idea of a state (being dead) rather than of *people* being dead.

The implied agent of Paul's resurrection is taken to be Christ rather than the Father because Christ is in focus in general in vv. 10–11 ('I want to know him' definitely refers to Christ). Thus Christ is also in focus as the life-giver in relation to Paul in 3:10b. Christ's agency in the resurrection can be seen in John 6:40, "For my Father's will is that everyone who looks to the Son and believes in him shall have eternal life, and I will raise him up at the last day" (NIV), and in the implications of John 11:25–26.

## BOUNDARIES AND COHERENCE

The final boundary of this unit is taken to be v. 11 since vv. 12–14 form the *basis* for the APPEAL in v. 15.

## PROMINENCE AND THEME

The basic orientation of the 3:7–11 paragraph is Paul's giving up as worthless what he once considered gain (7a, 8a, 8d, 8e) in order that he might know Christ (7b, 8b, 8c, 10) and be united with him (8f, 9). The theme statement is based on this fact.

# DIVISION CONSTITUENT 3:12–21 (Hortatory Section: Appeal₂ of 3:1–4:1)

*THEME: Follow my example of constantly striving to become more and more like Christ rather than following the bad example of those who are lustful and think only about earthly things. As for us, Christ will transform our earthly bodies to be like his heavenly body.*

| MACROSTRUCTURE | CONTENTS |
|---|---|
| APPEAL₁ | 3:12–16 Since you desire to be perfected and since you have my example of not considering that I am already perfect but of constantly striving to become more and more like Christ, follow my example. |
| APPEAL₂ | 3:17–21 Imitate me and those who live as I do since there are many people who are bad examples as shown by their lustful behavior, thinking only about earthly things. As for us, Christ will transform our lowly earthly bodies to be like his glorious heavenly body. |

## INTENT AND MACROSTRUCTURE

Both paragraphs in the 3:12–21 section are hortatory and their *APPEALS* are similar: 'follow my example', 'imitate me and those who live as I do'. In the first paragraph the example is Paul's alone. In the second paragraph Paul not only mentions the good example of others who live as he does, but the bad example of immoral people that is not to be imitated.

## BOUNDARIES AND COHERENCE

The coherence of this section is seen in the similarity of the *APPEALS*.

## PROMINENCE AND THEME

The *APPEAL* of the second paragraph is completely generic in form, but it certainly has ties with the content of the *APPEAL* of the first paragraph concerning Paul's example of striving to be more and more like Christ. But even this example is quite generic. The first paragraph focuses on Paul's good example, and the second focuses on the bad example of the libertines, an example to be avoided.

Both paragraphs have a reference to heaven (14b and 20–21). The second of these references to heaven is a motivating *basis* for the *APPEAL* and probably also serves as an introduction to the *summary* (4:1). It is therefore included in the theme statement.

# SECTION CONSTITUENT 3:12–16 (Hortatory Paragraph: Appeal₁ of 3:12–21)

*THEME: Since you desire to be perfected and since you have my example of not considering that I am already perfect but of constantly striving to become more and more like Christ, follow my example.*

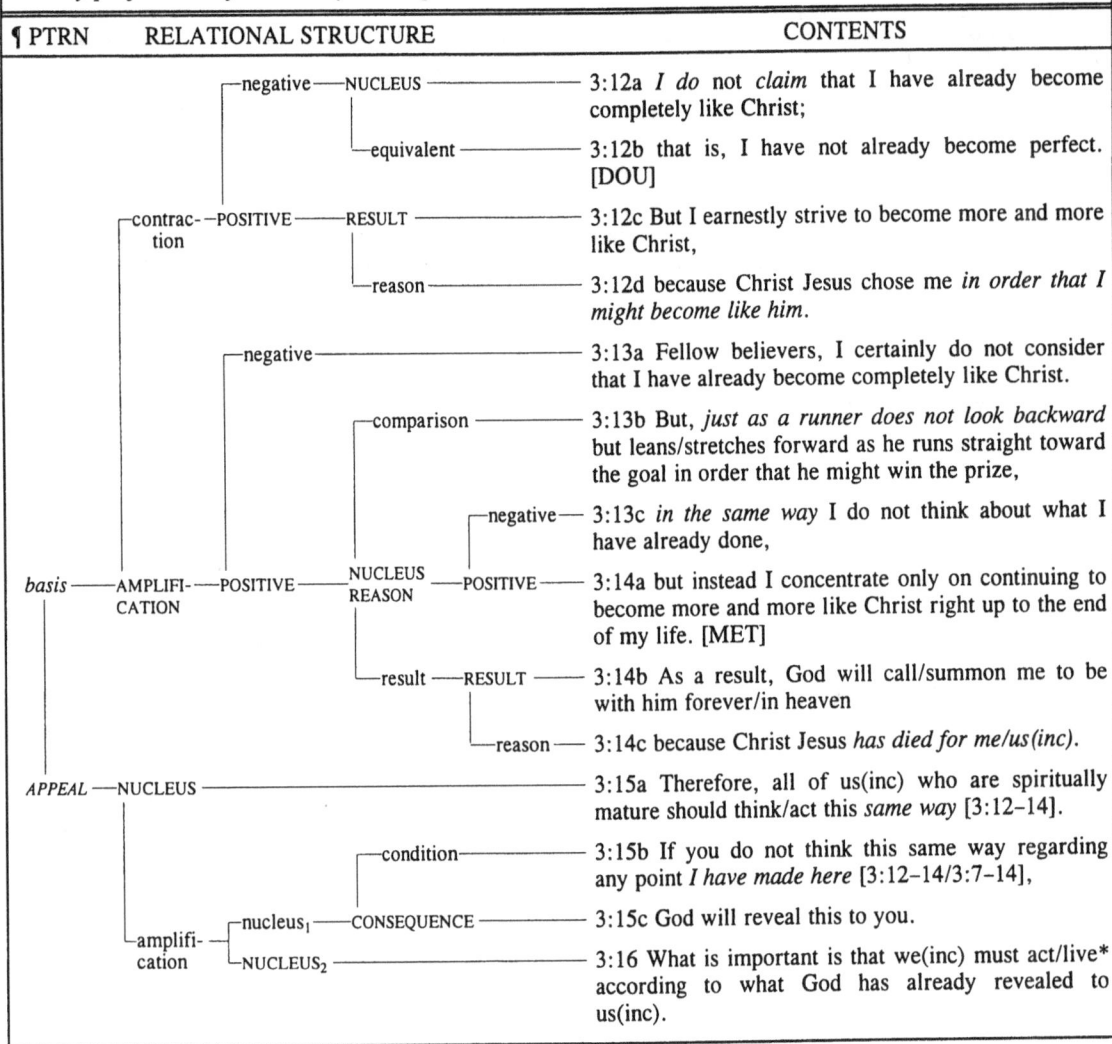

## INTENT AND PARAGRAPH PATTERN

At the beginning of 3:15 οὖν 'therefore' occurs and is followed by an exhortation, a clear signal that this exhortation is based on what comes before it. Therefore, the paragraph pattern of the 3:12–16 unit is *basis*-APPEAL. The *basis* is of an exemplary type. Paul gives the example from his own life and then in the APPEAL asks the readers to follow his example (i.e., take the same attitude). A second APPEAL follows in v. 16, but appears to be more generic. It does not necessarily follow upon the 3:12–14 *basis*.

## NOTES

**3:12a *I do not claim* that** Commentators point out that οὐχ ὅτι is an elliptical expression in which the verb (with subject marker) does not appear but only the negative marker οὐχ 'not' and the content marker ὅτι 'that', and thus the full expression would be 'I do not say that', 'I do not mean that'. Some languages have grammatical signals more or less similar to οὐχ ὅτι 'not that' in form and with the similar function of negating the clause or sentence as a whole or emphasizing the negation, but which are not necessarily elliptical. For translation there are at least three choices, depending on the patterns of the language: one is to fill in the ellipsis ('I do not mean that' or 'I do not claim that'); a second is to use the negative as a modifier of both clauses ("Not that I have already obtained all this, or have already been made perfect," NIV); a third is to use the negative with both verbs ('I have not already become like Christ; that is, I have not already become perfect').

**I have already become completely like Christ** The Greek is ἤδη ἔλαβον 'I already have taken, grasped, obtained, attained, received'. There is an implicit object here. What is it that Paul has not yet obtained? One rule to apply here is that when an object of a transitive verb is not made explicit, it is most likely to be suggested by the preceding context. Either there will be some specific word (the closer the more likely) or a more generic constituent that functions as a whole. (This rule casts doubt on the viewpoint of those commentators who would take βραβεῖον 'prize' in v. 14 to be the implied object here.) A second consideration is that if the verb occurs in a parallel structure, as here, the parallelism may give a clue as to what the object is.

The immediately preceding specific antecedent here is τὴν ἐξανάστασιν τὴν ἐκ νεκρῶν 'the resurrection from the dead'. But this, taken literally, is so obvious that Paul would not say it; and the context shows that it is indeed literal. So it is much more probable that the implied object of ἔλαβον is the nearest preceding generic constituent, namely vv. 10–11, which has as its generic statement τοῦ γνῶναι αὐτόν 'to know him (Christ)'. Not only is it the most immediate generic whole, it is so forcefully presented that it is the most likely antecedent constituent to be in Paul's mind when he comes to v. 12, and it is the one most likely to be in the minds of the addressees as well.

As for the parallelism in 12a, note the construction:

οὐχ ὅτι
not that

ἤδη ἔλαβον
already I-obtained

ἢ ἤδη τετελείωμαι
or already I-have-been-perfected

διώκω δὲ εἰ καὶ καταλάβω
I-pursue if even I-may-take-hold-of

The conjunction ἤ 'or' may signal one of two opposite meanings: that the items it joins are either similar or different. Because of the similarity in form and meaning of ἔλαβον 'I obtained' and καταλάβω 'I may take hold of' it is clear that the latter is continuing on with the idea of the former. This suggests that τετελείωμαι 'I have been perfected' is similar or equivalent to ἔλαβον 'I have obtained', rather than being different. In fact, Paul's very purpose for using τετελείωμαι may have been for clarification of the meaning of ἔλαβον, something which is obviously needed with the object of ἔλαβον left implicit. Vincent says, "Τετελ. explains ἔλαβον more definitely, or puts literally what ἔλ. had put figuratively."

The context strongly suggests that the perfection intended here does not refer to some state Paul (or anyone else) would reach on this earth. In fact, many commentators understand Paul to be teaching against some false doctrine that preaches an attainable state of perfection on this earth, a state which the proponents of the doctrine had already reached.

Bruce (1989) comments as follows:

> His growing knowledge of Christ, his sharing here and now both in his sufferings and in the power of his risen life, are bringing him nearer the goal, but so long as he is in the body, that goal still lies ahead. He will never in this life attain perfection in the sense that no further spiritual progress is possible and nothing is left to aim at beyond the point he has reached.

Thus, 'knowing Christ' is to be understood in vv. 12–14 in the sense Paul focuses on in v. 10: conformity to Christ and his will in all things no matter how difficult it may be. Vincent says, "The perfection referred to is moral and spiritual perfection." In all likelihood, Paul is not only referring to negating his own desires but also to fulfilling all of Christ's positive purposes for his life and becoming more and more like him. This is the idea chosen for the propositionalization of ἔλαβον 'I have obtained' here.

**3:12b I have not already become perfect** The question here is the significance of the passive form τετελείωμαι 'have been perfected, made perfect'. The tense is perfect. Greenlee (1986) describes the function of the perfect tense in Greek as signaling a "present state resulting from past action" (p. 50). The idea of "perfect" is itself stative rather than an action. Words representing states tend to marginalize agents. We might say that passive forms in general place less focus on the agent than active forms do and that verbs representing states place even less focus on the agent. BAGD (p. 810.2eα) gives active meanings such as 'become perfect' to some of the passive forms of τελειόω. Also there is the consideration that the whole context has to do with Paul's initiative. In fact, propositionalizing as '*God* has not yet made me perfect' would downplay Paul's responsibility, which is the whole point of what Paul is saying in vv. 12-14.

'Become what God intended me to become' would be an alternate propositionalization of τετελείωμαι 'am perfected' (cf. Meyer).

**3:12c I earnestly strive to become more and more like Christ** There is no reason to take εἰ 'if' in διώκω δὲ εἰ καὶ καταλάβω 'I pursue if I may attain/apprehend' as signifying a conditional construction. NIV has "I press on to take hold of that for which..."; NEB has "I press on, hoping to take hold of that for which..." It would appear that the reason Paul uses εἰ 'if' rather than ἵνα 'in order to', the normal purpose marker, is to communicate the necessity of striving wholeheartedly to attain this goal. On the other hand, he is not focusing on the doubt of his attaining it.

The intensity of striving signaled by εἰ is communicated in the display text by the use of 'earnestly', 'I earnestly strive to become more and more like Christ' (cf. v. 11).

**strive** The word διώκω might be translated as 'run' or 'press on'. However, it is difficult to know if the figure of the race is already in Paul's mind when he uses the word here. He may instead be using it with the meaning 'pursue', which is probably a more common sense. This would be appropriate here since there is an object that is being sought, as καταλάβω 'apprehend, take hold of' shows. Also, διώκω is quite far removed from the figurative words used later of the race. As entry 4b in BAGD (p. 201) shows, διώκω often expresses the idea of 'strive for', suggesting that in some of its uses it is a dead metaphor. For English at least, what was a MEANS construction (διώκω 'I pursue') becomes an auxiliary verb ('strive'), while the purpose is expressed as the main verbal idea ('become like'). There is no direct translation of καί 'even' since καί here seems to mark καταλάβω 'I apprehend' as more intensive than διώκω 'I pursue' on the grammatical level. On the semantic level the intensive force applies to the construction as a whole. This is indicated by 'earnestly striving' in the display.

**3:12d because Christ Jesus chose me *in order that I might become like him*** There is a question as to whether ἐφ' ᾧ here means 'for which' or 'because'. It is very difficult to know which sense Paul intended: 'for which' is a literal rendering; 'because' is an idiomatic substitution for ἐπὶ τούτῳ ὅτι meaning 'for this reason that, because'. The latter is used by Paul in other passages such as Rom. 5:12, ἐφ' ᾧ πάντες ἥμαρτον 'because all have sinned', and 2 Cor. 5:4 (see ἐπί, BAGD, p. 287.II1bγ). In Phil. 4:10, however, ἐφ' ᾧ cannot mean 'because'; there it means 'on behalf of which, for which' (Meyer) or 'with reference to which' (Vincent).

In taking ἐφ' ᾧ to mean 'for which' here in 3:12, Heyward propositionalizes 12c-d as 'But I am earnestly striving to *know Christ perfectly*, which is what Christ Jesus intended when he chose me *to belong to himself*. If ἐφ' ᾧ were taken to mean 'because', the propositionalization would be 'But I am earnestly striving to *know Christ perfectly* because Christ Jesus chose me *to belong to himself*. Here 'chose me *to belong to himself*' is the nonfigurative rendering for 'apprehended me', and 'to belong to himself' is supplied to fill out the purpose of 'chose'. (This is an obligatory function in some languages.) However, if the implied purpose of 'chose' is stated to be 'in order that I might know him', there would be little difference between a propositionalization based on ἐφ' ᾧ as 'for which' and one based on ἐφ' ᾧ as 'because':

> I am earnestly striving to know Christ perfectly, which is what Christ Jesus intended for me when he chose me to belong to himself.

> I am earnestly striving to know Christ perfectly because Christ Jesus chose me *in order that I might know him*.

The rendering in the display is similar to the latter; this more clearly shows what the relationships are. It fairly well represents either of the interpretations of ἐφ' ᾧ.

**3:13a Fellow believers** The vocative ἀδελφοί 'brothers' functions to foster rapport and, at the same time, mark prominence on the following statement or statements.

**I certainly do not consider that I have already become completely like Christ** By using the free form ἐγώ 'I' together with ἐμαυτόν 'myself' Paul further emphasizes his statement that he does not consider himself to have attained perfection. But is he contrasting himself with others who say that they have attained perfection ('I myself do not consider that I have already conformed completely to Christ'), or is he simply emphasizing the fact that he does not consider that he has attained perfection? Paul does not make it explicit anywhere in this section that some people take the view that they are already perfect (though it is certainly a good possibility that Paul is arguing against the position of such people here), so for this reason 'I myself' is not used in the display. Instead, 'certainly' is used to signal the emphasis on the reality of Paul's statement. TEV handles this with "Of course ... I really do not think that I have already won it."

**3:13b–c** *just as a runner does not look backward ... I do not think about what I have already done* There is a question as to whether τὰ ὀπίσω 'the (things) behind' refers to all of the accomplishments and happenings of Paul's life—whether failures or successes—or just to his attainments. There are at least two reasons why τὰ ὀπίσω 'the (things) behind' might refer only to his attainments. The first is that if he is seeking to show his opponents that it is not possible to reach full perfection in this life, something which they claim for themselves, he might well be saying that he himself forgets whatever attainment he already has as he presses on to becoming more and more like Christ. The second reason for seeing 'the (things) behind' as attainments is that in the figure of a race 'what is behind' refers to the part of the race that has already been accomplished and attained.

However, serious questions arise if τὰ ὀπίσω is taken to refer only to attainments. Paul has not explicitly referred to his attainments. But he has referred to his lack of attainment, twice in v. 12 and again in 13a even more strongly. This explicit referral to lack of attainment signals to the reader that 'the things behind' must at least include what Paul has not yet attained. In discourse one does not switch from one topic to its antithesis without explicitly signaling the switch. It seems best to render τὰ ὀπίσω 'the (things) behind' generically: 'what I have already done' or 'the things of the past', not 'what I have attained'.

Since τὰ μὲν ὀπίσω ἐπιλανθανόμενος 'forgetting the (things) which are behind' could be seen as nonfigurative, a figurative part is required here to balance the figurative 'stretching forward to the things which are before', hence 'does not look backward' in the display.

*just as a runner ... leans/stretches forward as he runs straight toward the goal* The participle ἐπεκτεινόμενος 'stretch forward, strain forward' is very graphic: it pictures the runner leaning forward, stretching out to win the race. This participial phrase modifies the main verb διώκω 'I run' in v. 14; it describes the manner in which Paul is running. To maintain the contrast between what is behind and what is before, the idea of running is supplied here (from διώκω in v. 14): '*just as a runner does not look backward* but leans/stretches forward as he runs straight toward the goal'.

**in order that he might win the prize** Once the verb 'runs' is introduced in the propositionalization of 13c along with 'the goal', the latter being necessary or helpful to make specific the sense of the forward direction, it is unnatural and counterproductive to repeat these figurative concepts in 14a. It is best to include the figure of the prize as part of the figure of the race here.

**I do not think about** Paul is referring to an intentional forgetting here. Forgetting generally is not something done on purpose; in fact, in some languages 'forget' would not be appropriate here at all. Therefore, it is better to propositionalize it as 'I do not think about' or 'I ignore'.

**3:14a I concentrate only on** In v. 13 of the Greek text the word ἕν 'one (thing)' is an elliptical form that is usually rendered "one thing I do" (NIV, TEV, etc.). The question is whether it refers to the main verb διώκω 'I run, press on' or to one or both of the participial phrases. 'Forgetting (not thinking about) the things which are behind' is not so much part of the one thing that Paul *does* as it is a statement of what he does *not* do. But 'stretching out to the things before' and 'pressing on toward the goal for the prize' refer to one action, so clearly they are the 'one (thing)' that Paul concentrates on. In English, however, 'this one thing I do' would not relate grammatically to the participial phrases but to the main clause: 'this one thing I do' and the participial phrases are all modifiers of the main clause. For translation into other languages, the concept of 'this one thing I do' may be signaled in the surface structure either before both participial phrases, or before the second participial phrase, or before the main clause, depending on the language constraints.

**continuing to become more and more like Christ right up to the end of my life** One of the difficulties in the interpretation and propositionalization of vv. 12–14 is the mismatch between the figures and their nonfigurative meaning. Paul is pursuing something resolutely, and he repeatedly says that he has not yet attained it. We have taken that something to be perfection in the sense of knowing Christ perfectly, a complete conformity to Christ and his will. It is implicit in the context that he will not attain that goal in his earthly life. So in the real world reference what he is pursuing is continued and ever-increasing conformity to Christ right up to the end of his life on earth. This is the goal. The only other way to look at this is to see final perfection as the goal. But final perfection is a goal that is not reached by running and striving; it is a gift. Therefore, if the goal is being presented by Paul as something that he must strive for continually, the reference must be to continual striving to be ever-increasingly like Christ till the end of life on earth. Paul may also have final perfect conformity in mind, but it is questionable that it should be included in the propositionalization as, for example, 'I concentrate only on continuing to become more and more like Christ right up to the end of my life and then I will be made completely perfect by him'.

**3:14b As a result** Some commentators (Kent, Silva, O'Brien 1991) take εἰς in εἰς τὸ βραβεῖον 'for the prize' as signaling a purpose relationship, and this relationship is used in the display to render the figurative side, 'in order to win the prize', in 13b. There is certainly intention and action on Paul's part. But for the nonfigurative aspect, it is not easy to decide whether the relationship is MEANS-purpose or REASON-result. It may be that when there are two agents both acting from intention and one is the grantor of the intention of the other, MEANS-purpose would be an appropriate classification if the purpose is granted automatically, while REASON-result would be appropriate if the author sees the granting as not automatic (i.e., only because of the good will of the grantor). In propositionalizing the nonfigurative aspect here, MEANS-purpose does not seem appropriate.

**God will call/summon me to be with him forever/in heaven** One might think that Paul would explicitly state that the prize is the gift of final perfection, complete knowledge of Christ, and conformity to him, in heaven. However, he describes the prize more generically as τὸ βραβεῖον τῆς ἄνω κλήσεως τοῦ θεοῦ ἐν Χριστῷ Ἰησοῦ 'the prize of the upward call of God in Christ Jesus'.

In BAGD (pp. 76-77) the listing of the NT references of ἄνω 'above, upward' does not include any reference to a figurative meaning other than that which is associated with a high place. In other words, the sense of 'noble, excellent' certainly does not seem to be a primary meaning of ἄνω, though it is possible as a secondary meaning. It should also be noted that the meaning of ἄνω here is probably *not* 'from above'. (That idea is usually communicated by ἄνωθεν; its primary meaning is 'from above'.)

Some commentators say that τὸ βραβεῖον τῆς ἄνω κλήσεως τοῦ θεοῦ 'the prize of the upward call of God' cannot mean that the prize is the calling upward since the words for 'call' in the New Testament, whether the noun or the verb, always refer to the act of calling and never to the thing to which one is called. But it is doubtful that the act of calling itself can be so easily distinguished or separated from the purpose of the call. In Rom. 11:29, for instance, in ἀμεταμέλητα γὰρ τὰ χαρίσματα καὶ ἡ κλῆσις τοῦ θεοῦ 'for the gifts and call of God are irrevocable', κλῆσις 'call' has no meaning without the purpose of the call. (This becomes quite evident when one is obligated to translate 'call' into certain languages with a full specification of the purpose of the call.) Also, if κλῆσις 'call' always refers only to the act of calling, then ἐπουρανίου 'heavenly' in κλήσεως ἐπουρανίου μέτοχοι 'sharing in a heavenly calling' (Heb. 3:1) could refer only to God or Christ calling and would say nothing about the purpose of the call. This is possible, but it is hardly likely. It seems simpler to understand the purpose of the call as receiving the prize: God will summon me to receive a prize.

It is common, in English at least, for the genitive with "prize" to refer to the specific prize that is intended, for example, "a prize of fifty dollars." This is probably also the case with τὸ βραβεῖον τῆς ἄνω κλήσεως τοῦ θεοῦ 'the prize of the upward call of God'. It is noteworthy that both unit 10-11 and unit 12-14, which are thematically very similar, end with a reference to eternal life. It is a reference to the prize or the reward after the striving is finished. And note that this prize implies not only getting to know Christ perfectly but also getting to know God.

**be with him forever/in heaven** The fact that the call is from God and that it is described with the word ἄνω 'upward' implies that it refers to the call of God for Paul to come and be with him permanently. This might be described temporally by the term 'forever' or as a locative: 'in heaven' (cf. 2 Cor. 5:1).

**3:14c because Christ Jesus *has died for me/us(inc)*** It seems best to take ἐν Χριστῷ Ἰησοῦ 'in Christ Jesus' as the one through whom the call is made possible. Taking it to mean that Christ Jesus is the one through whom the calling is announced is probably too narrow a meaning, since Christ has not only announced, but more importantly, has made possible the call and its fulfillment through his death and resurrection.

The fact that God is the agent in the call implies that ἐν Χριστῷ Ἰησοῦ 'in Christ Jesus' indicates action taken by Christ rather than by Paul. That is, it refers primarily to Christ's making possible the call and only secondarily to Paul's trusting or abiding in Christ to receive what Christ has made possible.

**3:15a Therefore** 'Therefore' is an appropriate translation for οὖν when it signals an *APPEAL* based on a preceding *basis* as is the case here. However, when the *basis* is an example from the writer's life, we would expect some tie-in between the example and the exhortation to show why his example should be followed. As will be shown in the following two notes, ὅσοι τέλειοι 'as many as are mature' provides that tie-in.

**all of us(inc)** The Greek is ὅσοι οὖν τέλειοι, τοῦτο φρονῶμεν 'as many as therefore (are) mature, this (is how) we should think'. It is unnatural in English to represent the same persons twice like this and it must be handled in some other way, as in the phrase 'all of us' (NIV, TEV).

**spiritually mature** The correct meaning of τέλειοι at the beginning of v. 15 is difficult to determine. Usually in discourse a word or its close cognates will tend to retain the same meaning in the same general context unless there are good reasons for the meaning to be different. This is especially true if the words are pivotal in the argument as would seem to be the case here. After Paul has said that he is not yet perfect (τετελείωμαι) in v. 12, he includes himself with the τέλειοι, a word which could mean 'the perfect ones'. Therefore he is either using τελειόω and τέλειος (the verb and the adjective) with different senses or he is not really including himself with the τέλειοι. If he is not really including himself with the τέλειοι, then the τέλειοι are either at a more advanced state than he is, which the context denies, or he is using the word ironically, meaning 'those who presumptuously think that they are perfect'. If he is using τέλειος with a different meaning from τελειόω, then there should be some other way in which that different meaning is signaled other than only the fact that he has just said he is not yet perfect.

Although a good number of commentators (though probably not a majority) do take τέλειος to be ironical here, that solution raises some major problems. It is difficult to see why Paul would include himself among those who declare that they are perfect. Used ironically τέλειοι must mean 'those who declare that they have already become perfect'. Paul has just declared that he has *not* already become perfect. It is highly improbable that he would now say, "All of us who declare that we are perfect should have this attitude I have: that I have not already become perfect." Writers and speakers, including Paul, often include themselves with the others they are exhorting, even though they themselves do not fall into the specific classification of the addressees being dealt with at the moment. But there are certainly limits to this and compared to its use in some languages Paul is not excessive with it.

Also, if τέλειοι is taken ironically, then the τέλειοι are people who think differently from Paul, since he said he was not perfect. But Paul seems to differentiate somewhat between ὅσοι οὖν τέλειοι, τοῦτο φρονῶμεν 'therefore as many of us who are perfect should think this way' and καὶ εἴ τι ἑτέρως φρονεῖτε 'and if you think somewhat differently'. This may be a different set of people as TEV suggests, "But if some of you have a different attitude." Or it may be a different way of thinking as a more literal translation of καὶ εἴ τι ἑτέρως φρονεῖτε would suggest. If it is a different set of people, then one of the sets consists of the people who Paul says may think differently from himself (τι ἑτέρως φρονεῖτε), and the other of those who do not. But if τέλειος is ironical, then it also would refer to the people who did not think like Paul. The same would be true if a different way of thinking rather than a different set of people was intended by Paul.

If we take τέλειοι to refer to those who are aspiring to perfection, as Paul was, then v. 15 makes more sense. His inclusion of himself in such a class is consistent with his real actions.

But, if this is true, what should we say about the problem of τελειόω and τέλειος having a different meaning in the same context? The best answer seems to be that τέλειος is being used in another of its common senses, 'mature', which occurs several times in the New Testament, including in Paul, to mean 'spiritually mature'. If τέλειοι is more or less a technical term for Christians who are spiritually mature, then the switch in meaning is signaled by the use of the word in a context where perfection is clearly not intended.

It must be remembered that in analyzing the meaning of a word or larger construction in discourse, other things being equal, a normal, nonironical meaning takes precedence over an ironical meaning. There is no doubt that τέλειος meant 'adult, mature' in Greek. It is used in the sense of spiritually mature in 1 Cor. 14:20, Eph. 4:13, and Heb. 5:14 in contrast to νήπιος and παιδίον (those who are spiritually children, i.e., spiritually immature). In 1 Cor. 2:6 it has the meaning of 'spiritually mature' without explicit contrast to νήπιοι or παιδία, although νήπιοι does occur several verses later in 3:1. In Rom. 2:20 Paul talks about the Jews being teachers of the νήπιοι, which surely refers to the spiritually immature rather than to children. Thus it appears that in the church the words νήπιοι and τέλειοι were used for two classes of people, the spiritually immature and the spiritually mature. The use of τέλειοι in Phil. 3:15, then, would be taken by the addressees of this letter to refer to those who are spiritually mature, especially when his statement in 3:12 counterindicates its meaning of 'perfect'.

At the same time, Paul's inclusion of himself among the τέλειοι, right after he has stated his intense striving for perfection, implies that a recognized characteristic of the mature Christian in the early church was a striving for perfection. It is the words ὅσοι τέλειοι 'as many as are mature' and are thus aspiring to perfection that ties the *basis* (Paul's example) to the APPEAL ('let us have this attitude'): 'Since we are mature Christians aspiring to perfection, therefore let us follow this attitude of mine of striving for perfection'.

It may be difficult to translate 'spiritually mature' literally into some languages. Another problem (in English, as in most languages) is that by using 'mature' there may not be much tie-in with 'have already become perfect' in 12b, certainly not to the degree of τέλειοι with τετελείωμαι. Thus, especially for languages where the use of 'spiritually mature' is impossible, a translation such as 'all of us who aspire/desire to be perfect' might be proper for ὅσοι τέλειοι.

**think/act** The verb φρονέω 'think' has a generic meaning, but in passages like this the idea is more specific: 'have (this) attitude'. This abstract noun is not used in the display, however (see the note on 2:5a). The kind of thinking or attitude here (as there) is one that leads to action; it does not refer to thinking that does not result in action. Therefore, if a literal equivalent of 'think' does not communicate this idea in some languages, something like 'should do what I do' or 'should follow according to what I do' may be called for.

**this *same way*** [3:12-14] The demonstrative τοῦτο 'this' relates Paul's APPEAL most specifically to his example in vv. 12-14. TEV translates it as "should have this same attitude."

**3:15b** Since 3:15b begins with καί, our first expectation would be that some type of additive relationship is being signaled. This additive relationship is not one of a second APPEAL but of more details about the APPEAL in 15a, so it appears to be in an amplificatory relationship. This is discussed further under the note on 3:16.

**If you do not think this same way regarding any point *I have made here*** [3:12-14/3:7-14] It is most natural to take εἴ τι ἑτέρως φρονεῖτε 'if you think anything differently' to refer to disagreement with Paul in the matters he has just stated, most specifically in vv. 12-14, but also possibly going back as far as v. 7.

**3:15c God will reveal this to you** The τοῦτο 'this' in καὶ τοῦτο ὁ θεὸς ὑμῖν ἀποκαλύψει 'also/even this God will reveal to you' grammatically refers back to τί 'anything'; and τί refers to whatever they may be thinking that is different from the points Paul has just stated. To the extent that they differ, their thinking is in error. (Greenlee lists nine commentators taking this view.)

The implication of 'God will reveal this to you' is either (1) that they have not taken it as from God yet even though Paul made it known in vv. 12-14, or (2) that they do not yet understand certain details of God's desires for them. The second interpretation explains the occurrences of καί better than the first. The first suggests more of an adversative relationship. Based on the second interpretation, καὶ τοῦτο 'this also' would imply the following idea: 'God will make clear to you not only what I have already revealed to you about this subject but also those points still unclear to you'.

'God will reveal this to you' might be more fully propositionalized as 'God will reveal to you that you think differently at that point'.

**3:16 What is important** The word πλήν, which begins this verse, has an adversative sense in the Gospels, but in Paul's writings it tends to mark prominence. In BAGD (p. 669.1c) the occurrences of πλήν in Paul's writings (except for possibly Phil. 1:18) are grouped under "*only, in any case, however, but*, breaking off a discussion and emphasizing what is important." It is true that there is some adversative sense, but that sense has to do with a contrast in prominence, not a contrast between the basic meaning of the propositions themselves. It would be difficult to prove πλήν signals that the condition for God's further revelation is the carrying out of what he has already revealed.

As to the relationship of 3:16 with 3:15, 3:16 appears to be a generic axiomatic principle stated in exhortation form. Greenlee (1992) cites seventeen commentators who say that the infinitive στοιχεῖν 'be in line with' is used for an imperative. Thus it is an APPEAL in itself, but in effect, it supports the APPEAL of 15a since it provides motivation for carrying out that APPEAL. At the same time, it seems to be more a part of the APPEAL mechanism than a *basis* for the APPEAL. Therefore, in the display it is included under amplification of the APPEAL.

Verse 16 is conjoined with 15b-c, but there is contrast in prominence, as shown by the relational labels in the display.

**according to what God has already revealed to us(inc)** There is a question as to whether ἐφθάσαμεν 'we have attained' refers to what they had attained in spiritual knowledge (through revelation by whatever means) or attained in their spiritual life in general. It is obvious that στοιχεῖν 'keep in line with' refers to actions that are being exhorted, and εἰς ὃ ἐφθάσαμεν 'to that which we have attained' refers to a standard they are to keep in line with. The whole force of Paul's life and attitude, as he says in vv. 12-14, is that he is striving to go beyond what he has already attained in his spiritual life. Therefore ἐφθάσαμεν must refer to what is already known, what has already been revealed, rather than only to what is already attained (whether in spiritual life or behavior).

There are a number of different readings in the manuscripts for the second part of the verse. The UBSGNT text has τῷ αὐτῷ στοιχεῖν ('with that keep in line'), which is given an A rating ("the text is certain"). Hodges and Farstad have τῷ αὐτῷ στοιχεῖν κανόνι, τὸ αὐτὸ φρονεῖν, translated in the KJV as "let us walk by the same rule, let us mind the same thing." Various other readings are found in the manuscripts. O'Brien (1991:418) remarks on the text as follows: "The shorter and more difficult reading τῷ αὐτῷ στοιχεῖν has the most significant MSS support...and is to be preferred. As an elliptical expression this reading explains the Majority Text, which adds κανόνι, τὸ αὐτὸ φρονεῖν (with other variations in the textual tradition)." Metzger (p. 549) says, "The variety and lack of homogeneity of the longer readings make it difficult to suppose that the shorter reading...arose because of homoeoteleuton," that is, from the omission of a line by a scribe because of mistaking similar endings.

**we(inc) must act/live\*** BAGD (p. 769) glosses στοιχέω as "orig[inally] 'be drawn up in line', in our lit. only fig. *be in line with, stand beside* a pers[on] or thing, *hold to, agree with, follow*." The basic idea of the figurative use, then, in this context of exhortation is to abide by a standard.

## BOUNDARIES AND COHERENCE

In view of its *basis*-APPEAL paragraph pattern, 3:12-16 is taken to be a paragraph. A new APPEAL is signaled at the beginning of v. 17 with the imperative construction συμμιμηταί μου γίνεσθε 'be imitators of me'. The use of the vocative ἀδελφοί 'brothers' following this imperative can be understood as marking a new paragraph.

Paul's use of the cognates τετελείωμαι 'have already become perfect' in v. 12 and τέλειοι 'mature' in v. 15 helps to tie the paragraph together and marks the initial boundary of the *basis* for the APPEAL as the beginning of v. 12 rather than at an earlier point in Paul's example from his life (3:4b or 3:7).

## PROMINENCE AND THEME

In the 3:12-16 paragraph, with its *basis*-APPEAL pattern, the *basis* is the example of Paul's life, and in the APPEAL he exhorts the Philippians to follow his example. Therefore main elements of the *basis* should be included in the theme statement: for one thing, *basis* is always integral to the theme; moreover the content of this APPEAL is only identifiable in the *basis*, since the APPEAL is so generic. The question might be raised as to whether vv. 12-14 are really not part of the APPEAL, filling in the content for τοῦτο 'this', which is part of the APPEAL: 'Think *this* way', 'Have *this* same attitude'. But the presence of οὖν 'therefore' and of ὅσοι...τέλειοι 'whoever is mature', that is, 'whoever desires to be perfected', strongly suggests that vv. 12-14 act as a *basis* in that they are a prime example. So Paul is saying, "Since you are mature and desire to be perfected and you have this example of mine, you should follow it."

Most commentators understand 3:16 as an exhortation; but since it appears to support the major APPEAL of 3:15, it is not a full-fledged APPEAL on the paragraph-pattern level. For this reason it is not included in the theme statement.

## SECTION CONSTITUENT 3:17–21 (Hortatory Paragraph: Appeal₂ of 3:12–21)

*THEME: Imitate me and those who live as I do since there are many people who are bad examples as shown by their lustful behavior, thinking only about earthly things. As for us, Christ will transform our lowly earthly bodies to be like his glorious heavenly body.*

| ¶PTRN RELATIONAL STRUCTURE | CONTENTS |
|---|---|
| APPEAL — NUCLEUS₁ | 3:17a Fellow believers, *all of* you should unitedly imitate me |
|          NUCLEUS₂ | 3:17b and observe those people who act/live* as we(exc) act/live* *in order that you might imitate them also.* |
| negative exemplary basis — ITEM — CONTENT | 3:18a You should imitate me and those who act as I/we(exc) act rather than imitating anyone else. You should do this since there are many people *who say that they believe in Christ* who act *in such a way that shows* they are opposed to *the teaching that* Christ *died on* the cross *in order to enable humankind/us(inc) to stop sinning* [MTY]. |
|      prominence orienter | 3:18b I have told you about these people many times *before* and now I am even weeping *as* I tell you *about them again.* |
| description₁ of 'people' | 3:19a They will be destroyed* *by God* because they *act immorally.* |
| description₂ of 'people' | 3:19b They strongly desire to do what their bodies lustfully desire [MTY] rather than strongly desiring to do what God desires [MET]; |
| description₃ of 'people' | 3:19c they are proud of things which they should be ashamed of; |
| description₄ of 'people' | 3:19d they think only about *what unbelievers on this* earth *think about.* [MTY] |
| positive motivational basis — NUCLEUS₁ | 3:20a Imitate us(exc) (or, Instead of imitating them, be sure to imitate us(exc)) since we(inc) are citizens of heaven. |
|      NUCLEUS₂ | 3:20b And we(inc) are also eagerly awaiting a Savior to come from heaven; he is our(inc) Lord Jesus Christ. |
|      NUCLEUS₃ — CONCLUSION | 3:21a He will change/transform our(inc) lowly bodies to be like his glorious body, |
|          grounds | 3:21b since he is completely able to do/control* all things. |

### INTENT AND PARAGRAPH PATTERN

The presence of two imperatives in 3:17 followed by a γάρ 'for, since, because' at the beginning of 3:18 signals an APPEAL-basis hortatory paragraph pattern. However, the APPEAL-basis reasoning is not as direct as it often is in Paul's reasoning. Instead of saying, "Imitate us since we are good examples," he seems to be saying, "Imitate us since there are many people who are bad examples." He never actually states that they are bad examples, but he describes their bad character and resulting destruction. This might be called a *negative exemplary basis*. Following the description of these people there is another γάρ at the beginning of 3:20 with an ensuing reference to Paul and true believers. It may be that this γάρ intentionally signals a second, positive, *basis*. Instead of presenting the good example of Paul and true believers as a *positive exemplary basis*, there is a description of the great privileges of true believers and this is future oriented. The best explanation for this is that Paul is seeking to motivate the Philippians to properly follow him and Christ by describing the rewards awaiting the true believer. This is a *positive motivational basis*. It is true that the *negative basis* also has a motivational aspect to it, as 'whose end is destruction' shows.

## NOTES

**3:17a Fellow believers** The vocative reference to the addressees has been transferred to the beginning of the sentence in the display from its position after the first clause in the Greek text. This places it in close proximity to the subject reference to the addressees, 'all of you'. In the Greek text it is placed in close proximity to the subject reference, that is, the second person plural suffix on the verb γίνεσθε 'you should be'. In Greek, there is a tendency for the vocative and second person references to be in close proximity. Although this may not be a universal tendency, it seems best in English translation to maintain this close proximity. This necessitates the transferral of the vocative to the beginning of the sentence.

**all of you should unitedly imitate me** When συν- 'with, together with' is prefixed to μιμηταί 'imitators' a word results that might be translated as 'fellow imitators'. The comparison of this with συναιχμάλωτος 'fellow prisoner' (Rom. 16:7; Col. 4:10; Philem. 23) shows that συν- means existing in the same state or situation along with someone else or performing an action that someone else is also performing. It may include the idea of fellowship and unity as well. The fact that Paul used (coined?) this compound which has been found nowhere else and the fact that Paul calls the Philippians to unity elsewhere, as in 1:27 and 2:1-4, suggest that the idea of unity and fellowship may be in mind here in 3:17. However, imitating Paul is by far the most important concept in 17a. Putting undue focus on unity at the expense of imitation would result in an inappropriate translation. The following, for example, is the *wrong* focus: 'all of you should unite/join together in order that you may imitate me'. In changing the noun phrase 'fellow imitators' into a verb phrase in the propositionalization, the following are options: '*all of* you together should imitate me'; '*all of* you should unitedly imitate me'.

A minority view put forth by Bengel and others is that the meaning of συμμιμηταί μου γίνεσθε is 'be fellow imitators of Christ with me', but this does not suit the context, either the second part of the verse or Paul's example in 3:12-14. Another view is that the meaning is 'be fellow imitators with others of me' or (using a verb) 'join others in imitating me', in which 'others' refers to people who are already doing a good job of imitating Paul, namely, those referred to in the second part of the verse. But such a reference to others would need to be more explicit. When there is nothing in the verb phrase that explicitly specifies any participants other than Paul and the addressees themselves, it is not likely that participants other than these are being referred to.

Alternates for 'imitate' would be: 'act as I act', 'behave as I behave', 'conduct yourselves as I conduct myself'. The specific behavior Paul has in mind is his way of life as described in vv. 7-14, most particularly vv. 12-14.

**3:17b observe those people who act/live* as we(exc) act/live* in order that you might imitate them also** The verb σκοπεῖτε might be translated here as 'observe', 'take note of', 'pay attention to'. A purpose relationship is implied. BAGD (p. 756) renders 3:17b as "*notice those who conduct themselves thus*, i.e. in order to imitate them." Many commentators (see Greenlee 1992) also understand an implied purpose clause here.

There are two ways to understand καθὼς ἔχετε τύπον ἡμᾶς 'as you have us (as) an example'. One is to take οὕτω 'thus, so' as correlative with καθώς so that, in effect, the καθώς construction explains οὕτω, that is, the manner in which they walk or live: 'those who walk/live in such a manner as you have us as an example' or, more freely, 'according to the example which you have in us'. The second way is to understand οὕτω 'thus' as referring back to μου 'of me' or συμμιμηταί μου 'fellow imitators of me' ('observe those who walk/live thus [=imitating me]') and καθώς as meaning 'inasmuch as' ('inasmuch as you have us as an example').

The former appears to be the better solution for the following reasons:

1. When οὕτω and καθώς are in close proximity they are normally correlative, even though sometimes, as in Rom. 11:26, the occurrence of the two in close proximity can be taken in other than a strict correlative function, depending on certain other factors.

2. While taking οὕτω as referring backward to συμμιμηταί μου 'fellow imitators of me' gives a proper meaning in this context, it is more difficult to see an appropriate meaning for the καθώς construction other than a correlative one. 'Inasmuch as', which would probably function as signaling grounds, is too tautological to be seen as a good alternate solution: 'Imitate me and observe (and imitate) those who imitate me inasmuch as you have us for an example'. The only way this could be seen as grounds supporting the exhortations would be if the example were somehow qualified as to its appropriateness. This could be seen, possibly, if ἡμᾶς 'us' is considered as prominent because of its placement at the end of the sentence, bringing out the contrast with the bad example mentioned in the next two verses. But such an analysis probably does not have a clear enough validity to vie with the one that sees a correlative construction here.

It may be helpful to look at the verse as having two parts, divided by the vocative, ἀδελφοί 'brothers'. The first part deals only with Paul as an example. The second part deals with two sets of examples: those who are primary examples, that is, Paul and the others included in ἡμᾶς 'us' (presumably Timothy and possibly other companions of Paul) and those who are secondary examples, that is, those who walk according to the example of Paul and those he includes with himself in ἡμᾶς 'us'.

**we(exc)** There are three possible ways to understand ἡμᾶς 'us': (1) As a literary plural referring to Paul alone, (2) as a reference to Paul and those who are walking after his example as described in this verse, or (3) as a reference to Paul, Timothy, and possibly other associates. Once a correlative construction is understood here, option two is no longer applicable; it is only appropriate to taking καθώς as grounds. Hawthorne presents several arguments for taking ἡμᾶς as referring to Paul alone. The strongest of these arguments is that the literary plural was of common use among Greek authors and that Paul uses this on some occasions (according to Hawthorne in Rom. 1:5; 2 Cor. 11:6 [φανερώσαντες]; 1 Thess. 2:18; 3:1-5, especially vv. 3 and 5). This argument is strengthened by the fact that "the order and choice of words in this sentence imply that Paul differentiates between himself as model and others and considers himself to be the supreme model (τύπος), on a plane above other worthy models," even as an authoritative apostolic model. Hawthorne stresses the fact that τύπον 'model' here is in the singular. But it also appears in the singular in 1 Thess. 1:7 where it unambiguously refers to many people as models.

The plural form 'we' is used in the display because (1) the primary meaning of ἡμᾶς is first person plural, and (2) the verse may be divided into two parts with Paul presenting himself in the first part as a model and in the second part others as models with him.

**3:18a** *You should imitate me and those who act as I/we(exc) act rather than imitating anyone else. You should do this* **since** When γάρ follows imperatives, as here at the beginning of v. 18, it usually introduces support for the imperatives (i.e., *basis* ). But the cause-effect relationship between vv. 18-19 and v. 17 is not as transparent as it often is. KJV, for example, though translating γάρ as 'for', takes vv. 18-19 to be parenthetical. The best solution is that 'imitate me and those who act as I/we act' is to be understood as 'imitate me and those who act as I/we act to the exclusion of anyone else'. Unit 18-19 with its description of people whose behavior can be seen as a bad example is then appropriate as a *negative exemplary basis*.

**there are many people** *who say that they believe in Christ* There is a divergence of opinion as to who these people described in vv. 18-19 really are. There are three main views:

1. Some commentators consider them to be the Judaizers of 3:2, whose opposition to the cross of Christ might be seen in the fact that their doctrine demanding circumcision and keeping of the whole law actually repudiated the efficacy of the cross of Christ. But the people mentioned in vv. 18-19 could not be these Judaizers, who were strict observers of the law. The ones in vv. 18-19 obviously did not keep the law; they appear to have been sinfully self-indulgent and morally loose to the extreme.

2. Other commentators consider the people in vv. 18-19 to be the heathen, since their behavior is characteristic of heathen behavior. However, Paul's grief over their behavior does not suit a reference to the heathen. Heyward says, "Such deep emotion would be more likely to be evoked over professing Christians who acted in this way...Also, one wouldn't expect there to be a strong tempta-

tion to imitate the heathen, but the temptation to imitate those who profess to be believers would be a real problem and one which would warrant the safeguard in 3:17." The whole force of what Paul is saying has to do with contraexpectation, not the normal, expected heathen behavior.

3. Most commentators consider the people in vv. 18-19 to be those who professed to believe in Christ but failed to live a moral Christian life. Vincent describes them as "antinomian Libertines of Epicurean tendencies: nominal Christians of immoral life." They perverted the freedom and grace of the gospel by living a life without moral restraints. Neva Miller states, "Paul and other NT writers fought such a perversion of the grace of God into a license to sin with impunity. This is abundantly evident in the Pastoral Epistles, Corinthians, Romans, Peter's Epistles, Jude, etc." They were enemies of the cross of Christ in that they opposed its purpose of delivering mankind from the practice of sin.

The third interpretation best suits the context and is the one adopted for the display.

**who act** *in such a way that shows that* **they are opposed to** *the teaching that* **Christ** *died on* **the cross** *in order to enable humankind/us(inc) to stop sinning* It was their willful practice of sin that made them enemies of the cross of Christ, since Christ died on the cross not only to save us from the guilt of sin but also from the practice of sin (Rom. 6:6; 1 Peter 2:24). It would be possible to see 'enemies' as a metaphor: They are like enemies of the cross of Christ in that their conduct shows they oppose the teaching that Christ died to deliver us from the practice of sin.

'The cross of Christ' is a metonymy: what they are in opposition to is not the literal cross, but what Christ's death on the cross was meant to accomplish for them. Eadie regards Paul as here "speaking of the cross in its ultimate purpose, as pointing not so much to its expiatory agony, as to its sanctifying power."

**3:18b I have told you about these people many times** *before* **and now I am even weeping** *as I tell you* **about them again** This verse is complicated, both grammatically and semantically. The construction οὓς πολλάκις ἔλεγον ὑμῖν, νῦν δὲ καὶ κλαίων λέγω '(of) whom I have told you many times and now even weeping tell you' acts as an orienter for the CONTENT τοὺς ἐχθροὺς τοῦ σταυροῦ τοῦ Χριστοῦ '(they are) the enemies of the cross of Christ'. The verb λέγω 'I say/tell' with the content of what is said following is certainly in an orienter-CONTENT relationship. Note that this orienter was not really necessary to introduce speech in that Paul as writer is speaking all the time and these are not the words of someone else. Also note that the orienter word λέγω is modified with certain intensive-type qualifiers: πολλάκις 'many times' and καὶ κλαίων 'even weeping'. These facts show that this is the type of orienter that marks prominence on the CONTENT: 'pay special attention to what I am now going to say'.

Paul, in effect, inserts the orienting construction into the middle of the CONTENT. By placing the first part of the CONTENT at the beginning of the verse a strong contrast with ἡμᾶς 'us' at the end of v. 17 is produced. To render this complicated construction more simply and at the same time keep the contrast as close to the beginning of the verse as possible, the prominence orienter is placed after the CONTENT. NIV and TEV, however, place the orienter first.

We usually think of an orienter as an introducer, but even regular speech orienters may come after the CONTENT, in some languages at least. This is done especially when for reasons of prominence or contrast it is advantageous to place the CONTENT first.

As to whether Paul's weeping here is literal, there is no good reason to take it otherwise. Paul wept tears over these enemies of the cross of Christ as shown by καί 'even': it is *even* to the extent of physically weeping or crying. Hence this is not a metaphor. If he was *not* physically weeping, the words καὶ κλαίων 'even weeping' *would* be metaphorical. Since Paul is using a physical, outward sign to express an inward, emotional state, this inward, emotional state might be made explicit in translation in a language where it is necessary (e.g., 'I am so sad that I am even weeping'). But weeping is such a universal expression of grief that it is not made explicit in the display.

The participial phrase καὶ κλαίων 'even weeping' modifies the verb λέγω 'I tell', and so has a relationship of manner. But when a manner relationship is expressed by a full proposition, the two propositions often must take the form of NUCLEUS-circumstance, at least in English. Sometimes it is the naturally prominent proposition that has the role of circumstance, as here: 'now I am even weeping *as* I tell you about them again'.

This may be an idiosyncrasy of English; other languages have other ways to deal with this.

**3:19** In 3:19a, 'whose end is destruction' is the result of the behavior described in the rest of the verse, even though it is not explicitly signaled as result. Each of the segments of the verse is formally introduced either by a relative pronoun or the article acting as a relative pronoun (19b and c form one relative clause in the Greek text). The relative clauses are descriptive of the previously mentioned enemies of the cross. Though the first, 19a, may refer more to the outcome of their behavior than to a description of it, Paul does not choose to use logical, cause-effect markers, but descriptive ones. The descriptive genre is used here, though only for an embedded one-verse unit, so the descriptive style is maintained in the display. For translation into some languages a result-reason relationship between 19a and 19b-d may be preferable.

**3:19a They will be destroyed\* by God** An alternate propositionalization would be, 'They will be destroyed\* *in hell by God*'. 'Destroy' is marked with an asterisk since it is used here in a generic sense rather than as what may be its primary meaning in English, the destruction of the physical body. What Paul intends by ἀπώλεια 'destruction' here is eternal destruction (what Jesus describes in Matt. 10:28 as the destruction of both soul and body in hell), but it does not seem appropriate to explicate the exact nature of the destruction. The constraints of some languages, however, may demand a translation that is more specific in details.

**because they *act immorally*** Regarding τέλος, literally 'end', Vincent says: "Τέλος is more than mere termination. Rather consummation; the point into which the whole series of transgressions finally gathers itself up." This is supported by 2 Cor. 11:15, ὧν τὸ τέλος ἔσται κατὰ τὰ ἔργα αὐτῶν 'whose end will be according to their works', for which NIV has "Their end will be what their actions deserve." There is an inherent cause-effect relationship. Since 'end' in the sense intended here is an abstract noun and it carries this cause-effect relationship, the meaning of ὧν τὸ τέλος 'whose end' is propositionalized as a reason construction: 'because they *act immorally*'.

As previously stated (in the 3:19 note), description is more fitting here than cause-effect. However, on the lower level within 3:19a, result-reason seems better for our purposes. The result is placed first in the propositionalization to parallel the other descriptions of these people in 19b-d.

**3:19b They strongly desire to do what their bodies lustfully desire** Some commentators, both ancient and modern, have taken ἡ κοιλία 'the stomach' to have reference to the observance of Jewish food laws. If one takes the view that the people Paul is now talking about are the Jews or Judaizers mentioned in v. 2, this view necessarily follows. But Vincent says that to take it to mean "Jewish laws about meats, is fanciful." The impression that this is fanciful probably comes from the fact that 'the belly' normally suggests the desires or appetites of the belly, as 'flesh' suggests the sensual desires of the body in a more generic sense. But to take 'belly' to refer to the opposite of this—restrictions to what one eats—might indeed be seen as fanciful.

It is much more straightforward to take 'whose god is the belly' as referring to these people's sensual appetites, which control their lives. But a further question is whether ἡ κοιλία 'the belly' refers specifically to appetites for food and drink alone or whether a more general reference is intended. There is no other reference in the Greek Scriptures that unambiguously ties κοιλία with a more generic sense of sensual appetites. It does, however, have the wider sense of referring (frequently) to the womb and (occasionally) to the inner thoughts or possibly desires of a person: For Prov. 20:27 the LXX has Φῶς Κυρίου πνοὴ ἀνθρώπων, ὃς ἐρευνᾷ ταμιεῖα κοιλίας (translated by Brenton as "The spirit of man is a light of the Lord, who searches the inmost parts of the belly") and for Job 15:35, Ἐν γαστρὶ δὲ λήψεται ὀδύνας, ἀποβήσεται δὲ αὐτῷ κενά, ἡ δὲ κοιλία αὐτοῦ ὑποίσει δόλον (translated by Brenton as "And he shall conceive sorrows, and his end shall be vanity, and his belly shall bear deceit"). Therefore from a lexical point of view, it is possible that κοιλία in Phil. 3:19 refers to the sensual appetites of the person as a whole rather than only those related to food and drink.

As far as the context is concerned, it appears that it does have a wider reference than only a sinful appetite for food and drink. In fact, drunkenness usually leads to all kinds of sensual practices and αἰσχύνη 'shame' here is an appropriate description of such practices. Moreover, their belief system would seemingly allow them to participate in all kinds of sensual practices. It would seem that just as the word σάρξ 'flesh' is often used as a metonymy for the sensual, sinful desires of the body, here κοιλία 'stomach' has a similar figurative meaning.

**rather than strongly desiring to do what God desires** Here ὁ θεός 'god' is metaphorical; their sensual desires are being compared with the concept of 'god'. In Rom. 16:18, where a similar metaphor occurs, the point of similarity (serving) is made explicit: οἱ γὰρ τοιοῦτοι τῷ κυρίῳ ἡμῶν Χριστῷ οὐ δουλεύουσιν ἀλλὰ τῇ ἑαυτῶν κοιλίᾳ 'for such people do not serve our Lord Christ but (serve) their own bellies'. In Rom. 16:18 the word 'serve' is δουλεύω, referring to the type of service a servant or slave performs for his master. Since κοιλία is the metaphor for the thing served in Rom. 16:18, it is possible that the idea of 'serve', or something close to it, is intended in Phil. 3:19 also. The context in Phil. 3:19 suggests that there is no lack of desire in this service. Bruce (1989) says, "If their god is their 'appetites,' that means that their 'appetites' are their ultimate concern; they do not say so expressly, but that is the implication of their way of life." Also, an implicit contrast is intended between God's being their God and their appetites' being their god. Based on these various considerations, 'their god is their belly' might be propositionalized in several ways: 'they strongly desire to do what their body lustfully desires as though their body was their god', 'they strongly desire to do what their body lustfully desires as one should strongly desire to do what God desires', 'they strongly desire to do what their body lustfully desires rather than strongly desiring to do what God desires'.

**3:19c they are proud of** A contrast is intended in 19c between 'their glory/honor' and 'their shame'. The idea is that they boldly maintain that their practices, which Paul and any true Christian would immediately recognize as shameful, are honorable. They are proud of their practices. This might be propositionalized 'They are proud of things which they should be ashamed of' or 'They boast about things which they should be ashamed of'.

**things which they should be ashamed of** Greenlee (1992) notes a distinction of interpretations in the commentaries between "They glory in the things of which they ought to be ashamed" and "They glory in things which really bring shame on them." However, there is little real difference between the two interpretations because there is no shame involved unless the people concerned really *are* ashamed of what they are doing. These people obviously were not ashamed; they were proud of what they were doing. 'These things bring shame on them' in this context really means, 'these things cause them to be in a state/situation they *should be* ashamed of'.

**3:19d they think only about** A good English translation for φρονοῦντες here is 'they set their minds on' (BAGD, p. 866.2; similarly various versions and commentaries). Michael says, "The present phrase denotes that the whole trend and inclination of the life of these persons is towards the things of earth." However, 'set one's mind on' is idiomatic, so 'they think only about' is used in the display.

*what unbelievers on this* **earth** *think about* The Greek is τὰ ἐπίγεια 'the earthly (things)'. This is a metonymy in the sense that the earth is put for the associative idea of those things or activities which have their origin, as far as spiritual things are concerned, only on earth and are not from God in heaven. Since, however, this is a complex, extended figure, it has been propositionalized simply, without spelling out much detail.

**3:20a** *Imitate us(exc)* **(or,** *Instead of imitating them, be sure to imitate us(exc)***) since** It is difficult to know the function of γάρ at the beginning of 3:20. Semantically there is a definite contrast between vv. 18–19 and vv. 20–21 as to the people concerned, their actions, and their orientation (mind set on earthly things in opposition to heavenly citizenship). However, it would be difficult to prove convincingly that γάρ, lexically, has as one of its functions the signaling of contrast. This leaves us with the possibility that γάρ is either signaling reason/grounds for something immediately preceding it or *basis* for the APPEAL in v. 17.

To take it as signaling reason or grounds for something immediately preceding it, an implied statement must be understood. This is done by Vincent: "Their course is the opposite of ours; *for*, while they mind earthly things, our mind is set upon the interests of the heavenly commonwealth to which we belong." Meyer takes a similar view: "Justly I characterize their whole nature by the words οἱ τὰ ἐπίγεια φρονοῦντες ['they set their minds on earthly things']; for it is the direct opposite of *ours*; *our* πολίτευμα ['commonwealth'], the goal of *our* aspiration, is not on earth, but in heaven." Such implied statements tend to be superfluous and suggest that only one relationship, that of contrast, is operating at this level. But, if contrast is seen to be operating at the lower level, while *APPEAL-basis* is operating between 3:17 and 3:20-21 at the paragraph-pattern level, the relationships are clearer and it is more obvious why Paul used γάρ here rather than δέ 'but'. In fact, in a paragraph where there are *APPEALS* (v. 17) followed immediately by γάρ (v. 18) and the rest of the paragraph is built on a negative-positive contrastive relationship, we would normally expect everything within that relationship to support the *APPEALS*. And it would not be unnatural at all on the semantic level to understand a direct tie between the *APPEALS* and the positive support.

As far as γάρ signaling that support for the *APPEALS* of v. 17 is concerned, some commentators maintain that γάρ signals relationships for immediately preceding units rather than for units where there is intervening material. Eadie, however, appears to take γάρ as signaling support for v. 17 when he says, "Walk as ye see us walking, for our country is in heaven." Bengel and Lenski also take γάρ as signaling the reason why they should imitate Paul and others like him. Silva says, "Because the Philippians' need to follow the right example was Paul's main concern, vv. 20-21...were meant to support the apostolic command—and what better *reason* is available than the reminder that their true citizenship is a heavenly one?" According to BAGD (p. 152.1c), "γάρ is somet. repeated. It occurs twice either to introduce several arguments for the same assertion...or to have one clause confirm the other."

I take vv. 20-21 as the *positive motivational basis* for the *APPEAL* of v. 17, understanding γάρ as either an intentional signal of that relationship directly or perhaps more remotely. The tie-in with the *APPEAL* of v. 17 may be supplied as 'Imitate us/our(exc) example'. Or the contrast might be brought out as in 'Instead of imitating them, be sure to imitate us(exc)'.

**we(inc)** The switch here from an exclusive first person plural pronoun in the first half of 20a to an inclusive one ('we(inc)') in the second half may seem strange to some, but the excluding feature in some languages is so strong that the Philippian believers might not be seen as included if the exclusive form were used. They too are citizens of heaven.

**are citizens of heaven** For this verse Greenlee (1992) divides the major senses of πολίτευμα into two categories: "It refers to a place, a country...; [or] it refers to citizenship." Under the place category, the idea of 'colony' is also one of the significant senses of πολίτευμα. Other senses are 'commonwealth', 'state'. O'Brien (1991) says, "The meaning that is best attested in Hellenistic times and that is also most suitable for our context is 'state' or 'commonwealth' in an active and dynamic sense, a connotation that may be compared to βασιλεία as 'reign'." A. T. Lincoln (*Paradise Now and Not Yet*, pp. 99 and 220, as quoted in O'Brien 1991) points out that if Paul had used πολίτευμα in the sense of 'colony' "he would have spoken of πολίτευμα οὐρανῶν ἐπὶ τῆς γῆς ['a colony of heaven on earth'], whereas what he actually says is that the πολίτευμα is in heaven."

It may be that Paul means to communicate here the character of life (i.e., behavior) of the citizens of heaven. That is what τὰ ἐπίγεια 'earthly things' in v. 19 refers to, and we would expect the contrast in τὸ πολίτευμα ἐν οὐρανοῖς 'πολίτευμα in heaven' to have some reference to a similar orientation. At the same time, the orientation of the *positive basis* is somewhat different from that of the *negative basis*. The basic orientation of 3:18-19 as support for the *APPEALS* of 3:17 is the bad character of these people pointing up the fact that they are not good examples at all. As for 3:20-21, it is support for those *APPEALS* in that it states the reward of conducting themselves after Paul's good example. The reward of those with bad character is also stated in 'their end is destruction', which verifies the fact that Paul has rewards in mind as motivational support for carrying out his *APPEALS*.

Another factor to be considered is that ἡμῶν τὸ πολίτευμα 'our citizenship, our country' is a genitive expression. This implies a semantic relationship between 'we' and πολίτευμα: If πολίτευμα means 'country' or is a reference to a place or political entity, then the implied relationship is 'we are to live in the country which is heaven' or 'we belong to the country which is heaven'. If πολίτευμα means 'citizenship', then the relationship is 'we have citizenship in heaven' or 'we are citizens of heaven' or even 'we belong to heaven', 'we are to live in heaven' (depending on how much content the idea of citizenship is intended to have here). It appears, then, that in this context there is not a lot of difference in meaning between understanding πολίτευμα as 'country', 'state' or as 'citizenship'.

If the idea of conducting oneself as a citizen of heaven is present here, then 3:20a might be propositionalized as, 'we(inc) are citizens of heaven *and as a result we(inc) act as citizens of heaven should*'. But the reward theme of this *positive basis* for the APPEAL is more in focus, hence the proposition in the display. An alternative is 'we will live in heaven'.

**3:20b And ... also** Of the nine translations cited by Greenlee (1992), only KJV and NASB translate καί here. Greenlee lists only eight commentators who comment on it, with four different views. Vincent says, "Καί marks the correspondence of the expectation with the fact of the πολίτ. εν ούρ. ['commonwealth/citizenship in heaven']." The position of καί right after οὗ 'where', the relative pronoun referring to heaven, certainly might signal that Paul is making two statements about heaven: our citizenship or commonwealth is in heaven and it is *also* from heaven that we are eagerly awaiting our Savior, the Lord Jesus Christ. When propositionalized, the function of καί is realized as linking these two statements as conjoined propositions. It may be translated as 'and' or 'and also'. The conjoined propositions have the same function within the *basis*: both make very positive statements about the true believer's reward.

**we(inc) are also eagerly awaiting** BAGD (p. 83) glosses ἀπεκδέχομαι as 'await eagerly', and Greenlee (1992) lists eleven commentators who use 'eagerly' or a similar intensive modifier with whatever verb they use.

**eagerly awaiting a Savior to come from heaven; he is *our(inc)* Lord Jesus Christ** An alternate would be 'eagerly awaiting our(inc) Lord Jesus Christ to come from heaven; he is the one who saves those who trust in him'. Loh and Nida state that σωτῆρα 'Savior' "is without a definite article, and therefore is to be understood in a descriptive sense, not a title of reference. The emphasis is thus on the role or capacity of the Savior (NEB 'deliverer') in his final return." In fact, σωτῆρα is in an emphatic position, forefronted before the verb ἀπεκδεχόμεθα 'we eagerly await', while κύριον Ἰησοῦν Χριστόν 'Lord Jesus Christ' comes after the verb. But it is difficult to know what difference these considerations mean for translation. If in the target language it is difficult to render 'Savior' as a noun anyway, the verbal form would certainly be in order here. If a language has a good term for 'Savior', a verbal form would not necessarily be required, since the noun form would carry the 'saving' idea. A verbal form would be called for only if the noun lacks the proper force of the basic idea of one who saves. What is involved here is not a difference in content but a difference in focus.

Regarding σωτήρ 'savior, deliverer' here, O'Brien (1991) says, "At Phil. 3:20 this saving function has to do with the end time, that is, the final salvation. A real parallel is found at 1 Thes. 1:10, where the Saviour (ὁ ῥυόμενος) who is awaited from heaven will effect deliverance from the coming wrath." There probably is an intended contrast between the salvation of the true believers (20b) and the destruction of the enemies of the cross of Christ (19a). What one is saved from is a component of meaning implicit in the word 'save', and in some languages this must be made explicit. Therefore an alternate propositionalization for translation in some languages would be 'And we(inc) are also eagerly awaiting *our(inc) Lord Jesus Christ to come from heaven in order to save us(inc) from the destruction which God has planned for those who do not trust in him*'.

**3:21a change/transform** The Greek is μετασχηματίσει, a verb glossed by BAGD (p. 513) as "*change the form of, transform, change.*" Its meaning is contextually determined by the process needed for lowly earthly bodies to become glorious heavenly bodies. The simplest and most generic word for this in English is 'change'; 'transform' is also appropriate.

**our(inc) lowly bodies ... his glorious body** The construction τὸ σῶμα τῆς ταπεινώσεως ἡμῶν is often translated literally as 'the body of our humble state'. But this is a secondary sense of the English word *humble*. The primary sense of *humble* in English has to do with a certain attitude of people, not their state. To use the word to describe a state rather than an attitude may be an idiomatic use, which would explain why it is impossible in many languages to translate *humble* literally in a context like this. In Greek, however, ταπείνωσις and its cognates can be used of both a humble attitude and a lowly state.

The similarity in grammatical construction, as shown below, enhances the contrast of ταπεινώσεως 'lowly state' with δόξης 'glorious state':

```
τὸ σῶμα  τῆς ταπεινώσεως ἡμῶν
τῷ σώματι τῆς δόξης       αὐτοῦ

the body of-the lowliness of-us
the body of-the glory     of-him
```

Given such a construction, it is probable that the words in contrast are antonyms. If the meaning of one, therefore, is known and the meaning of the other needs to be determined more precisely, we may draw on our knowledge of the known meaning to determine the knowledge of the other. We might say that 'glorious' describes something as having all the best qualities in the situation under consideration. The closest non-idiomatic antonym of 'glorious' in English in this sense is 'lowly', which is one of the main meanings of the ταπειν- group of words. Words such as 'weak', 'mortal', and 'vile' refer to specific characteristics of 'lowly' bodies and so are one step removed from a literal translation appropriate in this context. If a language has words that will maintain the 'lowly'/'glorious' contrast, this would be an adequate translation, other things being equal. Otherwise, specific characteristics of the lowly body may have to be used for 'lowly'. TEV, for example, has "weak mortal bodies." It is difficult to see how a translation that refers *only* to the sinfulness of our present bodies (and not their fragility or mortality) would be adequate, however.

**to be like** BAGD (p. 778) glosses σύμμορφος as "*having the same form, similar in form* τινός *as* or *to something.*" The use of this word with σῶμα 'body' shows that a change of physical form is intended, but this, of course, also includes a change in what is usually thought of as the "inward nature and quality" (Loh and Nida, see also Vincent).

**3:21b since he is completely able** Two interrelated problems arise here. One is determining the relationship of the κατά 'according to' construction with what comes before it. The other is how to handle the abstract noun ἐνέργεια 'power, (out)working, action'. The context shows that the κατά construction refers to the all-encompassing capability that Christ has which enables him to transform our bodies and do anything he pleases in the universe. It may be that ἐνέργεια 'power' and τοῦ δύνασθαι αὐτόν 'of his being able' emphasize different aspects of that capability. O'Brien (1991) has "the outworking of his ability," for example (see also Hawthorne). Still the reference is basically to Christ's all-powerful capability. Of course, 'capability' is an abstract noun; the verb form would be 'he is able' or, because of the emphasis created by the double reference to capability, 'he is completely able'.

When 'capability' is expressed as a verb, the κατά construction is in a reason or grounds relationship with what comes before it: 'He will change our lowly bodies to become like his glorious body because/since he is completely able to do all things'. Regarding κατά BAGD (p. 407.II5aδ) says, "Oft[en] the norm is at the same time the reason, so that *in accordance with* and *because of* are merged." Here the κατά construction is not the reason he transforms our bodies but the reason he is able to do it, which is either close to or may actually be grounds. Since the verb in the main clause is future, CONCLUSION-grounds is possible, though the form of the statement in general and the context are not argumentative. However, there is a syllogism involved:

Major premise: Christ is able to subject all things to his power and control.
Minor premise: Our earthly bodies are included in 'all things'.
Conclusion: Therefore, Christ is able to subject our earthly bodies to his control, transforming them into heavenly bodies.

Martin (1959), Meyer, O'Brien (1991), and Silva appear to support a CONCLUSION-grounds relationship.

**to do/control\* all things** To determine an appropriate rendering for ὑποτάξαι, the following must be considered: Though BAGD (pp. 847-48) glosses ὑποτάσσω generally as "*subject, subordinate*" and in active voice with "τινά *bring someone to subjection*" or with "τινί τινα *or* τι [*bring*] *someone* or *someth.* [*to subjection*] *to someone,*" there is an amount of personification in these glosses. In some languages there would be a collocational clash between 'bring to subjection', an action that implies subjecting an entity with a will, and 'all things', which includes things without a will. Moreover, willful resistance would not be in focus at all in the action of changing lowly earthly bodies to glorious heavenly bodies. Thus it is better to use a generic word in the display. Since 'control' is not will-oriented, it is a good choice, but one problem with the word 'control' is that it does not necessarily fit in the same semantic domain as 'change' since 'control' can have the idea of 'rule over' instead of fundamental change. For this reason, the more generic 'do' is used in the display, with 'control' as an alternate but marked with an asterisk to alert the reader to its special sense here, that of being able to fundamentally change a person or entity.

# SECTION CONSTITUENT 3:17–21

## BOUNDARIES AND COHERENCE

Verses 17–21 are analyzed as a paragraph with an *APPEAL-basis* paragraph pattern since there are two imperatives in v. 17 followed by two occurrences of γάρ (v. 18 and v. 20). The most probable function of γάρ in each of these occurrences is that of signaling *basis* for the *APPEALS*. The vocatives and summarizing nature of 4:1 mark it as a new unit. See the further discussion on this subject in the note under 4:1b.

## PROMINENCE AND THEME

The only difference between the two parts of the double-headed *APPEAL* is that different people are involved. So basically it is one *APPEAL* in content. Both the *negative exemplary basis*, which is the bad example, and the *positive motivational basis*, which is the glorious hope of the true followers, are integral to the theme. Since each *basis* contains three or four conjoined constituents, the theme statement summarizes the information in them and at the same time maintains the important contrastive points between the two.

# DIVISION CONSTITUENT 4:1 (Hortatory Paragraph: Summary of 3:1–21)

*THEME: My dear friends, on the basis of all that I have told you [3:1–21], continue to believe firmly in the Lord Jesus Christ according to what I have just taught you [3:1–21] and act accordingly.*

| ¶ PATTERN | CONTENTS |
|---|---|
| *rapport basis* — | 4:1a My fellow believers, whom *I* love and whom *I* long for *and* who *make* me happy [MTY] and proud*, |
| APPEAL ——— | 4:1b on the basis *of all that I have told you* [3:1–21], continue to believe firmly in the Lord according to what I have just taught you [3:1–21] and act accordingly, dear friends. |

## INTENT AND PARAGRAPH PATTERN

The highly emotional buildup in 4:1a might be seen as a *rapport basis* to motivate the Philippian believers to carry out the APPEAL in 4:1b. This relationship is not based on words in Greek that normally signal cause and effect but on the semantic effect produced from the use of the vocatives in 4:1a.

## NOTES

**4:1** The adjectives that modify ἀδελφοί μου 'my brothers' are ἀγαπητοί 'beloved' and ἐπιπόθητοι 'longed for'. They basically express events rather than attributes. Then follow two nouns in the vocative. The first, χαρά 'joy', is abstract and the second, στέφανος 'crown', is used figuratively. At the end of the verse ἀγαπητοί occurs again and could be glossed as either 'beloved' or 'beloved ones'. Vocative abstract nouns or adjectives cannot be translated literally in many languages. (One wonders how universal abstract vocatives are.) In the display all of these abstract vocatives except the one at the end of the verse are rendered as full descriptive propositions (relative clauses). This results in a rather long representation of the vocatives. If they were to be kept in the same order as in the Greek text, they would interrupt the logical sequence of the argument: (1) chapter 3 as support for the appeal of 4:1, (2) ὥστε 'therefore', (3) the APPEAL οὕτως στήκετε ἐν κυρίῳ 'thus stand firm in the Lord'. Even so, the vocatives need to come before the APPEAL since they build rapport for it. The best way to handle this is to render ὥστε with a generic referring to the support elements in chapter 3 ('on the basis *of all that I have told you* [3:1–21]'), placing it after the modifiers of the vocative.

**4:1a whom *I* love and whom *I* long for** The adjectives ἀγαπητοί 'beloved' and ἐπιπόθητοι 'longed for' modifying ἀδελφοί 'brothers' are propositionalized as 'whom *I* love and whom *I* long for' or 'whom *I* love and whom *I* long *to see*'. See the note on 2:26a concerning ἐπιποθέω 'long for'.

***and* who *make* me happy** Vincent says about χαρά 'joy', "Χαρά by metonymy for the subject of joy." In other words, the Philippian believers cause Paul to be happy. There seems no reason to understand it in other than a generic sense. As 4:14–18 shows, the Philippian believers have been a source of joy to Paul not only in the immediate past but from the very beginning of their relationship. They have been faithful in contributing to his needs, but this is too specific a cause of joy for this context. Their generosity is only a manifestation of something deeper that gives Paul real joy: their firm faith and all its manifestations.

**and proud*** The noun στέφανος in its primary sense refers to the victor's wreath (not a kingly crown, which is διάδημα). Three other passages give clues to the meaning of στέφανος in this verse: I Thess. 2.19, Prov. 17:6, and Job 19:9.

In 1 Thess. 2:19, στέφανος occurs with καύχησις 'boasting, pride' in a genitive construction στέφανος καυχήσεως 'crown of pride'; it refers metaphorically to the addressees just as it does here and means 'you are the ones who make us proud'. This is confirmed by ὑμεῖς γάρ ἐστε ἡ δόξα ἡμῶν 'for you are our glory' in the following verse (1 Thess. 2:20).

In Prov. 17:6 (LXX) στέφανος occurs in a doublet with καύχημα 'pride, glory', which shows that their intended meaning is virtually the same:

Στέφανος γερόντων τέκνα τέκνων,
καύχημα δὲ τέκνων πατέρες αὐτῶν

"Children's children are the crown of old men; and their fathers are the glory of children."
(Brenton)

Note that TEV translates both of the emotive ideas represented in 'crown' and 'glory' here with the one word 'proud': "Grandparents are proud of their grandchildren, just as children are proud of their parents." (Of course, the TEV translation is based on the Hebrew text rather than the Greek.)

In Job 19:9 (LXX) στέφανος 'crown' is equated with 'pride/glory' by being linked in a doublet construction:

Τὴν δὲ δόξαν ἀπ' ἐμοῦ ἐξέδυσεν,
ἀφεῖλε δὲ στέφανον ἀπὸ κεφαλῆς μου

"And he has stripped me of my glory,
and has taken the crown from my head."
(Brenton)

These three passages demonstrate not only the meaning of the figure στέφανος ('pride, glory, honor'), but they also show that it is not necessarily a live figure. While in Job 19:9 the taking of the crown from the head could be a live figure, it is difficult to see 'wreath/crown' as a live figure in Prov. 17:6, "Children's children are the crown of old men." The TEV translator appeared to recognize that στέφανος is not always used as a live figure: στέφανός μου 'my crown' is translated as "how proud I am of you" in Phil. 4:1.

If taken to be a live figure, στέφανός μου in 4:1 is a metaphor: the Philippian believers are said to be a 'crown'. They are called 'crown' because they bring Paul honor by the testimony of their lives. However, as already mentioned, there is good reason to see the occurrence of στέφανος here as a dead figure. Following TEV, 'proud' is used in the display without any reference to 'crown'. As long as 'proud' is understood as an exultant emotional reaction to the godly life of the Philippians, in which Paul has had real influence, without implying that Paul is boasting about this to others, 'proud' may be an acceptable translation. (In fact, no other English word seems appropriate.) But 'proud' here is marked with an asterisk to show that the sense of boasting or bragging often associated with 'proud' is not present. Since receiving a στέφανος, whether literal or figurative, is always the result of some appropriate action or situation, this causative idea is expressed in the display rendering with 'make'. An alternate would be 'cause to be'.

It needs to be remembered that this verse is very emotive. This should be maintained in translation. A rendering that is too involved would detract from its emotive power.

**4:1b on the basis *of all that I have told you* [3:1–21]** Two words in this verse, ὥστε 'therefore' and οὕτως 'thus, in this way', express a connection with what has come before. (Actually οὕτως could express a forward reference but that seems unlikely; see the note that follows on 'what I have just taught you'.) Since 'thus' is contained in the APPEAL to stand fast in the Lord ('stand fast thus in the Lord'), it most naturally refers to other hortatory material. Paul's words about his own example could be included in that hortatory material since the Philippians are told to follow it, and this topic is the basic hortatory material of 3:12–16 (it has connections with 3:7–11 also). The connector ὥστε 'therefore' usually refers back to *basis* material, and it is possible that 3:20–21 with its statements of the glorious rewards for the true believers is the *basis* intended: 'Since we will receive such glorious rewards, you should persevere in this way'. However, if 3:20–21 were seen as a *basis* for this statement in 4:1, and if 3:20–4:1 were taken as a paragraph in itself with a *basis*-APPEAL paragraph pattern, it would be difficult to know what the reference of 'thus' would be. Verses 3:20–21 do not refer to how one should behave.

It seems better to understand 4:1 as a summary of chapter 3 and to take Paul's intended meaning as 'Since I have shown you the way you should live/behave, therefore you should follow that way'. This is more generic and far-reaching than just the material in 3:20–21. Or, slightly different, ὥστε could be seen as standing for all the supportive material in 3:1–21, just as οὕτως στήκετε ἐν κυρίῳ 'in this manner stand firm in the Lord' stands for all the hortatory material. There are good reasons to expect 4:1 to be a generic statement. The massing of emotive vocatives is certainly signaling something prominent. And since vocatives are often used to introduce new units, such a massing is probably not introducing something at midparagraph, though single vocatives do occur midparagraph, as in 3:13. Verse 4:1 sounds like a summary. (Summaries are generic representations of specific, filled-out units.) Here στήκετε ἐν κυρίῳ 'stand (fast) in the Lord' and οὕτως 'thus' are certainly abbreviated in form and broad enough to serve as generic representations. And the idea of 'stand firm in the Lord' finds its best context in a situation where there is opposition. The situational context of chapter 3 is that of the opposing beliefs of the Judaizers (3:2), the libertines (3:18–19), and whoever those people are who claim they are already perfect (3:12). Thus it is very probable that 4:1 is a summary closing this part of the epistle. The next two verses are very personal exhortations. A number of loosely connected exhortations occur after that, so 4:1 would end a section of the epistle in which Paul deals with the *major* subjects he wants to communicate.

If 4:1 is a summary, then 3:20-21 has a significant part in the support for the exhortation of 4:1, especially because of its emotive overtones and its position right before the *APPEAL*. However, this does not exclude other information in 3:1-21 from also being signaled by ὥστε 'therefore' as support for the *APPEAL* in 4:1.

**continue to believe firmly ... and act accordingly** The imperative verb στήκετε here is often glossed as 'stand, stand firm, stand your ground', since the primary meaning of the verb στήκω is 'to stand'. However, in this context, these are really figurative. Though this might be called a dead metaphor in English, the sense in this context is built on the idea of not retreating but standing one's ground. In a situational context where there are, actually or potentially, opposing beliefs and practices being propagated by determined men (the Judaizers of 3:2 and the libertines of 3:18-19), and where the whole of chapter 3 has focused on how to deal with them, the nonfigurative meaning of στήκετε would be 'continue to firmly believe and practice what I have taught you'. Bruce (1989), Martin (1959), Loh and Nida, and O'Brien (1991) mention resistance to opposition. Bruce says, "In the present context he encourages them to be steadfast in resistance to those influences against which he has just warned them—influences that would undermine their Christian stability."

**what I have just taught you [3:1-21]** The imperative στήκετε 'stand' has two qualifiers here, οὕτως 'thus, in this manner' and ἐν κυρίῳ 'in the Lord'. It would be highly appropriate in this context for οὕτως to refer to what Paul has been teaching them about true belief and practice in chapter 3. Though οὕτως could refer forward, the idea of standing against opposition, which is a component of meaning present in στήκετε, is more appropriate to what has come before in chapter 3 than what follows in chapter 4.

**in the Lord** If we keep the figurative or semi-figurative sense of 'stand firm', then 'stand firm in your position in the Lord' would probably be as appropriate a translation as any in this context of forces opposing true Christian doctrine and practice. But since this is still using figures, and since 'position' is an abstract noun, better propositionalizations would be 'Continue to believe firmly in this true teaching [3:1-21] about the Lord and act/behave accordingly', 'Continue to believe firmly in what I have just taught you [3:1-21] about the Lord and act/behave according to it', or 'Continue to believe firmly in the Lord according to what I have just taught you [3:1-21] and act/behave accordingly'.

As to the word 'Lord', κύριος 'Lord' in Paul's writings more often refers to Jesus Christ than to God the Father, and there are factors that suggest that this is the case here. It is the Judaizers' and libertines' wrong understanding of who Jesus is which is the background of the discussion in 3:1-21. The Judaizers do not believe fully in his grace (3:2) and they do not glory in him but rely upon themselves for salvation (3:3). The libertines are enemies of the cross of Christ (3:18) because of their disbelief in his will or power to keep the Christian from sinning. By implication the Judaizers do not have saving faith and the libertines are clearly unbelievers as shown by the statement, 'their end is destruction'. Although 'Jesus Christ' is not supplied in the display, it may be necessary in languages where the Father and the Son must be distinguished.

**dear friends** Paul sandwiches his *APPEAL* between vocatives to show the Philippians how much he really does love them. The final one of these vocatives is ἀγαπητοί 'beloved (ones)'; it is rendered as a vocative, '*my* dear friends', at the end of 1b. Another possibility would be to include it with the representations of the earlier vocatives, but the same idea, 'whom *I* love', is already there in the representation of the earlier ἀγαπητοί.

Since 'dear' is close to being an abstract adjective, an alternate would be: '*my* friends whom *I* love'.

## BOUNDARIES AND COHERENCE

Verse 4:1 coheres as one Greek sentence. For boundaries, see the note on 4:1b concerning 'on the basis *of all that I have told you*'.

## PROMINENCE AND THEME

Vocatives, which represent the *basis,* form a good part of this verse. To express them in the theme statement, they are telescoped into '*my* good friends'. Since the *APPEAL* is a generic summary of 3:2-21, it is kept in full form.

# SUBPART CONSTITUENT 4:2–9 (Hortatory Section: Appeal₃ of 1:27–4:9)

*THEME: I urge Euodia and Syntyche to be reconciled with each other. Rejoice always and be gentle to everyone. Do not worry; pray instead. Think about all that is good and practice whatever you have learned from me and God will be with you and grant you peace.*

| MACROSTRUCTURE | CONTENTS |
|---|---|
| APPEAL₁ | 4:2–3 I urge Euodia and Syntyche to be reconciled with each other since they belong to the Lord, and I request that you, faithful comrade, help them in this since they have both proclaimed the good news faithfully together with me and my other fellow workers. |
| APPEAL₂ | 4:4–7 The Lord is near. Always rejoice, be gentle to everyone. Do not worry about anything, but pray to God instead. As a result, God will grant you profound peace. |
| APPEAL₃ | 4:8–9 Continually think about everything that is good and praiseworthy. Continually practice whatever you have learned from me. As a result, God will be with you and give you peace. |

## INTENT AND MACROSTRUCTURE

The 4:2–9 section continues the hortatory genre of the subpart with three more hortatory paragraphs. The first paragraph (4:2–3) is distinctive in that it applies the earlier general *APPEALS* to unity (2:1–4) to a very specific situation, the case of Euodia and Syntyche. The second paragraph (4:4–7) comes back to the theme of rejoicing, adding to it *APPEALS* not to worry but to pray instead. The third paragraph contains very general *APPEALS*. Both the second and third paragraphs have reference to peace.

## BOUNDARIES AND COHERENCE

In chapter 4, vv. 2–9 are distinct from vv. 10–20 in that every verse in 2–9 except v. 7 contains an *APPEAL* (all imperatives in form except for v. 2, which, however, does contain a strong *APPEAL*). No imperatives or other types of exhortation whatsoever are found in vv. 10–20. Also, vv. 10–20 deal with a subject that is not touched on at all in vv. 2–9, Paul's thankfulness for the Philippians' gift. Verses 10–20 belong to the final expressive part of the *BODY* of the epistle.

The coherence of vv. 2–9 derives not so much from content but from genre and style. With nine exhortations in eight verses, the unit is heavy on *APPEALS* and light on *basis*. Such a style is characteristic of final instructions at the point a writer is about to finish his discourse.

Still, there are some threads that give lexical or content coherence to vv. 2–9. The most obvious of these are ἡ εἰρήνη τοῦ θεοῦ 'the peace of God' in 4:7 and ὁ θεὸς τῆς εἰρήνης 'the God of peace' in 4:9. Both of these occur in result constructions after imperatives and act as *motivational bases* for carrying out the imperatives. Emotive content can also be seen in the commands to rejoice in v. 4 and the related idea of showing gentleness to all in v. 5. Even vv. 2–3 are emotive in that they deal with emotive relationships between individual Christians. Of course, not enough emotive content is present to suggest that the genre is expressive rather than hortatory.

Since τὸ λοιπόν at the beginning of 4:8 is not taken to mean 'finally' but 'as for a remaining matter', it is not necessary to see vv. 8–9 as in a different section from vv. 2–7.

## PROMINENCE AND THEME

The three paragraphs of the 4:2–9 section are all hortatory. They stand in a conjoined relationship to one another. The theme statement for the section comes from each of them. To make it as concise as possible only the *APPEALS* are used, except that the twice-repeated reference to peace (in v. 7 and v. 9) is represented at the end.

## SECTION CONSTITUENT 4:2-3 (Hortatory Paragraph: Appeal₁ of 4:2-9)

*THEME: I urge Euodia and Syntyche to be reconciled with each other since they belong to the Lord, and I request that you, faithful comrade, help them in this since they have both proclaimed the good news faithfully together with me and my other fellow workers.*

| ¶ PTRN | RELATIONAL STRUCTURE | CONTENTS |
|---|---|---|
| APPEAL₁ | | 4:2a I urge *you(sg)*, Euodia, and I urge *you(sg)*, Syntyche, to be reconciled with each other, |
| basis | | 4:2b *since you both belong to* the Lord. |
| APPEAL₂ | | 4:3a And, *my* faithful comrade/partner, I also request that you(sg) help them *to be reconciled*, |
| basis | NUCLEUS | 4:3b since they have *faithfully proclaimed* the good news together with me *even though many people have opposed us(exc)*, |
| | AMPLIFICATION—ITEM | 4:3c and *they have faithfully proclaimed the good news* together with Clement and the rest of my fellow workers, |
| | description of 'rest' | 4:3d whose names *are* in the book *in which God/Christ has written the names of all those people who will* live *forever/eternally*. |

### INTENT AND PARAGRAPH PATTERN

The 4:2-3 paragraph consists of two APPEAL-basis units, one of which is addressed to Euodia and Syntyche, the other to the 'true yokefellow' of Paul. The two *bases* are not clearly marked as such formally, but semantically it is clear that they are *bases*, as will be shown in the notes.

### NOTES

**4:2a I urge *you(sg)*, Euodia, and I urge *you(sg)*, Syntyche** This is clearly a hortatory statement, not a declarative one. The use of παρακαλῶ 'I urge' is one of the ways exhortation is signaled in Greek. The repeated παρακαλῶ is seen by many commentators as showing impartiality. It may also add emphasis to the urging (Hawthorne, Jones, Silva). The use of παρακαλῶ may be a more polite means of expressing the APPEAL than an imperative would be. This is the case in Philem. 8-9.

**Euodia . . . Syntyche** These are the names of two women, as shown both by the feminine form of the names and also by the use of the feminine pronominal forms αὐταῖς 'them' and αἵτινες 'who' in v. 3.

**to be reconciled with each other** The Greek is τὸ αὐτὸ φρονεῖν 'to think the same thing'. A similar expression occurs in 2:2b: τὸ αὐτὸ φρονῆτε, literally, 'you might think the same thing'. (See the note there.) This expression is probably idiomatic to some extent. It may be translated 'to agree with one another'. Several of the versions translate it 'agree' or 'agreement' (e.g., NJB, NIV, REB, TEV). In the display, however, it is translated 'be reconciled with each other'. (Vincent's paraphrase is "to be reconciled"; this is also close to NASB's "live in harmony" or TNT's "settle their differences.") The reason is that, in view of the clear lack of fellowship between two people, it is somewhat more appropriate in English to use 'be reconciled with each other' than 'agree with each other'; 'agree' tends to focus on specific issues, while 'be reconciled' focuses on relationship.

**4:2b *since you both belong to* the Lord** Paul's use of ἐν κυρίῳ 'in the Lord' here may well be motivational: 'Since you both belong to the Lord, you should be reconciled to each other'. Their relationship with the Lord demands that they be reconciled to each other. Christ's giving of himself to unite us with himself demands that we give ourselves to one another in unity and harmony.

In propositionalizing ἐν κυρίῳ 'in the Lord', subjects must be stated. A decision must be made as to whether Paul is addressing these two women directly or indirectly, that is, 'since you both belong to the Lord' or 'since they both belong to the Lord'. Since there is no overriding reason to see them as not being addressed directly, direct address has been chosen for the display. They are, after all, the ones being exhorted. For translation into other languages, the choice between direct address ('you') and indirect address ('they') will depend on the rules of the target language for rapport and address in such a situation as this.

**4:3a And** The word ναί, in its functions of answering a question in the affirmative or agreeing with someone else's statement, is appropriately translated into English as 'yes' and might be translated likewise in other languages. However, the reference here is classified by BAGD (p. 533.3) under "in emphatic repetition of one's own statement," in this case where "the repetition can consist in the fact that one request preceded and a similar one follows." The primary use of the word is in dialogue. Its use in monologue, as here, is to capture some of the dynamic of dialogue. A vocative has this same function. Both here and in Philem. 20 ναί is used with a vocative. There it occurs right before the vocative in the emotional appeal. While 'yes' is a possible English translation in Phil. 4:3, it is not a very natural translation and in many languages it would be even less natural to use the equivalent to the 'yes' of dialogue in this context. A more natural rendering here in English would be 'and', though it is true that 'yes' is more emphatic than 'and'. A few manuscripts read καί 'and' instead of ναί 'yes', and KJV follows that reading with 'and'. However, modern versions which use 'and' probably do so to maintain natural English; it is not that they follow the καί reading (see Greenlee 1992).

**also** Since παρακαλέω 'I urge, request' and ἐρωτάω 'I ask, request' are similar in meaning, ἐρωτῶ καὶ σέ most likely means 'I urge them and I urge you also'. That is, Paul has two requests, one for the women, and one for Paul's faithful comrade. O'Brien (1991) says that καὶ σέ "means 'you also', that is, in addition to the two women directly exhorted. It may be difficult for Euodia and Syntyche to come to a common mind on their own, so Paul requests his trusted colleague to help them." However, Lenski says regarding καὶ σέ, "'Also thee' means 'thee' especially and thus in a way requests also others who may be able to lend assistance." But the fact that no one else except Paul and the two women has been introduced thus far makes it unlikely that others are also in focus, since, at least in English and presumably in Greek, in signaling participants, 'also' signals the addition of a participant(s) to those already named.

**comrade/partner** There has been much conjecture as to who is being referred to by γνήσιε σύζυγε 'faithful yokefellow'. For translators, the identity problem is not whether it is Epaphroditus or Luke or Silas, as various commentators have suggested. The question is whether σύζυγος is the personal name of someone among the addressees of the epistle or whether it identifies someone among the addressees as having a special relationship to Paul or to the two women. For this person to know that he is the one being addressed, γνήσιε σύζυγε must be clearly identificational to him. If it is his personal name, he would immediately know. However, according to TDNT (vol. 7, pp. 748-50) and also BAGD (p. 775, citing A. Fick-F. Bechtel, Die griech. Personennamen 1894:132), σύζυγος has not yet been found as a personal name in any Greek literature or inscription.

Though σύζυγος was sometimes used to refer to one's spouse, probably as 'partner' is in English, it is hardly likely that Paul is calling on his own wife to help settle this dispute as some commentators have suggested, or that he is calling on the husband of one of the women to help.

If it is not a proper name, and if the relationship referred to by συν- 'with' refers to the relationship of Paul with this person, then most likely it is one of these three options: (1) an expression that Paul often used for this person, (2) an expression appropriate for some person in a unique relationship with Paul, the only one who could see himself so identified, or (3) an expression identifying a person already singled out to perform this task by Paul through some means other than in this epistle.

While it is difficult to know exactly what Paul had in mind, it seems best to translate γνήσιε σύζυγε fairly literally, but in a way that is contrastive to συνεργοί μου 'my fellow workers' in the latter part of the verse. The use of σύζυγος is, at the very least, a means of contrasting this person with the rest of Paul's fellow workers for identificational purposes. 'Comrade' and 'partner' are given as alternates in the display. 'Yokefellow' is not used because it is based on the figure of the yoke.

**faithful** While the primary sense of γνήσιος is 'genuine, real', it is not likely that Paul means to contrast this genuine comrade with comrades who are not genuine, but rather to emphasize the faithfulness of this comrade. Also, 'faithful comrade' is a more natural collocation in English than 'genuine comrade'.

**4:3b since** We would expect the APPEAL συλλαμβάνου αὐταῖς 'help them' to be followed by a *basis*. While ὅστις (αἵτινες) is a type of relative pronoun, one of its functions in some contexts is to signal *basis* or grounds. BAGD (p. 587) lists this function under 2.b, "to emphasize a characteristic quality, by which a preceding statement is to be confirmed." Greenlee (1992) lists fifteen commentators and three versions that take the function of αἵτινες here as giving "the reason why these women should be helped."

**they have** *faithfully proclaimed* **the good news together with me** *even though many people have opposed us(exc)* The συν- 'together with' of συναθλέω 'contend together with, struggle together with' refers to struggling or fighting side by side with one's comrades, unitedly struggling against someone or something else.

'Struggled with me in the gospel' is elliptical as far as full propositionalization is concerned: They struggled side by side in proclaiming the good news. The struggle was not one of physically fighting with the opponents of the good news, however. Therefore the words 'struggle' or 'contend' are not used in the display. Rather, the component of opposition found in συναθλέω 'struggle along with' is represented by 'even though many have opposed us(exc)'. 'Faithfully' represents the component of meaning of faithfulness and steadfastness implied in 'struggle along with'. The concept of struggle in a context such as this implies not only opposition but also serious effort in opposing the opposition.

It should be noted that Paul's life itself was full of struggle against the opponents of the good news, whether human or spiritual, and this was the case for his fellow workers also. This then is taken to be what Paul intended by συναθλέω rather than some weaker sense.

It is difficult to know whether the implicit 'us' is inclusive or exclusive. While the faithful comrade addressed here would also be in the same general situation of being opposed by many people, Paul does not explicitly include him along with the other fellow workers mentioned when he says 'they have struggled together with me in the good news', and so the exclusive form may be the best choice. Of course, the final test is the choice of the mother tongue speaker, once he or she understands the situational context well.

**4:3c the rest of my fellow workers** The Greek is τῶν λοιπῶν συνεργῶν μου 'the rest of my fellow workers'. It might also be rendered 'the rest of those people who have worked together with me' or 'the rest of those people who have proclaimed the good news together with me'.

**4:3d whose names** The relative clause ὧν τὰ ὀνόματα ἐν βίβλῳ ζωῆς 'whose names (are) in the book of life' is taken to refer to the unnamed fellow workers of Paul, since a relative pronoun usually relates back to its nearest antecedent.

Also, the fact that these fellow workers are unnamed here but are named in the book of life would seem to be Paul's reason for including this relative clause. Otherwise it is difficult to know how this relative clause fits the theme. It would appear that Paul uses this clause for reasons of rapport. He feels that he must name Clement, but for reasons of space or otherwise, he chooses not to name his other fellow workers. To show that he also holds these other fellow workers in highest respect, even though he has not named them, he says that their names are in the book of life. This, of course, is more important than their names appearing in the letter.

Since this is formally a relative clause and its role is not clearly that of any other communication relation, it has been labeled in the display as "description of 'rest'," that is, of the rest of the fellow workers. This description maintains rapport between Paul and these fellow workers. Another option would be to label it a "comment" or "rapport comment"; but this is a relation reserved for units that are incidental to the theme, and it would be inappropriate to consider all units dealing with rapport as incidental to the theme.

Greenlee (1992) lists fourteen commentators who take ὧν 'of whom, whose' as referring "to the unnamed others of Paul's fellow workers" and only three who take it as referring "to all the persons mentioned in this verse." Certainly all the persons mentioned in the verse have their names written in the book of life, but the interpretational problem is, Which ones does Paul focus on in this relative clause?

**in the book** *in which God/Christ has written the names of all those people who will* **live** *forever/eternally* The clause ὧν τὰ ὀνόματα ἐν βίβλῳ ζωῆς 'whose names in book of life' has no verb. The simple stative verb 'are' might be supplied. However, in order to propositionalize the genitive construction 'book of life' with its abstract noun 'life', it is much clearer to use 'are written' or 'are recorded'. To do so an agent must be stated: either God or Christ. In Rev. 3:5 Jesus says, "I will never blot out his name from the book of life, but will acknowledge his name before my Father and his angels" (NIV).

## BOUNDARIES AND COHERENCE

Verses 2-3 of chapter 4 are considered a unit since their *APPEAL-basis* paragraph patterns are closely interrelated thematically, both dealing with Euodia and Syntyche's reconciliation. The

APPEAL in 4:1 is to the Philippian believers in general as also are the APPEALS in the rest of the section (4:4-9); the APPEALS in 4:2-3 are to individuals. Difference in participants usually signals paragraph boundaries.

## PROMINENCE AND THEME

Since there are two APPEAL-basis paragraph patterns in this unit, elements from each APPEAL and each basis are included in the theme.

## SECTION CONSTITUENT 4:4-7 (Hortatory Paragraph: Appeal₂ of 4:2-9)

THEME: *The Lord is near. Always rejoice, be gentle to everyone. Do not worry about anything, but pray to God instead. As a result, God will grant you profound peace.*

| ¶ PATTERN | RELATIONAL STRUCTURE | CONTENTS |
|---|---|---|
| APPEAL₁ | NUCLEUS | 4:4a Rejoice always *because you belong to* the Lord. |
| | equivalent | 4:4b I say again, rejoice. |
| APPEAL₂ | | 4:5a Always be gentle to everyone. |
| *motivational basis* | | 4:5b The Lord is near/close by. |
| APPEAL₃ | REASON — negative | 4:6a Do not worry about anything; |
| | POSITIVE — NUCLEUS₁ | 4:6b instead, in everything/every situation pray *to God*, tell him what you need, and ask him *to help you*. [DOU] |
| | NUCLEUS₂ | 4:6c Also thank *him that/because he helps you always*. |
| | RESULT — NUCLEUS — RESULT — NUCLEUS | 4:7a As a result, God will cause you not to worry *about anything* [MTY] (*or,* God will protect your minds *in every way*), [PRS] |
| | equivalent | 4:7b *that is,* he will cause you to be peaceful, |
| | reason | 4:7c *because you trust* in Christ Jesus. |
| | amplification | 4:7d *You* will not be able to understand how you can be so peaceful *in such difficult circumstances*. |

### INTENT AND PARAGRAPH PATTERN

The imperatives of the 4:4-7 paragraph mark it as hortatory. However, emotive ideas do pervade the paragraph: χαίρετε 'rejoice' (v. 4 twice), μηδὲν μεριμνᾶτε 'be anxious about nothing' (v. 6), ἡ εἰρήνη 'peace', and καρδίας 'heart' (both v. 7). In fact 'rejoice' and 'do not be anxious' are quite close in meaning. But what of 'let your gentleness (ἐπιεικές) be known to everyone' (v. 5a), which comes between these two related ideas? Silva (p. 224) says, "Several commentators have suggested that the word [ἐπιεικής] reflects an attitude of contentment with one's state, even when one has not been treated justly. Although it would be difficult to prove that this nuance is a basic semantic component of the word, the context of the letter as a whole supports it." Eadie (p. 245) says, "If this joy in the Lord were felt in its fulness, the spirit so cheered and exalted would cease to insist on mere personal right, and practise forbearance." It could almost be said that the state of mind that Paul exhorts in χαίρετε 'rejoice' and μηδὲν μεριμνᾶτε 'be anxious about nothing' focuses on an inner attitude, while τὸ ἐπιεικὲς ὑμῶν γνωσθήτω πᾶσιν ἀνθρώποις 'let your gentleness be known to everyone' focuses on manifesting that attitude toward others.

The display shows three separate APPEALS as each having 4:5b, 'The Lord is near/close by', as a *motivational basis*. Another option is to see 4:5b as a *motivational basis* for 4:5a only.

## NOTES

**4:4a Rejoice always *because you belong to* the Lord** The exhortation χαίρετε ἐν κυρίῳ 'rejoice in the Lord' also occurs in 3:1a (see the note on 3:1a).

This is a deep joy, not merely a superficial one. Martin (1959) quotes Bonnard who says: "The Pauline appeals to joy are never simply encouragements; they throw back the distressed churches on their Lord; they are, above all, appeals to faith." In the semantic systems of some languages, it is unnatural to exhort an emotive concept such as joy; however, to exhort an action that would result in joy is possible, for example, 'trust fully in the Lord so that you will be completely happy'.

**4:5a Always be gentle to everyone** BAGD (p. 292) glosses the adjective ἐπιεικής as "*yielding, gentle, kind.*" Here in 4:5 it is the substantive that occurs: τὸ ἐπιεικὲς ὑμῶν, glossed as "*your forbearing spirit.*" One of the clearest indications of the meaning of ἐπιεικής in the New Testament is found in its *contrast* with πλήκτης 'bully, violent person' in 1 Tim. 3:3. Another clue is the co-occurrence of ἐπιεικής with what would seem to be a close synonym, ἄμαχος 'not quarrelsome, peaceable', in 1 Tim. 3:3 and Titus 3:2. There is no reason to think that its meaning would be different in Phil. 4:5 since in each of these passages the context indicates that a primary sense of the word is in focus. 'Kind' would be an alternative to 'gentle' in the display, though 'kind' tends to have a greater range of meaning and refers to many different types of positive acts toward other people, while 'gentle' focuses more on the passive side.

There is a mismatch in 4:5a between the grammatical form of the substantive τὸ ἐπιεικές 'gentleness, forbearing spirit' and its semantic realization. 'Gentleness' represents either a state (in this case an attitude) or an attribute of an event, though the event is implicit. That event might be represented by 'act' ('act gently toward everyone'). Of course, in English it is more natural to say, 'Be gentle toward everyone', and this would be appropriate for the passive idea of not reacting in the wrong way.

The use of the imperative verb γνωσθήτω 'let it be known' (from γινώσκω) is an extended sense of 'let it be known': the usual sense is making something known by verbal or written communication. But here it is making known by way of life. The rendering in the display is a restatement of 'let your gentleness be known to everyone' in words with primary senses. The imperative γνωσθήτω 'let it be known' and the substantive τὸ ἐπιεικὲς ὑμῶν 'your gentleness' are seen as two representations of the same action, and the double representation is taken as intensifying that action. This is then translated with only one verb and some type of intensifier: 'Always be gentle to everyone', 'Be completely gentle to everyone', 'Be sure you are gentle to everyone'.

Another possible rendering is to use 'be gentle' as the imperative and express the 'making known' component as a purpose clause: 'Be gentle to everyone in order that everyone will know that you are gentle people' or 'Be so gentle to people that everyone will know that you are truly gentle people'. In these renderings 'know' must have a content (e.g., 'that you are truly gentle people').

**4:5b The Lord is near/close by** The Greek is ὁ κύριος ἐγγύς, literally, 'the Lord is near'. Most commentators take this as the soon coming of the Lord Jesus. Good evidence can also be found to support the meaning of the Lord's perpetual presence. This latter sense was common in the Old Testament. Psalm 119:151 (118:151, LXX) is very similar to Phil. 4:5b, Ἐγγὺς εἶ Κύριε 'You are near, O Lord'. Paul was grateful for the Lord's nearness in a similar situation to that of the setting for his Philippian letter when he wrote in 2 Tim. 4:17, ὁ δὲ κύριός μοι παρέστη καὶ ἐνεδυνάμωσέν με. NIV renders this "But the Lord stood at my side and gave me strength."

The evidence is rich, however, that ὁ κύριος ἐγγύς is intended here to mean 'the Lord is coming soon'. The New Testament contains many references where ἐγγύς 'near' or some other word with a similar meaning is used in the sense of nearness in time. The closest to the Phil. 4:5 occurrence may be Matt. 24:33, γινώσκετε ὅτι ἐγγύς ἐστιν ἐπὶ θύραις, which NIV translates as "you know that it is near, right at the door" with a marginal note of "or *he*" (i.e., he, the Son of Man, is near, right at the door).

Formally, the context does not give clear clues to the intended meaning since no connectors mark the relationship of 4:5b with the units before or after. As far as the semantics is concerned, however, several commentators (Martin 1959, Meyer, and others) have pointed out that the sense 'The Lord is coming soon' would be appropriate support as motivation for the Philippian believers to be gentle and forbearing with those who have done them wrong since the Lord will soon come to right all wrongs. This would parallel James 5:8, "You too, be patient and stand firm, because the Lord's coming is near" (NIV, cf. 5:9). Structurally, this solution would be appropriate in the sense that it would provide an explicit *basis* for the APPEAL of 4:5a and thus be a full paragraph pattern, which is expected in discourse, though not obligatory. The absence of connectors might be explained by viewing this unit as an emotive peak of the epistle. The concise style would be appropriate to a peak.

On the other hand, the Lord's presence is such an encouragement and comfort to believers who are passing through hard times that 'the Lord is near' might be seen as motivational support for each of the APPEALS of 4:4–7. 'Rejoice always' and 'do not be anxious about anything' certainly have to do with emotional encouragement; 'be gentle and forbearing to everyone' is also related to these concepts, as previously noted. As writers such as Bruce (1989) and Newman have suggested, the Lord is always near his people, and the nearness of his presence brings encouragement whether that nearness is his invisible presence now or the expectancy of his imminent visible presence. O'Brien (1991) cites Ernst, Merk, and Michaelis as taking 4:5b as support for each of the exhortations in 4:4–7 regardless of whether they see 4:5b referring to Christ's invisible nearness or his soon coming, or both. O'Brien himself takes this view. It should be noticed, however, that ὁ κύριος 'the Lord' refers to the Lord Jesus elsewhere in Philippians while it is God the Father who is in focus in 4:6–7.

A literal rendering of ὁ κύριος ἐγγύς is used in the display. Unless ὁ κύριος ἐγγύς was a common expression in the early church meaning 'The Lord is coming soon', ὁ κύριος ἐγγύς would not have any more of an obligatory temporal meaning than 'The Lord is near' would have in English. Therefore it seems best to leave it unconnected and ambiguous in the display, as in the Greek text. This is especially necessary since the temporal representation would demand a nonambiguous rendering in the display, while a literal rendering could be taken either way. For many languages, however, it may have to be translated unambiguously.

Although 4:5b is shown in the display as a *basis* for each of the three APPEALS, the rendering of 4:5b does not explicitly signal this. It would be difficult to signal this relationship. Moreover, there is no formal signal in the Greek. It seems best in this case to rely on the context to signal any support which 4:5b may have for the APPEALS in this paragraph. The other option is to understand 4:5b as a *basis* for 4:5a alone.

**4:6a Do not worry** In this context the verb μεριμνάω means either 'be anxious' or 'worry'.

**4:6b instead, in everything/every situation**
The conjunction ἀλλά with the imperative typically signals an opposite action or state to be sought after, that is, one that is opposite to the immediately preceding negated action or state. Here it is 'worry' that is negated (by μηδέν 'nothing'); in the ἀλλά construction the Philippians are exhorted to carry out an action (prayer) that will result in a state opposite to worry, namely, peace. This is somewhat different from the more typical negative-POSITIVE relationship where the positive concept is the antonym of the negative. There the two parts are almost equivalent in meaning. Even so, the action in 6b is still substitutionary to that of 6a, and 'instead' is an appropriate signal.

There is an intended contrast between μηδέν 'nothing' and ἐν παντί 'in everything'. They should worry about *nothing*, but instead should let God know about *every* area where they have needs, that is, every area where there would be a tendency to worry.

**pray *to God*...ask him *to help you*** The Greek is τῇ προσευχῇ καὶ τῇ δεήσει. This might be translated as 'by prayer and petition' since προσευχή may be thought of as the more general term for 'prayer' and δέησις sometimes focuses more on the idea of 'supplication, petition'. Here, however, there is no distinguishing context and so the use of these synonyms is taken to have some function other than a meaning difference. Note too that τὰ αἰτήματα ὑμῶν γνωριζέσθω πρὸς τὸν θεόν 'let your requests be made known to God' is also similar in meaning. One common function of the piling up of synonyms is to signal comprehensiveness: here, then, the meaning might be 'pray in all kinds of ways'. But this does not seem to fit. The intended function may be that of emphasizing that prayer is the definitive answer to their worries. Bruce (1989) says that Paul "uses three different Greek words for 'prayer' here. There are slight differences of nuance between one word and another, but the main effect of the use of all three is to emphasize the importance in Christian life of constancy in believing and expectant prayer."

In propositionalizing, some of these distinguishing aspects of prayer must be retained, especially since the abstract noun phrase τὰ αἰτήματα ὑμῶν 'your requests' must be translated as a verbal phrase: 'ask him to help you' or 'ask him to grant what you need'. In the display, 'pray to God' is intended in the general sense; this is one of the meanings of προσευχή 'prayer', and it thus sets the stage for more specific references to prayer. This kind of rendering helps to stress the importance of prayer in solving one's worries, just as the multiple references to prayer do in the Greek text. In some languages other means may be necessary to stress the importance of prayer.

**tell him what you need** The Greek is τὰ αἰτήματα ὑμῶν γνωριζέσθω πρὸς τὸν θεόν 'let your requests be made known to God'. Of all the words and phrases Paul uses for prayer and thanksgiving in 6b-c this is the one he wants to stress the most as seen by his use of the imperative. (The others, however, though abstract nouns in the Greek text, are nevertheless hortatory from the semantic standpoint.) Since God knows what we need (Matt. 6:32), why are the Philippians told to make known their requests to him? O'Brien (1991) says, "Not because he is unaware of either the petitions or their content. Rather, by bringing to him their αἰτήματα ['requests'], which reflect every possible cause of anxiety, they are laying out their troubles before him [cf. Michael, p. 198], or casting all their cares upon him (cf. 1 Pet. 5:7)." In this sense, 'make known to God' is appropriate. However, in some languages, a literal translation of 'make known to God' would be inappropriate since 'make known' is normally used of teaching and one does not teach God.

**4:6c thank** *him that/because he helps you always* The word εὐχαριστίας 'thanksgiving' is an abstract noun and would be propositionalized in basic form as 'thank *him*'. But when 'thanksgiving' is propositionalized as only 'thank him', its connection with the context is somewhat vague. If a reason for the thanksgiving is to be supplied in the display, we must first determine whether the thanksgiving is for past and present blessings or is specifically for the blessings asked for at the time of prayer. Many commentators take it to refer only to past and present blessings (Bruce 1983, 1989; Loh and Nida, Meyer, O'Brien 1991, Vincent, among others), that is, as a general expression of thanksgiving, which leads to confidence that God will answer one's present requests too, and so peace. One might say, however, that the person who thanks God that his request is *going* to be fulfilled shows even more confidence and will experience peace. Miller and Rountree render it "tell him what you need, and then thank Him (because He is going to help you)." It would seem best, however, to understand the thanks as more general (e.g., 'Also thank *him because he helps you always*'), since nothing in the context forces us to understand future blessings to be in focus more than past blessings or vice versa.

Note that the supplied clause should focus on the reason or occasion for the thanks rather than the grounds for it: 'thank him *for* what he does for you always' rather than 'thank him, *since* he always helps you'.

**4:7a As a result** As the context shows, καί at the beginning of this verse signals result, a not uncommon function of καί, especially after an imperative or other hortatory construction (BAGD, p. 392.I2f). Thus v. 7 is the result of the imperative action of v. 6. This result is to some extent motivational and so might be seen as a *motivational basis* for carrying out the APPEAL. However, it is treated as only a result in the display diagram since it is not marked in the Greek surface structure as grounds and it does not seem especially helpful to double label it.

This result (of carrying out the APPEAL) is considered to be marked as prominent and is therefore included in the theme statement. What marks it as prominent is the description of the peace of God as surpassing all understanding.

**God will cause you not to worry** *about anything* (*or*, **God will protect your minds** *in every way*) The literal rendering is 'the peace of God...will guard your hearts and minds', a personification: peace acts as a guard. But even when this is adjusted to 'God will guard your hearts and minds', there may still be a figure if 'guard' is taken in the sense of a soldier guarding people or property. Many commentators mention this graphic and effective figurative sense which communicates both the right meaning and feeling. However, φρουρήσει 'he will guard' might also be translated 'protect', 'watch over', or 'take care of', which, at least in some languages, would not be figurative. (Of course, the way 'heart' and 'mind' are rendered, whether as figures or not, will affect the overall rendering in respect to figurative language.)

An alternative solution is to take φρουρήσει 'he will guard' as nonfigurative and translate it as 'prevent' with the addition of an object or content of 'prevent' ('will prevent you/your hearts and minds from worrying'). Since worry is, as it were, the opponent in focus in vv. 6–7, it is appropriate to see worry as that which the heart and mind are defended from. Note that 'guard' or 'protect' always implies an opponent whom one is to be protected from. The rendering in the display, however, is even further removed from the figure; it follows normal SSA rules for propositionalization.

Some of the older commentators took φρουρήσει in the sense of 'keep' with a meaning of 'the peace of God will keep your hearts and minds in Christ Jesus', that is, keep them in place in their union with Christ. But, as Meyer points out, the verb is φρουρήσει 'guard, protect' rather than τηρήσει 'keep'.

The meaning of καρδία 'heart' is broad. It may refer to "the seat of physical, spiritual and mental life" (BAGD, p. 403.1). It can mean not only the faculty of thought but the thoughts themselves. The basic meaning of the other noun here, νόημα, is *"thought, mind"* (BAGD, p. 540.1). Thus the meaning of the two words partially overlaps. Paul's purpose in using two overlapping words is to emphasize the comprehensiveness of God's protective care over every area of our inner life that is subject to worry and anxiety. Likewise, the repetition of the article and the pronoun in τὰς καρδίας ὑμῶν καὶ τὰ νοήματα ὑμῶν 'the hearts of you and the minds of you' is to emphasize the whole by emphasizing the inclusion of all its parts.

As Louw and Nida (26.3) state, καρδία 'heart' does not occur in the New Testament in its literal sense. Also, it is what the figurative heart and the mind *do* that is in focus here rather than the heart and mind as entities. Therefore, 'heart' and 'mind' are not used in the first of the two options given in the display rendering. (Many languages do use organs of the body in ways similar to Greek, and their use may be appropriate here in those languages.) Instead of using 'heart' and 'mind' in the first option in the display rendering, the emotions and thoughts that they represent are referred to: 'worry *about anything*'. That is, God guards our thoughts by preventing them from being worries. 'About anything' represents the comprehensiveness signaled in 'your hearts and your minds'. The second of the two options given in the display has 'in every way' for the same reason.

For translations where it seems best to represent καρδία 'heart' and νόημα 'mind' by either body organs or the activities associated with them, καρδία should be rendered by some word(s) appropriate to the emotions of worry and peace. For example, for translation into English, this might be either 'heart' or 'emotions', even though in Greek emotion is only one of the senses of καρδία and not even the basic one. By such a translation of καρδία, together with that of νόημα, the parts of the whole inner being that are in focus in this context are covered.

**4:7b** *that is* There is a question as to whether 4:7a, 'God will cause you not to worry *about anything*', and 4:7b, 'he will cause you to be peaceful', are in a NUCLEUS-equivalent relationship or in a NUCLEUS-amplification relationship. In the display it is taken as NUCLEUS-equivalent; 7b is basically equivalent to 7a.

**he will cause you to be peaceful** The phrase ἡ εἰρήνη τοῦ θεοῦ 'the peace of God' means 'the peace which God gives'. Some commentators who take this meaning also say that this peace is God's in the sense that it is part of God's nature. While this may be true, it is not focal in vv. 6–7 and need not be made explicit in the proposition. The fact that this peace is received from God in answer to prayer to overcome the Christian's worry means that it is an inward peace and tranquility.

Since 'peace' is an abstract noun, 'the peace of God' is propositionalized as 'God will cause you to be peaceful'.

**4:7c** *because you trust* **in Christ Jesus** Commentators agree that ἐν Χριστῷ Ἰησοῦ 'in Christ Jesus' indicates, as Vincent says, "the sphere in which divine protection will be exercised." That is, the protection is available only to those who are in union with Christ Jesus. This might be propositionalized as '*because you are united* to Christ Jesus' or '*because you trust* in Christ Jesus'.

**4:7d** *You* Since the addressees, and especially those who carry out the APPEAL of 4:6, are the focal participants of 4:7b, it is they who are unable to understand how they can be so peaceful. The implication is that no one else can understand either.

**will not be able to understand how you can be so peaceful** *in such difficult circumstances* It is difficult to know whether ἡ ὑπερέχουσα πάντα νοῦν means 'which surpasses all understanding' or 'which surpasses all reasoning'. Though this second interpretation, reasoning out one's problems and so achieving peace, may not be so commonly known, it is held by some well-known commentators such as Lightfoot, Meyer, Plummer, and Vincent, among others. In support of the first sense Loh and Nida say the basic meaning of νοῦς "is 'the mind' as the faculty of thinking and reflection, not 'cleverness' or 'inventiveness.'" It is true, however, that 'reasoning' or 'reasoning ability' is a verifiable sense of νοῦς in some contexts such as Rev. 13:18, where ὁ ἔχων νοῦν ψηφισάτω τὸν ἀριθμὸν τοῦ θηρίου might be translated as 'whoever has reasoning ability, let him calculate the number of the beast'. But the point is that 'reasoning out one's own peace' is a more complicated concept than simply understanding God's peace. If the context does not clearly signal that such reasoning is in focus, the simpler concept is the one more likely to have been intended by Paul and understood by the addressees.

It is characteristic of Paul's mode of thought to say God's peace is beyond human understanding. The same idea can be seen in Eph. 3:20, τῷ δὲ δυναμένῳ ὑπὲρ πάντα ποιῆσαι ὑπερεκπερισσοῦ ὧν αἰτούμεθα ἢ νοοῦμεν 'now to him who is able to do infinitely more than all we ask or think'.

What is there about the peace of God which surpasses all understanding? It is presumably not so much the essence of the peace itself as its surprising effect on the person in difficult circumstances. This becomes apparent in propositionalization when peace is not treated as an abstract noun (i.e., as an entity) but as an attribute.

## BOUNDARIES AND COHERENCE

The phrase τὸ λοιπόν 'concerning other matters' or 'as for a remaining matter' at the beginning of v. 8 is typically an introducer of a new topic. Therefore, this paragraph's final boundary is the end of v. 7. What binds the paragraph together is the emotive focus of Christian joy and peace. The Philippians are instructed to rejoice always in the Lord, not to worry but to pray to God instead and as a result receive the peace that passes all understanding.

## PROMINENCE AND THEME

Something from each of the three conjoined *APPEALS* is included in the theme statement. The marked prominent RESULT of the third *APPEAL* is also included, as well as the *basis*, which is basic to the paragraph pattern.

# SECTION CONSTITUENT 4:8–9 (Hortatory Paragraph: Appeal₃ of 4:2–9)

*THEME: Continually think about everything that is good and praiseworthy. Continually practice whatever you have learned from me. As a result, God will be with you and give you peace.*

| ¶ PTRN | CONTENTS |
|---|---|
| APPEAL₁ | 4:8 As for a remaining matter (*or*, In conclusion), fellow believers, whatever is true, whatever is noble, whatever is right, whatever is morally pure, whatever is pleasing,* whatever is admirable, whatever is good, whatever *people* praise, these are the things which you should continually think about. |
| APPEAL₂ | 4:9a Those things which I have taught you and passed on to you, those things which you have heard me *say* and which you have seen me *do*, those are the things which you *yourselves* should continually do. |
| motivational basis (result) | 4:9b As a result *of your doing this* [4:8-9a], God will be with you *and will cause you to* be peaceful. |

## INTENT AND PARAGRAPH PATTERN

The 4:8–9 paragraph has two APPEALS. Their form in the Greek text is imperative. The result construction of 4:9b acts as a *motivational basis* for carrying out these APPEALS. Paul ends the hortatory part of the epistle with these generic exhortations.

## NOTES

**4:8 As for a remaining matter (*or*, In conclusion)** The Greek is τὸ λοιπόν (see the note on 3:1a). The final subject of the epistle, Paul's thanks for the Philippians' gift (covered in 4:10-20) is quite distinctive from the matter Paul discusses in 4:8–9; it is not in view at this point as another 'remaining matter' and therefore τὸ λοιπόν is rendered in the singular. Clearly 4:8–9 belongs to the hortatory part of the epistle, while 4:10–20 belongs to the final expressive part of the epistle.

Since 4:8–9 is the final paragraph of the hortatory part of the epistle and since its content is to some extent a summary, τὸ λοιπόν could be rendered 'in conclusion' (TEV). Note, however, that this conclusion is in reference to the hortatory part of the epistle *only*.

**true** Paul's use of so many attributes in this list is for the purpose of comprehensiveness. Therefore 'true' here should be understood in a comprehensive sense, including any sense of 'true' that is appropriate to this context of moral and spiritual values.

**noble** The components of meaning for σεμνός are 'morally good' and 'above the commonplace'. It is difficult to find a good English word to translate σεμνός in this generic context. If people were being referred to, 'respectable' or 'respected' might be the best translation, but if something abstract is being referred to, the use of 'respectable' or 'respected' would create a collocational clash in English. In many other languages a collocational clash would be even more likely. Some English translations use 'noble' (NIV, REB, TEV, TNT), which is appropriate here as Funk and Wagnalls' first definition under entry 2 shows: "Characterized by or displaying superior moral qualities."

**right** The primary meaning of δίκαιος has to do with conformity to a moral standard (BAGD, p. 195.1). This is also the meaning of English *right* (see Funk and Wagnalls).

**morally pure** According to BAGD (p. 11), ἁγνός 'pure, holy' was "originally an attribute of the divinity and everything belonging to it ... then transferred to moral sense." In some contexts it refers specifically to chastity (2 Cor. 11:2; Titus 2:5), but here it has a more general sense and might be defined as 'that which is untainted by sin'. In the display 'morally' is used to modify 'pure' since 'pure' by itself refers to anything that is untainted, whether abstract, animate, or inanimate.

**pleasing*** For προσφιλής BAGD (p. 720) states, "in our lit. only pass[ive] *pleasing, agreeable, lovely, amiable*." Although 'pleasing' is used in the display, it might be more finely propositionalized as 'whatever people are pleased with'. The literal meaning is 'lovely, lovable', but 'love' is not used in the display because its meaning across languages is so different.

What is pleasing to humans is not always pleasing to God, so in translation any such negative implication of 'whatever people are pleased with' should be avoided. The general sense here is those things which are *morally* pleasing to both

God and people. Bruce (1983) understands ὅσα προσφιλῆ as those things which "commend themselves by their intrinsic attractiveness and agreeableness. They give pleasure to all and cause distaste to none, like a welcome fragrance."

**admirable** The adjective εὔφημος is formed from εὖ 'well' and the φημ- stem, which has to do with 'saying, speaking'. Lightfoot says of the meaning, "not 'well-spoken of, well-reputed,' for the word seems never to have this passive meaning; but with its usual active sense, '*fair-speaking*,' and so 'winning, attractive.'" In classical Greek literature it was used in the second sense Lightfoot mentions; in the NT this is its only occurrence. The NAB translation 'decent' is probably based on the second sense Lightfoot mentions. Some commentators argue for this sense as the intended meaning. O'Brien (1991) says that the word "implies essential worthiness" (with a footnote reference to Vincent, Plummer, Michael, Martin 1980, and Hawthorne). Little difference can be detected between the two meanings *in this context*, since that which has essential worthiness is of good report and admirable. The cognate noun εὐφημία has a clear meaning of 'good report, good repute' in 2 Cor. 6:8. Therefore the word 'admirable' is used for the display. It might be more finely propositionalized as 'whatever people admire', in which the implication is *morally* admirable.

**whatever is good** At this point the phrasing switches from ὅσα ἐστίν 'whatever is' followed by an adjective (in the early part of the verse) to εἴ τις 'if any' followed by a noun. But 'if any virtue' or 'if there is any virtue' is really quite vague. It does not mean 'even if there is a little (i.e., any) virtue or praise in it, think about it'. It helps our understanding to realize that the two phrases, 'whatever is' and 'if any', have the same semantic function. The words εἴ τις, in fact, are commonly translated elsewhere as 'whatever' (see BAGD, p. 220, entry VII under εἰ). When εἴ τις is translated as 'whatever (is)' or as 'if anything (is)' (NIV), then the Greek noun that follows εἴ τις is translated as an adjective: NIV has "if anything is excellent."

Many commentators take the last two constituents of the series ('if any virtue and if any praise') to be generic representations of the preceding constituents, but the evidence for this is not strong enough to merit translating the verse with explicit specific-generic phrasing or to choose words for the attributes that only have a specific-generic relationship. In the Greek itself, it would be very difficult to prove a specific-generic relationship, for instance, between εὔφημος 'of good report/repute, admirable' and ἔπαινος 'that which is worthy of praise'. The same is true of προσφιλής 'lovely, lovable, pleasing, admirable' and ἔπαινος, which Moore (p. 50) classifies as near-synonyms along with εὔφημος. Moreover, nothing in the syntactical arrangement supports a specific-generic relationship.

The change in the phrasing is most likely stylistic. It may not be appropriate to change the phraseology at this point when translating into other languages.

**good** BAGD (p. 105.1) places this occurrence of ἀρετή under its usual meaning: 'moral excellence, virtue'. For English, *virtue* is defined in Funk and Wagnalls as "The quality of moral righteousness or excellence; rectitude," but this is a rather vague term to the modern English reader. Moreover, as Loh and Nida correctly point out, "'Excellence' in modern usage has very little to do with moral conduct." They suggest that "the only word which may have nearly all the force of the original is 'goodness.'" TEV renders ἀρετή as 'good' here. (NIV has 'excellent' here but translates ἀρετή as 'goodness' in 2 Pet. 1:5.) Wikgren in the vocabulary of his book *Hellenistic Greek Texts* glosses ἀρετή as 'goodness' along with 'excellence' and 'virtue'. We might ask if moral excellence is essentially the same thing as goodness or whether they are two somewhat different things. Another question is whether moral excellence is in some way a superior attribute to goodness. It may be that the component of superiority implied by 'excellence' is simply rhetorical. Thus TEV's "those things that are good" is as appropriate a translation as NIV's "if anything is excellent."

**whatever *people* praise** The abstract noun ἔπαινος 'praise' refers to an event, the agent of which is people in general.

**you should continually think about** In many of the occurrences of the verb λογίζομαι in the New Testament its meaning is 'consider, reckon, take into account'. In all these occurrences it has, or at least tends to have, a content or a double object or is the basis for some further action. However, in 1 Cor. 13:11, ὅτε ἤμην νήπιος... ἐλογιζόμην ὡς νήπιος 'when I was a child...I *reasoned* as a child', the meaning of λογίζομαι is more general since it does not have a content or double object nor is it the basis for further action. Here in Phil. 4:8 where there is no explicit content and the context is general, it does not seem appropriate to supply a purpose construction. It appears that a more general sense of 'think' is in focus as in 1 Cor. 13:11. The mind is constantly thinking and there is a deplorable human tendency to think about things that are opposite to the good things here. Not everything the mind thinks about is for the purpose of acting upon the thought. It is true, of course, that actions do issue from how the mind thinks.

The rendering in the display is based upon these considerations. (There are idiomatic expressions that would be appropriate for English-speaking readers: TEV has "fill your minds with" and REB has "fill your thoughts with.")

Note that in English when the focus is maintained on 'these things' by forefronting this phrase before the verb (as in the Greek text), it is natural to switch from an imperative to a 'should' construction. Propositionalizations with an imperative are possible, for example, 'continually think about these things'. The implication is, of course, that these are the things which the Christian should continually think about, as the present tense shows.

**4:9a Those things which** There is no conclusive evidence of an explicit relationship between the qualities mentioned in v. 8 which the Philippians are to fill their minds with and the things which the believers have learned from Paul that they are to put into practice. Of course, they are the same general qualities, but the question is how explicitly Paul intended to connect them here because the construction beginning with ἅ '(the things) which' is one that may occur even when there is no possible antecedent to ἅ. In other words, ἅ here does not refer to an antecedent but relates forward to, or relates to the same things as, ταῦτα 'these (things)' later in the verse. A similar example is 2 Tim. 2:2: καὶ ἃ ἤκουσας παρ' ἐμοῦ διὰ πολλῶν μαρτύρων, ταῦτα παράθου πιστοῖς ἀνθρώποις 'and the things which you have heard from me before many witnesses, these things entrust to faithful people'. In this example there is certainly no antecedent in v. 1. Another consideration is that ὅσα...ταῦτα 'whatever...these (things)' of Phil. 4:8 and ἅ...ταῦτα '(the things) which...these (things)' of 4:9 are intended parallel constructions.

Even if we understand the καί which immediately follows ἅ '(the things) which' to mean 'also', nothing in the καί itself necessitates taking the things Paul mentions in v. 9 as a reference to the things in v. 8, as Meyer's rendering shows:

"Whatever also has been the object and purport of your instruction, etc., that do."

**I have taught you and passed on to you, those things which you have heard me *say* and which you have seen me *do*** Four verbs describe what the Philippians are to do or practice: 'learned', 'received', 'heard', 'seen'. There is a question as to why Paul uses words here that seem synonymous. The answer: Paul is doing in v. 9 what he did in v. 8, namely, using a number of synonyms for the rhetorical effect of stressing the completeness with which the Philippians should carry out the things they have learned from Paul. In such a listing the lexical meaning of the individual words, even their arrangement, is not as primary as the total effect. It is not helpful to argue over the generic-specific relationships between the words or other such relationships, especially since they are related in the Greek text only by the use of καί 'and'.

In translation, language-specific requirements may change the arrangement. For example, NIV has "Whatever you have learned or received or heard from me, or seen in me—put it into practice." This makes a slight distinction between the first three elements and the fourth element, probably because the first three words may collocate with 'from me' in English but 'seen' must collocate with 'in me'.

There is some evidence, however, to suggest that double pairing is intended. Since the occurrence of καί before a word and a second occurrence of καί between that word and the next word signals a construction that may be translated into English as 'both...and', some commentators see 4:9 translatable as 'those things which you have both learned and received (from me), which you have both heard (from me) and seen in me'. Also, the fact that εἴδετε 'you have seen' is the only one of the four verbs that is definitely contrastable with the others and its primary lexical contrast would be with ἠκούσατε 'you have heard' suggests that they are a pair, leaving the first two as a pair. The relationship between the two pairs would be that the latter pair is based on how the information is taken into the mind, that is, through hearing or seeing, while the former pair possibly deals with two types of information according to content. Therefore it is possible to translate in pairs, but not necessary. In some languages, the first two, or even three, verbs may need to be translated as one verb only since they are basically synonymous.

Note that the things Paul is referring to in the four verbs all have to do with actions to be performed, since he tells them to 'do' or 'practice' these things.

**I have taught you** The verb ἐμάθετε 'you have learned' is rendered 'I have taught you' in the display. This verb is generic in meaning. It does not necessarily refer to formal teaching as Matt. 24:32 shows: Ἀπὸ δὲ τῆς συκῆς μάθετε τὴν παραβολήν 'Learn this lesson from the fig tree'. The reciprocal of 'learned' is used in the display to harmonize better with the rendering of the next verb as shall be seen.

**passed on to you** The verb παρελάβετε 'you have received' is rendered 'passed on to you'. This verb is often used as the reciprocal of παραδίδωμι 'give' to refer to the receiving of παράδοσις 'tradition' and other such things that are passed on. These are things which did not originate with the teacher. But παραλαμβάνω is not restricted to the receiving of things which were first passed on to the teacher and here the context does not clearly demand such a translation. It does not seem obligatory, then, to translate with a specific mention of tradition or the receiving of what Paul had first received from someone else. Such a translation would be acceptable, however, since it would add to the comprehensiveness of the total construction and would provide a distinction between items one and two. (This would be in keeping with the distinction that exists between items three and four.) One problem in translation into some languages would be that the rendering of 'received' in this restricted sense would be too involved—it might throw things out of focus. In English propositionalization it is less involved if the reciprocals of 'learn' and of this restricted sense of 'received' are used: 'Those things which I have taught you and passed on to you'.

**which you have heard me** *say* **and which you have seen me** *do* The next pair of verbs is 'you have heard' and 'you have seen', and it is the verbal contrast that appears to be the primary feature in this pair so that it is not necessary to try to figure out how what is heard is distinctive from what was learned and received.

**those are the things which you** *yourselves* **should continually do** BAGD (p. 698.1a) glosses the primary, transitive meaning of πράσσω as "*do, accomplish*," saying that it is "oft[en] used without distinction betw[een] itself and ποιεῖν," the most common word for 'do'. Many commentators and versions translate πράσσετε here as 'practice' or 'put into practice'. The Philippian believers had learned what was right from Paul by word and example. They were to be sure to put these things they had learned into practice. 'Do' is used in the display since it is more easily translated across languages and is not an inadequate translation; 'continually' is called for because of the present tense of πράσσετε 'do, put into practice'. In English, 'practice' has a component of meaning of continuity of action. It is difficult to know whether πράσσω has more of that sense than ποιέω 'do' does.

**4:9b As a result** *of your doing this* **[4:8-9a]** As in 4:7, καί immediately after the imperatival construction signals result. The question is, Does Paul intend this result, the God of peace being with the Philippians, to be seen as coming from their carrying out of the APPEAL of v. 9, or of both v. 8 and v. 9? Since v. 8 and v. 9 are so similar in construction and intent, and since as far as content is concerned the result would naturally follow from v. 8 as it does from v. 9, it is probably better to see the result as based on the APPEALS of both. This would yield a more complete paragraph pattern since the result would act as a *motivational basis* for both APPEALS. Martin (1959) says, "A life which is modelled on these patterns of apostolic example and teaching will be blessed with the gift of God's peace (verse 7) which comes from *the God of peace* Himself. There is no higher blessing from God; and no finer incentive to 'think on these things' (verse 8)."

**God will be with you** *and will cause you to* **be peaceful** In English 'the God of peace' might be taken as identificational, that is, 'the/that God who gives people peace' or 'the/that God who is characterized by peace'. But here the semantic focus is not on the identification of God. It is either on a description of God ('God, who gives peace'; 'God, who is characterized by peace') or on the activity of God in respect to peace as far as his obedient children are concerned ('God will give you peace'). The description in itself without focused realization of that peace in the hearts and lives of people is not adequate semantically in this context. Thus the display rendering is 'God will be with you *and he will cause you to* be peaceful'. The Greek can express this with a genitive construction, but many languages cannot. For them the best expression of it is not with a relative descriptive clause but with two separate declarative clauses.

There is no adequate reason to suppose that 'peace' here is different from the 'peace' mentioned in 4:7. Therefore it is rendered 'cause you to be peaceful' here as it is there. See the note in 4:7b for understanding this as inward peace and tranquility.

## BOUNDARIES AND COHERENCE

Verses 8–9 cohere as two parallel imperatival units of similar construction (see the note on 4:9a concerning 'those things which'). The two *APPEALS* appear to have the same *motivational basis*: 'the God of peace will be with you'.

## PROMINENCE AND THEME

Since 4:8 mentions eight different qualities of the Christian life, a generic representation is made for the theme statement. While the final two qualities do not stand out in a specific-generic relationship with the others to the degree that it should be made explicit in translation, they are, nevertheless, a good generic representation for the theme. Because the purpose of the 4:8 listing is to stress completeness, 'everything' is used in the theme statement to represent this. Perhaps 'only' would be more natural ('Continually think only about what is good and praiseworthy'), but that is not quite appropriate to the listing of so many qualities.

For 4:9a, 'learned' is generic enough to cover the other three words that also describe what Paul is asking them to do.

The *motivational basis* is also represented in the theme statement since it is an integral part of the paragraph pattern.

# PART CONSTITUENT 4:10–20 (Expressive Section: Nucleus₃ of 1:3–4:20)

*THEME: I rejoice greatly because, even though Christ enables me to be content in every situation, you have given me a very generous gift by way of Epaphroditus, just as you have helped me from the very beginning. God will abundantly supply your every need also. Let us praise him forever and ever.*

| MACROSTRUCTURE | CONTENTS |
|---|---|
| REACTION₁ | 4:10-14 I rejoice greatly because you have once again demonstrated your concern for me by giving to meet my needs, though it is true that Christ enables me to be content in every situation. |
| REACTION₂ | 4:15-17 You Philippians yourselves know that in the early days of preaching the good news in your region you were the only congregation that sent me gifts; not that I desire your gifts but I desire that God would abundantly bless you for aiding me. |
| REACTION₃ | 4:18-20 I have received your very generous gift; God is very pleased with this gift, and he will abundantly supply your every need also. Let us praise him forever and ever. |

## INTENT AND MACROSTRUCTURE

In the 4:10–20 section Paul expresses his reaction to the gift that the Philippian believers sent by way of Epaphroditus. The first word of the section, ἐχάρην 'I rejoice' (4:10a), signals the expressive genre and the first REACTION. The *situation* (the sending of the gift) is stated both in the 4:10-14 paragraph and the 4:18-20 paragraph: ὅτι ἤδη ποτὲ ἀνεθάλετε τὸ ὑπὲρ ἐμοῦ φρονεῖν 'that/because you have now after some time revived your concern for me' (4:10b); συγκοινωνήσαντές μου τῇ θλίψει 'having shared my affliction' (4:14); ἀπέχω δὲ πάντα... δεξάμενος παρὰ Ἐπαφροδίτου τὰ παρ' ὑμῶν 'I have received in full everything...having received from Epaphroditus the things from you' (4:18). In the 4:18-20 paragraph the latter *situation* is followed by REACTIONS in the rest of v. 18 and all of v. 19.

The middle paragraph (4:15-17) expresses REACTIONS (in the form of a commendation and a wish) to their having aided him from the very beginning of their acquaintance with one another.

## BOUNDARIES AND COHERENCE

The coherence of the 4:10-20 section is indicated by its all being expressive and by the fact that there is one *situation* (the Philippians' gift to Paul) to which he expresses a number of REACTIONS throughout the section. Paul also reacts in 4:15-17 to their having given him gifts from the very beginning of their acquaintance.

The difficult question is where the doxology in 4:20 belongs. Since 4:20 is a REACTION to 4:19, it has been included in paragraph 4:18-20. (For a more detailed discussion of this, see "Boundaries and Coherence" under 4:18-20.)

## PROMINENCE AND THEME

Each of the paragraphs in the 4:10-20 section is in a conjoined relationship with one another; the theme statement, therefore, is drawn from all of them. They are all made up of *situation*-REACTION paragraph patterns. The first and last have only one basic *situation*, the giving of the gift by the Philippians to Paul, so in the theme that *situation* is not repeated, but the separate REACTIONS are mentioned. The *situation* in the middle paragraph (the giving of gifts by the Philippians to Paul from the very beginning of his ministry among them) is mentioned. Along with the thematic *situations* and REACTIONS is a concession component (given in some detail in 4:11-13, 17a), namely, Paul's statements that he does not desire gifts, that he has learned to be content with whatever he has. This concession has marked prominence, shown by the balanced repetition in 4:12-13, and so is represented in the theme also.

# SECTION CONSTITUENT 4:10–14 (Expressive Paragraph: Reaction₁ of 4:10–20)

*THEME: I rejoice greatly because you have once again demonstrated your concern for me by giving to meet my needs, though it is true that Christ enables me to be content in every situation.*

| ¶ PTRN | RELATIONAL STRUCTURE | CONTENTS |
|---|---|---|
| REACTION | | 4:10a I rejoice greatly *and thank* the Lord |
| situation | NUCLEUS | 4:10b because now after some time you have once again demonstrated that you are concerned about me. |
| | └ amplification | 4:10c Indeed you were concerned about me all the time, but you had no opportunity *to demonstrate that you were concerned about me.* |
| | concession ─ NUCLEUS | 4:11a I am saying *this* [4:10] not because *I am concerned that I* lack *what I need.* |
| | └ AMPLIFICATION ─ NUCLEUS ─ GENERIC | 4:11b In fact, I have learned to be content in whatever *situation* I am. |
| | └ specific | 4:12a *Specifically,* I know how *to be content when* I do not have what I need and I know how *to be content when* I have plenty. |
| | amplification₁ ─ GENERIC | 4:12b I have learned how *to be content* in any and every *situation* [DOU]. |
| | └ specific | 4:12c *Specifically,* I have learned how *to be content when* I have enough to eat and I have learned how *to be content when* I am hungry. I have learned how *to be content when* I have plenty *of what I need* and I have learned *how to be content when* I lack *what I need.* |
| | amplification₂ ─ RESULT | 4:13a I am able to cope with every situation |
| | └ reason | 4:13b because Christ enables me *to cope with every situation.* |
| amplification | CONTRAEXPECTATION ─ ORIENTER (evaluative) | 4:14a Nevertheless, you did *very* well |
| | └ CONTENT | 4:14b *in that* you *helped me (or, gave me a gift)* while I have been suffering hardship; you have expended yourselves in order that you might help me. |

## INTENT AND PARAGRAPH PATTERN

The 4:10–14 paragraph is expressive as signaled by its first words: ἐχάρην δὲ ἐν κυρίῳ μεγάλως 'I rejoice greatly'. The *situation* causing this REACTION of joy is the Philippians' expression of concern in sending Epaphroditus with a gift for Paul. The *situation* is stated in 4:10b. Silva (p. 233) has outlined this paragraph as follows:

(1) commendation, v. 10a [display's 10a–b]
(2) first qualification, v. 10b [display's 10c]
(3) second qualification, vv. 11–13
(4) commendation restated, v. 14

The qualification in 10c clarifies Paul's ambiguous use of φρονεῖν 'think, be concerned' in 10b. In the second qualification Paul expresses his attitude toward material needs: he has learned through Christ's enabling to be content in every situation whether he has what he needs or not. This second qualification functions as the concession to his final remark in the paragraph, an expressive reiteration of the REACTION-*situation*.

## NOTES

**4:10a** As to the function of δέ at the beginning of v. 10, it is (as it often is) a high-level marker of a transition to a new subject. In most cases, as here, it is not appropriately translated as 'but', and a translation using the nontemporal, transitional 'now' can be misleading. It is best left untranslated here, but how it is translated in other languages will depend on the types of high-level markers used in the language.

**I rejoice** The tense of ἐχάρην 'I rejoiced' is aorist, but to translate it with a past tense does not seem appropriate in English. Some commentators have maintained that ἐχάρην is an epistolary aorist. In other words, the act of rejoicing on receiving the gift was a present event when Paul wrote the letter, but it would be a past event when the Philippians read it. However, since Paul is writing some time after he first received the gift brought by Epaphroditus (as shown by 2:25-30), his great rejoicing on receiving that gift would already be a past action by the time he wrote the letter. Instead of an epistolary aorist, it seems more likely that what is in view is the point of intensity when Paul first received the gift without regard to the duration of the state of rejoicing. In English we tend to focus more on the duration of the state of the rejoicing; if a past tense is used, it suggests that the state of rejoicing is over (or greatly diminished). This is certainly not what Paul intended. Bruce (1989) says, "The aorist *echarēn* ('I rejoiced') refers back to the moment of Paul's receiving the gift, but his joy persists into the present." In English the present tense would be used to maintain the focus on the joy (cf. NEB, NIV, TEV).

***and thank* the Lord** Some commentators say that ἐν κυρίῳ 'in the Lord' describes the nature of the rejoicing which takes place (Eadie, Ellicott). However, using a construction that usually indicates a locative to translate this concept is unacceptable grammatically in many languages. As already mentioned, the verb ἐχάρην 'I rejoiced' signals an expressive paragraph pattern of REACTION-*situation*. If ἐν κυρίῳ relates primarily to the *situation* as we have taken it in 4:4, then the Lord would be the causer, the one who provides the initiative and resources for giving the gift: 'I rejoice greatly because the Lord has prompted you'.

However, the better solution is to take ἐν κυρίῳ as relating to the REACTION, 'I rejoice greatly and thank the Lord'. Though this does not explicitly mention the Lord as causer, it does so implicitly. Bruce (1989) has, "'I gave joyful thanks to the Lord' (when I received your gift)."

**4:10b now after some time** In BAGD (ἤδη, p. 344.1c) ἤδη ποτέ is glossed as "*now at length.*" There is no good reason to doubt that this is the general meaning here as it is in Rom. 1:10, the only other occurrence in the New Testament. The context does not suggest that Paul intends to reproach the Philippians by stressing the undue length of time since the last material expression of their concern. Any translation, then, that does stress this point would be inappropriate. It would be better, for instance, to translate as 'now after some time' rather than 'now after such a long time'. Nothing in ἤδη ποτέ literally means 'long time', though idiomatically it may have that meaning in some contexts.

**you have once again demonstrated that you are concerned about me** Commentators are divided as to whether ἀνεθάλετε 'you revived' is transitive here ('you revived your thinking/care about me') or intransitive ('you revived to think of that which concerned me', 'you revived as regarded the thinking concerning me'). (The above glosses are based on Vincent's presentation.) The word occurs only here in the New Testament. But in the Septuagint it occurs both as intransitive and transitive. (There are occurrences with a transitive function in Ezek. 17:24; Sirach 1:18; 11:22; 50:10.)

The transitive function appears more straightforward here in Phil. 4:10b. But if ἐφ' ᾧ in 4:10c is taken literally ('for which'), ᾧ 'which' would relate most straightforwardly to τὸ ὑπὲρ ἐμοῦ 'that which concerned me', a phrase that would be functional only if ἀνεθάλετε 'you revived' is being used intransitively (see Meyer). The intransitive use of ἀνεθάλετε 'you revived' has been understood by some commentators as expressing a revival in concern not dependent on the will of the Philippians. This is in contrast to the transitive use, which expresses a revival of concern dependent upon the will. Thus, they feel, it could more easily be taken as a reproach against the Philippians' lack of concern for Paul.

Another factor in deciding whether ἀνεθάλετε τὸ ὑπὲρ ἐμοῦ φρονεῖν means 'you have revived your thinking on my behalf' or 'you have revived to think of that which concerned me' is that it must refer to a revival not only of the thought itself but also to the concrete expression of the thought in the gift. This is clearly the *situation* which Paul reacted to with great rejoicing. Also, 4:10c shows that Paul recognizes that the Philippians were really concerned about him all along but had no opportunity to express that concern. These considerations do not favor taking ἀνεθάλετε 'you revived' as intransitive: Paul was not purposely avoiding reference to the Philippians' will in the revival of interest in him. All in all, therefore, it seems better to understand ἀνεθάλετε 'you revived' as transitive.

In propositionalizing, the best way to render φρονεῖν 'think, care' in its contextual meaning here of both thought and the concrete expression of the thought is with 'show' or 'demonstrate' ('you have once again shown/demonstrated that you are concerned about me'). However, this may not be usable in all languages. A good alternate translation would be 'you have once again given me aid/gifts'.

**once again** The verb ἀνεθάλετε 'you have revived' functions semantically as an auxiliary here. That is, it does not refer to a separate action but describes the revival of the action in focus, the 'thinking' or 'concern'. This auxiliary function can be expressed in English and other languages by adverbs or particles, or even some other means, and it is necessary to use an adverb here in the propositionalization in order to avoid an abstract noun or substantive construction.

**4:10c Indeed** The 4:10c qualification of 10b is necessary because Paul has used φρονεῖν 'think' in an ambiguous way. It might be taken wrongly as meaning that he felt the Philippians were not really concerned about him for a considerable period of time and had only now revived that concern. Paul immediately reassures them by telling them that he knows they were really concerned all along but had no opportunity to express that concern. This qualification is introduced by ἐφ' ᾧ, a phrase which literally means 'for which', but in its other uses by Paul (Rom. 5:12; 2 Cor. 5:4; probably Phil. 3:12) has the idiomatic meaning of 'because'. (For more on this use, see the discussion on ἐφ' ᾧ in 3:12d.) Here in 4:10c 'because' does not make sense. A literal translation of 'about which, in regard to which' (Hendriksen has 'with reference to which') does make sense: 'You have revived your thinking about my concerns, about which (concerns) you have been thinking all along but did not have opportunity (to meet them)'. As far as connection between the clauses is concerned, this function of ἐφ' ᾧ is basically anaphoric only; it does not clearly signal a communication relation. Some versions (NASB, NIV, NRSV) begin this clause with 'indeed'. In BAGD (ἐπί, p. 287.II1bγ) ἐφ' ᾧ is glossed here as 'for, indeed'. Contextually 'indeed' seems very appropriate. The relationship between 10b and 10c is a type of NUCLEUS-amplification in which a statement is elaborated to make the author's thought clearer, or in this case, unambiguous.

**you were concerned about me all the time** The verb ἐφρονεῖτε is in the imperfect tense to stress the duration of the Philippians' concern. This is brought out clearly by the phrase 'all the time'.

**you had no opportunity *to demonstrate that you were concerned about me*** The meaning of the verb ἠκαιρεῖσθε here is 'you had no opportunity'. It semantic function is auxiliary, being close in meaning to 'you were unable to'; it is therefore potentially translatable as such in those languages where a word for 'opportunity' does not exist. The fact that it does have this auxiliary function means that it is necessary to supply the primary action in the propositionalization. An alternate would be: 'You were unable *to give me gifts/help me*'.

**4:11a I am saying *this* [4:10]** Paul's second qualification (in vv. 11–13) relates not only to the rejoicing but to all of v. 10. It has to do with needs, which is what 10b–c also refers to, as shown by the phrases τὸ ὑπὲρ ἐμοῦ φρονεῖν 'your concern for me/my (needs)', ἐφρονεῖτε 'you were concerned', and ἠκαιρεῖσθε 'you had no opportunity' in v. 10.

**not because** The combination οὐχ ὅτι 'not that' seems to be a formula for introducing a negative qualification. It is used this way in John 6:46; 7:22; 2 Cor. 1:24; 3:5; Phil. 3:12. It may be that here οὐχ ὅτι modifies (grammatically) the whole construction. But many versions translate this as a simple negative, "I am not saying this" (NIV, TEV, TNT) and "I do not say this" (NAB, NJB), even though Paul is saying this. This works well in English, but to translate this with the negative modifying 'say' would not be appropriate in many other languages. In the semantic structure the negative semantically modifies either the reason clause ('I am saying *this* not because *I am concerned that I* lack *what I need*') or the construction as a whole ('It is not that I am saying this because *I am concerned that I* lack *what I need*'). The former is given in the display since it is somewhat simpler, but it is difficult to know which alternative would transfer better across languages.

One of the functions of κατά is to signal reason (BAGD, p. 407.II5aδ). This is obviously the function of κατά here, and it is therefore rendered 'because'.

***I am concerned that I* lack *what I need*** BAGD (p. 849) glosses ὑστέρησις as "*need, lack, poverty.*" Paul is not saying that he has sufficient supply for his needs from other sources; he is saying that whatever needs he may have are of no real concern to him. He does not see them as needs. This is the point of his explanation (beginning with γάρ 'because') in 4:11b–13: in whatever situation he finds himself he has learned to be content and satisfied.

**4:11b In fact** In the Greek text the γάρ construction (4:11b) is a reason for Paul's statement in 11a that his words in v. 10 are not based on a felt lack of the necessities of life. As mentioned, 11a is a negative qualification modifying v. 10. In argument, qualifications are often followed by the grounds for them, but since Paul is talking about his own experience there is no argument and so 11b (and its specific and amplification, vv. 12–13) are reason instead. When it comes to propositionalizing 11a with its negative reason, the reasoning becomes complicated and it is better to state 11b in the form of an amplification instead. (Amplification and reason/grounds are *sometimes* difficult to distinguish anyway.)

**I** The reason or amplification for the statement in 11a is given in 11b. It begins with the pronoun ἐγώ 'I'. Most of the commentators mentioned by Greenlee (1992) take the view that the emphatic ἐγώ 'I' here "means that, whatever may be the experience of others, [Paul] has learned to be content." It is normal for free pronouns to be used in contrast, but here there is no other explicit pronoun or noun to contrast with. It may be that ἐγώ here emphasizes the personal quality of the experience, which is more or less the point of most commentators.

**have learned** It is quite obvious that the kind of learning here is learning through experience. BAGD (p. 490) classifies this occurrence of μανθάνω under entry 4, "*learn, appropriate to oneself* less through instruction than through experience or practice." The tense of ἔμαθον is aorist, 'I learned'. Most commentators take the aorist here as not referring to having learned at one point in time but to some other use befitting the situation of learning through experience. O'Brien (1991) says, "As a constative (or complexive) aorist it sums up his learning experiences to the moment of writing and views them as a whole." Also, μεμύημαι 'I have learned the secret' in v. 12, which is parallel to ἔμαθον in this context, is in the perfect tense. Martin (1959) takes a different point of view than the one here: he says, "The lesson he learnt came to him in a moment of time, as the aorist tense of the verb indicates." That moment, according to Martin, was at his conversion.

**to be content** BAGD (p. 122) glosses αὐτάρκης for Phil. 4:11 as "*content*, perh. *self-sufficient.*" This, for the Stoics, was a prime virtue. Eadie says, "The epithet αὐτάρκης means self-sufficing, having within one what produces contentment." Bruce (1989:151) says, "The Stoic emphasis on *autarkeia* in the sense of self-sufficiency goes back to Socrates who, when asked who was the wealthiest person, replied, 'The one who is content with least, for contentment (*autarkeia*) is nature's wealth' (Stobaeus, *Florilegium* 5.43)." Thus Paul is using αὐτάρκης not in the sense of always being able to provide one's own material needs, but of being, as Bruce (ibid.:150) says, "God-sufficient". He was able, by God's help, to handle the situation from within himself; in other words, he was content.

**in whatever** *situation* **I am** The prepositional phrase ἐν οἷς εἰμι 'in which(pl) I am' may be translated in English as "*in the situation in which I find myself*" (BAGD, εἰμί, p. 225.III4). The expansion of this phrase in the following verse to all kinds of differing circumstances shows that Paul is not referring only to the circumstances he is in at the moment but to whatever kind he has experienced.

**4:12a** *Specifically*, **I know how** *to be content when* Verse 12 is an expansion of 11b. The expansion can be seen in the use of words similar to those in 11b. There are two occurrences of οἶδα 'I know (how)' and one of μεμύημαι 'I have learned the secret of' that repeat the idea or function of ἔμαθον 'I have learned' in 11b. The expansion can also be seen in the specific situations which come under the generic ἐν οἷς εἰμι 'in whatever (situation) I am': ταπεινοῦσθαι 'to be abased', two occurrences of περισσεύειν 'to abound', χορτάζεσθαι 'to be well fed', πεινᾶν 'to be hungry', ὑστερεῖσθαι 'to lack'. Also, ἐν παντὶ καὶ ἐν πᾶσιν 'in everything and in all things' is a restatement of ἐν οἷς εἰμι 'in whatever (situation) I am'.

Note, however, that there is no repetition or explicit expansion of αὐτάρκης εἶναι 'to be content', though this is what Paul learned. This suggests that in the expansion a different semantic relationship exists between the verb and the infinitive constructions than exists in 4:11b. One possibility is that αὐτάρκης εἶναι 'to be content' is implicit in the expansion after each repetition of the idea 'I have learned'. For example, the full statement for the first part of the repetition would be, 'I know how to be content when I am abased and I know how to be content when I abound'. Otherwise, 'I know how to abound/have plenty' can only mean 'I have experienced having plenty' or 'I know how to handle having plenty', though the latter would only be a generic representation of 'I know how to be content when I have plenty'.

In the rendering of NIV, "I have learned the secret of being content in any and every situation whether well fed or hungry, whether living in plenty or in want," the implicit "being content" is supplied in the latter part of the verse, but the two occurrences of οἶδα 'I know' are not treated as meaning 'I know how to be content', but as 'I have experienced need and plenty' ("I know what it is to be in need, and I know what it is to have plenty").

Many commentators, however, seem to take οἶδα 'I know' with a meaning similar to ἔμαθον 'I have learned'. Greenlee (1992) lists eight who support the sense of οἶδα as knowing how to do something. Vincent states, "Paul says, 'I know how to be abased and not crushed; to be in abundance and not exalted.'" O'Brien (1991) points out that when οἶδα is followed by an infinitive it "usually signifies 'to know how' or 'to be able'," which he footnotes with references to BAGD (p. 556, οἶδα, entry 3) and Robertson (pp. 1045, 1103) and others. Since 4:11b-12 is built on parallelism formally, it seems better to keep the parallelism semantically to the extent possible. Thus, not only ἔμαθον 'I have learned' and μεμύημαι 'I have learned the secret' are expressions of learning how to be content, but also the two occurrences of οἶδα have a similar meaning.

**when I do not have what I need** By far the most common meaning of ταπεινόω in the New Testament has to do with humiliating someone or being humbled. (The cognate nouns have a similar meaning.) But this is not necessarily the primary meaning of the verb. BAGD (p. 804) glosses ταπεινόω generally as "*lower, make low,*" and under entry 1, the literal (in contrast to the figurative) entry, has a reference to Luke 3:5 (from Isa. 40:4) glossed as "*level a mountain, hill.*" Loh and Nida say that "this Greek word may be used of the dropping of water level in a river." And since the intended antithesis to ταπεινοῦσθαι here is περισσεύειν 'to have more than enough, abound' and what is in focus in this context is material needs, there is substantial reason to translate ταπεινοῦσθαι as 'to be in need'. (NIV and TEV render it without any component of humbleness or abasement.)

**and I know how** *to be content* In the Greek text, οἶδα 'I know, I know how' is repeated and the reason for this may well be for emphasis (Lenski, Lightfoot, O'Brien 1991, Vincent). O'Brien says, "In order to drive home the point that he knows the one secret as well as the other Paul breaks the normal construction by the emphatic repetition of οἶδα."

The structure of v. 12 in the Greek text is parallel and rhythmic. Hence in the rendering there is an attempt to follow this structure to some extent. Translators should use the receptor language's appropriate corresponding style.

**I have plenty** The meaning of περισσεύω is 'to have more than enough, to have in abundance, to have plenty'.

**4:12b I have learned how** Louw and Nida (27.14) define μυέω or μυέομαι as "to learn the secret of something through personal experience or as the result of initiation—'to learn a secret.'" In BAGD (p. 529) this word is described as a "t[echnical] t[erm] of the mystery religions" meaning "*initiate (into the mysteries).*" It also has a general (nontechnical) meaning, according to BAGD, glossed for Phil. 4:12 as "*I have learned the secret.*" There are problems, however, with translating 'I have learned the secret' into some languages since 'secret' is an abstract noun and, as Loh and Nida point out, what Paul had learned from experience on how to be satisfied with what he had was not a secret in the sense of hidden information. In English, 'I have learned the secret' is somewhat idiomatic, since it does not necessarily mean that something deliberately hidden from others is involved. It was thought best to simply use 'I have learned how' in the display. Paul uses different verbs in 11b-12 (ἔμαθον 'I have learned', οἶδα 'I know', μεμύημαι 'I have learned the secret'), but they all express the same general meaning and their content is basically the same. Their lexical variation enhances the style, and also the inclusiveness and importance of this topic.

*to be content* See the first note under 4:12a for the reason for supplying 'to be content' here (cf. NIV).

**in any and every** *situation* The Greek is ἐν παντὶ καὶ ἐν πᾶσιν 'in every (thing) and in all (things)', in which the singular form of πᾶς 'every, all' occurs first, then is repeated in plural form. The repetition of πᾶς signifies comprehensiveness more than it signifies any specific categorization. It is therefore best translated idiomatically in a form that will express comprehensiveness appropriate to this context. Formally it is an expansion of ἐν οἷς εἰμι 'in whatever (situation or circumstance) I am' in v. 11, which gives even greater emphasis to these words in v. 12. Therefore, it is important to maintain great emphasis in translation. This can be done in English by 'in any and every situation' ('any' and 'every' actually refer to the same thing but are used to signal comprehensiveness) although it is to some extent idiomatic.

**4:12c Specifically, I have learned how *to be content when*** There is a GENERIC-specific relationship between ἐν παντὶ καὶ ἐν πᾶσιν 'in every and in all (situations)' and the four infinitives at the end of the verse, which describe situations of deep need and plenty. This relationship may be propositionalized as follows: 'I have learned how *to be content* in any and every *situation. Specifically*, I have learned how *to be content when* I have enough to eat and I have learned how *to be content when* I am hungry', etc.

Another way to propositionalize this is to transform 'in every and in all (situations)' into a GENERIC circumstantial proposition that relates to the specific circumstantial propositions transformed from the infinitives 'to be filled', to hunger', 'to abound', 'to lack': 'I have learned *how to be content,* whatever happens to me, *specifically*, whether I have enough to eat or whether I am hungry', etc.

**I have enough to eat** BAGD (p. 883) glosses the passive form of χορτάζω as "*eat one's fill, be satisfied.*" Here it is the opposite of πεινάω 'to be hungry'.

***when* I have plenty *of what I need* and ... *when* I lack *what I need*** Paul again uses περισσεύω, which occurred earlier in v. 12 and was rendered in the display as 'I have plenty', but he uses a different word for the antithesis to plenty, the passive form of the verb ὑστερέω. BAGD (p. 849.2) glosses the passive of this verb as "*lack, be lacking, go without, come short of.*" (The cognate noun ὑστέρησις 'need, lack' occurs in v. 11.)

**4:13a I am able to cope with** The finite verb here, ἰσχύω, has a basic meaning of 'have power/strength, be able'. In many of its occurrences it is followed by an infinitive which expresses the action one is able to do. Here, however, it is not followed by an infinitive. The translation 'I am able *to do* all things' is not based on 'do' being explicit as a separate word in the Greek text, though ἰσχύω by itself can mean 'I can do all things' if the context is appropriate. Furthermore, 4:13a restates 4:11b-12. The beginning word of v. 13, πάντα 'all things', is the final mention of the category which was first brought up in 11b, ἐν οἷς εἰμι 'in whatever (situation) I am', then followed up in 12b by ἐν παντὶ καὶ ἐν πᾶσιν 'in every and in all (situations)' (and actually also referred to by each of the antitheses). As O'Brien (1991) says, the verb ἰσχύω here "signifies that Paul can handle or cope with all these things." While 'do' is very generic in English, it is probably not the most appropriate word for this context. For many languages a literal translation of 'do' would be inappropriate to the extent that it would tend to exclude the situations of 11b-12 rather than include them. Hence it is not used in the display.

**every situation** As already noted, πάντα 'all (things)' refers to basically the same things as the multiple references in 11b-12, but the fact that both πάντα and these references signify comprehensiveness means that πάντα does not have to be seen as referring back to them as antecedents. This may explain why πάντα occurs without the article. In English it is more effective to say, 'I can cope with all things', rather than, 'I can cope with all those things'. Moreover, they mean the same thing.

**4:13b because** The preposition ἐν 'in, by, through' often signals means, but here Paul's ability to cope with every situation is not the result of what he does but of what Christ does, and therefore the relationship is RESULT-reason.

**Christ** The word Χριστῷ 'Christ' does not occur in some Greek manuscripts. The UBSGNT does not have Χριστῷ in the text and considers its absence to be certain (an A rating). The text of Hodges and Farstad does have it. In any case, for SSA purposes a noun indicating the agent (subject) would have to be supplied to replace 'the one'. In a similar passage to this one there is no question that Christ is the explicit agent of the strengthening: Χάριν ἔχω τῷ ἐνδυναμώσαντί με Χριστῷ Ἰησοῦ τῷ κυρίῳ ἡμῶν 'I thank the one who has strengthened me, Christ Jesus our Lord' (1 Tim. 1:12).

**enables me *to cope with every situation*** The verb ἰσχύω in the earlier part of v. 13 was rendered in the display as 'I am able to cope with'. In view of that, ἐνδυναμοῦντι is rendered as 'enables' rather than 'strengthens'.

**4:14** Since the *situation* which Paul thanks the Philippians for in 4:10 is the same one which he praises them for in 4:14, it is possible to see 4:11-14 as an amplification of the REACTION-*situation* in 4:10, rather than a separate REACTION-*situation* paragraph pattern.

**4:14a Nevertheless** Verse 14 begins with the conjunction πλήν, one of whose functions is to signal contraexpectation. Paul is saying, 'Even though I am not concerned about my needs, nevertheless it was good of you to share in my affliction'. The concession is 4:11–13.

**you did *very* well** The expression καλῶς ἐποιήσατε 'you did well, you did nobly' is not only an evaluative statement but also one of praise. It is a REACTION to the *situation* of the Philippians' contribution to Paul. It is to some extent a restatement of the REACTION in 4:10, ἐχάρην ἐν κυρίῳ μεγάλως 'I rejoice in the Lord greatly'. Bruce (1989) says that "in the past tense *kalōs poiein* conveys the sense of 'thank you'" and cites "Acts 10:33, *kalōs epoiēsas paragenomenos* 'it was good of you to come' (NIV) or 'thank you for coming.'" Expressing thanks is certainly appropriate to the context. Also, in some languages where the verb 'praise' has a public component, making the good deed known to people other than those who have done the deed, 'thanks' may be especially appropriate here.

As for more traditional translation, καλῶς ἐποιήσατε is often translated into English as "it was good of you" (Hawthorne, NJB, NIV; cf. TEV) or "it was kind of you" (NAB, NRSV, REB, TNT; cf. BAGD under καλῶς, p. 401.4). These translations are probably more idiomatic than 'you did well' and for that reason 'you did well' is used in the display. The intensive modifier 'very' is added since 'you did well' is rather weak in English.

***in that*** If the Greek text is understood as non-idiomatic, the events expressed in καλῶς ἐποιήσατε 'you did well' and συγκοινωνήσαντές μου τῇ θλίψει 'having shared my affliction' might at first be taken to be one and the same. In this case, the two representations of the event would be in a restatement relationship, such as generic-specific. However, this would be a failure to recognize the function of καλῶς ἐποιήσατε 'you did well' as an evaluative statement and also a statement of praise, even thanks. An evaluative statement of this type is labeled as an evaluative orienter (Beekman, Callow, and Kopesec, pp. 93–94). In this case it is an evaluative orienter also functioning as a REACTION to the *situation* of the Philippians' gift. Although evaluative orienters are usually less prominent than the content they orient, here the double function of orienting and REACTION suggests that 14a is possibly the more prominent.

**4:14b you *helped me (or, gave me a gift)* while I have been suffering hardship; you have expended yourselves in order that you might help me** While v. 14 might be translated freely as 'Nevertheless it was good of you to share with me in my troubles', this rendering could be understood in two different ways. It could be understood as meaning that the Philippians shared of their material things with Paul while he was suffering hardship, which, of course, is what they did. Or it could be understood in the sense that by giving of their material things they expended themselves on Paul's behalf and in this sense they participated in the hardships of Paul. The second interpretation has merit since συγκοινωνήσαντές μου τῇ θλίψει means 'having participated in my affliction'. (In the other two NT occurrences of συγκοινωνέω, Eph. 5:11 and Rev. 18:4, the accompanying word in the dative, paralleling θλίψει 'affliction' here, indicates what the persons participated in.)

Participation in the hardships of others means that just as it is costing the primary sufferer in some way, those who participate in his hardships willingly bear some cost in aiding him. In this instance undoubtedly both senses are encompassed: 'participating in the afflictions' thus refers to participating in aiding the sufferer as an expression of their feelings of oneness with him. There is the sense that those who so participate *expend* themselves in some way in helping him. Meyer explains it this way: "He who renders the aid enters into the relation of a participant in the position of the afflicted one, inasmuch as by his very work of love he, in common with the latter, shares and bears his θλῖψις." Vincent translates this as "that ye made common cause with my affliction." NEB has "to share the burden of my troubles." The Philippians' participation in Paul's troubles in the sense of being persecuted themselves does not seem appropriate in this context, even though they well may have been persecuted at the same time.

**suffering hardship** The expression 'suffering hardship' used in the display does not meet the SSA goal of eliminating abstract nouns, but it is difficult to render θλῖψις 'affliction' in English without an abstract noun since the use of the verb 'suffering' by itself has the primary sense of physical suffering.

## BOUNDARIES AND COHERENCE

Since all of the section from 4:10 through 4:19 or 4:20 deals with the Philippians' gift to Paul, some commentators do not subdivide it. Among those who do, there is not complete agreement as to where the breaks are. Some commentators end the first part at 4:13, while others end it at 4:14. But ending the paragraph at v. 13 would break the low-level concession-CONTRAEXPECTATION relationship. Verses 10-14 function well as a paragraph as shown by the paragraph-pattern structure described earlier under "Intent and Paragraph Pattern."

## PROMINENCE AND THEME

For this paragraph pattern of REACTION-situation it is necessary to represent both parts in the theme statement. The concession (the second qualification) forms the greater part of this paragraph in volume. Therefore it is considered as marked prominent and is included in the theme statement also.

## SECTION CONSTITUENT 4:15-17 (Expressive Paragraph: Reaction₂ of 4:10-20)

THEME: *You Philippians yourselves know that in the early days of preaching the good news in your region you were the only congregation that sent me gifts; not that I desire your gifts but I desire that God would abundantly bless you for aiding me.*

| ¶ PTRN | RELATIONAL STRUCTURE | CONTENTS |
|---|---|---|
| REACTION₁ (commendation) | ORIENTER | 4:15a You Philippians yourselves know |
| | NUCLEUS — circumstance | 4:15b that during the time *I first proclaimed* the good news *to you*, at the point that I left Macedonia *province*, |
| | NUCLEUS — NUCLEUS | 4:15c you were the *one and* only group of believers [LIT] who *sent me* gifts in order that I might help/teach others just as I had helped/taught you. |
| | amplification | 4:16 Even *when I was* in Thessalonica *city*, you sent *gifts* to me two different times [IDM] in order to *supply* what I needed/lacked. |
| REACTION₂ (wish) | negative | 4:17a It *is* not that I desire that you aid me; |
| | POSITIVE | 4:17b rather, I desire that you be abundantly blessed *by God* as a result of *your aiding me*. |

## INTENT AND PARAGRAPH PATTERN

As expected of a unit that expresses thanks for gifts sent, the 4:15-17 paragraph is expressive in genre. Typical words of thanks are not explicit, but a strong commendation is expressed through Paul's reminding the Philippians (οἴδατε δὲ καὶ ὑμεῖς Φιλιππήσιοι 'you Philippians yourselves know', 4:15a) of their consistent and unique aid to him (4:15b-16). Note that, while 4:15-16 is the commendation, and thus a type of REACTION, it also includes elements of the *situation* which brought that commendation.

Verse 17 begins with οὐχ ὅτι 'not that', which typically introduces a qualification, that is, a statement to correct any wrong ideas the addressees might get from the preceding statement. However, the basic relationship here is between the negative part of the corrective statement and the following POSITIVE statement beginning with ἀλλά 'but, rather'. This statement, ἀλλὰ ἐπιζητῶ τὸν καρπὸν τὸν πλεονάζοντα εἰς λόγον ὑμῶν 'but I desire the fruit that abounds to your account', is itself expressive: it expresses Paul's good feelings and intentions toward the Philippians, and might even be called a wish. In fact, one of the glosses that BAGD gives for ἐπιζητέω is "*wish, wish for*" (p. 292.2a).

This paragraph is similar to the preceding one in structure in that it begins with a REACTION followed by a qualification (4:17a). Then follows a second REACTION, which basically parallels the *amplification* of the REACTION in the 10-14 unit.

## NOTES

**4:15a** Although this paragraph begins with the conjunction δέ, there is no obvious adversative sense between this paragraph and the preceding one on any level. So δέ is taken as a transitional marker at the paragraph level. As such it is often left untranslated in English, as here.

**You Philippians** The occurrence of the pronoun ὑμεῖς 'you' signals emphasis on the Philippians as does the use of καί before ὑμεῖς and the use of Φιλιππήσιοι 'Philippians' after ὑμεῖς. This strong emphasis on the Philippians is part of the dynamics of commending them for their outstanding and unique role of supporting Paul from the beginning.

Most of the commentators mentioned by Greenlee (1992) consider Φιλιππήσιοι 'Philippians' a noun of direct address ('you know, Philippians'), but most of the versions translate it as in apposition with 'you' ('you Philippians know'). The function of this word is to stress their identity as a unit in contrast with other units. Translators may feel this function is carried out better in English, or at least is more natural, with the appositional use. In translation into other languages, also, one of these choices may be more appropriate than the other. The appositional form is used in the display. The alternate propositionalization as direct address would be: 'O Philippians, you yourselves know...' or 'You yourselves know, O Philippians...'

**4:15b during the time *I* first *proclaimed* the good news *to you*** The context bears out that ἐν ἀρχῇ τοῦ εὐαγγελίου 'in the beginning of the gospel' speaks of ἀρχή 'beginning' from the standpoint of the Philippians. It refers to the time when the gospel was first preached to, and believed by, them. To make it refer to a more general sense of 'beginning of the gospel' is fraught with problems. See O'Brien (1991) for a summary of such views and his conclusion that "it is better...to regard the expression from the standpoint of the Philippians."

The phrase ἐν ἀρχῇ τοῦ εὐαγγελίου 'in the beginning of the gospel' contains what is in effect two abstract nouns, and for the display it is necessary to change them to verbs: τοῦ εὐαγγελίου 'the gospel' might be changed to 'I proclaimed the good news' or its reciprocal, 'you believed the good news'. Since the cognate verb εὐαγγελίζω means 'to proclaim the gospel' or just 'proclaim, preach', one might say that the meaning 'to proclaim' is implicit in εὐαγγέλιον 'gospel' in this context. On the other hand, since Paul is speaking from the standpoint of the action of the Philippians in contributing to his needs when they first became Christians, 'believe the good news' might be more appropriate. For the display 'proclaimed the good news' was used, but 'believe' might just as well have been used. The choice between 'proclaim' and 'believe' in a translation may depend on the dynamics of the particular language.

To change ἀρχή 'beginning' from its abstract noun form, 'began' is suitable ('during the time when I began to proclaim the good news to you'); 'first' is another possibility ('during the time I first proclaimed the good news to you'). The full alternate propositionalization with 'believed' instead of 'proclaimed' would be 'during the time when *you* first *believed* the good news'.

**at the point that I left Macedonia** If the aorist tense of ἐξῆλθον 'I went out' is taken in its primary function of indicating past time, it would mean, 'when I left Macedonia', that is, at the point of Paul's departure. But if it is taken as having the sense of a pluperfect, 'when I had left Macedonia', it would refer to sometime after Paul's departure. It could, then, possibly refer to the help Paul received while he was in Corinth as mentioned in 2 Cor. 11:9: "And when I was with you and needed something, I was not a burden to anyone, for the brothers who came from Macedonia supplied what I needed" (NIV). It is difficult to know which of these was intended by Paul, but it seems better to take the aorist with its primary function, especially since Paul seems to be emphasizing the fact that they committed themselves to sending him gifts at the very earliest stages of their Christian experience. This can be seen through the use of ἐν ἀρχῇ τοῦ εὐαγγελίου 'in the beginning of the gospel' and the reference in the next verse to the gifts sent while he was in Thessalonica, which would be the very earliest they could have sent gifts (see Meyer). Also, the fact that they did send him gifts while he was in Thessalonica shows that it is plausible to think that he received a gift from them on his departure from Macedonia (Acts 17:14).

The relationship between 'during the period I first proclaimed the good news to you' and 'at the point that I left Macedonia' is a temporal specification relationship, one in which the specific representation refers to a point in a span of time, the span being the early preaching of the gospel in Macedonia. Paul refers to the 'beginning of the gospel' because he wants to emphasize the early date of their beginning to help him; the second reference to time is to a specific point within that period.

*province* 'Province' is supplied in the display to clarify the entity referred to in the text by the name 'Macedonia'.

**4:15c you were the *one and* only group of believers** Again, as at the beginning of the verse, Paul uses an emphatic construction to stress the uniqueness of the Philippians in aiding him: οὐδεμία ἐκκλησία εἰ μὴ ὑμεῖς μόνοι 'no church except you only'. The construction is a litotes: what normally would be stated positively, 'you were the only church', is, for emphasis, stated with a negative, 'no church but you alone'. The display follows Vincent's paraphrase, TEV, and TNT in using 'you were the only church'. In some languages a negative statement followed by 'except' involves a rather complicated structure. At the same time, however, it would be good to express Paul's emphasis in some other way. For this reason 'one and only' is used in the display, though it is somewhat idiomatic.

**who *sent me* gifts in order that I might help/teach others just as I had helped/taught you** The Greek is ἐκοινώνησεν εἰς λόγον δόσεως καὶ λήμψεως 'shared (or, were partners) in the matter of giving and receiving'. It is difficult to know exactly what Paul means by this. Does 'giving and receiving' refer to the Philippians' giving and Paul's receiving, as some commentators believe, or is it reciprocal, as other commentators take it. Martin (1959) says, "Material gifts passed from the church to the apostle, and spiritual blessings flowed the other way. This agrees with 1 Corinthians ix. 11 (cf. Rom. xv. 27)." In 1 Cor. 9:11 Paul says, "If we have sown spiritual seed among you, is it too much if we reap a material harvest from you?" (NIV).

Other features in this paragraph indicate that the focus is on a two-way transaction. The primary meaning of κοινωνέω 'participate, share, fellowship, be a partner with' has to do with reciprocity. In v. 17 Paul mentions the Philippians' receiving: οὐχ ὅτι ἐπιζητῶ τὸ δόμα, ἀλλὰ ἐπιζητῶ τὸν καρπὸν τὸν πλεονάζοντα εἰς λόγον ὑμῶν 'not that I seek the gift but I seek the fruit/profit that shall abound/multiply to your account'. NIV renders this "Not that I am looking for a gift, but I am looking for what may be credited to your account." Thus δόμα 'gift' and καρπός 'profit' may be representations of δόσις 'giving' and λῆμψις 'receiving'. Even v. 19 indicates two-way blessing. The Philippians have given abundantly, God will supply for them abundantly more.

The two-way focus in 4:15c might be propositionalized as 'you were the *one and* only group of believers who *sent me* gifts in order that I might help/teach others just as I had helped/taught you'. This gives specific representations of the 'fellowshipping' or 'acting as partners'. This propositionalization avoids the second reference to this that would be made if the generic terms were used also.

While ἐκοινώνησεν εἰς λόγον δόσεως καὶ λήμψεως could be translated figuratively with accounting terms (e.g., NEB has "my partners in payments and receipts"), it is not so evident that Paul intended a live figure that a figurative rendering is required. It seems best, then, to propositionalize it nonfiguratively (see the notes on 4:17b and 4:18a).

**4:16 Even *when I was* in Thessalonica *city*** The conjunction at the beginning of this verse is ὅτι, which usually has one or the other of two distinct functions. One is to signal content ('that'); the other, reason or grounds ('because' or 'since'). But like γάρ 'for', ὅτι can also be used to signal relationships that are difficult to classify as either of these. BAGD classifies them under "The subordination is oft. so loose that the transl. *for* recommends itself" (p. 589.3b). As with the corresponding category under γάρ, these relationships are probably most often ones of amplification. A majority of the commentators mentioned by Greenlee (1992) maintain that ὅτι represents grounds for the statement in the preceding verse. But note that if ὅτε ἐξῆλθον ἀπὸ Μακεδονίας 'when I left Macedonia' is taken to mean when Paul actually left the province of Macedonia from Berea (Acts 17:14), or afterward, the ὅτι construction is not grounds for such a statement, since the ὅτι construction deals with what the Philippians did before Paul left Macedonia. This may mean one of the following: (1) v. 16 as grounds supports the idea of their aiding Paul at the beginning of his evangelization in Macedonia and Achaia in general, not just on his departure from Macedonia; (2) ὅτε ἐξῆλθον ἀπὸ Μακεδονίας 'when I left Macedonia' and ἐν Θεσσαλονίκῃ 'in Thessalonica' refer to the same general time; (3) ὅτι signals a second CONTENT construction oriented by οἴδατε 'you know', which occurs at the beginning of v. 15; or (4) ὅτι signals what

BAGD calls loose subordination (p. 589.3b). Note also that an argument here would not be an argument in the normal sense of trying to persuade the addressees of the truthfulness of a certain claim. It is something that is a part of the experience of the Philippians themselves, something that they do not need to be persuaded of.

Meyer objects to taking this second ὅτι as meaning 'that':

> The rendering of ὅτι by *that* (Rheinwald, Matthies, Hoelemann, van Hengel, Rilliet, de Wette, Lünemann, Weiss) is to be set aside, because while the emphatic οἴδατε καὶ ὑμεῖς, ver. 15, accords doubtless with the exclusion of other churches in ver. 15, it does not accord with ver. 16 ("*ye also* know that ye have sent...to me!"), to which it would stand in an illogical relation, even apart from the uncalled-for *inversion of the order of time*, which would result.

But would it not be just as illogical for Paul to use the sending of their own gifts as a grounds to prove to them that they had been the only church to help Paul. The only way the second ὅτι construction makes sense as truly argumentative is if Paul is trying to show them that they are the only church that helped him by reminding them that obviously Thessalonica did not help him since he had needs while he was there that the Philippians had to supply. But if this were true, why does he say nothing about Berea, the very church that would have been most handy to send him off from Macedonia with a gift?

The simplest solution is to take ὅτι as nonargumentative and understand it as signaling amplification, either on the basis of ὅτι acting as a second CONTENT marker after the orienter οἴδατε 'you know' (Hawthorne, Kennedy) or on the basis of what BAGD categorizes as loose subordination. Some versions use no connector here (TEV, Phillips).

**two different times** The phrase καὶ ἅπαξ καὶ δίς 'both once and twice' is no doubt an idiom of some type since it is found elsewhere (1 Thess. 2:18; 1 Clement 53:3 [Deut. 9:13]). It is also quite clear that, whether the number signaled by the idiom is two or is indefinite, the idiom has the function of emphasizing the value of the multiplicity of the actions. Thus, even though Ellicott takes it as meaning 'twice', he says it is an emphatic idiom. This interpretation suggests the English expressions 'not once but twice', 'more than once', 'two different times'. As for other occurrences of this idiom in Greek, it is not clear whether a definite 'twice' is meant or not. Though it is difficult to know the exact meaning of the idiom, it would seem that if Paul intended more than two times, he would have used a different expression. 'Not once but twice' and 'more than once' are more idiomatic than 'two different times' and so the latter is used in the display.

**you sent *gifts* to me...in order to *supply* what I needed/lacked** The UBSGNT text here is εἰς τὴν χρείαν μοι ἐπέμψατε 'you sent to me for the need', but it is given a C rating, indicating difficulty in deciding which variant to place in the text. Other readings are εἰς τὴν χρείαν μου ἐπέμψατε 'you sent for my need' and τὴν χρείαν μοι ἐπέμψατε 'you sent to me the need', that is, 'you sent to me what I needed'. There does not appear to be a significant semantic difference between these various readings.

The sense of 'send' in this context is to send by means of someone. In this verse there is no explicit representation of the gift, though it is clearly implicit. Many languages will need an explicit representation, which may be simple enough to supply. However, if a decision must be made in translation as to the nature of the gift, money may be the best choice, though it is difficult to prove that was the actual case.

**4:17a *It is* not that** As in 3:12 and 4:11a, οὐχ ὅτι 'not that' introduces a negative qualification. The negative qualification is followed by a positive statement beginning with ἀλλά 'but' in the second half of the verse. An alternate propositionalization with the purpose of making the connection between 4:15-16 and 4:17 clearer would be, '*It is* not that *I am saying this* [4:15-16] *because* I desire that you aid me'. However, this is rather complicated.

***It is* not that I desire that you aid me** The verb ἐπιζητέω 'I seek' in this context denotes an attitude of the mind rather than specific action. The second entry for ἐπιζητέω in BAGD (p. 292) has the glosses 'strive for, wish, wish for, demand, desire'.

The noun δόμα 'gift' involves an action, giving freely, even though it denotes a material item here. While many languages have a generic noun for 'gift', others do not, so the action is expressed with a verb in the display. An alternative is 'It is not that I want you to give me things/money'.

**4:17b rather, I desire that you be abundantly blessed *by God* as a result of *your aiding me***

There are two major problems in 4:17b. One is to determine the nature of the figurative use of the words, the other the actual referential meaning. The word καρπός 'fruit' in ἐπιζητῶ τὸν καρπὸν τὸν πλεονάζοντα εἰς λόγον ὑμῶν 'I seek the fruit which abounds to your account' is figurative in some sense. O'Brien (1991) says that καρπός "can mean the 'advantage or profit' gained in a business transaction and thus here probably signifies 'interest'." But note that καρπός is not commonly found as a specific word for 'interest'. Regarding πλεονάζω, which has the primary meaning of 'increase, be present in abundance', O'Brien says, "Although there is no certain evidence that this word, which denoted large abundance, was a business term, in the light of the surrounding expressions it seems to take on commercial nuances." But Paul uses both καρπός and λόγος many times with no reference to business matters. As for εἰς λόγον, O'Brien says that it "was a technical phrase used in business transactions and signified 'to the account of'." But this could be taken in a more generic sense than just 'bank account'. However, there are so many words and phrases in this one paragraph that either were known to be used as business terms or that can be easily taken that way that Paul could well have planned this as one of the rhetorical features of the paragraph. In other words, he may well have used an extended figure to illustrate his commendation of them for their gifts. Other words or phrases that may be seen as business terms are εἰς λόγον in v. 15 together with δόσεως καὶ λήμψεως 'giving and receiving'. And in v. 18 there is ἀπέχω, which BAGD (p. 84) lists under entry 1, "commercial t[echnical] t[erm]" meaning "*receive* a sum *in full* and give a receipt for it."

For 4:17b, the words are neutral enough that a translator should not feel *obligated* to translate them with commercial technical terms, however.

As for the referential meaning of τὸν καρπόν 'the fruit', whether 'profit' or 'gain' or 'benefit', it must be something spiritual since there is no suggestion that material gain in itself is in focus. There is the idea that the gift produces τὸν καρπόν 'fruit'. That this is 'benefit' of some kind is suggested by Rom. 6:21-22, "What benefit [καρπός] did you reap at that time from the things you are now ashamed of? Those things result in death! But now that you have been set free from sin and have become slaves to God, the benefit [καρπός] you reap leads to holiness, and the result is eternal life" (NIV). Martin (1959) says, "At the last day such generous and unstinted service which expressed itself in practical monetary support would not go unrecognized or unrewarded." Other commentators such as Meyer, Alford, and Ellicott also limit the meaning to future reward, but, as Vincent says, this is arbitrary. Nothing in the context or in the meaning of the words themselves tends to delimit the καρπός 'benefit', so it is best to translate it generically. One possible propositionalization is in the display. An alternative is 'I desire that *God* abundantly bless you because *you have aided me*'. It would seem that Paul is using πλεονάζω 'increase, be in abundance' to stress the abundant reward or blessing that results for them. Vincent says, "The verb, which is often used by Paul, signifies large abundance."

If the expressions in v. 17b are taken as a whole as business terms, intended by Paul as figurative language, an alternate propositionalization would be, 'I desire that you *be abundantly blessed by God as a result of your aiding me, just as a person* receives high interest credited to his account *when he makes a good investment*'.

## BOUNDARIES AND COHERENCE

The words ὅτι 'that, because' at the beginning of v. 16 and οὐχ ὅτι 'not that' at the beginning of v. 17 are connectors that tend to be used within a paragraph. On the other hand, δέ, which occurs at the beginning of v. 15 and v. 18, tends to connect paragraphs. Such observations are not rules, however, but only tendencies, as shown by the fact that even in Philippians we have taken οὐχ ὅτι as beginning a paragraph (3:12-16) and δέ at the beginning of 4:19 as in the middle of a paragraph. So these tendencies must be verified by other features of coherence. The segment begun by οὐχ ὅτι 'not that' here (v. 17) is very short and closely tied to what comes before so it is considered a part of the same paragraph as 4:15-16. The same could be said about the construction that begins with ὅτι 'that, because, for' in v. 16.

## PROMINENCE AND THEME

This paragraph has two *REACTIONS*, and both are represented in the theme.

# SECTION CONSTITUENT 4:18–20 (Expressive Paragraph: Reaction₃ of 4:10–20)

*THEME: I have received your very generous gift; God is very pleased with this gift, and he will abundantly supply your every need also. Let us praise him forever and ever.*

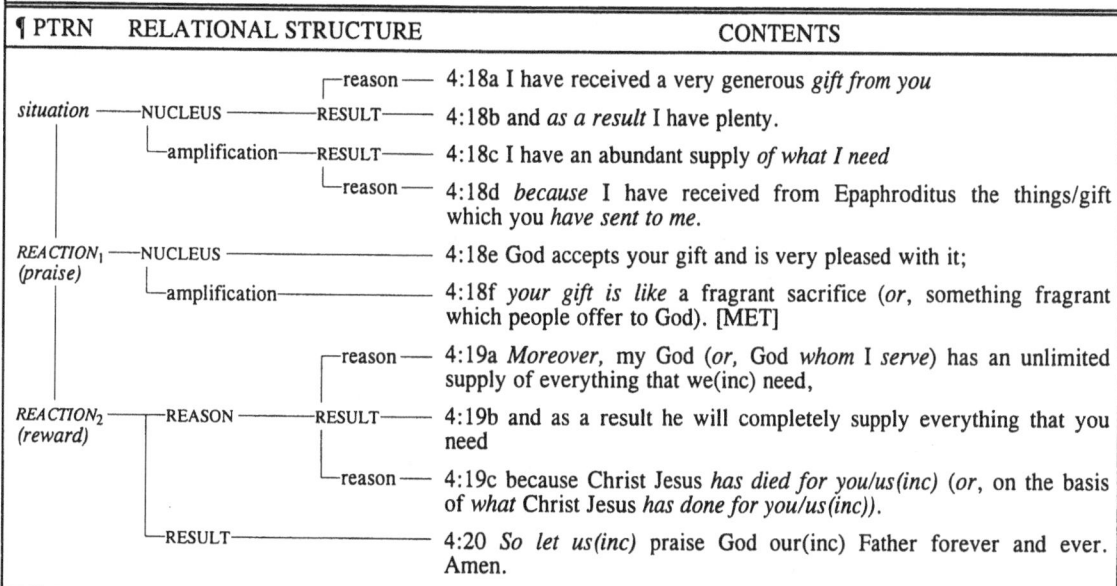

## INTENT AND PARAGRAPH PATTERN

The 4:18–20 paragraph is a continuation in the expressive section 4:10–20. Here Paul states the contemporary *situation* in the most specific terms he has yet used to describe it (4:18a–d). This is followed by two different REACTIONS. The first, in 4:18e–f, is an expression of praise of the value of the gift: 'it is like a fragrant, acceptable sacrifice to God which God is very pleased with'. The second REACTION, 4:19, is in the form of a promise: 'My God will completely supply your every need according to his glorious riches, through Christ Jesus'. In expressive terms, it would probably be better to call this a 'reward'. (The label in the display is not intended to signify a precise theological distinction between promise and reward in this context.)

Verse 20 might be labeled as a REACTION to v. 19. However, since it is not as thematic to the paragraph as the REACTIONS of vv. 18 and 19, it is treated as a prominent RESULT of v. 19.

## NOTES

**4:18a** The meaning of δέ here is not adversative ('but'). Its function appears to be to signal a new *situation-REACTION* paragraph pattern. As at the beginning of v. 15, δέ is a clue that this new unit is in a conjoined relationship with the preceding unit rather than in an amplificatory relationship, even though the general subject is the same.

**I have received a very generous *gift from you*** The word that begins this paragraph is ἀπέχω; it is in the present tense. The meaning components of ἀπέχω are (1) 'to have' or 'to receive' and (2) 'completeness', that is, what has been received has been received in full. In some extrabiblical contexts it means 'have receipted', and various commentators and translators (Hawthorne, O'Brien, NAB, TEV, TNT) understand that meaning here. (TEV has "Here, then, is my receipt for everything you have given me.") The completeness or abundance of the reception is in focus here. It is signaled not only in the verb itself but also by πάντα 'all, everything' and the two following verbs, περισσεύω 'I abound, have more than enough' and πεπλήρωμαι 'I am filled'. Therefore Paul had two good reasons for using ἀπέχω: One was to express the idea of having received a sum of money; the other was to express the completeness or abundance of the sum received.

Note that ἀπέχω does not have an obligatory component of 'payment'. The money or item received is not necessarily payment for some type of service rather than a gift. Brenton translates: ὅτι ἀπέχομεν τοὺς κλήρους ἡμῶν ἐν τῷ πέραν τοῦ Ἰορδάνου ἐν ἀνατολαῖς as "because we have our full inheritance on the side beyond Jordan eastward" (Num. 32:19b, LXX). Thus, in translating ἀπέχω πάντα here it is not necessary to use figurative language ('payment', 'receipt') to express the nonfigurative idea that Paul intended. While it is an option, since the component of receipting could be in focus, one needs to be careful not to overtranslate.

Some commentators translate ἀπέχω as 'I have' (Vincent: 'I have all things', 'I have to the full'; cf. Alford, Ellicott, Lightfoot, and Meyer). It is true that δεξάμενος παρὰ Ἐπαφροδίτου τὰ παρ' ὑμῶν 'having received from Epaphroditus the things from you' is an explanation of why Paul had everything he needed. The explanation would seem somewhat superfluous if Paul had already said 'I have received everything (that you have sent me). The three verbs or verbal phrases that express the idea 'I have everything I need and more' plus a reason for this abundance certainly do form a cohesive entity.

On the other hand, there are arguments for taking ἀπέχω to mean 'I have received' rather than 'I have'. The first two verbs, ἀπέχω 'I have' or 'I have received' and περισσεύω 'I abound', are joined by καί 'and', while there is no connector between περισσεύω and πεπλήρωμαι 'I am filled'. Then πεπλήρωμαι is connected to the subordinate participial phrase that follows it. This joining and division of the four verbs suggest a binary structure which is both repetitive and chiastic, but only if ἀπέχω means 'I have received'. The first and last elements of the chiasm deal with receiving the gift, and the middle elements with Paul's resulting state of abundance. This produces a reason-RESULT RESULT-reason structure:

A ἀπέχω       δὲ πάντα
  I-have-received   everything

B καί         περισσεύω
  and(as-a-result)  I-have-plenty

B' πεπλήρωμαι
   I-am-fully(supplied)

A' δεξάμενος         παρά
   (because)I-have-received  from

   Ἐπαφροδίτου τὰ    παρ' ὑμῶν
   Epaphroditus the(things) from you

Miller and Rountree translate ἀπέχω πάντα as 'I want you to know I have now received everything (you sent to me)'. An alternate translation might be, 'I have received a generous *gift from you*', 'I have received all *that I needed*'. Paul's use of πάντα 'everything' does not necessarily imply he was stressing that he had received the same amount that they had sent, in which case we might have expected τὰ πάντα, but it stresses the magnitude of the gift. Thus for the display ἀπέχω πάντα has been rendered as 'I have received a very generous *gift from you*'. Note that this would be the nonfigurative equivalent of NIV's figurative "I have received full payment."

**4:18b and *as a result*** See the previous note concerning the chiastic structure of the first half of v. 18, which shows 18b (and also 18c) as RESULT. The connector καί functions quite commonly as a marker of result (see BAGD, p. 392.I2f).

**I have plenty** The verb περισσεύω occurs twice in v. 12 and now here. It means 'be more than enough, be abundant'.

**4:18c I have an abundant supply *of what I need*** The basic meaning of πληρόω is 'to fill'. When the verb is in perfect passive form as here, a state is referred to. KJV translates it as "I am full." While 'full' or 'be filled' is meant literally in many contexts, here it is figurative. The primary meaning of 'fill, full' has to do with a container or space being supplied with as much as it can contain. Therefore a literal translation of 'full' in this context is not appropriate in many languages. Note too that πεπλήρωμαι in this context cannot project the image of a quantity less than that projected by περισσεύω 'I have more than enough, I have in abundance' in 18b, since that would be counterproductive as far as Paul's intended thought is concerned. Thus the idea represented by πληρόω in a context like this should not necessarily be limited by being translated as equal to some standard of measurement (the literal meaning of 'full'), such as 'all that I need'.

There are several ways πεπλήρωμαι 'I am filled' could be translated here. One is to render the concept signaled in πεπλήρωμαι as an adverb such as 'amply' and then supply a verb: "I am amply supplied" (following the translation of Hendriksen, NASB, NIV, and others). Another way would be to use an adjective that is a nonfigurative equivalent of 'full' such as 'I have an abundant supply *of what I need*'.

**4:18d *because*** The finite verb πεπλήρωμαι 'I am filled' is followed by an aorist participle, δεξάμενος 'having received'. This type of construction potentially signals a RESULT-reason relationship. Such a relationship is appropriate to the context: Paul was amply provided for (18c) because of the Philippians' gift to him through Epaphroditus.

**I have received from Epaphroditus the things/gift which you *have sent to me*** There are two παρά 'from' prepositional phrases here, παρὰ Ἐπαφροδίτου 'from Epaphroditus' and παρ' ὑμῶν 'from you'. The latter occurs in the substantive phrase τὰ παρ' ὑμῶν 'the (things) from you'. The first παρά phrase indicates from whom Paul had received the gift most directly; the second one indicates the originators of the gift. In both of these παρά phrases an action is implicit. TEV uses the reciprocal of 'receive' ('brought') to render the participle δεξάμενος 'having received' and at the same time indicate the action implied by the first παρά phrase: "now that Epaphroditus has brought me all your gifts." An alternate rendering using 'brought' would be 'I have received your gift which Epaphroditus *brought to me*'. The second παρά phrase might be rendered as 'you sent/gave': 'the gift which you *sent to me*', 'the things which you *gave to me*'.

**4:18e God accepts your gift and is very pleased with it** The similarity between the Philippians' gift and the fragrant sacrifice is explicit in the Greek text, δεκτήν, εὐάρεστον τῷ θεῷ 'acceptable, pleasing to God'. The words 'acceptable' and 'pleasing/well-pleasing' are adjectives that represent events, and because of this must be translated as verbs in many languages. They are translated as verbs in the display. Note, though, that the idea of 'accept' here has more than just the idea of 'receive'. It means "To receive with favor, willingness or consent" (Funk and Wagnalls' first entry). This idea is reinforced by the conjoined statement 'and is very pleased with it'.

**4:18f *your gift is like*** The Philippians' gift is described figuratively as 'a fragrant odor, an acceptable sacrifice, pleasing to God'. Since 'fragrant odor', 'acceptable', and 'pleasing' modify 'sacrifice' (whether implicitly or explicitly), the basic question here is the relationship of the gift to a sacrifice. Is the gift like an OT animal sacrifice offered to God? The best interpretation is to take ὀσμὴ εὐωδίας 'fragrant smell' and θυσία 'sacrifice' as figurative, having reference to animal sacrifices (burnt offerings), the fragrance of which is said to be pleasing to God (e.g., in Exod. 29:18, 41). TEV's translation here is "They are like a sweet-smelling offering to God, a sacrifice which is acceptable and pleasing to him."

The display rendering (also TEV's) compares substantives: 'your gift is like a fragrant sacrifice'. It is also possible to express the comparison between propositions: 'God accepts your wonderful gift and is very pleased with it, *just as he accepted and was very pleased with* fragrant sacrifices *that people offered to him*'.

**a fragrant sacrifice (*or*, something fragrant which people offer to God)** The two nouns in this phrase are ὀσμή 'smell, odor' and εὐωδία 'aroma, fragrance'. In this construction the second noun (the one in the genitive case) modifies the first like an adjective, 'fragrant odor'. But in English, at least, 'fragrant' in itself means 'fragrant odor'. This phrase occurs many times in the Septuagint referring to burnt offerings. See, for example, Gen. 8:21; Ex. 29:18; Lev. 1:9, 13.

In propositionalizing these figures, it is best to make only one explicit reference to 'offering' or 'sacrifice'. Also, it does not seem necessary to repeat the idea of 'acceptable' and 'pleasing' on the figurative side of the comparison.

Though the word 'sacrifice' here represents the thing sacrificed and not, specifically, the act of offering, still an event is involved. Thus, for those languages which have no verb or noun meaning 'sacrifice' it may have to be translated with a verbal construction such as 'something which people offer to God'. As the agents of the offering on the figurative side, 'people' has been used in the display. An alternative may be 'you' ('*your gift is like* a fragrant sacrifice/item which you offer to God') depending on how specifically or completely *the figurative side* is made to apply to OT sacrifices.

**4:19** The parts of v. 19 have been reordered so that reason proposition 19c representing ἐν Χριστῷ Ἰησοῦ 'in/through Christ Jesus' can be attached more naturally.

**4:19a *Moreover*** The Greek text represented by 4:18e-f is formally only a description of the gift, in which adjectives modify the gift. This is a REACTION of praise to 18a-d; 4:19-20 is a second REACTION to 4:18a-d. To signal this, 'moreover' is supplied.

The function of δέ at the beginning of v. 19 is probably signaling switch of agent. Levinsohn (1995:63) classifies the occurrence of ὁ θεός μου 'my God' at the beginning of this verse as "topicalization in connection with the provision of a new point of departure...(a shift from 'I' to 'my God')." In 4:18 Paul describes how *his* needs have been fully met by the Philippians. Now he says, 'My God, in turn, will fully supply all *your* needs'.

**my God** (*or*, **God, *whom* I *serve***) Paul's use of ὁ θεός μου 'my God' is not identificational but most likely an allusion to the fact that God, whom Paul served, would supply their needs on his behalf. O'Brien (1991:545, fn. 215) says, "The balancing pronouns, ὁ θεός μου ['my God'] and πᾶσαν χρείαν ὑμῶν ['your every need'], in the light of vv. 16 and 18, suggest that God will act on Paul's behalf: the Philippians had generously sent support to meet *Paul's need*; the God whom he serves will fully meet their *every need*. Cf. J. B. Lightfoot, 167." Loh and Nida say, "Paul could not repay the debt, but God whom he serves would repay it on his behalf."

See the note on 1:3a which gives the reasons the rendering 'God *whom* I *serve*' is presented as an alternative in the display whenever 'my God' occurs.

**has an unlimited supply of everything that we(inc) need** While πλοῦτος 'riches, wealth' may be used to describe an abundance of material possessions, it is often used by Paul in speaking about spiritual matters. In the spiritual sense the word is used figuratively to refer to 'an abundance' of God's blessings. It does not seem appropriate in translation to take πλοῦτος 'riches, wealth' as a live metaphor and retain the figure while also giving the nonfigurative meaning, though that is possible if it comes across naturally. For this context, a possible nonfigurative translation would be 'My God has an unlimited supply of everything that we need', though 'supply' may be an abstract noun in this sense. A less complicated alternative would be 'My God can do all things'.

**unlimited supply . . . completely supply** There are several different views as to the meaning of ἐν δόξῃ 'in glory' here. According to Greenlee (1992), of the commentators he mentions some take ἐν δόξῃ as connected with πληρώσει 'he will supply', telling how (and perhaps when) the needs will be met; other commentators and versions take it as describing πλοῦτος 'riches'; one commentator (Bengel) takes it as referring to both of these; and one other commentator (Lenski) says that ἐν δόξῃ tells where the riches are located.

Vincent mentions that in the New Testament where δόξα 'glory' occurs with πλοῦτος it is always in a genitive construction, 'the riches of glory' (see Rom. 9:23 and cf. Eph. 1:18; 3:16; Col. 1:27). He also says that ἐν δόξῃ 'in glory' "is always used in connection with a verb (see 2 Cor. iii. 8, 11; Col. iii. 4), and so are all similar phrases, as ἐν ἀληθείᾳ, ἐν δυνάμει, ἐν δόλῳ, ἐν ἐξουσίᾳ, ἐν ἀδικίᾳ, ἐν ἀγάπῃ, etc. There is not in the N.T. a phrase like πλοῦτος ἐν δόξῃ ['riches in glory']." It should be noted that while in English it is natural to take 'in glory' with 'riches' because of proximity this is not necessarily the case in Greek. Proximity rules are different for Greek; moreover, it is normal constituent order in Greek for prepositional phrases to come after the object (see Levinsohn 1992:76).

Among those commentators who do take ἐν δόξῃ 'in glory' with πληρώσει 'he will supply', three different interpretations emerge: Some take it as referring to the manner in which their needs will be supplied ('gloriously, generously'). Others take ἐν 'in' as having a spatial or temporal sense and referring to the coming Messianic glory, "by placing you in glory" (Lightfoot). Still others take ἐν in the sense of 'with', meaning that God will supply all their needs 'with (i.e., by giving them) Christ's glorious riches'.

In the final analysis it would appear that, except for the matter of the time when God will supply the needs of the Philippians, there is really no great difference in any of these views that affects the total meaning of the verse. (The differences in interpretation only have to do with Paul's emphasis on the magnitude of the supply in relationship to meeting the needs of the Philippians.) Since κατά 'in correspondence to' simply denotes the concept of equivalence between each side of the relationship, 'God will gloriously supply your every need in correspondence to his riches' is essentially the same as 'God will supply your every need in correspondence to his glorious riches'. Either way, it is implied that his riches are limitless. While the grammatical argument for connecting ἐν δόξῃ 'in glory' with πληρώσει 'will completely supply' appears stronger than for connecting it with τὸ πλοῦτος 'the riches', in translation the meaning difference is so small that taking 'glorious' with 'riches', if that made for a more effective and natural translation, would not be considered mistranslation. It is not appropriate to the context of 4:10–19, however, to take ἐν δόξῃ to imply that Paul was referring at this point only to God's supplying the Philippians' every need in the future Messianic glory. Not only did Paul have needs that were wonderfully met in the present, God would see that the Philippians' present needs would be met too, indeed all their needs forever.

Paul has so loaded v. 19 with intensive signals that it could be said that the propositionalization has reached a saturation point. Representation of ἐν δόξῃ is hardly needed. It could be said to be already represented in 'completely supply' or 'unlimited supply'. However, 'abundantly' could be added as a representation of ἐν δόξῃ 'in glory' as follows: 'he will completely and abundantly supply everything that you need'.

**4:19b and as a result** The occurrence here of the preposition κατά with the accusative case most likely comes under BAGD's entry II5 (p. 407), "of the norm, of similarity, homogeneity *according to, in accordance with, in conformity with, corresponding to*," hence 'My God will supply your every need according to, or in correspondence to, his riches'. The denotation is that the needs will be supplied in correspondence to the amount of God's riches; the connotation is that there is no end to that supply. The relationship signaled here by κατά is problematic: κατά is only followed by a noun phrase, which is not necessarily abstract. However, an implicit verbal sense of 'have, possess' may be present: 'according to (based on) his possessing great riches'. A potential relationship is that of result-reason, especially if 'on the basis of' is considered a type of reason. Under entry II5δ (p. 407) for κατά, BAGD gives not only the gloss "*in accordance with*" but also "*because of, as a result of, on the basis of.*" Therefore, the first part of this verse might be propositionalized as 'And God, whom I serve, will completely supply everything you need on the basis of his possessing great riches' or 'because he possesses great riches'. Another possibility is to reorder: 'God, whom I serve, possesses great riches and as a result he will completely supply everything you need'. Loh and Nida suggest "since my God has so much wealth through Christ Jesus."

**will completely supply** For the sense of πληρόω intended in this context Louw and Nida (35.33) give "to provide for by supplying a complete amount—'to provide for completely, to supply fully.'" The basic sense of πληρόω is 'to fill' and the context indicates what is to be filled. Here it is πᾶσαν χρείαν ὑμῶν 'every need of yours'. Since 'fill' is figurative, as mentioned in the note for 4:18c, the idea of 'fullness' is transferred to the adverb, 'fully, completely', and an appropriate verb is then needed, such as 'provide' or 'supply'.

A comparison is intended between πεπλήρωμαι 'I have an abundant supply' in the previous verse (4:18c) and πληρώσει 'he will completely supply' here in 19b: 'I have received an ample supply from you; my God will amply supply all your need'.

**everything that you need** Since Paul in this context is specifically talking about material needs, πᾶσαν χρείαν ὑμῶν 'every need of yours' must refer to material needs here also. The question is, Does it also refer to all their other physical and spiritual needs? O'Brien (1991), in favor of including spiritual needs, points out that in 4:17 Paul does not focus on their financial help (δόμα 'gift') "but the fruit (καρπόν), the ongoing, permanent gain that accrues to the Philippians in the spiritual realm." This focus on the spiritual side is seen elsewhere in this section in 4:10–14. O'Brien also points out that all through the epistle Paul has been most concerned with their spiritual needs and that the word for 'need', χρεία, "may denote a wide range of needs, both spiritual and material," in the New Testament. The references to spiritual needs, which he gives, are Matt. 3:14; Luke 15:7; Matt. 26:65; Mark 14:63; John 2:25; 1 Thess. 1:8; Heb. 5:12; 1 John 2:27; Heb. 10:36; Eph. 4:29. There is no good reason to restrict χρεία here to material needs alone, especially since the whole sense of the verse points toward a superabundant supply.

**4:19c because Christ Jesus *has died for you/us(inc)* (or, on the basis of *what* Christ Jesus *has done for you/us(inc)*)** The phrase ἐν Χριστῷ Ἰησοῦ 'in/through Christ Jesus' most likely is to be connected with the verb πληρώσει 'will supply': 'God will supply your needs through Christ Jesus'. The overwhelming majority of commentators in Greenlee (1992) take it this way. The sense here is not that of God's administering the supply through Christ, 'God will cause Christ to supply your needs', 'God will enlist Christ to supply your needs', but of God's supplying their needs on the basis or merit of what Christ has done for them in providing salvation. Meyer says, "That which is promised has its causal ground *in Christ*, who by His work has acquired for believers the eternal δόξα." To propositionalize this causal construction a verb is needed. One option is to use a specific verb: 'because Christ Jesus *died for you/us(inc)*' or 'on the basis of Christ Jesus' *dying for you/us(inc)*'.

Another option is to be generic: 'because/on the basis of *what* Christ Jesus *has done for you/us(inc)*'.

Greenlee (1992) lists only a minority of commentators as holding "that they will receive these benefits because they are in union with Jesus Christ." Another possibility, then, is to translate ἐν Χριστῷ Ἰησοῦ as 'because you are in union with Christ Jesus', 'because you believe in Christ Jesus'. But this is a step further removed: Christ died for them in order that they might be provided with all the benefits of salvation. These benefits are available through their believing, through their entry into union with him.

**4:20 So** Regarding v. 20, Vincent says, "The promise just uttered, by its wonderful range and richness, calls forth an ascription of praise." Verse 20 is an expressive REACTION to v. 19. However, since this REACTION is not as thematic to the paragraph as the REACTIONS of 4:18 and 4:19, which deal with praise and reward for the Philippians' gift, it is considered to be on the lower level and is labeled RESULT. If it were a REACTION, it would be the most prominent REACTION of the paragraph, which does not seem appropriate.

**let us(inc) praise** The Greek text of 4:20 has no verb. The majority of commentators in Greenlee (1992) say that the verb to be understood is the optative εἴη 'may it be', that is, 'may there be glory to our God and Father forever and ever'. But ἡ δόξα 'glory' in the sense intended here signifies an event, which should be propositionalized not with the verb 'to be' and the abstract noun 'glory', but with a verb such as 'praise' or 'glorify' (cf. BAGD, δόξα, p. 204.3).

As to who the agent for the semantic event might be, it is certainly not limited to 'you(pl)'. This outburst of feeling comes from within Paul and it would be inappropriate for him to exclude himself in the praise. At the same time, doxologies tend to be inclusively oriented, so it is better to understand a first person plural inclusive rather than first person singular. Paul's use of ἡμῶν 'our' in πατρὶ ἡμῶν 'our Father', which would have an inclusive sense, lends support to understanding the agent here as 'we(inc)'.

In the display, 'let us', the form for the inclusive exhortation in English, is used instead of the optative 'may' since in some parts of the world there is no optative form. 'Praise God our Father for ever and ever' might have been used if it were understood as inclusive and not second person plural only. This is probably a more natural way to express what Paul intends here, but it is not used because the agents would be ambiguous with this form.

**God our(inc) Father** This might also be rendered as 'God who is our(inc) Father'. It is possible to understand ἡμῶν 'of us' in τῷ θεῷ καὶ πατρὶ ἡμῶν 'to the God and Father of us' as also modifying θεῷ 'God' and not only πατρί. But since the collocation 'our God' would be unnatural in many languages, it is not used in the display. It also does not seem necessary to use a phrase in place of 'our' here such as 'God whom we serve'. The relationship intended by 'our' is well covered by '*our* Father'.

**Amen** The final word in the verse is ἀμήν, which is usually glossed as 'truly' or 'so let it be'. The Greek word used in the Septuagint translation of the Old Testament to render the Hebrew word for 'amen' is γένοιτο 'so let it be'. 'Amen' in the Old Testament, however, is always, or at least almost always, a response to something said by someone else. In the New Testament many of the occurrences are not the responses of dialogue but are found in monologue. BAGD (p. 45) classifies the sense here in Phil. 4:20 under entry 1, "liturgical formula, at the end of the liturgy" and more specifically as "at the end of a doxology." It seems that the original use of the word as a response of agreement, which was used in liturgy and the like, actually became part of the liturgy or spiritual discourse (such as doxology) even in a monologue situation. The response use is still practiced today whether to liturgy or more informally. But when the person uses 'amen' for his own statements, something different is happening semantically, since the primary function of 'amen' is within dialogue. Following are two possibilities:

1. The 'amen' at the end of a doxology or other spiritual discourse signals emphasis on what has been said. Its function is similar to its function in dialogue insofar as that can be accomplished by monologue.
2. The word has a formulaic sense only, as something spoken to signal the end of a liturgy or other spiritual discourse. It has no inherent meaning beyond its basic function of closure. Thus it means, simply, 'The end'.

The first option is the more purposeful, and it is likely that this is what Paul intends in the use of 'amen' here. The intense emotion at this point suggests that 'amen' is one of the doxology's signals of emphasis and intensity.

But for the rendering in the display, 'this is true' and 'so let it be' are inappropriate. They are appropriate only for dialogue and this is monologue. In fact, it may be that 'amen' was borrowed into English in the first place because there is no good equivalent, and the same may be true for other languages. For this verse Miller and Rountree (cf. Loh and Nida) suggest 'this is certainly what we should all do!' as an alternate to 'amen', but this is not natural for ending a doxology in English. It may be a starting point, however, for pursuing the idea further in some other languages.

## BOUNDARIES AND COHERENCE

The initial boundary is marked by δέ at the beginning of 4:18; it signals a further development in Paul's expressive acknowledgment of the gift. Verses 4:18–19 form a *situation-REACTION* paragraph pattern. At the beginning of v. 19 is another δέ but with a different function, that of signaling switch of agents. At the beginning of v. 20 is yet another δέ. It is difficult to know what its function is. There is a strong expressive carryover into v. 20 from v. 19. (See the note on 'So' in 4:20.) It is also quite common for doxologies to appear at this point in an epistle, as though they were an optional constituent of the macrostructure, part of the closure. A doxology is found at, or near, the end of Romans, 1 and 2 Timothy, 1 and 2 Peter, and Jude. However, in many places (1 Tim. 6:16; 2 Tim. 4:18; 1 Peter 5:11), as here in Phil. 4:20, the doxology is woven into, or closely connected with, the theme of a paragraph, being a reaction to something within a paragraph instead of standing alone as a macrostructure constituent might do. The tendency is for a doxology to be a reaction to the glorious things that God will do in the future (Phil. 4:20; 2 Tim. 4:18; 1 Peter 5:11), to a description of God (1 Tim. 6:16; Rom. 11:36), or to the glorious things God has done for the author (1 Tim. 1:17).

Here in this unit, because of the close connection between Phil. 4:19 and 4:20, 4:20 is considered to be part of the paragraph beginning in 4:18.

## PROMINENCE AND THEME

The theme statement of an expressive paragraph pattern must always state not only the *REACTIONS*, but also the *situation*. Hence the prominent elements of the *situation* and the two *REACTIONS* are all summarized in the theme of 4:18–20. The doxology is also included since doxologies are constituents often found near the end of epistles.

# EPISTLE CONSTITUENT 4:21-23 (Expressive Section: Closing of the Epistle)

*THEME: In closing, all of us here greet all of you. May the Lord Jesus Christ bless you spiritually.*

| MACROSTRUCTURE | CONTENTS |
|---|---|
| REACTION$_1$ (greetings) | 4:21-22 I and all of the rest of God's people here, including those who serve God with me and those who work at the emperor's palace, greet each one of God's people there. |
| REACTION$_2$ (benediction) | 4:23 May the Lord Jesus Christ bless you spiritually. |

## INTENT AND MACROSTRUCTURE

The greetings and benediction are emotive in nature. They are two different expressions of REACTION to the close bond which Paul and those with him have with the Philippians. They are also two parts of the formulaic structure of a letter.

## COHERENCE

The final greetings and the benediction cohere in that they are expressive and are characteristic units of the closing of an epistle.

## PROMINENCE AND THEME

This section is composed of two distinct REACTIONS. Both of them are represented in the theme.

# SECTION CONSTITUENT 4:21-22
## (Expressive Paragraph: Reaction$_1$ (greetings) of 4:21-23)

*THEME: I and all of the rest of God's people here, including those who serve God with me and those who work at the emperor's palace, greet each one of God's people there.*

| ¶ PTRN RELATIONAL STRUCTURE | CONTENTS |
|---|---|
| REACTION$_1$ | 4:21a Greet *for me/us(exc)* every one of God's people *there, that is, each person who trusts* in Christ Jesus. |
| REACTION$_2$ — NUCLEUS$_1$ | 4:21b The fellow believers who *serve God together* with me here greet you. |
| NUCLEUS$_2$ — GENERIC | 4:22a All of God's people *here* greet you. |
| SPECIFIC | 4:22b Especially the *fellow believers who work* at the house/palace of the emperor greet you. |

## INTENT AND PARAGRAPH PATTERN

As greetings the 4:21-22 paragraph is expressive in nature. The constituents of this paragraph are in a conjoined relationship with one another, each being built on the event 'greet'. No explicit stimulus-response relationship is indicated. However, there is an implicit stimulus-response relationship. The greetings are a REACTION to the implicit *situation* of the closeness that those mentioned have with those they greet, whether their bond is that of personal acquaintance or as believers in Christ Jesus.

While there is an imperative here, 'greet (ἀσπάσασθε) all the saints in Christ Jesus', it only occurs in one of the greeting constituents and only involves the means of carrying out the greeting and so does not signal that 4:21-22 is hortatory in genre.

## NOTES

**4:21a Greet *for me/us(exc)*** Paul does not say, "I greet all the saints in Christ Jesus" but "you(pl) greet [imperative] all the saints in Christ Jesus." He is asking the leaders of the church (most likely the ἐπίσκοποι 'overseers' and διάκονοι 'deacons' addressed in 1:1) to greet each of the believers on his behalf, or possibly on both his behalf and the behalf of all those he mentions here as sending greetings: 'Greet on my/our(exc) behalf each of the saints in Christ Jesus'.

While 'greet' is quite generic in English and covers salutations when people meet each other and well-wishes conveyed through writing or through the medium of another person, this is not the case in many languages. The intended meaning, therefore, in 4:21-22 of conveying good wishes will need to be translated to fit each language.

**every one of God's people** The word ἅγιος 'saint' is discussed in the note on 1:1b.

*that is, each person who trusts* **in Christ Jesus** Grammatically the prepositional phrase ἐν Χριστῷ Ἰησοῦ 'in Christ Jesus' could be connected with the verb ἀσπάσασθε 'greet' or with πάντα ἅγιον 'every saint', that is, 'every saint in Christ Jesus'. The latter is basically the same as πᾶσιν τοῖς ἁγίοις ἐν Χριστῷ Ἰησοῦ 'all the saints in Christ Jesus' in 1:1, where there is no verb and so no ambiguity. However, in 1 Cor. 16:19 Paul writes, ἀσπάζεται ὑμᾶς ἐν κυρίῳ πολλὰ Ἀκύλας καὶ Πρίσκα. NIV translates this as "Aquila and Priscilla greet you warmly in the Lord," the prepositional phrase ἐν κυρίῳ 'in the Lord' modifying the verb ἀσπάζεται 'greet'. It is clear that this latter construction is manner-focused as is shown not only by Paul's adverbial use of ἐν κυρίῳ 'in the Lord' but also by his use of πολλά 'much, warmly'. But there is nothing in Phil. 4:21 to signal manner, and in view of the phrase 'saints in Christ Jesus' in 1:1, it is better to assume that 'in Christ Jesus' connects with 'saints' here in 4:21. Vincent, who says that "the evidence is rather in favor" of the phrase modifying ἅγιον 'saint', goes on to say: "It is true that ἅγ[ιον] implies ἐν Χ[ριστῷ] Ἰ[ησοῦ]; but the same reason may possibly apply here which is given by Chr[ysostom] for the phrase in i. 1; namely, that he speaks of them as 'saints,' in the Christian as distinguished from the O.T. sense."

**4:21b The fellow believers who** *serve God together* **with me here** The substantive phrase οἱ σὺν ἐμοὶ ἀδελφοί 'the brothers with me' is composed of two identifying terms, ἀδελφοί 'brothers' and σὺν ἐμοί 'with me'. Both of these terms have wider denotations in other contexts. As Paul calls the believers at Philippi ἀδελφοί 'brothers' (e.g., in 3:17; 4:1, 8), so he would also call all the believers at the location he is writing from ἀδελφοί. And all the believers at that location are in a real sense σὺν ἐμοί, that is, with him, rather than being at Philippi or elsewhere. But the contrast with πάντες οἱ ἅγιοι 'all the saints' shows that οἱ σὺν ἐμοὶ ἀδελφοί 'the brothers with me' refers to a smaller group. The majority opinion is that 'the brothers with me' identifies Paul's close companions or fellow workers. Besides Timothy (1:1), this would most likely include any of Paul's companions who had traveled with him to his present location or might have come later, and possibly local Christians who worked closely with him.

This may also be propositionalized as 'the fellow believers who *work together* with me here', 'the fellow believers who *live/stay* with me', or for some languages 'my companions'.

Potentially ἀδελφοί 'brothers' could be taken as referring to Philippian brothers: '*your* brothers who *are here* with me'. They would certainly want to send their greetings. But there is no reference elsewhere in the epistle to people from Philippi being with Paul (except for Epaphroditus who would be with the Philippians when the letter was read), and commentators do not mention this option.

**4:22b** *fellow believers who work* **at the house/palace of the emperor** It is widely held that the phrase οἱ ἐκ τῆς Καίσαρος οἰκίας 'those of Caesar's household' rather than referring to the emperor's family or relatives refers to believers who were either on the staff of the imperial residence in Rome or in the service of the emperor in general. There is support from writings and inscriptions that Καίσαρος οἰκία 'house/household of Caesar' has these meanings but little support historically for a reference to believers among the emperor's family. An alternate to the proposition in the display is 'the *fellow believers who work* for the emperor'.

**the emperor** While Caesar (Καῖσαρ) was originally a proper name, it came to have the meaning of 'emperor' (see BAGD, p. 395).

## BOUNDARIES AND COHERENCE

The greetings (4:21-22) are considered as a separate paragraph from the benediction (4:23) since their functions are different. Many versions also have them as a separate paragraph (NEB NIV, NRSV, RSV, TEV).

## PROMINENCE AND THEME

A very brief theme statement for the 4:21–22 paragraph would be 'All of us greet all of you'. But it may be better to expand it to include each of the groups mentioned. Prominence is marked on those who work at the palace of the emperor by the use of μάλιστα δέ 'especially', though in this context it does not necessarily mark them as more prominent than the saints in general or Paul's fellow workers.

# SECTION CONSTITUENT 4:23
## (Expressive Paragraph: Reaction₂ (benediction) of 4:21–23)

| ¶PTRN RELATIONAL STRUCTURE | CONTENTS |
|---|---|
| THEME: *May the Lord Jesus Christ bless you spiritually.* | |
| REACTION — orienter | 4:23a *I pray* |
|          CONTENT | 4:23b *that our(inc)* Lord Jesus Christ *will continue to* bless you spiritually. |

## INTENT AND PARAGRAPH PATTERN

Similar to the greetings, the benediction would appear to be a REACTION to the closeness and fellowship of the author with the addressees. The closer the bond the more dynamic would the REACTION be. In this case, where Paul has just finished thanking the Philippians for their abundant gift, the benediction cannot be anything but heartfelt.

## NOTES

**4:23a-b** *I pray that our(inc)* **Lord Jesus Christ** *will continue to* **bless you** See the notes on the BLESSING in the epistle's opening (1:2) for a similar construction. Note that 'bless' here in the display is a translation of χάρις 'grace', which was translated 'act graciously' in 1:2. 'Bless' is more appropriate here as far as natural English is concerned.

**spiritually** There are two interpretations of τοῦ πνεύματος ὑμῶν 'the spirit of you(pl)'. One is to understand this as a synecdoche, the part ('spirit') being put for the whole ('you'). The other is to take it literally. That some commentators take it in its primary meaning shows that it is not fully recognized as a 'dead' figure in this context. BAGD (p. 675.3b) classifies this occurrence of 'your(pl) spirit' and the similar ones in Gal. 6:18 and Philem. 25 under "it can mean simply a person's *very self*, or *ego*." But note that this is not necessarily synecdoche. There is a difference between a reference to one's inner self and simply 'you'. Semantically, it is more appropriate to understand μετὰ τοῦ πνεύματος ὑμῶν 'with your spirit' as meaning something more specific than just 'with you' because Paul is placing some focus on the inner being. The most natural English propositionalization would be '*I pray that our(inc) Lord Jesus Christ will continue to bless you spiritually*'.

In some languages it may be impossible or unnatural to translate 'spiritually' or even 'spirit(s)' literally in this context. Where that is the case, one option would be to use 'you' by itself: '*I pray that our(inc) Lord Jesus Christ will continue to bless you*'.

# BIBLIOGRAPHY

## COMMENTARIES, LEXICONS, AND OTHER GENERAL REFERENCES

Alford, Henry. [1871] 1980. *The Greek Testament*. Vol. 3. Grand Rapids: Baker.

Bauer, W.; W. F. Arndt; and F. W. Gingrich. 1979. *A Greek-English lexicon of the New Testament and other early Christian literature*. 2d ed. Revised and augmented by F. W. Gingrich and F. W. Danker from Walter Bauer's 5th ed., 1958. Chicago: University of Chicago Press.

Baur, F. C. 1875. *Paul, the apostle of Jesus Christ*. London: Williams and Norgate.

Beare, F. W. 1969. *A commentary on the Epistle to the Philippians*. Black's New Testament Commentaries, ed. Henry Chadwick. London: Adam and Charles Black.

Beekman, John, and John Callow. 1974. *Translating the Word of God*. Grand Rapids: Zondervan.

Beekman, John; John Callow; and Michael F. Kopesec. 1981. *The semantic structure of written communication*. 5th rev. ed. Dallas: SIL.

Bengel, John Albert. [1864] 1971. *New Testament word studies*. Vol. 2. Grand Rapids: Kregel.

Black, David Alan. 1985. Paul and Christian unity: A formal analysis of Philippians 2:1–4. *Journal of the Evangelical Theological Society* 28:299–308.

Blass, F., and A. Debrunner. 1961. *A Greek grammar of the New Testament and other early Christian literature*. A translation and revision of the ninth-tenth German ed. by Robert W. Funk. Chicago: University of Chicago Press.

Blight, Richard. 1979. A propositional display of Philippians. Photocopy. Dallas: SIL.

Braune, Karl. [1870] 1960. The Epistle of Paul to the Philippians. In *Lange's commentary on the Holy Scriptures*, vol. 11, ed. with additions by Horatio B. Hackett. Grand Rapids: Zondervan.

Bruce, F. F. 1983. *Philippians*. A Good News Commentary, ed. W. Ward Gasque. San Francisco: Harper and Row.

———. 1989. *Philippians*. New International Biblical Commentary, ed. W. Ward Gasque. Peabody, Mass.: Hendrikson.

Caird, G. B. 1976. *Paul's letters from prison*. The New Clarendon Bible. London: Oxford University Press.

Callow, John. 1982. *A semantic structure analysis of Second Thessalonians*. Dallas: SIL.

———. 1983. *A semantic structure analysis of Colossians*. Dallas: SIL.

Callow, Kathleen. Forthcoming. *Man and Message*. Lanham, Md.: University Press of America.

Culpepper, R. Alan. 1980. Co-workers in suffering: Philippians 2:19–30. *Review and Expositor* 77:349–58.

Eadie, John. [1884] 1979. *A commentary on the Greek text of the Epistle of Paul to the Philippians*. Grand Rapids: Baker.

Ellicott, Chas. J. 1865. *A critical and grammatical commentary on St. Paul's Epistles to the Philippians, Colossians, and to Philemon*. Andover: Warren F. Draper.

Funk, R. W. 1966. *Language, hermeneutic and Word of God*. New York: Harper and Row.

Funk and Wagnalls standard college dictionary. In *The Readers' Digest great encyclopedic dictionary*, iv–xvii, 1–1565. 1966. Pleasantville, N.Y.: Reader's Digest Association.

Garland, David E. 1980. Philippians 1:1–26: The defense and confirmation of the gospel. *Review and Expositor* 77: 327–36.

———. 1985. The composition and unity of Philippians: Some neglected literary factors. *Novum Testamentum* 27:141–73.

Greenlee, J. Harold. 1986. *A concise exegetical grammar of New Testament Greek*. 5th rev. ed. Grand Rapids: Eerdmans.

———. 1990. Saint Paul—perfect but not perfected: Philippians 3:12. *Notes on Translation* 4 (4):53–55. Dallas: SIL.

———. 1992. *An exegetical summary of Philippians*. Dallas: SIL.

Hawthorne, Gerald F. 1983. *Philippians*. Word Biblical Commentary, vol. 43, ed. Ralph P. Martin. Waco, Tex.: Word.

Hendriksen, William. 1962. *Philippians*. New Testament Commentary. Grand Rapids: Baker.
Heyward, Katharine A. n. d. A semantic structure analysis of Philippians. Draft. Dallas: SIL.
Jewett, Robert. 1970. The epistolary thanksgiving and the integrity of Philippians. *Novum Testamentum* 12:40-53.
Jones, Maurice. 1918. *The Epistle to the Philippians*. Westminster Commentaries, ed. Walter Lock. London: Methuen.
Kennedy, H. A. A. 1980. The Epistle to the Philippians. In *The Expositor's Greek Testament,* ed. W. Robertson Nicoll, vol. 3, 397-473. Grand Rapids: Eerdmans.
Kent, Homer A., Jr. 1978. Philippians. In *The Expositor's Bible Commentary*, ed. Frank E. Gaebelein, vol. 11, 93-159. Grand Rapids: Zondervan.
Kittel, G., and G. Friedrich, eds. 1964-76. *Theological dictionary of the New Testament*. Translated and ed. by Geoffrey W. Bromiley. 10 vols. Grand Rapids: Eerdmans.
Lenski, R. C. H. [1937] 1961. *The interpretation of St. Paul's Epistles to the Galatians, to the Ephesians and to the Philippians*. Minneapolis: Augsburg.
Levinsohn, Stephen. H. 1992. *Discourse features of New Testament Greek*. Dallas: SIL.
―――. 1995. A discourse study of constituent order and the article in Philippians. In *Discourse Analysis and Other Topics in Biblical Greek,* ed. Stanley E. Porter and D. A. Carson. *Journal for the Study of the New Testament,* Supplement Series 113, 60-74. Sheffield, England: Sheffield Academic Press.
Liddell, H. G., and R. Scott. 1968. *A Greek-English lexicon*. 9th ed. with supplement, rev. and augmented by H. S. Jones. Oxford: Clarendon.
Liddon, H. P. 1899. *Explanatory analysis of St. Paul's Epistle to the Romans*. 4th ed. London: Longmans.
Lightfoot, J. B. [1913] 1953. *St. Paul's Epistle to the Philippians*. Grand Rapids: Zondervan.
Loh, I-Jin, and Eugene A. Nida. 1977. *A translator's handbook on Paul's letter to the Philippians*. New York: United Bible Societies.
Louw, Johannes P., and Eugene A. Nida. 1988. *Greek-English lexicon of the New Testament based on semantic domains*. New York: United Bible Societies.
Martin, Ralph P. 1959. *The Epistle of Paul to the Philippians*. The Tyndale New Testament Commentaries, ed. R. V. G. Tasker. Grand Rapids: Eerdmans.
―――. [1976] 1980. *Philippians*. New Century Bible Commentary. Grand Rapids: Eerdmans.
Metzger, Bruce M. 1994. *A textual commentary on the Greek New Testament*. 2d ed. Stuttgart: German Bible Society.
Meyer, Heinrich August Wilhelm. 1885. *Critical and exegetical handbook to the Epistles to the Philippians and Colossians, and to Philemon*. Translated from the 4th ed. n.d. by John C. Moore. Rev. and ed. by William P. Dickson. Meyer's Commentary on the New Testament. New York: Funk and Wagnalls.
Michael, J. Hugh. 1928. *The Epistle of Paul to the Philippians*. The Moffatt New Testament Commentary, ed. James Moffatt. London: Hodder and Stoughton.
Miller, Neva, and Catherine Rountree. n.d. The Epistle to the Philippians. Analyzed translation with exegetical notes by Neva Miller. Prepublication draft. Dallas: SIL.
Moore, Bruce R. 1993. *Doublets in the New Testament*. (Revision of Doublets, *Notes on Translation* 43, 1972.) Dallas: SIL.
Moule, H. C. G. [1897] 1981. *The Epistle to the Philippians*. Grand Rapids: Baker.
Muller, Jacobus J. 1955. *The Epistles of Paul to the Philippians and to Philemon*. The New International Commentary on the New Testament, ed. F. F. Bruce. Grand Rapids: Eerdmans.
Newman, J. H. 1896. *Parochial and plain sermons*, vol. 6. London: Longmans.
O'Brien, Peter T. 1977. *Introductory thanksgivings in the letters of Paul. Novum Testamentum,* Supplement 49. Leiden: Brill.
―――. 1991. *The Epistle to the Philippians*. The New International Greek Testament Commentary, eds. I. Howard Marshall and W. Ward Gasque. Grand Rapids: Eerdmans.
Plummer, Alfred. 1919. *A commentary on St. Paul's Epistle to the Philippians*. London: Robert Scott.
*The Random House dictionary*. 1980. Jess Stein, editor in chief. New York: Ballantine Books.

Robertson, A. T. 1934. *A grammar of the Greek New Testament in the light of historical research.* Nashville: Broadman.

Schenk, W. 1984. *Die Philipperbriefe des Paulus.* Stuttgart: Verlag W. Kohlhammer.

Schubert, Paul. 1939. Form and function of the Pauline thanksgivings. *Zeitschrift für die neutestamentliche Wissenschaft* 20. Berlin: A. Töpelmann.

Sherman, Grace E., and John C. Tuggy. 1994. A semantic and structural analysis of the Johannine Epistles. Dallas: SIL.

Silva, Moisés. 1988. *Philippians.* The Wycliffe Exegetical Commentary, ed. Kenneth Barker. Chicago: Moody.

Swift, Robert C. 1984. The theme and structure of Philippians. *Bibliotheca Sacra* 141:234–54.

Tuggy, John C. 1992. Semantic paragraph patterns: A fundamental communication concept and interpretive tool. *Linguistics and New Testament Interpretation,* ed. David Alan Black, 45–67. Nashville: Broadman.

———. 1994. A semantic and structural analysis of the Johannine Epistles. Dallas: SIL.

Vincent, Marvin R. 1897. *A critical and exegetical commentary on the Epistles to the Philippians and to Philemon.* The International Critical Commentary, eds. Samuel R. Driver, Alfred Plummer, and Charles A. Briggs. Edinburgh: T. and T. Clark.

Watson, Duane F. 1988. A rhetorical analysis of Philippians and its implications for the unity question. *Novum Testamentum* 30:57–88.

Wikgen, Allen. 1947. *Hellenistic Greek texts.* Chicago and London: University of Chicago Press.

Wiles, G. P. 1974. *Paul's intercessory prayers: The significance of the intercessory prayer passages in the letters of St. Paul.* Cambridge: Cambridge University Press.

## GREEK TEXTS AND TRANSLATIONS

Aland, Kurt; Matthew Black; Carlo M. Martini; Bruce M. Metzger; and Allen Wikgren. 1993. *The Greek New Testament.* 4th rev. ed. Stuttgart: United Bible Societies.

Beck, William F. 1964. *The New Testament in the language of today.* Saint Louis: Concordia.

Brenton, Sir Lancelot C. L. [1851] 1986. *The Septuagint with Apocrypha: Greek and English.* Peabody, Mass.: Hendrikson.

Friberg, Barbara, and Timothy Friberg. 1981. *Analytical Greek New Testament.* Grand Rapids: Baker.

Hodges, Zane C., and Arthur L. Farstad. 1985. *The Greek New Testament according to the Majority Text.* 2d ed. Nashville: Thomas Nelson.

*The Holy Bible.* Authorized (or King James) version. 1611.

*The Holy Bible: New international version.* 1985. Grand Rapids: Zondervan.

*The Holy Bible: New revised standard version.* 1989. New York: Oxford University Press.

*The Holy Bible: Revised standard version.* 1971. New York: Thomas Nelson.

*Holy Bible: Today's English version.* 1992. New York: American Bible Society.

Knox, Ronald A. 1944. *The New Testament.* New York: Sheed and Ward.

*The new American Bible.* 1971. Camden, N. J.: Thomas Nelson.

*The new American standard Bible.* 1977. Nashville, Tenn.: Holman.

*The new English Bible New Testament.* 1961. Oxford University Press and Cambridge University Press.

*The new Jerusalem Bible.* 1985. Garden City, N. Y.: Doubleday.

Phillips, J. B. 1958. *The New Testament in modern English.* New York: Macmillan.

*The revised English Bible.* 1989. Oxford: Oxford University Press and Cambridge University Press.

*The translator's New Testament.* 1973. London: British and Foreign Bible Society.

*The twentieth century New Testament.* [1904] 1945. New York: Revell.

Williams, Charles B. 1963. *The New Testament in the language of the people.* Chicago: Moody Press.

www.ingramcontent.com/pod-product-compliance
Lightning Source LLC
Chambersburg PA
CBHW082041300426
44117CB00015B/2570